# State and Nation-Building in Pakistan

Religion, violence, and ethnicity are all intertwined in the history of Pakistan. The entrenchment of landed interests, operationalised through violence, ethnic identity, and power through successive regimes has created a system of 'authoritarian clientalism'. This book offers comparative, historicist, and multidisciplinary views on the role of identity politics in the development of Pakistan.

Bringing together perspectives on the dynamics of state-building, the book provides insights into contemporary processes of national contestation which are crucially affected by their treatment in the world media, and by the reactions they elicit within an increasingly globalised polity. It investigates the resilience of landed elites to political and social change, and looks at the impact on land holdings of population transfer in the years after Partition. It goes on to discuss religious identities and their role in both the construction of national identity and in the development of sectarianism. The book highlights how ethnicity and identity politics are an enduring marker in Pakistani politics, and why they are increasingly powerful and influential.

An insightful collection on a range of perspectives on the dynamics of identity politics and the nation-state, this book on Pakistan will be a useful contribution to South Asian Politics, South Asian History, and Islamic Studies.

**Roger D. Long** is Professor of History at Eastern Michigan University, USA.

**Yunas Samad** is Professor of South Asian Studies at the University of Bradford, UK.

**Gurharpal Singh** is Dean of the Faculty of Arts and Humanities at the School of Oriental and African Studies, University of London, UK.

**Ian Talbot** is Professor of History and Director of Post-Graduate Research at the University of Southampton, UK, and former Chair of the British Association for South Asian Studies.

# Routledge contemporary South Asia series

1 **Pakistan**
Social and cultural transformations in a Muslim nation
*Mohammad A. Qadeer*

2 **Labor, Democratization and Development in India and Pakistan**
*Christopher Candland*

3 **China–India Relations**
Contemporary dynamics
*Amardeep Athwal*

4 **Madrasas in South Asia**
Teaching terror?
*Jamal Malik*

5 **Labor, Globalization and the State**
Workers, women and migrants confront neoliberalism
*Edited by Debdas Banerjee and Michael Goldfield*

6 **Indian Literature and Popular Cinema**
Recasting classics
*Edited by Heidi R.M. Pauwels*

7 **Islamist Militancy in Bangladesh**
A complex web
*Ali Riaz*

8 **Regionalism in South Asia**
Negotiating cooperation, institutional structures
*Kishore C. Dash*

9 **Federalism, Nationalism and Development**
India and the Punjab economy
*Pritam Singh*

10 **Human Development and Social Power**
Perspectives from South Asia
*Ananya Mukherjee Reed*

11 **The South Asian Diaspora**
Transnational networks and changing identities
*Edited by Rajesh Rai and Peter Reeves*

12 **Pakistan–Japan Relations**
Continuity and change in economic relations and security interests
*Ahmad Rashid Malik*

13 **Himalayan Frontiers of India**
Historical, geo-political and strategic perspectives
*K. Warikoo*

14 **India's Open-Economy Policy**
Globalism, rivalry, continuity
*Jalal Alamgir*

15 **The Separatist Conflict in Sri Lanka**
Terrorism, ethnicity, political economy
*Asoka Bandarage*

16 **India's Energy Security**
*Edited by Ligia Noronha and Anant Sudarshan*

17 **Globalization and the Middle Classes in India**
The social and cultural impact of neoliberal reforms
*Ruchira Ganguly-Scrase and Timothy J. Scrase*

18 **Water Policy Processes in India**
Discourses of power and resistance
*Vandana Asthana*

19 **Minority Governments in India**
The puzzle of elusive majorities
*Csaba Nikolenyi*

20 **The Maoist Insurgency in Nepal**
Revolution in the twenty-first century
*Edited by Mahendra Lawoti and Anup K. Pahari*

21 **Global Capital and Peripheral Labour**
The history and political economy of plantation workers in India
*K. Ravi Raman*

22 **Maoism in India**
Reincarnation of ultra-left wing extremism in the twenty-first century
*Bidyut Chakrabarty and Rajat Kujur*

23 **Economic and Human Development in Contemporary India**
Cronyism and fragility
*Debdas Banerjee*

24 **Culture and the Environment in the Himalaya**
*Arjun Guneratne*

25 **The Rise of Ethnic Politics in Nepal**
Democracy in the margins
*Susan I. Hangen*

26 **The Multiplex in India**
A cultural economy of urban leisure
*Adrian Athique and Douglas Hill*

27 **Tsunami Recovery in Sri Lanka**
Ethnic and regional dimensions
*Dennis B. McGilvray and Michele R. Gamburd*

28 **Development, Democracy and the State**
Critiquing the Kerala model of development
*K. Ravi Raman*

29 **Mohajir Militancy in Pakistan**
Violence and transformation in the Karachi conflict
*Nichola Khan*

30 **Nationbuilding, Gender and War Crimes in South Asia**
*Bina D'Costa*

31 **The State in India after Liberalization**
Interdisciplinary perspectives
*Edited by Akhil Gupta and K. Sivaramakrishnan*

32 **National Identities in Pakistan**
The 1971 war in contemporary Pakistani fiction
*Cara Cilano*

33 **Political Islam and Governance in Bangladesh**
*Edited by Ali Riaz and C. Christine Fair*

34 **Bengali Cinema**
'An Other Nation'
*Sharmistha Gooptu*

35 **NGOs in India**
The challenges of women's empowerment and accountability
*Patrick Kilby*

36 **The Labour Movement in the Global South**
Trade unions in Sri Lanka
*S. Janaka Biyanwila*

37 **Building Bangalore**
Architecture and urban transformation in India's Silicon Valley
*John C. Stallmeyer*

38 **Conflict and Peacebuilding in Sri Lanka**
Caught in the peace trap?
*Edited by Jonathan Goodhand, Jonathan Spencer and Benedict Korf*

39 **Microcredit and Women's Empowerment**
A case study of Bangladesh
*Amunui Faraizi, Jim McAllister and Taskinur Rahman*

40 **South Asia in the New World Order**
The role of regional cooperation
*Shahid Javed Burki*

41 **Explaining Pakistan's Foreign Policy**
Escaping India
*Aparna Pande*

42 **Development-induced Displacement, Rehabilitation and Resettlement in India**
Current issues and challenges
*Edited by Sakarama Somayaji and Smrithi Talwar*

43 **The Politics of Belonging in India**
Becoming adivasi
*Edited by Daniel J. Rycroft and Sangeeta Dasgupta*

44 **Re-Orientalism and South Asian Identity Politics**
The oriental other within
*Edited by Lisa Lau and Ana Cristina Mendes*

45 **Islamic Revival in Nepal**
Religion and a new nation
*Megan Adamson Sijapati*

46 **Education and Inequality in India**
A classroom view
*Manabi Majumdar and Jos Mooij*

47 **The Culturalization of Caste in India**
Identity and inequality in a multicultural age
*Balmurli Natrajan*

48 **Corporate Social Responsibility in India**
*Bidyut Chakrabarty*

49 **Pakistan's Stability Paradox**
Domestic, regional and international dimensions
*Edited by Ashutosh Misra and Michael E. Clarke*

50 **Transforming Urban Water Supplies in India**
The role of reform and partnerships in globalization
*Govind Gopakumar*

51 **South Asian Security**
Twenty-first century discourses
*Sagarika Dutt and Alok Bansal*

52 **Non-discrimination and Equality in India**
Contesting boundaries of social justice
*Vidhu Verma*

53 **Being Middle-class in India**
A way of life
*Henrike Donner*

54 **Kashmir's Right to Secede**
A critical examination of contemporary theories of secession
*Matthew J. Webb*

55 **Bollywood Travels**
Culture, diaspora and border crossings in popular Hindi cinema
*Rajinder Dudrah*

56 **Nation, Territory, and Globalization in Pakistan**
Traversing the margins
*Chad Haines*

57 **The Politics of Ethnicity in Pakistan**
The Baloch, Sindhi and Mohajir Ethnic Movements
*Farhan Hanif Siddiqi*

58 **Nationalism and Ethnic Conflict**
Identities and mobilization after 1990
*Edited by Mahendra Lawoti and Susan Hangen*

59 **Islam and Higher Education**
Concepts, challenges and opportunities
*Marodsilton Muborakshoeva*

60 **Religious Freedom in India**
Sovereignty and (anti) conversion
*Goldie Osuri*

61 **Everyday Ethnicity in Sri Lanka**
Up-country Tamil identity politics
*Daniel Bass*

62 **Ritual and Recovery in Post-Conflict Sri Lanka**
Eloquent bodies
*Jane Derges*

63 **Bollywood and Globalisation**
The global power of popular Hindi cinema
*Edited by David J. Schaefer and Kavita Karan*

64 **Regional Economic Integration in South Asia**
Trapped in conflict?
*Amita Batra*

65 **Architecture and Nationalism in Sri Lanka**
The trouser under the cloth
*Anoma Pieris*

66 **Civil Society and Democratization in India**
Institutions, ideologies and interests
*Sarbeswar Sahoo*

67 **Contemporary Pakistani Fiction in English**
Idea, nation, state
*Cara N. Cilano*

68 **Transitional Justice in South Asia**
A study of Afghanistan and Nepal
*Tazreena Sajjad*

69 **Displacement and Resettlement in India**
The human cost of development
*Hari Mohan Mathur*

70 **Water, Democracy and Neoliberalism in India**
The Power to Reform
*Vicky Walters*

71 **Capitalist Development in India's Informal Economy**
*Elisabetta Basile*

72 **Nation, Constitutionalism and Buddhism in Sri Lanka**
*Roshan de Silva Wijeyeratne*

73 **Counterinsurgency, Democracy, and the Politics of Identity in India**
From warfare to welfare?
*Mona Bhan*

74 **Enterprise Culture in Neoliberal India**
Studies in youth, class, work and media
*Edited by Nandini Gooptu*

75 **The Politics of Economic Restructuring in India**
Economic governance and state spatial rescaling
*Loraine Kennedy*

76 **The Other in South Asian Religion, Literature and Film**
Perspectives on Otherism and Otherness
*Edited by Diana Dimitrova*

77 **Being Bengali**
At home and in the world
*Edited by Mridula Nath Chakraborty*

78 **The Political Economy of Ethnic Conflict in Sri Lanka**
*Nikolaos Biziouras*

79 **Indian Arranged Marriages**
A social psychological perspective
*Tulika Jaiswal*

80 **Writing the City in British Asian Diasporas**
*Edited by Seán McLoughlin, William Gould, Ananya Jahanara Kabir and Emma Tomalin*

81 **Post-9/11 Espionage Fiction in the US and Pakistan**
Spies and 'terrorists'
*Cara Cilano*

82 **Left Radicalism in India**
*Bidyut Chakrabarty*

83 **"Nation-State" and Minority Rights in India**
Comparative perspectives on Muslim and Sikh identities
*Tanweer Fazal*

84 **Pakistan's Nuclear Policy**
A minimum credible deterrence
*Zafar Khan*

85 **Imagining Muslims in South Asia and the Diaspora**
Secularism, religion, representations
*Claire Chambers and Caroline Herbert*

86 **Indian Foreign Policy in Transition**
Relations with South Asia
*Arijit Mazumdar*

87 **Corporate Social Responsibility and Development in Pakistan**
*Nadeem Malik*

88 **Indian Capitalism in Development**
*Barbara Harriss-White and Judith Heyer*

89 **Bangladesh Cinema and National Identity**
In search of the modern?
*Zakir Hossain Raju*

90 **Suicide in Sri Lanka**
The anthropology of an epidemic
*Tom Widger*

91 **Epigraphy and Islamic Culture**
Arabic and Persian inscriptions of Bengal and their historical and cultural implications
*Mohammad Yusuf Siddiq*

92 **Reshaping City Governance**
London, Mumbai, Kolkata, Hyderabad
*Nirmala Rao*

93 **The Indian Partition in Literature and Films**
History, politics, and aesthetics
*Rini Bhattacharya Mehta and Debali Mookerjea-Leonard*

94 **Development, Poverty and Power in Pakistan**
The impact of state and donor interventions on farmers
*Syed Mohammad Ali*

95 **Ethnic Subnationalist Insurgencies in South Asia**
Identities, interests and challenges to state authority
*Jugdep S. Chima*

96 **International Migration and Development in South Asia**
*Edited by Md Mizanur Rahman and Tan Tai Yong*

97 **Twenty-First Century Bollywood**
*Ajay Gehlawat*

98 **Political Economy of Development in India**
Indigeneity in transition in the State of Kerala
*Darley Kjosavik and Nadarajah Shanmugaratnam*

99 **State and Nation-Building in Pakistan**
Beyond Islam and security
*Edited by Roger D. Long, Yunas Samad, Gurharpal Singh, and Ian Talbot*

100 **Subaltern Movements in India**
Gendered geographies of struggle against neoliberal development
*Manisha Desai*

101 **Islamic Banking in Pakistan**
Shariah-compliant finance and the quest to make Pakistan more Islamic
*Feisal Khan*

# State and Nation-Building in Pakistan

Beyond Islam and security

**Edited by
Roger D. Long, Yunas Samad,
Gurharpal Singh, and Ian Talbot**

LONDON AND NEW YORK

First published 2016
by Routledge
2 Park Square, Milton Park, Abingdon, Oxon OX14 4RN

and by Routledge
711 Third Avenue, New York, NY 10017

*Routledge is an imprint of the Taylor & Francis Group, an informa business*

© 2016 selection and editorial matter, Roger D. Long, Yunas Samad, Gurharpal Singh, and Ian Talbot; individual chapters, the contributors.

The right of the editors to be identified as the authors of the editorial matter, and of the authors for their individual chapters, has been asserted in accordance with sections 77 and 78 of the Copyright, Designs and Patents Act 1988.

All rights reserved. No part of this book may be reprinted or reproduced or utilised in any form or by any electronic, mechanical, or other means, now known or hereafter invented, including photocopying and recording, or in any information storage or retrieval system, without permission in writing from the publishers.

*Trademark notice*: Product or corporate names may be trademarks or registered trademarks, and are used only for identification and explanation without intent to infringe.

*British Library Cataloguing in Publication Data*
A catalogue record for this book is available from the British Library

*Library of Congress Cataloging in Publication Data*
A catalog record for this book has been requested

ISBN: 978-1-138-90347-0 (hbk)
ISBN: 978-1-315-69690-4 (ebk)

Typeset in Times New Roman
by Wearset Ltd, Boldon, Tyne and Wear

# Contents

| | |
|---|---|
| List of illustrations | xiii |
| Notes on contributors | xiv |

**Introduction: themes, theories, and topics in the history of religion, violence, and political mobilization in Pakistan**    1
IAN TALBOT

1 **The impact of the redistribution of Partition's evacuee property on the patterns of land ownership and power in Pakistani Punjab in the 1950s**    13
ILYAS CHATTHA

2 **Elections, bureaucracy, and the law: the reproduction of landed power in post-colonial Punjab**    35
HASSAN JAVID

3 **Factionalism and indiscipline in Pakistan's party political system**    60
MARIAM MUFTI

4 **Constructing the state: constitutional integration of the princely states of Pakistan**    76
YAQOOB KHAN BANGASH

5 **Identity politics and nation-building in Pakistan: the case of Sindhi nationalism**    101
SARAH ANSARI

6 **Understanding the insurgency in Balochistan**    118
YUNAS SAMAD

7 **A sublime, yet disputed, object of political ideology? Sufism in Pakistan at the crossroads** 146
ALIX PHILIPPON

8 **The rise of militancy among Pakistani Barelvis: the case of the Sunni Tehrik** 166
MUJEEB AHMAD

9 **Pakistan's religious *Others*: reflections on the minority discourse on Christians in the Punjab** 180
TAHIR KAMRAN AND NAVTEJ K. PUREWAL

10 **Violence and state formation in Pakistan** 192
GURHARPAL SINGH

*Index* 207

# Illustrations

## Figures

| | | |
|---|---|---|
| 4.1 | West Pakistan in 1948 | 83 |
| 4.2 | West Pakistan in 1955 | 95 |
| 4.3 | Pakistan in 1973 | 97 |

## Tables

| | | |
|---|---|---|
| 1.1 | Exchange of population in rural West Punjab | 15 |
| 1.2 | Land ownership and cultivation patterns in West Punjab in 1947 | 16 |
| 1.3 | Refugee 'claims' transferred from congested districts to non-congested districts | 21 |
| 2.1 | Socio-economic characteristics of National Assembly members, 1985–97 | 40 |
| 2.2 | Profession of members of the Punjab Assembly, 2008 | 41 |
| 2.3 | Land revenue and agricultural income tax receipts and total revenue in the Punjab | 49 |

# Contributors

**Mujeeb Ahmad**, International Islamic University, Islamabad, received his PhD from the Quaid-i-Azam University, Islamabad, in History in 2008. He is now Assistant Professor in the Department of History and Pakistan Studies at the International Islamic University in Islamabad where he specializes in teaching and researching modern South Asian history and politics. His dissertation was 'Barelwis and their Religio-Political Parties in Pakistan, 1947–1971'.

**Sarah Ansari**, Royal Holloway, University of London, is Professor of History. Her research interests focus on the recent history of South Asia, in particular those parts of the subcontinent that became Pakistan in 1947. Apart from a number of individual publications and the popular history of Pakistan which she is currently writing for Cambridge University Press, she has co-authored 'The Flux of the Matter: Loyalty, Corruption and the Everyday State in Post-Partition India and Pakistan', *Past and Present*, 219, 1 (2013): 237–79. She is also the editor of the quarterly *Journal of the Royal Asiatic Society*. Her books include *Life after Migration: Community and Strife in Sindh: 1947–1962* (Karachi: Oxford University Press, 2005) and *Sufi Saints and State Power: The Pirs of Sind, 1843–1947* (Cambridge: Cambridge University Press, 1992).

**Yaqoob Khan Bangash**, Forman Christian College, Lahore, is Assistant Professor and Chair of the Department of History. His main area of research is modern South Asia with a focus on the creation and consolidation of Pakistan, particularly with regard to the integration of the princely states into Pakistan, as over half of the area that now comprises Pakistan were princely states. He completed his dissertation, 'The Integration of the Princely States of Pakistan 1947–55', at the University of Oxford in 2011. His publications include *Subjects to Citizens: Accession and Integration of the Princely States of Pakistan* (Karachi: Oxford University Press, 2013) and 'Three Forgotten Accessions: Gilgit, Hunza and Nagar', *Journal of Imperial and Commonwealth History* 38, 1 (2010): 117–43.

**Ilyas Chattha**, University of Southampton, received his PhD in 2009 at the University of Southampton where he is now at the Centre for Imperial and Post-Colonial Studies. He is carrying out research on the impact of Partition on

Punjabi Christians in Pakistan. His publications include: 'Faction-Building in Pakistan: Sir Francis Mudie and Punjab Politics, 1947–1949', *Contemporary South Asia*, 22, 3 (2014): 1–15; 'The Patterns of Partition Violence in West Punjab: A Study of Police Records', in Ian Talbot (ed.) *The Independence of India and Pakistan: New Approaches and Reflections* (Karachi: Oxford University Press, 2013), pp. 58–89; and the monograph, *Partition and Locality: Violence, Migration, and Development in Gujranwala and Sialkot, 1947–1961* (Karachi: Oxford University Press, 2011).

**Hassan Javid**, Lahore University of Management Sciences, is Assistant Professor of Political Science. He received his PhD, entitled 'Class, Power, and Patronage: The Landed Elite and Politics in Pakistani Punjab', in 2012 from the London School of Economics at the University of London. He writes book reviews for various media outlets including *Dawn* and *The Express Tribune*, and is columnist for *The Nation* where he comments on a wide variety of topics such as 'We Need to Talk about Punjab' (22 June 2014); 'Understanding Pakistan's Political Parties' (8 June 2014); 'Modi, Sharif, and the Need for Peace' (25 May 2014); 'The Problem with the PTI' (11 May 2014); 'Reforming Education in Pakistan' (15 June 2014); 'The Problem with "Honour"' (1 June 2014); and 'Prioritizing Peacocks' (22 March 2014).

**Tahir Kamran**, Allama Iqbal Chair at the University of Cambridge, and Fellow of Wolfson College. He is the former Head of the Department of History at Government College, Lahore, where he founded the journal, *The Historian*, and was an influential figure in the Higher Education Commission of Pakistan. His current research focuses on minorities in Pakistan, religious radicalization, and its various modes of articulation. His publications include *Election Commission of Pakistan: Role in Politics* (Lahore: South Asia Partnership – Pakistan, 2009) and *Democracy and Governance in Pakistan* (Lahore: South Asia Partnership – Pakistan, 2008).

**Roger D. Long**, Eastern Michigan University, President of the South Asian Muslim Studies Association, is Professor of History and teaches a wide variety of courses in British, British Empire, South and Southeast Asian history, and world history. He is editor of *A History of Pakistan* (Karachi: Oxford University Press, 2015), as well as such volumes as William S. Metz, *The Political Career of Mohammad Ali Jinnah* (Karachi: Oxford University Press, 2010); *'Dear Mr. Jinnah': Selected Correspondence and Speeches of Liaquat Ali Khan, 1937–1947* (Karachi: Oxford University Press, 2004); *Charisma and Commitment in South Asian History: Essays Presented to Stanley Wolpert* (New Delhi: Orient Longman, 2003); *The Founding of Pakistan: An Annotated Bibliography* (Lanham, MD: Scarecrow Press, 1998); and *'The Man on the Spot': Essays on British Empire History* (Westport, CT: Greenwood Press, 1995).

**Mariam Mufti**, University of Waterloo, is Assistant Professor in the Department of International and Area Studies. As a comparative political scientist she works on regime change and political participation in hybrid regimes. In particular her research focuses on the role of the military and political parties in the processes of recruitment and selection of the political elite in Pakistan as a way to understand the behaviour of political leadership and regime dynamics. She received her PhD, entitled 'Elite Recruitment and Regime Dynamics in Pakistan', in 2011 from Johns Hopkins University. Her publications include *Religion and Militancy in Pakistan and Afghanistan: A Literature Review* (Washington, DC: Center for Strategic and International Studies, 2012) and the co-authored *Religion, Politics and Governance in Pakistan* (London: UK Department for International Development, 2009).

**Alix Philippon**, Institute of Political Studies, Aix en Provence, is a postdoctoral scholar at the Institute of Political Studies, Aix en Provence, and Research Associate at the South Asia Institute at the School of Oriental and African Studies, the University of London. Her publications include 'The *'Urs* of the Patron Saint of Lahore: National Popular Festival and Sacred Union between the Pakistani State and Society?' *Social Compass*, 59 (2012): 289–97 and *Soufisme et Politique au Pakistan: Le Mouvement Barelwi à l'Heure de la Guerre Contre le Terrorisme* (Aix-en-Province: Karthala-Sciences Po Aix, 2011).

**Navtej K. Purewal**, School of Oriental and African Studies, University of London, is Deputy Director of the South Asia Institute. Her interests lie in the areas of the sociology of gender and in the social realm of religion. Her teaching and research have continued to engage with a number of areas of the social sciences which cross both spatial and disciplinary boundaries. She has an interdisciplinary background with a BA in Political Science from Vassar College, an MA in Area Studies, South Asia, from the School of Oriental and African Studies at the University of London, and a PhD in Development Studies, Lancaster University. She has a number of collaborative international links with universities in India, Ghana, Sudan, and Bangladesh and she has recently completed a large project on popular religious practices and transgressions of religious boundaries in South Asia. Her publications include *Son Preference: Sex Selection, Gender and Culture in South Asia* (New York: Berg, 2010) and *Living on the Margins: Social Access to Shelter in Urban South Asia* (Burlington, VT: Ashgate, 2000).

**Yunas Samad**, University of Bradford, is Professor of South Asian Studies and Director of Post-Graduate Research. His publications include: *Pakistan–US Conundrum: Jihadis, Military and the People – The Struggle for Control* (London: Hurst, 2011); *Muslim Community Cohesion: Bradford Report* (London: Joseph Rowntree Foundation, 2010); *Islam in the European Union: Muslim Youth and the War on Terror*, with Kasturi Sen (Oxford: Oxford University Press, 2007); *Faultlines of Nationhood*, with Gyan Pandey (New Delhi: Roli Press, 2007); *Community Perceptions of Forced Marriage*, with John Eade (London: Foreign and Commonwealth Office, 2003); *Culture*

*Identity and Politics: Ethnic Minorities in Britain*, edited with T. Ranger, and O. Stuart (Aldershot: Avebury, 1996); and *A Nation in Turmoil: Nationalism and Ethnicity in Pakistan 1937–58* (Santa Barbara, CA: Sage, 1995).

**Gurharpal Singh**, School of Oriental and African Studies, University of London, is Dean of the Faculty of Arts and Humanities and Professor in Inter-Religious Relations and Development in the Department of the Study of Religions. His publications include: *New Dimensions of Politics in India*, ed. with Lawrence Saez (London: Routledge, 2012); *The Partition of India*, with Ian Talbot (Cambridge: Cambridge University Press, 2009); *Ethnic Conflict in India: A Case Study of Punjab* (London: Macmillan, 2000); and *Region and Partition: Bengal, Punjab and the Partition of the Indian Subcontinent*, edited with Ian Talbot (Karachi: Oxford University Press, 1999).

**Ian Talbot**, University of Southampton, is Professor of History. He was Head of Discipline from 2009 to 2012, and Chairman of the British Association for South Asian Studies in 2011–14. He was the founding director of the Centre for Imperial and Post-Colonial Studies at the University of Southampton. He has published extensively on the history of colonial Punjab, the Partition of India, and the post-independence political history of Pakistan. His publications include: *Pakistan: A New History* (London: Hurst, 2012); *Pakistan: A Modern History* (London: Hurst, 1998; 2nd edn, 2009); *The Partition of India*, with Gurharpal Singh (Cambridge: Cambridge University Press, 2009); *The Deadly Embrace: Religion, Politics, and Violence in India and Pakistan, 1947–2002* (Karachi: Oxford University Press, 2007); *Divided Cities: Partition and its Aftermath in Lahore and Amritsar 1947–1957* (Karachi: Oxford University Press, 2006); *Khizr Tiwana, the Punjab Unionist Party and the Partition of India* (Karachi: Oxford University Press, 2002); *India and Pakistan* (London, 2000); and *Punjab and the Raj, 1849–1947* (New Delhi: Manohar, 1988).

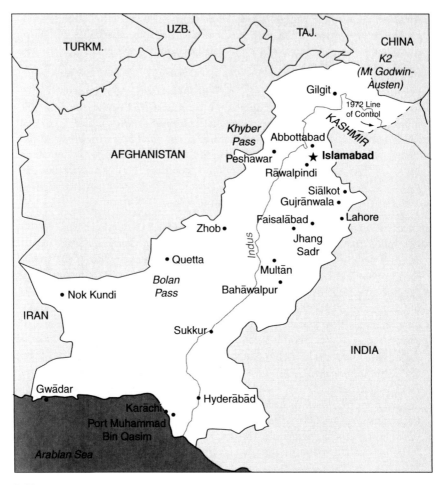

Pakistan.

# Introduction

Themes, theories, and topics in the history of religion, violence, and political mobilization in Pakistan

*Ian Talbot*

Pakistan was created in August 1947 after a seven year struggle by the All-India Muslim League under the leadership of Mohammad Ali Jinnah (1876–1948, Governor-General of Pakistan 1947–8). Despite a common administrative inheritance, the democratic experiences of post-independence India and Pakistan have taken divergent trajectories.[1] Pakistan has experienced long periods of military and military-backed rule. Ethnic tensions led to the breakaway of East Pakistan in 1971. Since then there have been renewed ethnic conflict in Balochistan and the rise of sectarian violence and Islamic militancy. The latter has threatened state control of the Tribal Areas adjoining Afghanistan. Tensions have also persisted with India, from time to time overflowing into armed conflict. The Kashmir dispute remains the symbolic focus of mistrust and enmity. While recent research has moved away from 'headline' accounts of Pakistan's state failure to seek to explain the resilience of the country, much work focuses on the themes of civil-military relations, ethnic conflict, and militancy. This introduction examines them in order to provide a context for readers, so that they can appreciate the fresh insights arising from the volume.

Pakistan inherited the more economically 'backward' and politically underdeveloped areas of British India at the time of the subcontinent's division. This has been termed by some writers a 'democratic deficit' which helps explain its struggles to consolidate a democratic system.[2] The dislocation brought by Partition compounded this inheritance. The fledgling government had to feed, clothe and house millions of refugees.[3] This monumental and unanticipated task, it has been argued, sharpened the contradictions between state consolidation and political participation.[4] Frequent military intervention has also been understood in terms of the country's geo-strategic situation with threatening neighbours giving birth to what has been called the 'garrison state' syndrome.[5] Since its creation, Pakistan has had especially difficult relations with its Indian and Afghan neighbours. These can be traced back to the state's creation, when many Pakistanis believed that India was trying to undo the Partition and Afghanistan was fermenting trouble with the Pashtun population of Pakistan because of its territorial ambitions. Pakistan has repaid India in the same coin, especially in Kashmir. The enduring rivalry has encouraged the nexus of ties between the Army, its intelligence agency, Inter-Services Intelligence (ISI), and *jihadist* groups in the pursuit of a 'proxy war' option.[6] This policy gave space for radicalism to flourish within Pakistan. This has created the circumstances for a 'creeping Talibanization' in the tribal areas. At the same time it also came at the price of rising sectarian conflict, as the *jihadist* groups had ties with militant Sunni groups within Pakistan such as *the Sipah-e-Sabha Pakistan* founded in Jhang by Haq Nawaz Jhangvi (1952–90) in 1985.

The post-9/11 period has transformed Pakistan's troubled regional relationships in three ways. First, the long-held tensions between the Afghan and Pakistan governments have resurfaced over issues of border security. Second, growing Indian influence in Afghanistan has increased Pakistan's anxieties about its encirclement. Finally, India has emerged as a strategic ally of the United States.

The Indian factor is never absent in Pakistan's politics. The Kashmir issue provides politicians with a means to both rally support and goad opponents. Moreover, diplomatic, economic, and strategic policy has all been skewed to counter the 'Indian threat'. Pakistan's political 'economy of defence' rather than of 'development' can only be explained with respect to Kashmir. The priority of building up the armed forces was spelled out by Prime Minister Liaquat Ali Khan (1895–1951, Prime Minister 1947–51) as early as 8 October 1948: 'The defence of the State is our foremost consideration ... and has dominated all other governmental activities. We will not begrudge any amount on the defence of our country.'[7] Pakistan's human development indicators lag behind other South Asian countries in part because of the long-term distortion of the economy arising from high rates of military expenditure. It has consistently remained at around 4.5 per cent of Gross Domestic Product (GDP), more than twice the total expenditure on public education. Illiteracy remains high, with only 68 per cent of adult males literate and only 40 per cent of female adults able to read and write. Moreover, a situation has arisen when *madrassah* education is all that is available for many poor families. Life expectancy has only risen slowly from 60 to 68 years in the period 1990–2012.

Yet until the 1990s, Pakistan experienced faster rates of economic growth than India. Indeed during the 1950s, the rate was almost double. From 2001 to 2006, Pakistan's macro-economic indicators were again impressive with GDP growing at around 6 per cent. In this period, those living below the poverty line declined by 10 per cent, although this still left 25 per cent of the population living below the poverty line. Since 2007, poverty has increased as the economy has suffered external shocks and the problems arising from terrorism; food and fuel prices have risen sharply. Inflation peaked at 12 per cent in 2011. Growth of GDP has been only 3 per cent since 2008 while the population in the same period has grown annually by 1.5 per cent. There has been a rise of the middle class linked with growth in the service sector. Nevertheless, this class is economically and especially politically much less influential than its Indian counterpart. Over 40 per cent of the labour force remains locked in the agricultural sector. During the height of the 1970s' Green Revolution, the rural sector grew rapidly, but it is now acting as a structural drag on growth. Rice and raw cotton remain major exports alongside textiles. There is the need for further diversification of the country's export base. Petroleum products are a major source of imports and have recently encouraged inflationary pressures. Telecommunications and financial services have been behind the growth of the service sector. There has not, however, been a similar IT boom to India's to spur economic growth. Overseas remittances have, however, played a very important role in Pakistan's economic performance since the 1980s. Remittances from overseas Pakistanis have been averaging about $1 billion a month since 2011.

A number of accounts explain Pakistan's contrasting democratic trajectory to India in terms of weak political institutionalization.[8] The weak institutional moorings of the Muslim League are traced to the fact that the All-India Muslim League, founded in 1906, was a 'latecomer' in the areas which eventually constituted Pakistan. Its heartland had always lain in the provinces of the United Provinces and Bombay where Muslims formed a minority. The League's lack of a mass base of support, outside of Bengal, even at the height of the freedom struggle, has been compared unfavourably with that of the All-India Congress Party founded in 1885. Many of the League's branches existed only on paper or were weakened by factional infighting. The League, in order to make a political breakthrough in the key Muslim majority areas, without which its Pakistan demand would lack credibility, had to accommodate itself to local mediators of power.[9] These included landlords, *biraderi* (kinship group) heads, and local religious leaders. This set in process a politics of clientalism which is still evident today.[10] Pakistan's clientalistic politics provides many openings for corruption. But charges of corruption have also been used to 'smear' opponents of sitting governments and to embroil them in court cases which undermine their room for political manoeuvre.

The Muslim League's ambiguous attitude to Islam has also been seen as a factor in weakening its nation-building ability.[11] It mobilized support either around the slogan of Islam in danger, or by means of local mediatory networks. Most of the Muslim League leaders, including Jinnah, were 'secular' in outlook, but used religious slogans to further their political cause in the final stages of the freedom struggle. Many of the Islamic scholars (*ulama*) opposed the Pakistan movement because of its secular leadership and placing national identity above commitment to the *ummah*. Once Pakistan was created they sought to Islamize it. The freedom movement had left unresolved the question whether Pakistan was a homeland for Indian Muslims, or an Islamic state. This issue further fed into the regional tensions between the Centre and East Pakistan, which contained a significant Hindu minority population. The Constituent Assembly's initial rejection of Bengali as a state language, coupled with a refusal to hold sessions in Dhaka, led to growing protests within Pakistan's eastern wing. The friction meant that it was not until nine years after independence that Pakistan's first Constitution was promulgated. By that stage a 'creeping authoritarianism' was in train with power slipping to the bureaucracy amidst an increasingly chaotic political scene.[12] US financial and military support proffered in the Cold War context and sought to counterbalance India, boosted the emerging bureaucratic-Army axis.[13] The process culminated in the country's first military coup in

October 1958. Far from being a decade of promise and democratic consolidation, the state's formative years had seen the creation of a path dependency that has continued to thwart democratization, with resultant military interventions and post-military withdrawal crises.[14]

Military intervention in politics has often been justified in terms of the Army's perception of itself as the bulwark of the country – the only institution which properly works. It is nevertheless undeniable that successive bouts of military rule in Pakistan (coups in 1958, 1977, and 1999 followed by long periods of direct military rule and 'guided democracy') have reinforced centrifugal ethnic, linguistic, and regional forces. Colonial recruitment policies from the so-called 'martial races' of the Punjab have continued.[15] This has made the Army appear as an alien occupying force when it has been deployed to quell unrest elsewhere in the country. Approximately 75 per cent of the Army is drawn from just three Punjab districts. Balochistan and Sindh together only make up about 5 per cent of Army personnel. Moreover, Army-backed governments have tended to view demands for autonomy in the smaller provinces of Pakistan as 'law and order' issues rather than legitimate demands which should be addressed by political compromise. The identification of the Army's interests with those of the Punjab has led elites from other provinces to talk about the 'Punjabization' of Pakistan.[16]

Military rule has perpetuated weak political institutionalization and undermined the growth of civil society. Depoliticization has been a tried and tested military solution to the problem of national unity. Parties have been banned and 'corrupt' politicians have been excluded through the operation of such measures as the Public and Representative Offices (Disqualification) Act (PRODA), enacted in 1949, and the Elective Bodies (Disqualification) Order (EBDO) of 1959. The Army has not, however, subjected itself to accountability. It has, however, increasingly expanded its role in commercial and industrial life.[17] The military runs its own schools, colleges, and universities, its own businesses and industries, and owns about 12 million acres of land. This has given it institutional motives as well as capacity for further political intervention. It has also encouraged 'authoritarian clientalism'. Political players have conceded power to the armed forces with the intention of maximizing their interests.[18] The Army has been used as a kind of umpire to avoid conceding space to the other. This kind of behaviour contributes to the 'short-termism' which is a notable feature of Pakistan politics. While elite politicians have benefited, national resources have been squandered by, for example, the award of generous loans from the state-controlled banking system to subsequent defaulters. Successive military regimes have claimed that they would clean up such practices.

The Army has expanded its recruitment base from the feudal elite to lower income groups. Indeed it is one of the few avenues to upward social mobility in Pakistan. Entry is controlled on ethnic rather than class lines. Advancement depends on performance, loyalty to its bureaucratic-organizational norms, and connections. Benefits include jobs after retirement. The Pervez Musharraf (b. 1943) regime (1999–2008) inducted about 5,000 individuals into various government postings. The concentration of the military welfare foundations' business activities in the Punjab is another cause of resentment amongst the smaller provinces.

The rule of Zia-ul-Haq (1924–88) between 1977 and 1988 had an especially pernicious impact on civil society because of its longevity and severity. Pakistan's first military ruler Ayub Khan (1907–74) muzzled the press during his 11-year period in power between 1958 and 1969, but it would have been unthinkable during his rule to flog journalists before the gaze of world opinion. In May 1978, however, four journalists were publicly flogged by bare-chested wrestlers in Lahore because they had gone on hunger strike to protest against the closure of the leading Pakistan People's Party (PPP) newspaper, *Musawat*.[19] Civil society was also exposed to the depredations of censorship and prayer wardens. Where co-option failed as in Sindh, brute force was deployed.

The long-standing debate about Islam's role in public life also took on a new dimension in the Zia era. The state for the first time sponsored Islamization through judicial, economic, and educational reforms and amendments to the Pakistan Penal Code.[20] There is debate as to whether Zia merely sought to legitimize his undemocratic regime in this way. Islamization thrived within the regional context of the Afghan conflict and domestically drew strength from the rapid socio-economic changes of the later 1970s and the truncation of the state following the emergence of Bangladesh.[21] Its legacy was to bring the *ulama* closer to power than ever before, although initially it was the lay activists of the Islamist *Jamaat-i-Islami* (JI) who were closest to the Zia regime. Differences between Sunni Hanafi jurisprudence and Shia interpretations became increasingly politicized and raised sectarian tensions between the Sunni majority and Shia minority (17 per cent of the population). The *Tehrik-e-Nifaz-e-Fiqh-e-Jafaria* from 1979 onwards led the Shia opposition.

Deobandi *madaris* (schools) proliferated in the Zia era as a result of state patronage and generous funding from Saudi Arabia. The Deobandis stood for a puritanical version of Islam which opposed not only Shia variants, but the Sufi practices of shrine-based Islam. Traditionalist Islam in Pakistan was organized through the Barelvi movement. Disputes over state management of shrines and mosques led to a major altercation between Deobandis and Barelvis at the Badshahi Mosque in Lahore in May 1984.[22] A small number of Deobandi institutions preached *jihad* and prepared students for military conflict in Afghanistan. Later, activities shifted to the Kashmir struggle. Subsequently, members of Deobandi-influenced militant groups, like *Sipah-e-Sahaba Pakistan* and *Lashkar-e-Jhangvi* (LeJ; Army of Jahangir), founded in 1996 as a splinter group from *Sipah-e-Sahaba*, have challenged the writ of the Pakistani state.[23] The catalyst was the military action in July 2007 against the militant Red Mosque (*Lal Masjid*), in the very heart of the Pakistani capital, Islamabad. The mosque was patronized during the Zia era because of its role in raising recruits for the Afghan *jihad*. It also became associated with hardline Sunni sectarianism. Its Deobandi students and their teachers in 2007 defied the state with a campaign to forcibly impose a strict interpretation of *shariah* law.[24] The Pakistan Army seized the

Red Mosque on 10 July 2007 in a bloody battle which claimed over 150 lives. The formation of the *Tehreek-e-Taliban Pakistan* (TTP) in December the same year as an umbrella organization for militant groups was a direct response.

South Punjab has emerged as a leading centre of Deobandi activity. Deobandi activities, even in the colonial era, were centred in this region because they wished to challenge its strong Sufi influence. Partition saw a number of Deobandi institutions re-established from Jullundur and Ludhiana in the region including Multan and Bahawalpur. *Wafaq ul Madaris ul Arabia* (established in 1959), which is a regulatory body of Deobandi *madaris* is also in Multan. In recent years, there has been both a proliferation of Deobandi religious institutions and considerable recruitment for the Afghan and Kashmir *jihads* from this area of Pakistan.[25]

Zia's Islamization coincided with the Afghan War which initiated two important processes continuing to impact on Pakistan. The first is the weaponization of the country, which has made religious, ethnic, and criminal activities deadly in their consequences. Second, the war encouraged the links between Islamic radicals and the Army and its intelligence wing, the ISI, which resulted in ambiguities in the approach to the post-9/11 'war on terror'. The military itself has been under attack as it has ventured into the tribal areas and as a result of the fall-out from the *Lal Masjid* episode.

Pakistan's history has been marked not only by contests over the role of Islam, but by the relationship between Pakistani nationalism and ethnic and linguistic allegiances. Their power in contrast with a state-centred identity of recent construction was summed up by the famous phrase of the Pushtun nationalist Wali Khan (1917–2006) when he declared in the 1980s: 'I have been a Pushtun for 4,000 years, a Muslim for 1,400 years and a Pakistani for 40 years.'[26] The Pakistan state has been manifestly unsuccessful in managing diversity. Recourse to centralizing solutions to the problem of state construction in a context of financial constraint and strategic insecurity lay at the heart of its failure. Attempts to establish a centralized state around the predominance of the Muslim League and the unifying symbols of Urdu and Islam created tensions with ethno-language groups in all the provinces, except Punjab which gradually emerged as the core of the new state. The gradual melding of Pakistan and Punjab identities had its longer-term historical roots in the colonial state's decision to make Urdu rather than Punjabi the official language of government.[27]

The Centre-province tussle became especially embittered in East Bengal. Alongside the Bengali language issue, there was a sense that the region's economic resources (the export of raw jute) were being exploited for the benefit of West Pakistan's development. Political marginalization made such notions even more combustible. The increasingly radical demands of Bengali nationalists were reflected in the Awami League's 6-Point Programme of May 1966 (the Awami League had been founded in 1949). This called for the establishment of full provincial autonomy in East Pakistan on the basis of the historic Lahore Resolution of 23 March 1940. The Centre was left only with the responsibility for defence and foreign affairs. The Awami League swept to power in East

Pakistan following Pakistan's first national election since independence in December 1970. The inability to secure a national-level power sharing agreement between it and the PPP led to the launching of the Army crackdown codenamed Operation Searchlight on 26 March 1971. Nine months of civil war and the third Indo-Pakistan War culminated in the defeat of the Pakistan Army on 16 December 1971 and the emergence of Bangladesh the following day.[28]

Some Pakistani authors have drawn parallels between the Bangladesh debacle and the situation in Balochistan which has been the focus of tribal insurgency and military intervention throughout much of the post-independence period. Eventually Zulfiqar Ali Bhutto (1928–79, President 1971–3, Prime Minister 1973–7) gave the Army a way back into political life, after the humiliation of its surrender to defeat by Indian forces in East Pakistan, by deploying it against what he termed an 'insurgency' by Baloch nationalists. The Bhutto era between 1971 and 1977 represented a lost opportunity for establishing civilian supremacy over the Army.[29] The return of a military regime led by Pervez Musharraf (b. 1943) in 1999 committed to the development of Balochistan in the national interest evoked long-standing antipathy. The establishment of cantonments in the wake of 9/11 made it appear that a Punjabi-led occupying force was taking over the province. Musharraf's encouragement of Pushtun Islamists further created a sense of Baloch marginalization. The circumstances were thus created for a new phase of militancy.[30] Musharraf denied it possessed a nationalist agenda, linking it instead to tribal leaders' resistance to any form of development which would undermine their autocratic power.

In the 1990s, the governments of Nawaz Sharif (b. 1949, Prime Minister 1990–3, 1997–9, 2013–present) and Benazir Bhutto (1953–2007, Prime Minister 1988–90, 1993–6) had to deal with a mini-insurgency in Karachi led by the *Mohajir Qaumi Mahaz* (MQM), the party which represented the interests of Partition migrants from India (*muhajir*). Its emergence in 1984 reflected the rise of ethnic political identity and the declining national political power of the *muhajir* community. Successive waves of migration have resulted in 5 per cent of the national population congregating in Karachi's urban sprawl. More Balochis reside in Karachi than in Balochistan and the city is a melting pot with significant Punjabi, *muhajir*, and Pushtun populations. Sindhis regard Karachi as an alien intrusion on their homeland. The politics of rural Sind differ significantly from those of Karachi. The city remains volatile, awash with weapons and the scene of ethnic, sectarian, and crime-related violence. Ethnic conflict in Pakistan's leading commercial centre again paved the way for military influence, as failure to provide law and order was a justification for the constitutional coups which removed Benazir Bhutto in 1990 and Nawaz Sharif in 1993. The Army's influence during the 1990s was exerted through the office of the Presidency. The controversial 8th Amendment to the 1973 Constitution, introduced by Zia in 1985, empowered the President to remove elected governments.

The MQM, until the emergence of Imran Khan (b. 1952) and his party, *Pakistan Tehreek-e-Insaf* (Movement for Justice), in 1996 as an important force, was the only Pakistan party with a middle-class base. Wealth and land constitute the basis for political influence. Parties field candidates who are influential in their localities. There is thus little scope for middle-class candidates. Just as it is difficult for middle-class politicians to make their way, so despite impressive reforms by Musharraf with respect to female representation, which saw 60 seats reserved for women in the National Assembly, independent women find it hard to make a political impact. Many of those elected are in the parliament to represent feudal family interests.

With the exception of the PPP and PML-N (Pakistan Muslim League (N)), Pakistan's parties lack the ability to move beyond regional and sectional appeals. The religious parties remain strongest in the more conservative areas of Khyber Pakhtunkhwa. The Deobandi *Jamiat-ul-Ulama-e-Islam* (JUI) is a party which appeals primarily to the Pushtun population and has more urban support amongst the lower middle class across Pakistan. The religious parties have been traditionally disunited and have lacked the ability to win more than a handful of seats in the National Assembly. In the 1993 elections, for example, they captured just nine. The 2002 elections saw a breakthrough for them in the Frontier and Balochistan. Their success was due to the hostility to US action against the Taliban government in Afghanistan and to the side-lining of the mainstream PPP and PML-N. The PPP's main powerbase is in Sindh and Southern Punjab where it has led demands for the creation of a new province. The PML-N has its greatest support in central Punjab. Pakistan's political geography means that support in Punjab is essential for a party to have a firm grip on power. Benazir Bhutto's 1988–90 government was seriously hampered at the national level by the hostility it faced in the Punjab from the provincial administration led by Nawaz Sharif. When the PPP has done well in elections it is because it has extended support from its heartland in Sindh to the Punjab. Explanations of the failure to consolidate democracy in the period 1988–99 point to the zero-sum game approach to politics of the two leading parties.[31]

Violence has been a marked feature of Pakistan's history. The country's bloody birth has been followed by a calamitous civil war in East Pakistan and the insurgencies in Karachi and Balochistan to which we have already referred. Since the Zia era there has been mounting sectarian violence, including bomb blasts and targeted killings. Militant struggle against the Pakistan state has seen the rise of suicide bombings. From 2002, the Pakistan Army has been engaged sporadically in military operations in the Tribal Areas. A large-scale military offensive was also required to restore the writ of the state in Malakand Division. From 2005, there was escalating violence once again in the troubled Balochistan province. There has been considerable Chinese investment in the development of its port facility at Gwadar but development projects in Balochistan remain controversial amongst Baloch nationalists. Some Pakistani analysts, however, see an Indian hand behind the insurgency in the strategically crucial province.

These insurgencies have dominated international headlines, but there have been a variety of outbreaks of violence in contemporary Pakistan. These have included protests against the state in response to shortages of electricity supply. The regular blackouts of recent years have led to angry protests from both domestic consumers and industrialists. Media reports put the energy shortfall in the range of 4,000–6,000 megawatts. Supplies will need to increase if growth rates are to be maintained and human development is to be improved. At present, 40 per cent of Pakistan households do not have access to electricity. At the same time government subsidies to the power sector which run annually at 220 billion rupees drain resources from improvements in education and healthcare.

There is also a strong gendered dimension to violence with repeated episodes of so-called 'honour killings', alongside brutal acts of domestic violence. The former are rooted in the prevailing notions of honour (*izzat*) and dishonour in Pakistani society, which allow for retribution to be meted out for violations of collective codes of sexual conduct. A number of explanations can be provided for the prevalence of violence. These must begin with reference to the asymmetrical power relations between rich and poor, and male and female, which enable criminal acts to be undertaken with relative impunity; the desperate conflicts over scarce resources; and the growth of the politics of identity based around sect and ethnicity in the past two decades. While the 'youth bulge' is a factor in economic dynamism – around 40 per cent of the population is below 14 years of age – it also is a factor in rising violence as a result of the recruitment of footloose and underemployed young men for a range of militant, ethnic, and criminal activities. In Karachi these coalesce with criminal activities, which are conducted under ethnic political cover. Lack of education could also be linked with violence in a society in which only 56 per cent of the population is literate, with the figure for women being much lower. Violence is not, however, the preserve solely of the uneducated, as seen in the lawyers' protests which began in March 2007.

A combination of Pervez Musharraf's liberal attitudes, mounting sectarian conflict, and the need to secure a favourable international image for his regime, led him to portray Pakistan as a moderate Islamic state which would act as a source of stability in a volatile West Asia region. Musharraf launched the concept of Enlightened Moderation at the 2002 Organization of the Islamic Conference meeting in Malaya. He also emphasized Sufi teachings as a counter to extremism. In November 2006, he launched a National Sufi Council amidst great fanfare. Sectarian violence, involvement of Pakistanis in acts of international terrorism, and a rising tide of suicide bombings which were introduced to Pakistan via the Iraq War (2003–11) belied this image. Government efforts ensured that a number of religious scholars headed by the chairman of the Barelvi education board, *Tanzimul Madaris Pakistan*, issued a *fatwa* on 19 May 2005 which forbade suicide attacks on Muslims and places of worship and public congregations. Deobandi *ulama*, in contrast, steadfastly refused to issue a blanket condemnation of suicide attacks. Even more damaging was the government's failure to clamp down on mushrooming 'hate literature', some of which glorified such attacks.

Many of the above themes are tackled in new and exciting ways in this volume. The dominance of work on Deobandi Islam is, for example, provided with a timely counterpoise in the chapters by Alix Philippon, 'A sublime, yet disputed, object of ideology? Sufism in Pakistan at the crossroads', and Mujeeb Ahmad, 'The rise of militancy among Pakistan Barelvis: the case of the Sunni Tehrik'. Philippon reveals the ways in which Sufism was projected during the Musharraf period as an alternative 'moderate' version of Islam to Deobandi-influenced radicalism. Her questioning of this construction is dealt with at length in the chapter by Ahmad. Its focus on the institutionalization of a Barelvi opposition to Deobandi activism through the formation of the Sunni Tehrik in 1990 not only extends our knowledge of Islamic institutions in Pakistan, but is a timely reminder that Sufism cannot be contained in quietist and peaceful stereotypes. The history of Sayyid Ahmad Shah (1786–1831), of Rae Bareilly's *jihad* against the Sikhs,[32] and the activities of Pir Pagaro (1928–2012), Pir Manki Sharif (1941–2012), and the Faqir of Ipi (1897–1960)[33] in the colonial era should in any case dispel 'easy' assertions of Sufi moderation.

The entrenchment of landed interests in Pakistan, which we have seen has encouraged clientalism, is the focus of chapters by Ilyas Chattha, 'The impact of the redistribution of Pakistan's evacuee property on the patterns of land ownership and power in Pakistani Punjab in the 1950s' and Hassan Javid, 'Elections, bureaucracy and the law: the reproduction of landed power in post-colonial Punjab'. Chattha reveals how the dislocation arising from the exodus of Sikh and Hindu landowners and the arrival of Muslim refugees from East Punjab did not undermine landed power in the Pakistan Punjab. Tenants were subjected to insecurities, but refugee landlords joined the existing landed elite in a system of landholding that was unchanged, despite the call by the left-leaning Minister for Refugees and Rehabilitation, Mian Iftikharuddin (1907–62) for land reform during his two-year term of office between 1947 and 1949. Javid reflects on the issue of 'authoritarian clientalism'. His chapter argues that landed elites in the Punjab have demonstrated the ability to accommodate themselves to both democratic and military rule. Again, this can be linked with longer-term regional trends. The desire to maintain local influence and power, and its basis, land, has influenced the Punjabi rural elite's response to changing regimes from at least the period of the Sikh kingdom of Lahore.[34] The way that the landed elite maintain their power through their influence over their tenants and in the community in a democratic system is partly explained by the lack of institutionalized and centrally organized political parties in Mariam Mufti's, 'Factionalism and indiscipline in Pakistan's political party system'.

Pakistan came about as the result of an ethnogenesis movement, that is, through the mobilizing of Muslims as an ethnic group in a demand for a political state to protect and further their political, economic, cultural, and religious interests. Yet once Pakistan was created every central government has attempted to dampen down ethnic identities and to emphasize allegiance to the state and not to an ethnic group. It failed in the case of the Bengalis as ethnic feeling led to a secession movement and the creation of Bangladesh in 1971. Ethnic identity remains strong in Pakistan and mitigates against the success of the nation-building project although the princely states in Pakistan have mostly been successfully integrated into the state, as Yaqoob Khan Bangash demonstrates in 'Constructing the state: constitutional integration of the princely states of

Pakistan'. Punjabi, Baloch, Pashun, and Sindhi, and now *muhajir*, identities make up the main ethnic identities in the country and often the first identity and allegiance Pakistanis feel; in the case of Balochistan it has led to the creation of an 'insurgency' against the state. Consequently, an understanding of ethnic movements and the way they impact society and politics in Pakistan is crucial to an understanding of the country's polity and society. Sarah Ansari looks at 'Identity politics and nation-building in Pakistan: the case of Sindhi nationalism', and Yunas Samad examines the often equally violent situation in Balochistan in 'Understanding the insurgency in Balochistan', while Tahir Kamran and Navtej Purewal turn to the minority discourse on Christians, in 'Pakistan's religious *Others*: reflections on the minority discourse on Christians in the Punjab'.

The volume concludes with an examination of the level and the role of violence in the creation of Pakistan and in its continuing existence in the body politic of the nation, Gurharpal Singh's 'Violence and State Formation in Pakistan'. Examining mass violence between 1917 and 1950, he shows that it was not only central to the creation of Pakistan but it has become a characteristic of its post-1947 polity. Political violence is deeply embedded in the country's state formation and the instrumental use of violence – against other religious sects, against minorities, ethnic or religious, rival political parties, or civilians by the military – has become institutionalized and part and parcel of life in Pakistan. Understanding the role of organized political violence is crucial for an understanding of the political and social life of not only the country but also the region.

## Notes

1 Maya Tudor, *The Promise of Power: The Origins of Democracy in India and Autocracy in Pakistan* (Cambridge: Cambridge University Press, 2013).
2 On the notion of the future West Pakistan areas forming a 'security state' under the Raj in which political participation was underdeveloped, see I. Talbot, *Pakistan: A Modern History* (London: Hurst, 1998), pp. 54–65.
3 Ian Talbot and Gurharpal Singh, *The Partition of India* (Cambridge: Cambridge University Press, 2009).
4 Ayesha Jalal, *The State of Martial Rule: The Origins of Pakistan's Political Economy of Defence* (Cambridge: Cambridge University Press, 1990).
5 K.M. Kamal, *Pakistan: The Garrison State* (New Delhi: Intellectual Publishing House, 1982); Ishtiaq Ahmed, *Pakistan. The Garrison State: Origins, Evolution, Consequences, 1947–2011* (Karachi: Oxford University Press, 2013).
6 Praveen Swami, *India, Pakistan and the Secret Jihad: The Covert War in Kashmir 1947–2001* (Abingdon: Routledge, 2007).
7 Cited in Chaudhuri Muhammad Ali, *The Emergence of Pakistan* (New York: Columbia University Press, 1967), p. 376.
8 L. Ziring, *Pakistan: The Enigma of Political Development* (Folkestone: Dawson, 1980); Safdar Mahmood, 'Decline of the Pakistan Muslim League and Its Implications (1947–54)', *Pakistan Journal of History and Culture* 15, 2 (July–December 1994), pp. 63–84.
9 Ian Talbot, *Pakistan: A New History* (London: Hurst, 2012), pp. 54ff.
10 See Anatol Lieven, *Pakistan: A Hard Country* (London: Allen Lane, 2011).

12  *I. Talbot*

11 For a sustained reflection on this argument, see Farzana Shaikh, *Making Sense of Pakistan* (London: Hurst, 2009).
12 Allen McGrath, *The Destruction of Pakistan's Democracy* (Karachi: Oxford University Press, 1996).
13 Yunas Samad, *A Nation in Turmoil: Nationalism and Ethnicity in Pakistan 1937–58* (New Delhi: Sage, 1995), p. 169.
14 See Mazhar Aziz, *Military Control: The Parallel State* (London: Routledge, 2008).
15 On colonial recruitment, see Clive Dewey, 'The Rural Roots of Pakistani Militarism', in D.A. Low (ed.), *The Political Inheritance of Pakistan* (Basingstoke: Macmillan, 1991), pp. 255–83.
16 Yunas Samad, 'Pakistan or Punjabistan: Crisis of National Identity', in Gurharpal Singh and Ian Talbot (eds) *Punjabi Identity: Continuity and Change* (New Delhi: Manohar, 1996), pp. 61–87.
17 Ayesha Siddiqa, *Military Inc.: Inside Pakistan's Military Economy* (London: Pluto Press, 2007).
18 Ibid., p. 103.
19 Iqbal Akhund, *Memoirs of a Bystander: A Life in Diplomacy* (Karachi: Oxford University Press, 1998), p. 366.
20 Talbot, *Pakistan: A Modern History*, pp. 270–83.
21 For further details, see Talbot, *Pakistan: A New History*, pp. 134ff.
22 *Al-Mushir* 26, 3 and 4 (1984), p. 202.
23 On development of the LeJ, see Tahir Kamran, 'Contextualising Sectarian Militancy in Pakistan: The Case of Jhang', *Journal of Islamic Studies* 20, 1 (January 2009): 55–85.
24 For a detailed study, see David Hansen, 'Radical Rhetoric – Moderate Behaviour: Perceptions of Islam, *Shari'a* and the Radical Dimensions among Inhabitants of Islamabad and Rawalpindi in the post-9/112 Pakistani Reality', Unpublished PhD Dissertation, University of Oslo, June 2010.
25 Ayesha Siddiqa, 'Terror's Training Ground', *Newsline* (September 2009), www.newsline.com.pk/NewsSep2009/bookmarksep.htm.
26 Talbot, *Pakistan: A Modern History*, p. 1.
27 See Tariq Rahman, *Language and Politics in Pakistan* (Karachi: Oxford University Press, 1996), Chapter 11.
28 Hassan Zaheer, *The Separation of East Pakistan: The Rise and Realization of Bengali Muslim Nationalism* (Karachi: Oxford University Press, 1994).
29 Talbot, *Pakistan: A New History*, Chapter 4.
30 See F. Grare, 'The Resurgence of Baloch Nationalism', *South Asia Project*, Pakistan Paper 65 (January 2006).
31 Talbot, *Pakistan: A New History*, Chapter 6.
32 Sayyid Ahmad Shah was trained in the Naqshbandi and Qadiriyya Sufi orders. For the significance of his death at Balakot in 1831 for contemporary *jihad* movements, see Ayesha Jalal, *Partisans of Allah: Jihad in South Asia* (Cambridge, MA: Harvard University Press, 2008).
33 The Faqir of Ipi was a Qadiriyya *pir* who led the 1936–7 Waziristan revolt against the British and continued his defiance until the end of the Raj. See Alan Warren, *Waziristan, the Faqir of Ipi, and the Indian Army: The North West Frontier Revolt of 1936–37* (Karachi: Oxford University Press, 2007).
34 The Tiwanas of the Shahpur District of the Punjab epitomize the adjustments of the rural elite to successive regimes. See I. Talbot, *Khizr Tiwana, the Punjab Unionist Party and the Partition of India* (Karachi: Oxford University Press, 2002).

# 1 The impact of the redistribution of Partition's evacuee property on the patterns of land ownership and power in Pakistani Punjab in the 1950s

*Ilyas Chattha*

The mass displacement created by the Partition of the Indian subcontinent in 1947 was phenomenal in its scale and impact. Around 20 million people were displaced by Partition, with Hindus and Sikhs migrating to India and Muslims migrating to Pakistan. Despite the scale of this refugee crisis, historians have only just begun to gauge its larger socio-economic and political impacts. This chapter looks at the history of the key province of the Punjab in Pakistan in the early post-independence period. It examines how the redistribution of evacuee land – the land abandoned by departing Hindu and Sikh landlords – impacted on patterns of land ownership and power in post-Partition West Punjab. A number of important points emerge, namely that the process further entrenched the larger landowners' power and that the aftermath of Partition could be as disruptive for indigenous populations as for refugees. Evidence of the disruption is clear in the case of local tenantry who faced hardship and dislocation because of the migration of their former Hindu and Sikh patrons when their holdings were allocated to resettle incoming Muslim refugees. The chapter sheds light also on the lengthy process of rural resettlement, the land grab situation, and on the factionalism which undermined the Punjab Muslim League. Finally, the chapter identifies the quest for a more egalitarian society raised by Mian Iftikaharuddin (1907–62), the first Minister for Refugee Rehabilitation (1947–8), through his proposals for land reforms. Their rejection was to have long-term consequences for political and socio-economic development in the Punjab, the core province of Pakistan.

Recent historiography has highlighted the profound impact of the mass influx of refugees on state formation and its legacies for ethnic and religious nationalism in South Asia's politics and culture.[1] One of the striking features of the studies is the consideration of the variety of ways in which refugees were assimilated into local communities and the contrasting ways in which they collectively emerged as a distinct political group.[2] But focusing solely on the urban experience overlooks the experience of rural residents who made up the vast majority of the population. Moreover, research on rural resettlement has largely focused on the Indian experience.[3] Most historians now acknowledge that one of the most significant consequences of the refugee crisis was that it fundamentally unbalanced the entire substructure on which Pakistan had been built. Early work of Ayesha Jalal and Ian Talbot, and more recently Farzana Sheikh, has persuasively suggested how the institutional balance of power quickly shifted in favour of the better-educated migrant bureaucracy and the well-entrenched military establishment in the early years of Pakistan's history.[4] Hamza Alavi's influential article on the state in post-colonial societies focussed on Pakistan and Bangladesh and pointed out that the new state inherited a strong military and bureacrative administrative apparatus. The 'centrality' of the post-colonial state, which evidently follows from these propositions, implies the 'centrality' of the state bureaucracy, which Alavi dubbed an 'oligarchy'.[5]

Partition changed everything. Remarkably, historians have yet to appreciate the extent to which the reallocation of refugees impacted landholding and political power. Land, which in Punjab's agrarian society was a major source of income, power, and status, was concentrated in a few hands. Both the pattern of ownership and the size of holdings varied from locality to locality. How strongly entrenched the big landowners were in the Punjab at the time of Partition is shown by the fact that they owned more than 50 per cent of the cultivable land. In some instances, the ownership concentration extended over hundreds of hectares.[6] However, landowners' role in politics and economic policy was much broader than the mere possession of land. Colonial rule in the Punjab sought ways to reinforce the rule of the 'landed gentry' in pursuit of political stability by granting large *jagirs* (land grants) to them from the late-nineteenth century onward.[7] Members of this group dominated the cross-communal Unionist Party, founded in 1923, that had governed the province since the 1920s.[8] Despite tremendous socio-economic and political change, they reproduced their power.[9] In the mid-1940s, many of this party's landlord leaders shifted their allegiance to the All-India Muslim League, founded in 1906, considering it a better vehicle for their interests.[10]

Despite many detailed studies of the ways in which the Punjab's traditional landowners controlled provincial politics, relatively few historical studies reach beyond the 1940s. Yet, the legacy of Partition for democratic practices arising from landlord retrenchment, the mishandling of evacuee property, factionalism, centre-province relations, and the increasing links between the refugee sections of the bureaucracy and migrant landlords, deserves special attention. This chapter suggests some of the ways in which the refugee crisis and the land grab situation in the Punjab undermined the attempt to establish democratic norms in early post-independence Pakistan. This has not been previously considered at length. Conventional accounts in nationalist historiography ignore local developments in their focus on personalities. However, the tension between the centre and the provinces, and the capture of the state by the bureaucracy and its landlord allies can only be fully comprehended through reference to studies of the local areas. Moreover, an assessment of the larger consequences of Partition is essential for historians to get down to the grass-roots level, not only as a study of agrarian history, but for a better understanding of the nature of socio-economic and political developments in Pakistan's early history. While the focus is on

West Punjab, this will be done through addressing major themes arising from the impact of mass displacements. It also represents a useful contribution to understanding the Indian refugee experience by highlighting how the failure to introduce tenancy and land reforms in the early years ensured that the Punjab followed a vastly different socio-economic and political trajectory from its Indian neighbour.

Certain points emerge. The refugee crisis opened up new opportunities for big landowners in West Punjab as they further tightened their grip over rural society and provincial politics through refugee resettlement. Some benefited by grabbing additional land, either by purchasing it at nominal prices from departing or incoming refugees or unlawfully occupying evacuee property; while some replaced the migrating Hindu *banias* (moneylenders) as the main source of rural and agricultural credit. According to one report, out of a total of 6 million vacated acres, over 1.8 million in West Punjab alone were 'illegally occupied by local residents'.[11] Hundreds of thousands of existing tenants faced economic hardship and dislocation as their holdings were allocated to incoming refugee cultivators. The latter were smallholders compared to the migrating Hindu and Sikh landlords. The possibility of land reform was raised by Mian Iftikaharuddin, who came from a wealthy and politically prominent Punjab family, and owned the *Pakistan Times*. Calls for land reform were not only met with stiff resistance by the ruling landowning politicians, but they also used their political clout to focus the state's attention on 'nationalisation' of the private estates of powerful 'rival' politicians, most notably the last Premier of colonial Punjab, Sir Khizr Hayat Tiwana (1900–75, Premier 1942–7). This was to have corrosive consequences for the democratic system.

## Agricultural refugees' dispersal and resettlement

In April 1948, the West Punjab authorities completed a refugee census and revealed that 5.5 million Muslim refugees had arrived in the province, representing over 28 per cent of the population.[12] The exchange of population increased the rural population of West Punjab from 5,841,000 to 7,134,000, an increase of no less than 22 per cent, as Table 1.1 illustrates.[13] Over 75 per cent of them were 'agriculturalists' or 'rural'.

This presented an unprecedented and unanticipated problem for the new government. Initially, an ad hoc 'Guzara Scheme' (a temporary allotment) for the

*Table 1.1* Exchange of population in rural West Punjab

| Occupation | West Punjab before migration | After migration | New/ increase | Percentage increase |
|---|---|---|---|---|
| Agriculturalists | 5,824,000 | 7,134,000 | 1,310,000 | 22.5 |
| Non-agriculturalists | | | 693,000 | 13.8 |
| Rural | | | 115,000 | 4.1 |

redistribution of land for the first two *rabi* (spring) and *kharif* (autumn) harvests was drawn up. The idea was that pushing refugees from camps to villages would not only save the government huge amounts of money but would assimilate them into the economic life of the villages. The authorities were particularly anxious that abandoned fields should not lie uncultivated during its incoming *rabi* crop and that the labour of refugee cultivators would avoid a food shortage. Another concern was the fear of illegal occupation of evacuee land. The temporary allotment, therefore, was based on 'an equal distribution of land', regardless of the land left by an individual in India. A fixed area of land was allotted to each family of five. The average unit was fixed at between six and eight acres in irrigated areas and up to 12.5 acres in non-irrigated areas. In this way, by the end of 1948, an official survey claimed that about 3.95 million refugees (90 per cent) had been dispersed on 3.39 million acres of evacuees' land in West Punjab.[14] While the refugee cultivators were quickly dispersed to villages, in actuality the process of settlement was much more difficult and lasted a lot longer.

An official survey in 1948 calculated that nearly six million acres of 'cultivable' or 'revenue paying' land was abandoned in West Punjab.[15] A major part of the land was, however, under Muslim tenant cultivation. As Table 1.2 indicates, more than 50 per cent of the vacated land was under cultivation by 'tenants-at-will' who had no security of tenure or legal and heritable rights.

Although the payment of rent varied from area to area and even from locality to locality, sharecropping was the most common method of payment of rent: landlords and tenants shared the crop on a 50–50 basis, although tenants were also required to render services of various kinds.[16] Without any formal contract tenants were liable to eviction without compensation, although many families had been cultivating the same land for generations on customary arrangements. As a result, they did not abandon their holdings willingly.

## Impact of refugee settlement on local tenantry

The impact of Partition could be as profound for those who did not migrate as those who were uprooted, as Joya Chatterji's recent work shows with respect to the impact on Bengali Muslims who did not cross to East Bengal.[17] In West Punjab, a large number of local tenants had to pay a heavy price as their holdings were either greatly reduced, or they were forced to abandon them completely in favour of peasant refugees. The resulting economic and social deprivation experienced by tenant families forced many younger male members

*Table 1.2* Land ownership and cultivation patterns in West Punjab in 1947

| Land owned/cultivated | Total acreage |
|---|---|
| Revenue paying land vacated by evacuees | 6 million |
| Owned and cultivated by non-Muslims | 2.7 million |
| Owned by non-Muslims, but cultivated by Muslims | 3.1 million |

to look for seasonal or permanent employment in nearby cities.[18] Many others were compelled to become casual labourers. A large number of them, however, turned to local landlords for employment. Hundreds of thousands became internally displaced, while a large number migrated to *kacha alaqa* (uncultivated areas); about one million people were relocated to unused state lands in southwest Punjab.[19]

As Table 1.2 shows, with such a large concentration of holdings in the hands of existing tenants, the state was in no position to eject them completely. Attempts to do so would spark both an economic and a political crisis. Against this background, local tenants were initially directed by revenue officers to pay their rent to the 'new refugee allottee landlords', instead of abandoning the land. This was not as simple as it sounds. In many instances tenants refused to pay the refugees, seeing it as the first step to their eviction. In 1950, in Lyallpur district 1,267 tenants were ejected from the land due to non-payment of rent. By early the following year tenant protests had spun out of control and hundreds were arrested in various parts of the province. Intelligence reports recorded that further evictions and arrests could lead to violent large-scale protests and mass protests aimed at the government. Assessing the consequences of the growing peasant movement, the authorities directed the deputy commissioners, who acted as district rehabilitation commissioners for the areas under their jurisdiction, that 'whatever the situation arose ... no arrest is made for the recovery of the cash rent, while all possible assistance should be given to the Lambardars [village headmen who assisted in revenue collection] in the matter of its recovery'.[20]

Refugee farmers and their representatives had long been protesting the failure to take possession of their allotted land. A spokesman for the Meo refugee community (which mainly came from Mewat), Chaudhry Mehtab Khan, during a speech in the Punjab Legislative Assembly in March 1952, complained that the government had allocated eight acres of land to Moes in ten villages in Lahore district but they had not got possession of the land five years later.[21] The plight of refugees was repeatedly raised in legislative assemblies and reported in local newspapers. As the pressure mounted, the Punjab government devised a plan to systematically reduce the holdings of existing tenants by 20 per cent. By the *rabi* crop in 1951, a total of 626,907 acres was cultivated by 498,732 refugees.

Accommodating refugees not only reduced the holdings of former tenants of Hindus and Sikhs, but also the holdings of local tenants of Muslim landlords. According to the rural settlement scheme, large landowners who owned more than 50 acres cultivated by tenants were to reduce the area farmed by tenants and to employ refugees. The plan was to resettle about 300,000 refugee tenants, and presuming that each tenant family had five members, 1,500,000 refugees would be resettled. The authorities argued that if refugees could be settled on six to eight acres per family then there was no reason why local tenants could not do the same. It was suggested that the reduction in the size of landholdings would overcome the shortage of bullocks which had come about as the result of migration.[22]

Efforts to evict local tenants sparked sporadic localised protests and clashes between local and refugee tenants. One of the immediate consequences was the lack of a unified peasant movement. Moreover, continued strife and uncertainty over possession of land provoked lengthy bouts of litigation in the courts and that partly contributed to the shortage of food in the Punjab in autumn 1951. In the areas where statistics are available, thousands of tenants were ejected by 1952 in such places as Lyallpur, Montgomery, Sargodha, and Mianwali. Resistance from tenants aside, landlords were averse to replacing their 'generations-old tenants for unknown and unwanted strangers' who not only lacked resources, but had little knowledge of local farming conditions.[23] Some landlord politicians criticised the Punjab government's policy of reducing the holdings of existing tenants. Abdul Sattar Niazi, a member of the Punjab assembly from Mianwali, told the refugee minister:

> Your policy is a kind of fraud, putting Ahmed's hat on Mahammad's head.... This not only opened up a plethora of litigations, but increased corruption and bribery at a shameful level.... It seems your resettlement project is creating a new group of local Muhajareen [emigrants] who would need rehabilitation soon.[24]

Clearly the process of refugee settlement in the Punjab did not affect all strata of the peasantry in the same way. Along with members of the local tenantry, the service classes also faced economic hardship and dislocation because of the migration of their former patrons. A great number of Christian *sepidars* (contractual labourers) were forcibly uprooted from the land they had been cultivating, although according to the rural settlement scheme they were entitled to two acres of land. According to one report, over 60,000 people had become unemployed in rural Punjab by January 1948. C. E. Gibbon, a Christian member of the Punjab Assembly, was especially outspoken in his criticism of the settlement policy. Pointing towards the ruling Punjab Muslim League leaders during a debate in March 1952, he declared that in seeking to satisfy some discontented people they had pursued a policy of robbing Peter to pay Paul and created a corrupt administration.[25]

This sentiment was widely shared and the situation was not conducive to establishing a legitimate democratic system in the Punjab or anywhere elsewhere in Pakistan. By the early 1950s the majority of tenants had been squeezed into between three and six acres, mainly in the productive canal colonies. Tenants with marginal holdings and extended families found themselves in a precarious situation. The Punjab refugee commissioner acknowledged that for tenants an economic holding for a family was considered to be about 12 acres and the decision to reduce the holding to six acres to absorb refugees meant that the holding could not now absorb the energies of a pair of bullocks and a family of workers. A survey commission, headed by the revenue commissioner, assessed the conditions of tenants who were cultivating 'different classes of land in the perennial and non-perennial' areas of Montgomery district and submitted his report in 1952. He stated that the system as it stood would only cause more trouble.[26]

The commission feared many landless peasants would not only turn to crime but also join a protest movement aimed at the government. For the immediate purpose, the commission recommended that the existing tenants should be charged the same rent as had applied to the refugee tenants. This was fixed at three times the land revenue compared to the local tenants who would pay double. At the same time, the commission warned that the 'big landlords' whose rents would be reduced might turn against the government. It believed that 'Desperate diseases call for desperate remedies.' Although 88,000 landowners employed tenants, they formed no more than 3.4 per cent of the total number of landowners in West Punjab. Compared with the total population of tenants this was an 'infinitesimal' number. The commission's recommendation was that three times the land revenue was fixed only for those tenants whose holdings were reduced to 12 acres or less.[27]

Predictably, this was unacceptable to the landlords. There were reports they systemically began ejecting tenants. Yet it is significant to note that, in marked contrast to the established landlords, the refugee landlords who owned more than 25 acres of land were prevented from evicting existing tenants on their allocated land. According to the rural settlement scheme, the refugee landlord was not granted the right to alienate land or eject any tenant except for non-payment of rent or for unlawful use of the land. This provision resulted in a number of clashes in ensuing months between refugee landlords and tenants. Many refugee landlords wanted to cultivate their allocated land and during the early 1950s they protested against this 'unfairness'. Chaudhry Akbar Ali Khan, a refugee landlord from Lyallpur district, raised this concern in the Punjab assembly in March 1952, although his listeners, predominantly the local landlords, were little impressed at his description of 'discrimination'.[28]

Attempts at evictions by refugee landlords resulted in direct clashes. One of the most serious incidents took place in Montgomery district in May 1952 when gunfire was exchanged between refugee landlords and local tenants resulting in the death of 20 people.[29] In Kabirwala *tehsil* (administrative district below the province), Multan, over 100 tenants and landlords were arrested to prevent an expected clash during the months of April and May 1953. While the authorities used force to evict tenants, in many places the tenants, with the support of their local patrons, effectively countered state violence and attempts at evictions. As the conflicts intensified in ensuing months, the matter became more a political issue than an economic one and a committee was set up by the government to look into the matter. The debate regarding the ejection of tenants was fought between refugee MLAs (members of the Legislative Assembly) and the representatives of tenants over three successive meetings held on 16, 18, and 23 April 1956. Ultimately, the refugee landlords won the right to eject existing tenants. The Punjab government declared that:

> Refugee allottee landlords would now exercise the same rights as enjoyed by the local owners ... whether they are evacuees or local owners now would be governed by the normal existing Tenancy Laws of the province ... the refugee landlords could keep more than 25 acres for khudkasht [cultivation on one's own land].[30]

Refugee landowners were not only discriminated against in regard to tenancy matters, but also with regard to landholdings. At the time of settlement they faced land ceilings that not only changed the landholding structure of the Punjab, but also hampered their sway over rural society, as well as the politics of the province. This was in marked contrast to the local landowners who in many ways benefited from such practices.

## Land ceilings on refugee landlords

There was a considerable degree of difference in relative fertility of land in both halves of the Punjab. It was considered unjust to regard each acre of land as equal to another when great diversity existed in terms of soil, irrigation, rainfall, and productivity. Moreover, the area available for allotment was markedly too small for the sheer number of refugees.[31] In order to adjust it equitably among the refugee peasants, it was considered necessary to reduce the amount of land allocated to them. The assessment of land in both halves of the Punjab was re-examined so as to 'give a fairer deal to refugees'.[32] It was, therefore, in order to evaluate the different classes of land on the basis of a comparable unit of value, that an 'index produce unit' was prepared in respect of all agricultural land so that claimants could get land of equal value. According to the scheme, refugees were classified according to the size of their holdings in India, expressed in 'produce unit' terms. A ceiling was placed on the size of holdings and the Punjab was divided into two categories of land: 'congested districts' (canal colonies) and 'non-congested districts' (uncultivated land). It was decided that every rightful claimant would get a share, and a cut of 50 per cent was imposed on claims beyond 20,000 units (roughly equal to 250 acres of irrigated land in Lyallpur) and that no allotment would exceed 36,000 units, which was roughly equal to 450 acres of irrigated land in Lyallpur.[33] No more than 20,000 produce index units would be allotted in the congested districts. In the case of allottees' surplus index units and claims over the 20,000, they were allotted land in the contiguous non-congested districts (see Table 1.3). Such stipulations on the refugee landlords not only limited the size of their holdings, but also caused fragmentations of their land. This was not acceptable to the big landlords who considered such provisions 'discriminatory'. 'If the argument was that the interests of the refugees/tenants were to be protected, then why the local landlords were exempted from the land ceilings', was beyond the understanding of Rao Abdul Rehman Khan, a refugee landlord from Multan district, as he stated in the Punjab assembly in 1952.[34]

The majority of the refugee cultivators wanted to resettle on the land in the fertile 'canal colonies'. A settlement survey in 1954 found that land in these districts had 'run out', despite the fact that there were still 83,933 'non-allottees' waiting for the settlement. These refugee farmers had been repeatedly requested by the authorities to get their claims transferred to other 'non-congested areas' where land was still available, but they continued to hope to obtain land there. Ultimately, the claims of these refugees, without their consent, were transferred to adjacent 'non-congested districts', as shown in Table 1.3.

*Table 1.3* Refugee 'claims' transferred from congested districts to non-congested districts

| Congested districts | Non-congested districts |
| --- | --- |
| Lyallpur | Jhang, Sheikhpura |
| Montgomery | Muzaffargarh |
| Multan | Dera Ghazi Khan |
| Shahpur | Mianwali |

Such forced transfers not only led to fragmentation, but also separated families. 'One brother is allocated land in Muzaffargarh; second is settled in Rawalpindi and third is settled in Campbellpur', Rao Abdul Rehman Khan, a spokesman for the Rajput refugee community, stated in the Punjab assembly. 'Half of their incomes [are spent] on railway fares to visit their relatives in such far places.'[35] Despite the forced transfers, many refugee families did not move away from their families and kin groups to these 'remote areas'. Some refugees sold their 'claims' to the local landlords at rock bottom prices, although there were many whose land was '*gum gki*' (lost). In other cases, their land was occupied by landowners who destroyed land records with the compliance of local revenue officers. As a result there was no mechanism by which land could be seized by refugees if powerful magnates were determined to hold on to it. Many landowners retained their possessions over the years, mainly by bribing officers and by dragging cases through the courts. At the local level, the revenue staff, such as the local *patwari* (village accountant) and *tahsildar* (tax collector), became the most important officials in the whole process. Whether it was the fertility of the agricultural land to be allotted, the location, or the actual possession of the property, many opportunities for bribery arose as 'discretion' lay in their hands. The cost of briberies was much higher in the fertile canal colonies where local officials liaised with officials at the district and provincial level.[36]

Resourceful migrant landlords defeated the land settlement scheme because their money and personal connections with officials and politicians gained them access to the most enviable vacated land. A fine example was the case of Sahibzadi Naseema Begum. This powerful landlady of Karnal district was politically astute and had personal connections with those in power. Despite the exchange of records between East and West Punjab, her 'claim' of land (36,000 units), like many others, could not be verified. However, she not only obtained hundreds of acres of agricultural land in different villages in Lahore and Kasur districts, and secured a great deal more than her share, but she also illegally sold them.[37]

The bulk of the refugees did not, of course, have high-level political access. They experienced petty corruption in their everyday dealings with the state. When successive governments were confronting the shortage of land to be allocated to the displaced peasantry, the archival record shows that attempts were made to siphon off a great deal of land to politicians and officials. An instance of this was noted by the statement of the Interior Minister after the dismissal of the Noon ministry in 1955:

> The Punjab Cabinet, which had been dismissed, had decided to allot land to all Major-Generals in the Army, the Deputy Commissioners in the Punjab or their relatives and most of the members of the Legislature. In addition it was proposed to allot land to certain members of the High Court and the Federal Court. The value of the land involved was Rs.32 crores. [This] was enough justification for the dismissal of the Ministry.[38]

This statement lays bare the fact that politicians, bureaucrats, powerful local notables, and enterprising refugee groups grabbed property by utilising their personal contacts. What emerged was a discourse of 'corruption' that was detrimental to the consolidation of democratic practices in the early years of Pakistan's history. Yet, even in these early years, there were some who pressed for more equitable redistribution of resources. One such case was the movement for land reforms in the 1950s in the Punjab, and this owed much to the leadership of Mian Iftikharuddin.

## Refugee resettlement and the dilemma of land reforms

The commitment to the equal distribution of resources dates back to the November 1944 manifesto of the Punjab Muslim League, as well as the socialistic slant of the 1945 draft plan of the All-India Muslim League Planning Committee.[39] In the election manifesto for the 1945–6 Punjab elections, the League had proposed radical land reforms so as to win peasant support for the Pakistan movement. But the party, being a coterie of landlords, gradually watered them down. At independence, the challenge of accommodating refugees increased the demands for land reforms. Mian Iftikharuddin, as refugee minister, came out with a radical solution for accommodating refugees, when he proposed breaking up the large estates and distributing the land to refugees. He insisted on a reorganisation of the agrarian sector and called for a 50-acre ceiling on landholdings and 'a graded tax' levy on the income of all landlords who owned more than 25 acres of land drawing more than 15,000 rupees per annum from their agricultural land. Iftikharuddin declared that over 40 per cent of land in the province was owned by a few large landlords, but they paid very little tax.[40] He urged a revision of the agricultural tax system and saw equitable redistribution of resources as the solution to the refugee problem. In the rural areas radical types of agrarian reforms would be 'the first step towards a transition to socialism'.

When the influential landlords prevented all attempts at land reform, Iftikharuddin resigned as the refugee minister. 'Why did I quit the ministry?' He explained his reasons to members of the provincial assembly a few months later in the March 1948 session of the Punjab assembly.

> Because I was sure the big zamindars would not allow me to levy agricultural tax and introduce any sort of reforms.... Our rulers say to impose tax on those landlords who own more than 25 acres is unfair; at the same time they claim that they would do their best for the settlement of refugees....

I asked them how they would do that ... and those who call for new system are said they are spreading fatina [chaos] ... [and they] are dismissed as the agents of Communist and enemies of the Government. Our rulers do fear that even to debate reforms would rag the landlords who might turn against the Government.[41]

He alleged that when the refugees needed help the governing Muslim League was instead thinking of acquiring all the evacuee property they could lay their hands on. On occasion, when he tried to raise the issue of corruption on the floor of the assembly, he was disallowed, stopped, and interrupted by the Speaker and opposition politicians.[42] He was of the opinion that the Mamdot government did not represent the people of the province; instead it represented the interests of some seven to ten big *zamindar* (landlord) families. He considered the government's 'extensive propaganda' concerning the settlement of 5 million refugees to be 'full of lies'. In fact, they allotted the land to the refugees 'on paper' with the result that half of the refugee population did not get possession of their allotted property.[43]

He stated that the existing provincial assemblies were elected on a restricted property or an educational franchise. Therefore, the Punjab assembly and government did not, in any real sense, represent the aspirations of the people and the assembly should be dissolved to hold new elections to bring in representatives who would enact extensive agricultural and social reforms. The assembly, he stated, was not representative of the people of the Punjab as the refugee community made up one-third of the population of the province, but their representation was only 5 per cent in the assembly. He called for fresh elections on the basis of a universal adult franchise so that the 'right spokesmen' would be elected: 'I say with 100% surety as long as this system remains, and the representatives of the people do not represent 90 per cent of the public, neither the needs of the ordinary people would [be met], nor the Punjab, which is the backbone of Pakistan, would be on the road to development.'[44]

While the demand for fresh elections was to gain ground the following year, the Punjab's ruling landed class blocked land reforms. They also sought ways to block the equitable redistribution of land by appealing to religious groups to underscore the sanctity of property in Islam, but also by using the politics of identity and appealing to 'provincialism'.[45] In addition, they marginalised Mian Iftikharuddin. Some rivals identified him a 'communist', a 'Congressite by instinct'; others described him as an 'urban exploiter' who, with money of the poorer people, owned a communist-line newspaper that regularly fanned vicious propaganda against the government and ministers. The revenue minister Sardar Shaukat Hayat (1915–98), himself a landlord, was especially outspoken in his criticism.[46] Another member of the provincial assembly Nawab Sir Muzaffar Khan Qizilbas (1908–82), who owned a great deal of rural and urban property in Lahore district, highlighted historical patron-client relations in rural Punjab, by opining that demands for land reforms and payment of higher agricultural tax always came from a few urban industrialists, rather than members of the rural populations.[47]

When the Punjab premier, the Nawab of Mamdot, himself a big refugee landowner from East Punjab, and his cabinet, which was dominated by landlords, refused to countenance Iftikharuddin's demands, the Pakistan–Punjab Refugee Council, a liaison body between the centre and the province, found the provincial government to be 'totally non-co-operative'. Its chairman, Raja Ghazanfar Ali Khan (1895–1963), criticised the Mamdot ministry's 'lack of vision'. Among other issues, the centre and the Punjab differed on the fixing of the land revenue. It was this decision of the council, in the absence of the premier, that caused the resignation of Mamdot from the council. The Punjab Governor Francis Mudie (1890–1976, Governor 1947–9) in an exasperated tone wrote to the Prime Minister Liaquat Ali Khan (1895–1951, Prime Minister 1947–51) on 26 March 1948:

> I write to you about a quarrel that has developed between Ghazanfar Ali and the West Punjab Government, particularly Mamdot, over the refugee question.... Main cause of the quarrel was the decision of the Council, in premier's absence, to collect a cash rent of six times the land revenue from tenants of non-Muslims evacuee landed properties in lieu of a grain rent.[48]

In the Punjab Assembly, Mamdot declared that he had decided to 'non-cooperate with the Refugee Council' and as a token of resistance had resigned from the council. 'It was impossible to co-cooperate with a Council which had no regard for the opinion of the West Punjab representatives', the Premier stated, and one which arrived at 'arbitrary decisions and interferes in the internal administration of the Province'.[49]

It is usually with respect to Sindh that disputes over refugee resettlement have often been seen as undermining centre-province relations in Pakistan's early years.[50] However, events in the Punjab reveal that they were present from the outset even in the so-called 'cornerstone' of Pakistan. The centre and the Punjab not only scuffled over evacuee property, but also on the settling of 'non-agreed refugees' (non-Punjabis) in the Punjab.[51] From the beginning, the Punjab representatives were of the view that property abandoned by Hindus and Sikhs should be allocated to the Muslim refugees from East Punjab. They took the view that there were simply not enough resources in the province to house all the refugees who flooded in. To favour the non-agreed refugees over their counterparts from East Punjab 'would lead to great discontentment'.[52] Their belief was that they had to be distributed in a further forced migration to other parts of Pakistan. For its part, the central government throughout 1948 cajoled other provinces to take in 'surplus refugees'. The Punjab's resistance to settle more Kashmiri refugees from Jammu and Kashmir on vacated land in the Punjab, and Sindh's refusal to take another 100,000 refugees from the Punjab, was condemned as 'anti-Islamic' by Raja Ghazanfar Ali: 'rehabilitation is [the] central government's responsibility', he added, 'and narrow provincialism [sh]ould not be allowed to interfere with the proper resettlement of refugees'.[53]

Mamdot not only quarrelled with the refugee council, but also protested about Mudie's 'arbitrary interference' in the Punjab, arguing he had presented 'a negative picture' of the activities of the provincial government to the centre. On occasion, he labelled Mudie a 'foreigner', 'pro-Unionist', and 'pro-Indian'.[54] On 12 April 1948 Mudie complained to the Prime Minister that Mamdot always double-crossed the Refugee Council by instructing his officers not to carry out the Councils' decisions. He even stated that Mamdot was staying in power in order to get his hands on more property.[55]

Apart from bickering between the centre and the Punjab, and rivalries within the provincial Muslim League, Mamdot's cabinet was heavily criticised in the press over the handling of refugees. The *Pakistan Times* – owned by Mian Iftikharuddin – was at the forefront highlighting accusations of corruption, embezzlement, and land grabbing. The newspaper played its part in developing a narrative of 'corruption' and this was used for political purposes with debilitating consequences for the consolidation of parliamentary practices. This is not to say that accusations of corruption and scandals were exclusively politically motivated by rival politicians or directed by the centre. The general extent of corruption meant that leaders would have found it difficult to deny them, even in the unlikely circumstances of their being impeccably honest. One British observer said Mamdot's ministry was 'unbelievably corrupt'.[56] Charges against Mamdot included the misuse of public funds to personally acquire about 2,000 acres of prime agricultural land at nominal rates in Montgomery district and working hand in glove with officials to do so. He was also alleged to have awarded hundreds of acres of land in the same district to his brother that belonged to the former Premier of the Punjab, Khizr Hayat Tiwana (1900–75, Premier 1942–7). In addition, Mamdot secretly deposited 100,000 rupees to one of his brothers from the 'Kashmir Fund'.[57]

The scramble for land intensified factionalism in the Punjab Muslim League and this was corrosive to the creation of democratic norms. Those in power actively tried to cultivate refugees as their new supporters by allocating them evacuee property. Indeed, migrant politicians needed to reward clients and kinfolk as they had no political base in Pakistan and wanted to keep their vote-banks intact. Mamdot was alleged to have lavishly awarded land to his followers and former tenants in order to keep his future vote-bank intact. He was also alleged by rival refugee politicians to have diluted their political base by systemically scattering their supporters throughout the Punjab. Some were calling for 'the district-wise settlement' of their groups and followers to keep their constituencies intact. Rao Abdul Rehman Khan, a spokesman for the Rajput refugee community, declared in the Punjab assembly that the government did not settle people district-wise with the result that in one *chak* (village) there were between 13 and 14 different refugee groups from different Indian districts and they clashed on a daily basis.[58] A member of the Punjab assembly bluntly declared on the floor of the House in March 1952:

> [B]ecause of this fear that if the refugee groups consolidated or compacted at places, they would emerge as big blocks during the election time; therefore, this fear led [to] their [forced] resettlement from districts to districts, places to places, localities to localities.[59]

Such claims were not without foundation. One of the immediate consequences of this was to appear in the first elections in the Punjab held on the basis of an adult franchise in 1951. Representatives of refugees made up 5 per cent of the provincial assembly although they comprised about one-third of the population.

Punjab politics continued to be dominated by the personal rivalries between Mian Mumtaz Daultana (1916–95), the Minister of Finance in the Punjab government, who was increasingly seen as the Centre's man, and Mamdot. Daultana resigned from the government and fought with the Premier over control of the provincial Muslim League. Daultana won and in November 1948 became the president of the Punjab Muslim League. From that position he initiated a campaign to oust the Punjab government. Having secured support from three Punjabi ministers in the central government, especially the Minister for Foreign Affairs, Sir Zafarullah Khan (1893–1985, Minister 1947–54), Daultana wrote to Liaquat Ali Khan that '[a]ny Central support for Mamdot would split the West Punjab from end to end'.[60] The centre, however, saw an opportunity to oust Mamdot and his clique. Zafarullah Khan, along with two other Punjabi ministers in Karachi, wrote to Liaquat Ali Khan asking him to dissolve the Punjab assembly and on 24 January 1949, the Governor-General, Khwaja Nazimuddin (1894–1964, Governor-General 1948–51) ordered Mudie to dissolve the legislature assembly and take over the provincial administration under the aegis of the central government.[61]

## Tenancy reform

The end of the Mamdot government instigated a fresh debate about refugee resettlement. In rural Punjab, the Azad Pakistan Party, founded in November 1949 by Mian Iftiqaruddin, and the Kisan Party, were stoking agrarian discontent. The mounting protest movement pressed the new administration to seriously consider more comprehensive tenancy legislation. In 1949 the Muslim League Agrarian Reforms Committee, with Daultana as its chairman, discussed tenancy reform and fixed a ceiling of 150 acres for irrigated land and 300 acres for non-irrigated land. Estates, the committee added, should be liquidated without compensation over two generations or moderate compensation paid. The committee suggested that the scale of compensation should be six times the annual value of the yield of the first 1,500 acres and less for additional holdings. To secure more land for refugees the committee urged the 'abolition of landlordism' by recommending that the state should resume all grants of land made by the British Government in lieu of services.[62]

While such recommendations, to some extent, reflected Iftikharuddin's early views on equitable land redistribution, they were regarded as unacceptable by influential landholding interests. They were, nonetheless, highlighted in the Punjab Muslim League's manifesto for the provincial elections in March 1951 when the party immediately attracted the support of tenants who had been granted the right to vote. Financially and politically supported by the centre, Daultana's Muslim League won the elections against Mamdot's Awami Muslim

League founded in 1949.⁶³ Not surprisingly, about 80 per cent of the members elected were landlords. Daultana's cabinet, which contained one refugee politician, was characterised by one observer as the 'cabinet of landlords'.⁶⁴ With such a concentration of political power in the hands of landed groups, the state was unable to extract concessions from them to empower tenants. After prolonged dithering, at the end of September 1951, the government introduced land reforms with various safeguards for landlords. In theory, tenants were given full security of tenure as long as they continued to pay their rent and took good care of the land. Ejection of tenants was totally banned. The First Five-Year Plan commented on the provincial government's restoration of tenancy rights:

> An interesting aspect of these reforms was that they had been initiated by the ministry through the legislature with the help of the Muslim League Party which consisted mainly of landlords.... [Reforms give] a new sense of freedom, dignity and self-respect, by releasing them from the ever-present fear of ejectment which kept them in a state of terror and helplessness.⁶⁵

Daultana claimed that the agrarian reforms enacted by the Punjab assembly were the 'most progressive in the world' in so far as they ensured security of tenure for tenants-at-will.⁶⁶ For all the hue and cry about the reforms, they were characterised by critics as merely cosmetic. They made no reference to a ceiling for large estates and merely tried to increase the tenants' share of the produce by 10 per cent from 50 to 60 per cent. Consequently, it rarely reached the stage of implementation, as many tenants did not demand their increased share as this would annoy their patrons. Even these nominal reforms, however, were unacceptable to landlords. There were reports that tenant evictions increased after the introduction of these tenancy reforms.

This matter reached the Punjab assembly when an editorial was published in the 14 January 1952 issue of the Urdu newspaper, *Afaq*, about the harshness of some landlords to their tenants, with the suggestion to tenants: 'if zamindars treat you harshly, first of all retaliate by slapping shoes on their faces, then throw them out in the fields.' In reality, regulations and legislation were of limited effect and Punjabi landlords tried to divert attention towards the private *jagirs* (grants of land) held by rival politicians who had opposed the Pakistan movement. Publically their position was to suggest pooling more ordinary land for the peasantry: the archival evidence, however, reveals a political vendetta.

## Abolition of Jagirs Act

On 12 August 1951, the Punjab Government issued an ordinance appointing a committee to scrutinise all cases of grants of Crown lands made in the Punjab since 1857.⁶⁷ The proposed abolition of *jagirs* was met with strong resistance, causing several landlords to go against the government, which became embroiled in debates within the cabinet. Many opposed the specific provisions that aimed 'to scrutinize all cases of grants of Crown lands made in the Punjab since 1857', as its implementation was to affect many sitting in the Punjab assembly. Fearing a political crisis, the provincial League assembly party, through negotiation and compromise, produced a compromise formula heavily weighted in favour of the landlords. The provisions were thus limited to 'certain influential persons' who were given grants 'as a price for the unpatriotic and anti-national activities' in the pre-independence days.[68] It is of special significance that the period was compressed to 1945–7, the period of office of the Unionist administration of Khizr Tiwana immediately prior to Partition. Having provided the maximum possible latitude to the landowning interests, the act enabled the government to resume without compensation any grants of land made during that period which 'proved to have been made in disregard of public interests'. Sheikh Fazal Ilahi Piracha, the Minister for Rehabilitation and Colonies, that is, the minister for refugees, explained the modified provisions of the act in the Punjab assembly in January 1952.

> During the Governor's regime an Act has already been passed where its powers were given to Government to confiscate all land grants given during the time of the Khizar regime or earlier, to those who were anti-Pakistan and against our struggle for freedom.... No compensation shall be claimed by any one affected by the provisions and no court shall have jurisdiction to entertain any suit or other proceedings instituted by or on behalf of any person claiming any sum or other benefit in respect of a jagir.[69]

The actual implementation of the act was problematic, partly because of the difficulties in exactly defining a 'jagir'. It was suggested that the act would affect a great number of ex-soldiers, as Chaudhry Mohammad Shafiq of Montgomery district, an opposition member in the Punjab assembly, warned.[70] As a result, the scope of the act was narrowed further when 'specific military grants' were exempted. The argument advanced to justify this was that 'military jagirs were not granted by the provincial government, but by the pre-Partition government of India on the recommendation of the Commander-in-Chief'.[71] In this way, in addition to the land of individual army officers, the larger 'military farms' and estates – about 70,000 acres in the Punjab alone – were exempted.

According to one observer the act was 'discriminatory, vicious and anti-social ... the object of this Act was to enable Government to resume grants of land made by the Unionist Ministry of Sir Khizr Hayat Tiwana in 1945–7.'[72] In Tiwana's hometown Shahpur alone, the total amount of land likely to be taken over was 10,000 acres. At the same time, the Punjab Minor Canals (Amendment May 1952) Bill was introduced in order to take over Tiwana's privately owned canals (in Shahpur district, the Lower Jhelum Canal, and the River Jhelum), which gave the owners 'opportunities of undue exploitation of their neighbour zamindars to charge as much as four to five times the abiana [revenue] rates, charged on the areas irrigated by the Government inundation canals'.[73]

An alarmed Khizr Tiwana, then in exile in America, immediately wrote to the British government:

> You must intervene with regard to the injustice of measures that are being taken by the Provincial Government, rather than to any general policy at the Centre. People everywhere were complaining of the growing amount of corruption amongst administrators. If a free plebiscite could be held, and the return of the British was a practical possibility, the great mass of the population would vote for this – in fact all Pakistanis, except those whose pockets had benefited directly from the new regime.[74]

The Lord Privy Seal replied a few days later that the British government could not intervene in the internal affairs of a member of the Commonwealth.[75] A frantic Tiwana immediately flew to London and tried, unsuccessfully, to persuade British officials that not only would Unionists be affected but also ex-soldiers. However the assessment of British officials went against Khizr, now a deserted collaborator.

> Sir Khizar Hayat has a large personal financial interest in the land affected by these ordinances and that his concern is probably for these interests rather than the interest of the ex-sepoys who may also be affected.... The actual target would not be ex-soldiers and other small fry ... it seems certain that their intended prey is the large landowners who are political opponents of the Muslim League.... It is he and other large grantees, and not the general body of ex-soldiers, who are likely to suffer severely from the operation of legislation now in force or being considered. The number of ex-soldiers settled in the Province is so great that I cannot believe that any large-scale dispossession of small tenants could hardly be materialised.[76]

The challenge of accommodating displaced populations at independence threatened the established rural order and offered opportunities to introduce reforms for the redistribution of land. Mian Iftikharuddin's proposals for land reform raised the possibility of a more equal and just rural landholding society. But powerful landowning interests, despite their political rivalries, not only effectively blocked all calls for reforms, but further entrenched their power. They defended their claims by appealing to Islam's unequivocal defence of private property and by marginalising those who called for an equal landholding structure, labelling them communist. At times, they also resorted to 'provincialism' by defending the rights of sons of the soil against non-Punjabi migrants. As a whole, they successfully prevented all attempts at meaningful land reform until the imposition of martial law in Pakistan in 1958. The failure to reform the landholding structure in the early years meant that West Punjab followed a vastly different socio-economic and political trajectory than its Indian neighbour and eastern wing.

Punjab's traditional landowners benefited from refugee settlement by acquiring additional land, either by purchasing it at rock bottom prices from incoming refugees or by illegally taking possession of evacuee property. The process of settlement further entrenched their sway over rural society and provincial politics, partly because their political constituencies were further extended as a large number of tenants depended on them. The deployment of more people on the land meant the expansion of their political base. Often overlooked in discussions about the larger consequences of Partition, this study has revealed that the impact of displacement could be as profound for those who did not migrate as for those who were uprooted. The scale of the internal displacements have yet to be determined. Divisions within the peasantry minimised the risk of any immediate threat from below of the kind that could have forced an equitable landholding structure. While settlement for the tenantry ended a chance of more equitable economic policies, the mishandling of refugee resources led to the emerging narrative of the politicians' inability to deliver. Moreover, the appropriation of refugee resources encouraged a discourse of 'corruption' in which the whole political elite was increasingly seen to be dishonest. Dealing with the refugee crisis greatly strained relations between the centre and the provinces. While the lengthy process of refugee settlement, the land grab situation, and factionalism played a part in undermining the democratic process, the state's discourse of 'corruption' was specifically political. Not only was it deployed to justify the dismissal of successive provincial governments in the 1950s, but it unwittingly strengthened the ever-encroaching power of the military and the bureaucracy.

Richer migrant landlords were in a position to acquire the cream of vacated property. Their money, influence, and personal connections with officials and politicians were assets employed in not only grabbing the best pickings, but also in acquiring a great deal more than their share. By using their political clout, refugee politicians such as Mamdot cultivated refugees and added them to their new vote-bank by siphoning off vacated land and giving it to their supporters and tenants. They retained their political base and emerged as rural patrons. At the same time, they dispersed the followers of rival politicians in order to shrink their political constituencies. The powerful effects of such developments were corrosive to democratic practices in the Punjabi heartland of the country. The ruling Punjab Muslim League victimised rival politicians by taking over their private estates in the guise of refugee settlement. Vendettas against opponents were detrimental to the spirit of give and take central to the parliamentary system. Moreover, the preference for hasty executive ordinances over the process of sustained political debate in elected assemblies infringed on the centre's role in provincial affairs as well as established the bureaucracy's sway over the entire political process.

## Notes

1 I. Talbot and G. Singh, *The Partition of India* (Cambridge: Cambridge University Press, 2009); J. Chatterji, *The Spoils of Partition: Bengal and India, 1947–1967* (Cambridge: Cambridge University Press, 2007); T. Y. Tan and G. Kudaisya, *The Aftermath of Partition in South Asian* (London: Routledge, 2000).
2 I. Talbot, *Divided Cities: Partition and Its Aftermath in Lahore and Amritsar* (Karachi: Oxford University Press, 2006); S. Ansari, *Life after Partition: Migration, Community and Strife in Sindh, 1947–1962* (Karachi: Oxford University Press, 2005);

Y. Khan, *The Great Partition: The Making of India and Pakistan* (London: Yale University Press, 2007); G. Pandey, *Remembering Partition: Violence, Nationalism and History* (Cambridge: Cambridge University Press, 2001); V. F. Zamindar, *The Long Partition and the Making of Modern South Asia* (Karachi: Oxford University Press, 2008); N. Nair, *Changing Homelands: Hindu Politics and the Partition of India* (Cambridge, MA: Harvard University Press, 2011); R. Kaur, *Since 1947: Partition Narratives among Punjabi Migrants of Delhi* (New Delhi: Oxford University Press, 2007); D. Rahman and W. V. Schendel, 'I Am Not a Refugee: Rethinking Partition Migration', *Modern Asian Studies*, 37, 3 (July 2003), pp. 551–84.

3 G. Kudaisya, 'The Demographic. Upheaval of Partition: Refugees and Agricultural Settlement in India, 1947–67', *South Asia*, 18, special issue (1995), pp. 73–94; M. S. Randhawa, *Out of the Ashes: An Account of the Rehabilitation of Refugees from West Pakistan in Rural Areas of East Punjab* (Chandigarh: Public Relations Department, 1954); V. V. S. Tyagi, *Economic Impact of Partition on Indian Agriculture and Related Industries* (PhD Dissertation, American University: Washington, D.C., 1958); S. M. Rai, *Punjab since Partition* (Delhi: Durga Publications, 1986).

4 A. Jalal, *The State of Martial Rule: The Origins of Pakistan's Political Economy of Defence* (Cambridge: Cambridge University Press, 1990); I. Talbot, *Pakistan: A Modern History* (London: C. Hurst, 2005); F. Shaikh, *Making Sense of Pakistan* (London: C. Hurst, 2009); and also see K. B. Sayeed, 'Collapse of Parliamentary Democracy in Pakistan', *Middle East Journal*, 13, 4 (1959), pp. 389–406; H. Alavi, 'Nationhood and Nationalities in Pakistan', *Economic and Political Weekly*, 24, 27 (July 1989), pp. 1527–34; M. Waseem, *Politics and the State in Pakistan* (Lahore: Progressive Publisher, 1989); Y. Samad, *A Nation in Turmoil: Nationalism and Ethnicity in Pakistan 1937–1958* (New Delhi: Saga, 1995); P. R. Newberg, *Judging the State: Courts and Constitutional Politics in Pakistan* (Cambridge: Cambridge University Press, 2002).

5 H. Alavi, 'The State in Post-Colonial Societies', *New Left Review*, 74 (July/August 1972), pp. 59–82; and also see C. Leys, 'The "overdeveloped" post colonial state: a re-evaluation', *Review of African Political Economy*, 3, 5 (January 2007), pp. 39–48.

6 For the concentration of land ownership in Pakistan, see M. Ahmad, 'Land Reforms in Pakistan', *Pakistan Horizon*, 12, 1 (1959), pp. 30–6; T. Maniruzzaman, 'Group Interests in Pakistan Politics, 1947–1958', *Pacific Affair*, 39, 1, 2 (1966), p. 85.

7 I. Ali, *The Punjab under Imperialism, 1885–1947* (Princeton, NJ: Princeton University Press, 1988).

8 I. Talbot, *Khizr Tiwana: The Punjab Unionist Party and the Partition of India* (London: Richmond, 1996).

9 Following the logic of 'path dependence', see H. Javid, *Class, Power, and Patronage: The Landed Elite and Politics in Pakistani Punjab* (PhD Dissertation, London School of Economics, 2012); and Class, Power, and Patronage: Landowners and Politics in Punjab', *History and Anthropology*, 22, 3 (2011), pp. 337–69.

10 I. Talbot, *Punjab and the Raj: Provincial Politics and the Pakistan Movement, 1849–1947* (New Delhi: Manohar, 1988); D. Gilmartin, *Empire and Islam: Punjab and the Making of Pakistan* (Berkeley: University of California Press, 1988).

11 *Inquilab* (Lahore), 10 February 1948, p. 2.

12 National Documentation Centre, Islamabad (henceforth NDC), File no. B50, 20/CF/48, appendix A, 'Pakistan Ministry of Refugees and Rehabilitation', p. 9.

13 National Archives, Kew Gardens, London (henceforth NA), DO142/28, 'Economic effects of the distribution of the Punjab', 20 January 1948.

14 Pakistan National Archives, Islamabad (henceforth PNA), Governor-General Reports on Refugees and Rehabilitation, File no. 803, PMS/48, p. 2.

15 Punjab Secretariat Archives, Lahore (henceforth PSA), West Pakistan Year Book 1956, E1 (12), p. 95.

16 For the colonial legislations on tenant rights, see M. Darling, *The Punjab Peasant in Prosperity and Debt* (London: Lightning Source, 2011).

17 Chatterji, *The Spoils of Partition*.
18 A number of the uprooted peasants from South Punjab sought employment opportunity in the rapidly emerging industrial city of Karachi, which by the mid-1950s had over 28 per cent of large-scale industry in Pakistan; for details, see S. S. Mehdi, 'Internal Displacement in Pakistan', *Refugee Survey Quarterly*, 19, 2 (2000), pp. 89–100.
19 By 1959, about one million acres of land in the newly set up schemes, such as the Thal Project, Taunsa Barrage Project, and the Ghulam Muhammad Barrage, had been given to displaced tenants, Christian *sepidars*, army personnel and landless locals. See, for example, PSA, West Pakistan Year Book, 1960, File no. E1 (12).
20 PSA, Resettlement of Refugees on Land in West Punjab, 1 July to 31 December 1954, E33, Part XIII, p. 15.
21 Proceedings of the Punjab Legislative Assembly Debates (henceforth PLAD), March 1952, File no. D50 (4), PSA.
22 PNA, Governor-General Reports on Refugees and Rehabilitation File no. 804, PMS/52, p. 3.
23 Ibid., p. 25.
24 PLAD, March 1952, File no. D-50 (4).
25 Ibid.
26 PNA, Governor-General Reports on Refugees and Rehabilitation, File no. 804, PMS/53, p. 5.
27 Ibid.
28 PLAD, 11 March 1952, File no. D-50 (4), p. 598.
29 PLAD, 23 May 1952, File no. D-50 (4).
30 PSA, Resettlement of Refugees on Land in West Punjab, 1 July to 31 December 1954, E33, Part XIII, p. 9.
31 The amount of land per head of the population (arrived at by dividing the total acreage by population) was calculated as 5.3 acres in West Punjab before the migration and 4.4 acres after the exchange of population. The difficulties of absorption were not necessarily proportionate to numbers. The majority of Muslims who had migrated from East Punjab were accustomed to very small holdings of land in compare to West Punjab's Sikhs and Hindus. Therefore, in theory, West Punjab could have readily absorbed an additional 1.3 million net rural population, while East Punjab would have the greatest difficulty in resettling in a contented state refugees from West Punjab, even considerably less in number than those who had moved out of the province.
32 PSA, Punjab: A Review of First Five-Years, 1947–1952, File E1 (9), A 82 (2), p. 49.
33 PSA, West Pakistan Year Book 1956, E1 (12), p. 96. Similar types of land ceilings were imposed on the Hindu and Sikh refugees who migrated to India; for example, those who owned 10 acres in West Punjab were given seven acres and those who owned 50 acres were given 27 instead. A maximum limit of allotment was fixed at 376 acres. For details, see NA, DO142/28, 'Economic effects of the distribution of the Punjab', 20 January 1948. For the Indian Punjab's experience of rural settlement, see Kudaisya, 'The Demographic Upheaval of Partition'; Rai, *Punjab since Partition*.
34 PLAD, 11 March 1952, File no. D50 (4), pp. 614, 616.
35 Ibid.
36 I. Chattha, 'Competitions for Resources: Partition's Evacuee Property and the Sustenance of Corruption in Pakistan', *Modern Asian Studies*, 46, 5 (September 2012), pp. 1182–211.
37 Lahore High Court Records (henceforth LAC), The Supreme Court Survey 1966, Mrs Sahibzadi Naseem Begum versus Settlement and Rehabilitation Commissioner (judgement order: NLR–1982-SCJ–1965).
38 NDC, microfilm no. 2161, 'Dismissal of Noon Ministry', Records of the meeting of the cabinet, held on Wednesday, 25 May 1955.
39 I. Talbot, 'Planning for Pakistan: The Planning Committee of the All-India Muslim League 1943–46', *Modern Asian Studies*, 28, 4 (1994), pp. 875–89.

40 He stated that over 1.6 million of Punjab's *zamindars* averagely paid less than Rs.250 tax annually, while only 7,180 paid little more than this amount. See for example, PLAD, 18 March 1948, File no. D50 (4), p. 126.
41 Ibid.
42 Ibid., 23 March 1948, p. 230.
43 Ibid.
44 Ibid., p. 234.
45 S. V. R. Nasr, 'Pakistan: State, Agrarian Reform and Islamization', *International Journal of Politics, Culture, and Society*, 10, 2 (1996), pp. 249–72; and also see Sheikh, *Making Sense of Pakistan*.
46 PLAD, 24 March 1948, File no. D50 (4), p. 303.
47 Ibid., 6 April 1948, p. 481.
48 PNA, Governor-General Reports on Refugees and Rehabilitation, File no. 262, PMS/48, pp. 36–7.
49 NDC, Ministry of Refugees and Rehabilitation, File no. B50, Appendix C, p. 11.
50 Ansari, *Life After Partition*.
51 The authorities in Pakistan divided the places of origin of migrants in India into two main categories. The refugees who came from East Punjab, the East Punjab States, and Delhi areas fell in the category of 'agreed areas', while refugees who came from other areas (out of 'the disturbed areas' of the Punjab) were placed in the category of 'non-agreed areas'.
52 NDC, Ministry of Refugees and Rehabilitation, File no. B50, Appendix C, p. 11.
53 NA, DO/142/386, Mr Stephenson's (Deputy Higher Commissioner, Lahore) memorandum on political events in the West Punjab.
54 Ibid.
55 PNA, Governor-General Reports on Refugees and Rehabilitation, File no. 262, PMS/48, pp. 36–7.
56 NA, DO/142/386, Mr Stephenson's (Deputy Higher Commissioner, Lahore) memorandum on political events in the West Punjab.
57 Ibid.
58 PLAD, 11 March 1952, File no. D50 (4), pp. 614, 616.
59 Ibid., 10 March 1952, p. 414.
60 NA, DO/142/386, Mr Stephenson's (Deputy Higher Commissioner, Lahore) memorandum on political events in the West Punjab.
61 The government announcement said:

> Public life has been demoralised by corruption and service discipline has been destroyed by intrigue. The main cause of the administration's dereliction of duty had been the failure of members of the Legislative Assembly to rise to the greater responsibilities which independence brings.

See, for example, 'Corruption Charge: An Election in West Punjab Ordered', *Western Australian* (Perth), 26 January 1949, p. 9.
62 NA, DO 35/3189, West Punjab and N.W Frontier Province Land Reform Legislation: Resumption of Punjab Land Grants.
63 For the elections results, see Jalal, *The State of Martial Rule*.
64 NA, DO/142/386, Mr Stephenson's memorandum on political events in the West Punjab.
65 PSA, Punjab: A Review of First Five-Years, 1947–1952, File E1 (9), A 82 (2), p. 6.
66 'Land Reforms in Punjab, Pakistan', *Times of India* (New Delhi), 19 January 1952, p. 7.
67 NA, DO 35/3189, West Punjab and N.W Frontier Province Land Reform Legislations, Punjab Abolition of Jagirs Act 1952.
68 Ibid.
69 PLAD, 11 January 1952, File no. D50 (4), p. 780.

70 Ibid., pp. 818–9.
71 Akhtar Hussein, the Financial Commissioner (resettlement and colonies) explained this in an official memo.
72 NA, DO 35/3189, Mr. Jasper's (Deputy High Commissioner, Lahore), fortnightly report.
73 *The Punjab Gazette* (Lahore), 27 May 1952; and also see PLAD, 11 January 1952, File no. D50 (4), p. 795.
74 NA, DO 35/3189, Record of Conversation between the Lord Privy Seal and Sir Khizr Hayat Khan Tiwana, 21 March 1952.
75 Ibid.
76 NA, DO 35/3189, the Deputy High Commissioner, Lahore, Jasper to Sir P. Liesching, 12 December 1951.

## 2 Elections, bureaucracy, and the law

The reproduction of landed power in post-colonial Punjab

*Hassan Javid*

Very soon after achieving independence from colonial rule, it became abundantly clear that Pakistan would not be following a trajectory of substantive, participatory democratization. The first decade of freedom from British rule, although formally democratic, was marked by internecine warfare between rival political factions in the country's eastern and western wings, and the imposition of military rule by Ayub Khan (1907–74, President 1958–69) in 1958 served to eliminate the faint hope for change that had accompanied the promulgation of the Constitution of 1956. Following the toppling of the Ayub regime in 1968, Zulfiqar Ali Bhutto's (1928–79, President 1971–3, Prime Minister 1973–7) Pakistan People's Party (PPP), founded in 1967, emerged as a potentially progressive panacea for Pakistan's political ills, particularly after the secession of Bangladesh in 1971. The promise of the PPP would prove to be illusory, however, and the question of whether it could have ultimately transformed Pakistan's politics for the better would be rendered moot by General Zia-ul-Haq's (1924–88, President 1977–88) military coup in 1977. When Pakistan finally started making another transition to democracy in 1988, it was one that was marked by the factional conflict of the past, abetted by the interference of a military establishment reluctant to relinquish its role in politics. Where General Zia-ul-Haq's hanging of Zulfiqar Ali Bhutto on 4 April 1979 was history as tragedy, General Pervez Musharraf's (b. 1943, President 2001–8) exile of Nawaz Sharif (b. 1949, Prime Minister 1990–3, 1997–9, 2013–) and Benazir Bhutto (1953–2007, Prime Minister 1988–90, 1993–6) in 1999 was surely history as farce, once again derailing Pakistan's tentative moves towards democracy. Over a decade later, with Musharraf gone and the PPP having succeeded in becoming the first party in Pakistan's history to complete an elected term of five years in office in 2013 (a notable achievement amidst an otherwise abysmal record), it is still unclear as to whether or not military interventions in politics are likely to remain a thing of the past.

What is clear, however, is that the elite character of Pakistani politics is unlikely to change. One of the most notable things about the cyclical shift between authoritarianism and democracy described above is that, for the most, a property-owning political elite has been able to maintain control over the apparatuses of representative government regardless of the regime type in place. Indeed, during times of military rule with 'elections', as well as periods of formal democracy, landlords and industrialists have been at the heart of government, and have succeeded in deeply entrenching themselves within the institutional framework of Pakistani politics. As members of parliament, leaders of political parties, bureaucrats, local government officials, and even officers within the armed forces, the propertied elite have been able to use the resources at their disposal to maintain their capacity to continually exercise power whatever the constitutional configuration.

Focusing on the Punjabi landed elite[1] who continue to dominate the rural political landscape of Pakistan's most populous province, this chapter attempts to outline some of the institutional mechanisms through which elite politics and power are articulated, pursued, and reproduced under conditions of formal democratic rule. In particular, this chapter will examine how elections and the party system, the bureaucracy, and legislative politics have all played a crucial role in this process. The importance this chapter places on periods of democracy, as opposed to authoritarianism, is deliberate; while the mechanisms that will be outlined below also exist under military regimes, and indeed are often produced or accentuated by military interventions in politics, the emphasis on democracy sheds light on precisely how elite politics is reproduced *despite* the possibility for the emergence of a more participatory and popular mode of politics. Furthermore, understanding how elite politics functions under democracy can help identify some of the limits to democratization in Pakistan in terms of its capacity to ensure greater representation for the people, and its potential as a political system through which historically constituted grievances and imbalances around the cleavages of class, ethnicity, and religion can be addressed. By identifying these constraints, this chapter hopes to make a contribution towards understanding both the scale of the challenge involved in radically transforming Pakistan's politics, and strategies through which to overcome these impediments.

The argument presented in this chapter is one that draws on my framework for understanding the reproduction of landed power in the Punjab.[2] Arguing that the relationship between the state and the landed elite in the Punjab is one that is best conceptualized as a bargain in which the latter provide the former with support in exchange for patronage, I suggest that this bargain has been reinforced and reproduced over time as part of a process of path-dependent institutional development that was initiated in the mid-nineteenth century by the British colonial government and has persisted to the present day. As authoritarian colonial and postcolonial regimes have constantly sought to cultivate alliances with powerful local political actors possessing the capacity to aid them in the pursuit of their political objectives, the landed politicians of The Punjab have consistently been able to use their position as recipients of state patronage to reinforce their position and pursue their interests, thereby increasing their utility to the state and further entrenching themselves within the political structure. As the very metaphor of a bargain implies, this relationship is mutually constitutive, in that the state and its landed allies both play a role in developing an institutional framework of politics that is reciprocally beneficial to both actors, and the use of the apparatuses of representative government to achieve this goal is an essential part of this process.

Before proceeding, it is necessary to qualify the argument presented in this chapter by recognizing that the Punjabi landed elite are not a 'ruling' class in and of themselves, given that they share power with landed elites from other parts of Pakistan, as well as elements of the national and metropolitan bourgeoisie.[3] It is also important to recognize that the balance of political power in the Punjab itself has not remained static over time; capitalist development, land fragmentation, and urbanization have all slowly eroded both the economic strength and geographical base of landed power, and recent debates on the rise of a 'middle' class in the province's small towns and cities illustrate the province's potential political future.[4] This chapter also acknowledges that the Punjabi landed elite do not always constitute a unified class bloc, particularly given their predilection for factional conflict. However, as will be explained below, it is possible to discern how, despite the presence of rival classes and intra-class rivalries, the Punjabi landed elite have nonetheless been able to maintain their power and influence by manipulating the institutional framework of politics in the province. Finally, it must also be clarified that the mechanisms listed below through which landed power is reproduced do not represent an exhaustive account of the ways in which elite domination of politics is perpetuated. While electoral, bureaucratic, and legislative mechanisms are important, they exist in parallel with other economic and ideological means through which the landed elite, as well as other members of the ruling class, cement their power.

The chapter is divided into three main sections. First, it examines how electoral and party politics in post-colonial Pakistan have contributed to reinforcing landed power, explaining how the enduring power of the landed elite and the constraints imposed by a predominantly rural electorate have resulted in the landed elite establishing their position as indispensable electoral assets. This will be followed by an analysis of the ways in which the landed elite have continued to use networks of bureaucratic power as a mechanism for ensuring their continued access to state patronage, and to dispense it at the local level. Finally, the chapter concludes with a detailed examination of the landed elite's use of legislative power to protect and pursue their interests; in particular, attention will be paid to how the landed elite have successfully circumvented successive attempts at imposing an agricultural income tax that would have impinged upon their economic interests.

## The electoral race to the bottom and the class composition of Pakistan's political parties

By successfully aligning themselves with Pakistan's different military regimes, landed politicians in the Punjab have been able to sustain their political power and influence in periods of authoritarian rule over long stretches of time characterized by a lack of elections, representative government, and party politics. The ability of the landed classes to do this has been rooted in their enduring economic and social power at the local level, as well as their ability to manipulate their networks of patronage in pursuit of their interests. However, the very same attributes that made landed politicians such a vital asset for military regimes would also hold true for civilian parties and governments seeking to win elections, gain legitimacy, and stave off potential challengers.

When Ayub Khan banned political parties and temporarily excised these landed politicians from formal politics at the start of his tenure, his measures had the effect of dismantling extant party apparatuses without really impinging on the power of the politicians he ostensibly opposed. This can be seen by the fate of the Muslim League, whose funds were first frozen by the federal government in 1958, and again in 1970 when the Muslim League (Councillor)[5] was forced to forfeit its own funds after the reimposition of martial law under General Yahya Khan (1917–80, President 1969–71) in 1969. Almost 20 years later, in response to a letter from Shaukat Hayat Khan (1915–98), the president of a reconstituted Muslim League, the Interior Ministry confirmed that the funds could not be returned because any party now formed, regardless of the name it took, would be treated as if it were an entirely new entity.[6] The Muslim League was not the only party to be deprived of its funding, with the same fate befalling all the other parties as well when martial law was imposed and parties were banned. Additionally, many political leaders and workers were also incarcerated and persecuted, particularly when they refused to acquiesce to the new political dispensation. The result of this was that when parties were re-allowed by Ayub Khan, they lacked established organizational apparatuses and identities. While this was arguably not true for parties like the Jamaat-i-Islami, founded in India in 1941, whose clearly defined ideology and politically committed cadre allowed it to emerge relatively unscathed as an organized body, the larger, national-level parties in West Pakistan were necessarily cobbled together on the basis of factional loyalties; membership with the Muslim League (Convention)[7] and the Conference Muslim League (CoML) was defined primarily by pro- or anti-Ayub sentiment, rather than any broader party programme, and was in any case subject to change depending on the regime's willingness to include previously disqualified or marginalized politicians.

More important, however, were the electoral calculations that went into the selection and recruitment of members for these parties. The necessity of recruiting landed elites was not simply linked to their proven capacity to mobilize support at the local level; it was also a reflection of nature of the Pakistani (and Punjabi) electorate. Indeed, in 1951, only 17.8 per cent of the population of West Pakistan lived in urban areas, with this percentage increasing only slightly to 22.5 per cent in 1961.[8] The demographic reality of Pakistan's rural electorate was accentuated by the way in which both rounds of Basic Democracy elections under Ayub Khan were designed to exploit this rural bias, exemplified by how nearly all of the otherwise urban parts of the Punjab were lumped together with large swathes of countryside when electoral constituencies were delimited.[9] Gerrymandering in this fashion was not something that was new to the Punjab; in addition to the state, many of these landowners themselves used the local level machinery of the state to shape the electoral environment in a way that would be of benefit to them. An example of this can be found in the 1952 elections to the District Boards in

Sargodha, which were the subject of a rare official enquiry due to allegations of electoral misconduct on the part of the incumbents. As noted in the report, there was 'little room for doubt that the Daultana Ministry had drawn up a plan of winning the Local Bodies' elections by hook or by crook',[10] with the mechanisms adopted for doing so being the amendment of electoral rules, and the redrawing of electoral constituencies to favour particular candidates. Much more recently, the transition to democracy following the end of the Zia regime in 1988 was accompanied by the creation of new districts 'under political influence' to ensure that local-level politicians could have easier access to state patronage and more direct control over the administrative apparatus in their areas.[11] Ultimately, shaping electoral constituencies to favour rural politicians had the effect of diluting an urban vote not as amenable to control as the rural one.

The Ayub regime's success in co-opting land-owning politicians to its side in a predominantly rural electorate posed a dilemma for opposition parties seeking to challenge the regime. Given the regime's demonstrated commitment to the pursuit of the interests of the propertied classes, and its willingness to work with politicians that it itself had expended considerable energy on discrediting, one possible route to electoral success would have been to rely on new candidates, potentially drawn from the subordinate classes, to campaign on a relatively progressive platform of socio-economic change. In some respects, this is precisely what Bhutto was able to do in the 1970 elections, albeit under very specific historical circumstances. By and large, though, opposition parties under Ayub chose instead to rely on traditional politics to establish their political power. The reasons for this were twofold; first, the regime's opponents were, for the most part, drawn from the same class background as the regime's supporters. The Conference Muslim League, for example, was mainly a party of landed interests, with its opposition to the regime being dictated more by the factionalism of the Punjab's politics than any principled opposition to dictatorship.

Second, however, was the fact that at the local level, even in the contemporary period, kinship and economic power,[12] as well as the historically reinforced role played by landlords in resolving disputes, mediating interactions with courts and the police, providing credit and economic support, and delivering access to the state and public services, continues to form the basis for landed power.[13] Not choosing an elite platform for politics brought with it the risk of political marginalization. The established capacity of landed politicians to monopolize votes at multiple levels of representative government through the use of their historically reinforced position and resources meant that the chances of a non-landed candidate prevailing in the rural electoral arena were slim at best. This was a problem compounded by the nature of the parties themselves; lacking a strong organizational apparatus as well as a defining ideology or policy programme, both a result of the Ayub regime's attempt to dismantle the party system, new parties were inevitably forced to rely on the localized power of individual politicians to capture votes.

In a real sense, therefore, political parties in Pakistan found themselves engaged in an electoral race of the bottom, continually seeking to co-opt landed factions in an attempt to strengthen their electoral chances. Repeated episodes of military rule would only serve to strengthen this tendency, as these governments would inevitably ban or curtail the activities of established parties, thereby preventing them from maturing as organizations even as pliant landed elites aligned themselves with the military in order to strengthen themselves. The ability of landed politicians to adapt to, and even strengthen their power under, military governments, even as parties as organizations suffered tremendously, only reinforced the electoral indispensability of these traditional elites in periods of 'democratic' government. Attempts by successive governments to preserve, and even enhance, the enduringly rural nature of the electorate confirm this fact. For example, in the run-up to the elections of 1977, there is considerable evidence to suggest that the Bhutto government, having by then thrown in its lot with landed politicians, actively sought to manipulate the delineation of electoral constituencies in a way that would favour rural politicians in league with the regime.[14] Even in the contemporary period, the constituencies drawn up for the elections of 2008 reflected the same kind of rural bias that had existed in 1962, with only 25 per cent of constituencies for the National Assembly being purely urban, even though approximately 36 per cent of the population was now estimated to live in cities. Of the remaining constituencies, approximately 49 per cent were purely rural, while the remaining 25 per cent were semi-urban constituencies in which urban centres, both small and large, were paired with surrounding villages that, more often than not, contained a larger number of voters than the cities, towns, and fragments of both that they were linked to.[15]

The utility of the landed elite to Pakistan's parties is also demonstrated by an examination of their class composition. As shown by Maniruzzaman, nearly 80 per cent of legislators in the Punjab in 1952 were members of the traditional landed aristocracy.[16] Between 1985 and 1997, there was little evidence to suggest that this situation had changed in any significant fashion, as shown by the evidence presented by Saeed Shafqat on the class composition of the National Assembly, reproduced in Table 2.1 below.[17]

Unfortunately, Shafqat does not cite the source of his data, which makes it difficult to ascertain whether or not there were any cases of overlap in this period between the categories of landlord and industrialist. Nonetheless the fact remains that throughout this period, including a decade of purely democratic rule, leadership

*Table 2.1* Socio-economic characteristics of National Assembly members, 1985–97

|  | 1985 | 1988 | 1990 | 1993 | 1997 |
| --- | --- | --- | --- | --- | --- |
| Landlords and tribal leaders | 157 | 156 | 106 | 129 | 126 |
| Businessmen/industrialists | 54 | 20 | 38 | 37 | 39 |
| Urban professionals | 18 | 9 | 46 | 26 | 32 |
| Religious leaders | 6 | 15 | 11 | 8 | 3 |
| Retired military officers | 0 | 7 | 3 | 5 | 2 |
| Other | 3 | 0 | 3 | 3 | 2 |
| Total | 238 | 207 | 207 | 207 | 207 |

of Pakistan's most powerful political parties remained firmly in the hands of the propertied classes, with the landed elite being the single largest group within this category. At the provincial level, comparable data on the class composition of the Provincial Assemblies during this period is not readily available. However, using data provided on the website of the Punjab Provincial Assembly, it is possible to see that the legislators elected to office in 2008 displayed economic and social backgrounds that are not dissimilar to those presented above, and which do not represent a significant departure from the claims that 80 per cent and 63.3 per cent of the Punjab's legislators were drawn from the landed elite in 1951 and 1972 respectively.[18] This data is given in Table 2.2.

It is worth noting that these statistics do not present a complete picture of the class composition of the Punjab Assembly for two reasons. First, the information is incomplete, as details have not been provided for 150 members of the assembly. Second, as noted in some of the profiles of individual members, the categories of 'businessman' and 'agriculturalist' often overlap. The net result of this is that despite decades of economic change in the Punjab, with the growth of both cities and industry, traditional landed elites have been able to retain their control over political parties and the representative organs of government. This finding is one that is not restricted to the national and provincial legislatures, as confirmed by recent research on the socio-economic profile of elected representatives at the local level.[19]

One final factor that can help to explain the continued dominance of landed politicians in the party system deals with the institutional design of electoral politics in the Punjab. Having inherited a first-past-the-post electoral system from the colonial government, Punjabi party politics remained a two-party system as predicted by Duverger's Law.[20] While national-level politics has proven to be much more fragmented, largely due to the emergence of strong ethnic parties like the Awami National Party (ANP) and Mohajir Qaumi Mahaz (MQM) in the smaller provinces (not to mention Bengal's Awami League prior to 1971), the Punjab itself has rarely had more than two major parties competing in elections. Even in situations where opposition parties have coalesced together against incumbents, as was the case with the Muslim League governments of the 1950s, or the Bhutto regime, more often than not these opposition coalitions have remained dominated by single formations of landed interests, with smaller parties from the religious right and the left remaining largely marginal to actual

*Table 2.2* Profession of members of the Punjab Assembly, 2008

| Profession | |
|---|---|
| Agriculturalist | 82.37% |
| Businessmen/industrialists | 59 |
| Urban professionals | 51 |
| Others | 23 |
| Total | 219 |

electoral politics. This was also true in the 1990s, when the PPP and the Islami Jamhoori Ittehad/Pakistan Muslim League IJI/PML-N were the only two parties capable of winning sufficient seats to form provincial governments, albeit sometimes with the support of much smaller parties and factions of independents. The tendency of Punjabi politics to gravitate towards two-partyism has had the effect of erecting barriers to entry for new parties seeking to challenge the status quo, and the winner-takes-all nature of the voting system has reinforced the need to field candidates possessing the potential to actually win in their constituencies. Once again, given the rural nature of the electorate, the voting system itself has served to incentivize political parties to recruit landlords to their fold.

The electoral race to the bottom that has been described above has extremely important implications for democratization in Pakistan. Although their electoral importance derives from their continuing ability to mobilize support at the local level, the entrenchment of the landed elite in party politics has provided them with a mechanism through which to reinforce their formal political power and, consequently, their capacity to more effectively pursue their interests as individual politicians, and as a class. Over time, reliance on the landed elite for electoral support has only deepened as the costs of selecting alternative candidates in the countryside have increased. In turn, these landed politicians have used their position within the party system to further develop the very same attributes that have made them so essential to the electoral process, thereby setting up a cycle of dependence from which parties have largely been unable to escape. Just as the path-dependent nature of institutional development put in motion by the colonial government solidified the position of landed politicians within Punjab's politics, similar mechanisms of entrenchment and reinforcement have underpinned the capture of Pakistan's political parties by the Punjabi landed elite.

## Networks of power and patronage

> By way of gift, something is to be given by the ruling party to its friends. There is my friend, the embodiment of generosity, Kazi Fazlullah Sahib. He has appointed his friend Jatoi Sahib as President of the Local Board of Dadu. Now everybody knows that Jatoi Sahib will be re-elected as a member of the Assembly; he had just to give him a gift. If the cousin of Abdul Hamid Jatoi is appointed as President of the Municipality, where is the harm; it is a gift to a friend. If another friend of Kazi Sahib, Ghulam Mustafa Jatoi, is appointed President of the Local Board, Nawabshah, where is the harm. It is also a gift and a friend will be elected ... if gifts are distributed, we should not grudge the Government this distribution of gifts. That is after all what they have got in their hands.[21]

During the colonial period, the vertical chains of patronage that linked the local to provincial and national politics were buttressed by linkages between the landed elite and the colonial state apparatus. A significant portion of the Punjabi bureaucracy was drawn from land-owning sections of the populace, and military recruitment from the province also disproportionately favoured these groups. The net result of this was to create a situation in which landed politicians seeking to mobilize support or pursue their own interests could call upon their networks within both the military and bureaucracy to do so. Following independence in 1947, it was this very fact that was at least partially responsible for the dominance of landed politicians in the West Pakistani government; the military-bureaucratic establishment was overwhelmingly Punjabi, and remained sympathetic to the very same Punjabi landlords that it had worked with so closely under the British.[22]

While this situation has changed to an extent, most notably after the 1970s following administrative reforms by the Bhutto government that opened the bureaucracy up to increased recruitment from the smaller provinces, as well as the middle classes,[23] the fundamental nature of the bureaucracy as a source of patronage to be accessed and distributed by the political elite has remained constant. Personal ties of loyalty and kinship continue to provide the basis for rent-seeking and preferential access to the state,[24] with the bureaucracy's broader recruitment base making it less insular and more open to clientelism, thus increasing the capacity of the state to dispense patronage to different social groups, and for the urban middle classes to exercise greater amounts of political power.[25] In the countryside, however, local landed influentials have largely retained their role as the primary sources of access to the state, and have continued to use their power to reinforce this position by providing services and negotiating with the state on behalf of their subordinates. The link between landed power and the state in the Punjab also continues to be influenced by the nature of recruitment into the military. Even though the military, like the bureaucracy, has widened access to include groups outside of the traditional landed elite, it remains an institution with roots in the Punjabi countryside.[26]

In order to understand the precise mechanisms through which the relationship between the Punjabi landed elite and the state has reinforced and reproduced the power of both actors over time, it is useful to begin by noting how, even in the contemporary period, the landed elite remains bound to the state by family ties. In his analysis of Punjabi politics in the years leading up to Bhutto's electoral victory in 1970, Craig Baxter made the observation that, in addition to having a significant number of family members who had previously or currently been involved in politics, many of the landed politicians of the Punjab had family members who occupied top positions in the bureaucracy, military, and industry.[27] Where these ties did not involve direct family, marriage was used as a strategy through which different landed politicians and factions could maximize the size and geographical spread of their networks. This point is also made by Sayeed,[28] Alam,[29] and LaFrance,[30] who all argue that the alliance between urban bureaucrats, military elites, and dominant economic groups is one cemented not only through the exchange of patronage, but also through marriage. These findings broadly hold true for the current crop of Punjabi legislators as well.[31] The vast majority of Assembly members have relatives who have held elected office, and many also have direct familial links to the bureaucracy and military.

Significantly, these links are not always restricted to the upper echelons of government, nor are they necessarily restricted to the constituencies of the legislators themselves; many of the relatives of these legislators have been involved in local government, and these ties have often been spread out over significant parts of the Punjab, if not Pakistan.

The implications of this for the exercise of landed power are clear. In his work on class in the Punjab, Saghir Ahmad noted that part of the power the traditional aristocracy held over the subordinate classes was linked to the size and cohesion of their networks; tenants or workers seeking to leave one village for another would often find themselves receiving unsympathetic treatment from neighbouring landlords with ties to those in their original village.[32] By cultivating direct links with functionaries in the bureaucracy and military, the landed elite is able to ensure that their control is maintained not only through the exercise of their power within their own domains, but also through proxies performing different roles within and outside of the state.

Marriage and family are not the only factors that have allowed the Punjab's landed politicians to maintain their networks of influence within the bureaucracy. The receipt and provision of patronage have also been key to this process, with the landed elite using their position as elected representatives to repay the military and bureaucracy for their services. As was the case under colonialism, this has most often taken the form of land grants to different government and military personnel. Following Partition, the various bureaucratic committees and boards tasked with managing evacuee property and allocating it to refugees were constantly criticized for cronyism as successive administrations used them as a tool through which to reward their subordinates.[33] Similarly, when the Feroz Khan Noon (1893–1970, Prime Minister 1957–8) government was dissolved in 1958, one of the reasons cited for its dismissal was the corrupt way in which it

> had decided to allot land to all Major-Generals in the army, all Deputy Commissioners in the Punjab or their relatives and most members of the legislature. In addition, it was proposed to allot land to certain members of the High Court and Federal Court.[34]

However, the fact that the Noon government had engaged in these activities was hardly a surprise. Indeed, as negotiations were being undertaken to finalize the One Unit scheme, imposed in 1955, a dispute arose between the Federal Government and the Punjab over the right of the provincial government to allocate land which was to be brought under cultivation following the imminent expansion of the irrigation network.[35] Given that the provincial governments of West Pakistan were to be merged into a single entity, the Governor-General had ordered all land allocations to be put on hold until the new government could take final decisions on them. In addition to the financial difficulties imposed on the provincial government by this decision, relating largely to how it impeded the government's ability to lease out land for short-term cultivation,[36] a number of objections to this were raised by the Punjab government, ranging from the 'categorical commitment to earmark an area of hundred thousand acres for men and officers of the armed forces',[37] to the need to confer 'proprietary rights on holders of certain categories of grants ... including *lambardari* [revenue official] grants'.[38]

Conferring grants of land to select groups, particularly in the army and bureaucracy, was not something that was restricted to any one government or landed faction. Rather, it was a vital part of the process through which the landed elite used their position to strengthen their networks and reproduce their power, and represented the continuation of a practice that had been in place since the colonial era. Despite their acrimonious conflicts of interest with each other, the use of land as patronage by rival groups was something that was arguably seen by landed politicians as being inherent to the process of government in the Punjab, and necessary for the perpetuation of their interests as a class. This was illustrated in a letter written by Feroz Khan Noon to the Finance Minister in response to the fear that many of the grants his government had already made would be reversed. Noon argued that

> whatever land was granted by Malik Khizar Hayat Tiwana [1900–75], the last Premier [1942–7] of the Punjab before Partition, at the time of elections and to which objection could have been taken, the Daultana ministry did not cancel any of these grants. Similarly, this ministry has not cancelled a single grant made by the Daultana ministry. Therefore ... whatever land ... has been allotted to people, the Central Government is honour bound not to cancel this.[39]

Using land as patronage would become common practice under both civilian and military governments, with a variety of different schemes being set up to award land to bureaucrats, army officials, and other groups whose support the regime in power would want to cultivate. For example, in the first five years of its rule, the Ayub Khan government conferred several thousand acres of land to some of the province's highest-ranking civil servants from departments including Health, Electricity and, ironically, Anti-Corruption.[40] In 1968, in a village in Sialkot where many inhabitants had been displaced by a flood, it was revealed that during the process of resettlement, half of the land had now been allocated to military personnel, with the displaced persons being resettled elsewhere.[41] In the same session of the Punjab Assembly, legislators were also informed that although the government had no plans to award any land to the province's landless cultivators,[42] 37,914 acres of land had been awarded to provincial-level bureaucrats, a further 10,417 acres had been granted to national-level bureaucrats, and 56,191 acres had been allocated to members of the three branches of the armed forces since 1960.[43] At the start of the Bhutto government, a question asked in the Punjab Assembly showed that the practice of granting land to the military continued unabated, with a significant amount of prime agricultural land being allotted to serving and retired soldiers in the district of Sargodha.[44] Furthermore, by 1975 the government had moved beyond just cultivating links with the military and bureaucracy, and had also started to award land to groups like lawyers and journalists.[45]

The landed elite have also cultivated their networks within the state by using their legislative power to directly reward a very particular set of government officials. The proceedings of the different Punjab Assemblies are replete with instances of landed politicians actively seeking to address the concerns of striking *patwaris* (village accountants or revenue officials),[46] resolve disputes between the local revenue administration and the police,[47] increase *patwari* wages,[48] challenge the transferral and removal of *patwaris*,[49] and facilitate recruitment into local-level administrations on the basis of favouritism rather than merit.[50] That legislators place such an emphasis on looking after the needs of members of the local revenue administration is not surprising; *patwaris* maintain exclusive access to records of land ownership and, therefore, play a fundamental role in determining the revenue landowners have to ultimately pay. Furthermore, in disputes over land, *patwari* records are key to any kind of adjudication or litigation. Without *patwari* support, it would not be possible for landlords to work with district and provincial administrations to manipulate the receipt and disbursement of funds and patronage.[51] The power of Pakistan's estimated 14,000 *patwaris* can be gauged not only by their ability to successfully block attempts at reforming an archaic revenue system,[52] but also by examining a revenue case from 1968 involving no less a personage than Zulfiqar Ali Bhutto. In a case brought against Bhutto alleging that he had illegally acquired 500 acres of land, the entire matter was dropped once it was discovered that the single existing copy of the local *patwari*'s record of land rights could not be used as evidence because the entry for Bhutto was not legible, making it impossible to determine if he owned five or 500 acres of land in that particular area![53]

Finally, during the colonial period, the institution that best embodied the nexus between the bureaucracy and the landed elite was that of the District Boards, which oversaw public works projects and development at the local level, and which would be replaced post-Partition by a variety of similar institutions. The first of these was the Village Industrial Development Programme, which was initiated in 1952 and envisaged a process of rural uplift that would be spearheaded by the bureaucracy at the local level. However, the plan would prove to be short-lived, partly due to tensions within the bureaucracy itself but also due to a lack of political commitment from the Muslim League.[54] This situation would change in 1959 with the initiation of the Rural Works Programme (RWP), a project that was envisaged by the Ayub Khan government as being a means through which to link the elected BD (Basic Democrats) members to the bureaucracy at the local level in order to ensure the effective implementation of developmental policies. In the words of Shaid Javed Burki (1969), who was the Director of the West Pakistan RWP, the plan ultimately led to the 'forging of an alliance between the Civil Service of Pakistan, West Pakistan's landed aristocracy, and a group of foreign advisors working in the country'.[55] Essentially, when the Ayub Khan regime began its rapprochement with the landed elite in the early 1960s, the involvement of landed politicians with the RWP illustrated enduring capacity to shape local level politics while also allowing them to use the programme as a means through which to distribute patronage, with the help of the bureaucracy, and claim credit for any developmental progress that took place. Like the District Boards, very large amounts of funding were placed at the disposal of the RWP, with Rs. 232,655,000 being spent on social welfare, agriculture, education, health, sanitation, communication, irrigation, and other areas between 1963 and 1966.[56] For Burki, the ability to influence the way in which these resources were used played a very important role in reinforcing the power of the landed elite during the Ayub years.

Although the RWP came to an end with the Ayub regime, its successor, the People's Works Programme (PWP) would perform a similar role under Bhutto, as would the Integrated Rural Development (IRD) Programme under Zia, with provincial and national-level legislators being given a direct role in the management of the local organizations charged with rural development.[57] Indeed, by 1985, legislators had been provided with annual grants worth Rs.5 million, channelled through the district administration, for use on 'local development'. More often than not, these funds were either appropriated by politicians themselves, or used to cultivate support through the disbursement of patronage.[58] More recent experiments with local government and rural development have yielded similar results. Under Musharraf, the Local Government Plan's provisions for the creation of associations for participatory development in individual villages remained hamstrung by bureaucratic control and elite influence.[59] As such, while the exact specifications of each of these schemes would differ, their fundamental character remained unchanged; rather than facilitating community-based, participatory development, these organizations would remain under bureaucratic control, and would essentially be 'communication channels between the local bureaucracy and the landlord factions'.[60]

Where political parties and the organs of representative government have provided the landed elite with an important means through which to acquire access to state patronage, their links with the bureaucracy and the military have allowed for the perpetuation of the mechanisms that have underpinned the reproduction of their power at the local level. Since independence, the Punjab's landed politicians have remained tied to the state by blood and treasure, deploying their own power and influence to curry favour with state functionaries in exchange for services related to the protection of their economic interests, the persecution of their rivals, and the pursuit of their political goals. That this relationship between the state and the landed elite bears considerable resemblance to that which existed under colonialism is yet another illustration of the path dependent nature of landed power in the Punjab; the nexus between local bureaucrats and landlords, and the use of state institutions for the pursuit of their common goals, was a system put in place by the colonial government and subsequently reproduced in a post-colonial context in which the state did not experience a significant rupture with the previous model of administration. The reciprocal nature of the relationship between the state and the landed elite has only deepened over time.

## Legislative power

> There are days when I hear capitalists speak the language of Socialists and there are days when I hear Socialists speak the language of capitalists. If there is anything which touches the pocket of the rich, then party discipline is thrown to the winds, and adequate time is given for discussion on the floor of the House. If there is any matter that affects the interests of the poor, then party discipline is invoked, and graveyard silence prevails in this House.[61]

After independence, Pakistan was governed using the Government of India Act of 1935, with many of the laws enshrined in this document either being retained in their entirety, or used as a template for subsequent legislation, even after the promulgation of the Constitution of 1956. The institutional implications of this for the Punjab can be seen in how modified versions of the Punjab Revenue and Tenancy Acts remained in place until the late 1990s, and the Alienation of Land Act, while not always enforced, remained on the statute books in an essentially unchanged form. While there were some significant legal changes, most notably with the introduction of laws aimed at bringing rules of female inheritance in line with Islamic teachings, the landed elite possessed the capacity to exploit loopholes in these laws, or even evade them altogether, thus ultimately lessening their impact.[62] The same was true for questions of land reform and taxation; in both cases, landed legislators used their influence to circumvent or dilute measures that directly impinged upon their economic power. By focusing on the failure to impose an Agricultural Income Tax in the Punjab, this section will show precisely how legislative power was used by the landed elite to shape the environment in which they could pursue their economic interests, thereby reinforcing their power as a class.

### *Agricultural income tax in the Punjab*

Unlike Pakistan's largely failed experiences with land reform, both rounds of which were initiated under conditions of military rule,[63] and which were essentially measures over which the landed elite had no direct control, laws governing revenue and taxation largely remained the sole domain of the Punjab Legislative Assembly, allowing landed politicians to design them in a way that would allow them to pursue and protect their interests more effectively. This was not entirely dissimilar to the way in which legislation had been created and used under the British, although there were a few important differences. The more formally democratic and competitive nature of post-independence politics, even during periods of military rule, meant that elected representatives had, at some level, to respond to the needs of the electorate, and thus limit the extent to which legislation had an explicit pro-elite bias. This was also a function of the presence of more rival groups in the Assembly; the ever-present threat of landed factionalism, coupled with the increasing number of capitalists, urban professionals, and even smaller landholders involved in lawmaking, particularly after the 1970s, added to the obstacles the landed elite had to overcome. More often than not, however, conflict was avoided due to the overlap between these different categories, as well as the clear demarcation of spheres of interest, such as land revenue, that did not necessarily involve a clash of interest between different groups. Lawmaking in the post-independence period was also reflective of the strong fiscal constraints experienced by both the federal and provincial governments which, as will be explained below, sometimes had a bearing on the shape of legislation relating to taxation. Finally, and perhaps most importantly, there remained the fact that formal laws and rules did not necessarily matter at the local level. As argued by Matthew Nelson, one of the keys to the enduring power of the landed elite at the local level has been their enduring capacity to evade the law in circumstances where it could work against them.[64] Alternatively, given that evasion necessarily entailed costs of its own, formally shaping the institutional arena through legislation remained an important means through which the landed elite reinforced their power.

Before examining the debates that surrounded the passage of laws regarding agricultural taxation, it is useful to first briefly review the history of such legislation in post-colonial Punjab. As has been pointed out in the literature on this subject,[65] one of the most striking features of Pakistan's taxation regime is that agriculture, despite contributing to over a quarter of Pakistan's GDP even in the 1990s,[66] and employing over half of the total labour force, accounts for a negligible amount of government revenue. In the Punjab, agriculture contributes to almost 30 per cent of total economic output and employs nearly half the workforce, Table 2.3 provides an indication of the revenue derived from the agricultural sector.

The relatively marginal contribution of the agricultural sector to government revenue is doubly surprising because agricultural incomes and productivity have grown tremendously since independence, not least due to a relatively high level of government investment in the sector.[67] For Sarfraz Qureshi,[68] the explanation for this lies in the failure of rural voters to establish the link between government taxation and expenditure, with the argument being that a tax system designed to highlight private returns from public expenditure might incentivize politically dominant agrarian elites to contribute more to the public exchequer. However, as

Table 2.3 Land revenue and agricultural income tax receipts and total revenue in the Punjab

|  | 1961–2 | 1967–8 | 1971–2 | 1977–8 | 1987–8 | 1991–2 |
|---|---|---|---|---|---|---|
| Land revenue (Rs. millions) | 144 | 163 | 120.748 | 100.10 | 239.5 | 501.2 |
| Agricultural income tax (Rs. millions) | 3 | 5 | n/a | 12.0 | 0.5 | n/a |
| Total revenue (Rs. millions) | 534 | 1165 | 742.683 | 700.15 | 2314.5 | 4649.6 |
| Agricultural taxation as percentage of total revenue | 27.5 | 20.3 | 16.25 | 16.01 | 10.3 | 10.78 |

Alavi,[69] Hussain,[70] and Husain[71] point out, it is precisely the exercise of landed political power that allows the elite to benefit from government expenditure while profiting from a very low tax burden. Rather than being the result of a flawed tax system, the low levels of revenue generated by agriculture are largely due to the ability of the landed elite to prevent the imposition of higher taxes, and their ability to impede the effective implementation of the taxation regime that does exist.

Part of an explanation for the low level of agricultural taxation lies in the legacy of colonialism; under the All-India Income Tax Act of 1925, the right to levy a tax on agriculture was granted to the provinces rather than the federal government, with this particular provision being bequeathed to both India and Pakistan following independence. Concurrently, the amount of revenue generated from agriculture continued to be determined by the various Provincial Revenue Acts which, in the Pakistani case, remained in place unchanged until 1967, at which point the West Pakistan Land Revenue Act essentially reproduced and imposed the Punjab Revenue Act in the rest of the country.[72] Although the Revenue Act included provisions for the payment of certain dues in addition to land revenue itself, such as the local rate, the development cess, and the water rate, the cumulative effect of these measures remained small. Similarly, while an agricultural income tax was imposed in the Punjab relatively early on in 1948 it was, as will be discussed below, extremely marginal, and justified only by the government's precarious financial position. While there was an abortive attempt to impose a more stringent tax regime by the Bhutto government in 1977, which abolished land revenue entirely in favour of an agricultural income tax, these measures were reversed by the Zia-ul-Haq government (1977–88) soon after it came to power in 1977. The situation would remain unchanged until the mid-1990s, when the dictates of international financial institutions, as well as Pakistan's worsening economic condition, provided the conditions under which the question of agricultural income tax could be raised once more. Again, however, the strength of the Punjab's landed lobby prevented the new taxation system from becoming any more severe than the one it replaced.

Starting with the debate over the imposition of an agricultural income tax in 1948, it is possible to see precisely how the landed politicians in the Assembly maneuvered to dilute the impact of the proposed law. When the law was first put to the Punjab Assembly, it was referred to a Select Committee comprised almost entirely of landed politicians including Mumtaz Daultana, Firoz Khan Noon, and Jamal Laghari.[73] As an initial response to the bill, Noon argued that the provisions contained within it imposed an unfair burden on individuals by taxing them on the basis of their revenue demand, rather than their actual income.[74] During the subsequent debate, Nurullah Ahmad repeated Noon's claim that the level of taxation outlined in the bill was too high, particularly for landowners like himself who paid between Rs.1,000 and Rs.5,000 in revenue and would thus have to pay twice this amount as tax.[75] Ahmad followed this up with the assertion that the income tax would lead *zamindars* to lose all interest in agriculture, and that it would ultimately be self-defeating as it would lead to a drop in food production.⁷⁶ Taking a slightly different approach, another legislator argued that it would make more sense for the government to generate income from the urban sector by taxing capitalists and their industries.⁷⁷ This point was also made by Muzaffar Ali Qizilbash, who felt that as the 'backbone' of the country, *zamindars* were willing to make this sacrifice, but that it only made sense to also tax capitalists and the urban sector at the same level, if not higher, since all were now equal citizens of Pakistan bearing the responsibility to help the nation progress.⁷⁸ Finally, in a particularly impassioned speech littered with couplets bemoaning the tragic circumstances of the province's landlords, Chaudhry Asghar Ali declared that the '*zamindar*' government of the Punjab had managed to accomplish that which even the Congress had been unable to do with regards to victimizing landowners. Bitterly criticizing the government for turning its back on the province's agriculturalists, Asghar Ali claimed that the government had reneged on its promise to create an Islamic state by attempting to impose a tax that had no basis in Islam and, indeed, no parallel in the rest of the world.⁷⁹

These members were not alone in raising these objections, which were echoed by the majority of the legislators present during the passage of this Bill. However, while these opinions were representative of the widespread and deep-seated opposition the landed elite had to any revision of the economic *status quo*, it is important to note that the Bill of 1948 was only to be applied for a year, as clarified by the Revenue Minister during the debate. Moreover, it was also clarified that the Bill was only being introduced on this temporary basis because of the precarious financial situation the Punjab government found itself in post-Partition, particularly given the need to support the millions of refugees streaming across the border with India.⁸⁰ This point had also been made a month earlier, with it being stated that the cost of rehabilitating the refugees from India was extremely high, and that while there was 'concern at the continual subjection of the resources of a small and mutilated province, which has barely recovered from the cruel wounds inflicted by the sword of Partition, to the incidence of such a vast unproductive expenditure',⁸¹ it was nonetheless necessary to impose an agricultural income tax on large landowners who could afford to pay it in light of the profits they had been able to make in recent years due to rising agricultural commodity prices.⁸² It was only in the face of this clear financial imperative that the Punjab's legislators acquiesced, albeit reluctantly, to the passage of the Bill.

Mild as the Bill was, it would eventually only be passed following amendments that guaranteed the temporary nature of the tax, ensured that transfers of land would not be rendered invalid, and allowed the Government to exempt individuals and groups from the payment of the tax.⁸³ After a year the Bill of 1948 lapsed, only to be replaced by the Punjab Agricultural Income Tax Act of 1951. This tax, which like the Bill of 1948 was really just a surcharge on the land revenue rather than a tax on actual income, represented an extremely marginal increase in the total amount of agricultural taxation. However, as can be seen in the debate on amendments to the Act that were proposed just a year later, the landed elites in the Punjab Assembly made effective use of their legislative power to further reduce the impact of this new law. As mentioned in the aims and objectives of the proposed amendments, the government sought to change the existing Income Tax Act to bring it in line with the changes that had been made to the terms of tenancy under the Punjab Protection and Restoration of Tenancy Rights (Amendment) Bill passed earlier in the year. Under the terms of this new legislation, the government argued that the incomes of landowners had been reduced by 10 per cent and, as such, it was only fair that the income tax burden on the province's landlords also undergo a reduction.

As always, when the Amendments were presented before the Assembly, much of the criticism took the form of allegations that the government was trying to destroy the livelihoods of the province's agriculturalists. This tendency was epitomized by Mian Abdul Bari, a member of the Opposition from Lyallpur, who claimed that big and small landowners were being robbed by the government in the name of the refugees, and that he could not understand why 'the Chief Minister [Daultana] has gotten it into his head that landowners are rolling in money'.[84] Bari then claimed that as a result of the tax, agriculturalists could no longer afford food, medicine, and education, and that even those owning 250 acres of land now found themselves in dire financial straits, with the gravity of the situation also being reflected in the way that most of the province's landlords could not even think of buying a car.[85] Instead, Bari suggested that the proposed law be amended to apply to individual harvests, rather than financial years, saying that this would reduce the burden of taxation to a level that would be more bearable for smaller and medium landowners.[86] In response, the government said that this simply was not possible since the tax only applied to big landowners who could afford it, and that even those owning 50 acres of land had average incomes of Rs.4,000–5,000 a year which was more than enough to bear the weight of an income tax. More importantly, the government argued that implementing Bari's proposals would lead to the total yield from the income tax being reduced by half.[87]

The government's response to Bari's proposed changes illustrated the way in which the fiscal constraints faced by the Punjab government limited the extent to which the economic demands of the landed elite could be accommodated. Even then, however, there is evidence to suggest that the government's own amendments to the law had already diluted its impact tremendously. This can be seen in the arguably more cogent criticisms of the Bill by the Assembly's urban members. Mian Amin, an Opposition lawyer from Lahore, accused the government of amending the law to protect the province's biggest landowners at the expense of smaller ones. As proof of this, he pointed to the fact that the biggest beneficiaries of the changes to the law would be the 14 largest estates in the province, including those of Khizr Hayat Tiwana and the Nawab of Mamdot (1906–69).[88] Amin argued that Khizr Hayat, as a former Unionist loyal to the British government before Partition, would reap a profit of Rs.150,000 due to the proposed amendments, and that the total amount of revenue yielded from the tax would drop from Rs.7 million to Rs.3 million per year, with the difference going back into the pockets of the same landowners the government claimed to be targeting.[89] Furthermore, according to Amin, loopholes in the law regarding the transfer of land would facilitate tax evasion by the landed elite and that even if that did not happen, the basis of the tax on outmoded and extremely low revenue assessments, rather than on actual income, would ensure that its financial impact would remain limited.[90] Urban frustration with the government was also voiced by Sheikh Hussain Qadri, another lawyer from Lahore who, when faced with opposition to an amendment he proposed seeking to base the tax on income rather than land revenue, asked the government, 'why are you afraid of big landowners?'[91] Not unexpectedly, the proposed amendment was rejected.

On a different note, Qadri also accused the government of trying to curry favour with the Punjab's landowning politicians. Referring to the factional conflict between Mamdot and Daultana, he said that the 'Government is legislating to keep a few big landowners happy for fear that they might defect', and that this also explained why the government was now willing to tax settled refugees while providing relief to people like Khizr Hayat.[92] This point was expanded upon by Chaudhry M. Shafiq, a lawyer from Sahiwal, who criticized a part of the Bill that gave the government authority to exclude any individual or group from the payment of income tax as an escape clause for the landed elite. Arguing that no such provision had been kept when it came to taxing refugees, Shafiq claimed that the government was simply interested in 'class war', and that retaining the power to waive taxation arbitrarily would lead to widespread corruption, bribery, nepotism, and tax evasion.[93] Furthermore, the clause allowing the government to waive the tax was deemed to be necessary in case of unforeseen circumstances that rendered particular individuals or groups incapable of paying the tax.[94] When the estion was then made that the clause be rewritten to prevent its abuse, the government declined to do so.

The debates over income tax in the late 1940s and early 1950s would set the tone for this particular aspect of agrarian revenue generation till the end of the Bhutto years, after which Bhutto's abortive attempt at imposing a more stringent tax would lead to the elimination of the income tax altogether until the late 1990s.[95] It was not coincidental that the Agricultural Income Tax Act of 1997 was prompted by IMF dictates instructing the imposition of the tax as a condition for the granting of loans to the federal government.[96] Once again, it was only under conditions of financial duress that the government was able to pass taxation legislation that impinged upon the economic interests of the landed elite. All was not lost, however; the legislation that was passed was not very dissimilar from the one that had existed decades earlier, and essentially reproduced the same kinds of safeguards that had existed then, allowing the government at the time to claim it had successfully imposed the tax even though it made little difference on the ground.[97] More importantly, the imposition of the tax was accompanied by the repeal of the venerable Land Revenue Act, a law that had shaped the agrarian economy for over a century, and which, even at this stage, found defenders who argued it was preferable to the new and unknown system of taxation being introduced to the province.[98] However, fears that the new income tax would burden the landed elite in any way would soon prove to be unfounded. Agitation by landlords throughout the province led to the introduction of amendments that diluted the law even further, and evidence from across the Punjab also suggested that the rate of tax collection had been very low.[99] Having failed to prevent the passage of the law, the landed elite simply exercised their capacity to evade it.

In this chapter, an attempt has been made to show how the Punjab's landed elite have used their relationship with the state to reinforce their power and entrench themselves further within the institutional framework of Pakistan's politics. Three mechanisms have been identified through which this has been done. First, the landed elite in the Punjab have been successful in maintaining a stranglehold on the province's electoral politics. Partly due to the impact of military rule and partly due to the rural bias in the electorate, landed politicians have been able to maintain their position as the pre-eminent source of rural support by using their historically evolved sources of power to mobilize votes for rival political parties. This has had the effect of setting up an electoral race to the bottom in which political parties, in an attempt to win elections by the most expedient means possible, have continued to curry favour with the landed elite at the expense of developing their organizational and ideological apparatuses. Like the Unionists and the Muslim League during the colonial period, the political parties of contemporary the Punjab remain beholden to landed interests, increasingly incapable of reorienting themselves towards a more programmatic, participatory form of politics.

The capture of the party system by the landed elite has been supplemented by their use of bureaucratic power and networks as a mechanism through which to reinforce their power. The ties of kinship, family, and politics that bound the Punjabi landed elite to the colonial military and bureaucracy have persisted throughout Pakistan's history, providing the former with ready access to state patronage, particularly through the organs of local government. The landed elite have returned the favour by using their own influence to further the interests of their allies in government, perpetuating a system of mutually beneficial, self-reinforcing nepotism and rent-seeking that has strengthened the relationship between the state and the landed elite over time.

Finally, attention has also been paid to legislation, and the way in which the capacity to shape and evade it has been crucial to the maintenance of landed power in the Punjab. In particular, it has been shown with reference to the case of agricultural income tax in the Punjab that, despite the economic arguments in favour of such a tax, its imposition was only possible in periods of economic stress, and even then in a form that rendered it relatively marginal to the economic interests of the landed elite. Similar processes underpinned the neutering of legislation related to land reform and land revenue, underlining the extent to which legislative politics has historically played a role in cementing landed power.

## Notes

1 The landed elite, as conceptualized in this chapter, are the members of the traditional aristocracy and rich peasantry who own more than 50 acres of land. At present, about 1 per cent of the Punjab's land-owners would fall in this category, collectively controlling 14 per cent of the total cultivated area. Following the argument presented in this chapter, this particular section of the land-owning populace is significant not

only because of its economic power, but also because of the way in which its power has been reinforced and reproduced over time. See Hassan Javid, 'Class, Power, and Patronage: Landowners and Politics in Punjab', *History and Anthropology*, 22, 3 (2011): 337–69.
2 Javid, 'Class, Power, and Patronage'.
3 This triadic conception of the ruling class in Pakistan is rooted in Hamza Alavi's characterization of the class structure of postcolonial Pakistan. See Hamza Alavi, 'The State in Post-Colonial Societies: Pakistan and Bangladesh', *New Left Review*, 1, 74 (July/August 1972): 59–81.
4 See Asad Sayeed, 'Growth and Mobilisation of the Middle Classes in West Punjab: 1969–1970', in P. Singh and S. Thandi (eds), *Globalisation and the Region: Explorations in Punjabi Identity* (London: Association for Punjab Studies, 1996).
5 The Muslim League (Councillor) was the anti-Ayub Khan faction of the Muslim League.
6 File No. 192/CF/72, 'Funds Belonging to Muslim League – Embezzlement of', President's Secretariat (Cabinet Division), 11 October 1977, National Documentation Centre, Islamabad (NDC). Following his ouster in 1977, Zulfiqar Bhutto accused the military establishment of using about Rs.20 million in confiscated PML funds to finance and then support the group of Opposition parties that constituted the IJI. See Zulfiqar A. Bhutto, *If I am Assassinated* (Lahore: Classic Book House, 2008 [1978]). Similar accusations were made by the PPP against the IJI in the late 1980s and early 1990s. At the time of writing this article in 2012, these accusations were being investigated by the Supreme Court as part of its hearings into the Asghar Khan Petition.
7 The Pro-Ayub Khan faction of the Muslim League.
8 W.M. Phillips, Jr., 'Urbanization and Social Change in Pakistan', *Phylon*, 25, 1 (1964), p. 37.
9 As can be seen in the lists of constituencies provided in the official report on the elections of 1962, many of the Punjab's cities were joined with villages located around them. In fact, with the exception of a few constituencies in Lahore, there were no purely 'urban' constituencies in the Punjab. Election Commission of Pakistan, 1962, *Pakistan General Elections 1962*, Appendix III, Punjab Civil Secretariat Library, Lahore (PSCL).
10 A.M.K. Leghari, *Report on the Sargodha District Board Elections 1952–53* (Lahore: Government of Punjab, 1954), p. 3.
11 Saeed Shafqat, 'Democracy and Political Transformation in Pakistan', in Imran Ali, Jean-Luc Racine, and Soofia Mumtaz (eds), *State, Society and Democratic Change in Pakistan* (Karachi: Oxford University Press, 2002), p. 218.
12 Hamza Alavi, 'Rural Bases of Political Power in South Asia', *Journal of Contemporary Asia*, 4, 4 (1974): 413–22.
13 See Muhammad A. Chaudhry, *Justice in Practice: Legal Ethnography of a Pakistani Punjab Village* (Karachi: Oxford University Press, 1999); Stephen M. Lyon, *An Anthropological Analysis of Local Politics and Patronage in a Pakistani Village* (Lampeter: Edwin Mellen Press, 2004); Ali Cheema and Shandana K. Mohmand, 'Accountability Failures and the Decentralisation of Service Delivery in Pakistan', *IDS Bulletin*, 38, 1 (2007); and Matthew J. Nelson, *In the Shadow of the Shari'ah: Islam, Islamic Law and Democracy in Pakistan* (New York: Columbia University Press, 2011).
14 Government of Pakistan, *White Paper on the Conduct of the General Election in March 1977* (Islamabad: Government of Pakistan, 1978), pp. 43–60.
15 The constituency categories described here have been determined with reference to the constituency maps provided on the website of the Election Commission of Pakistan, www.ecp.gov.pk/Delimitation/Constituency/Maps/NA.aspx. Constituencies are delineated on the basis of population. For the purposes of the 2008 elections, it is

important to bear in mind that the population figures used to delineate the constituencies were based on the Census of 1998. Given the explosive growth of the urban population in the decade between the Census and the elections, the rural vote was even more over-represented than the official report would suggest. Indeed, as argued by R. Ali, it may now be possible to make the claim that the increasingly blurred distinction between 'rural' and 'urban' in Pakistan means that over 50 per cent of the population might now qualify as urban. See R. Ali, 'Underestimating Urbanisation?', in S. Akbar Zaidi (ed.), *Continuity and Change: Socio-Political and Institutional Dynamics in Pakistan* (Karachi: City Press, 2003).

16 Talukdar Maniruzzaman, 'Group Interests in Pakistani Politics, 1947–1958', *Pacific Affairs*, 39, 1/2 (1966): 83–98.

17 Saeed Shafqat, 'Democracy in Pakistan: Value Change and Challenges of Institution Building', *The Pakistan Development Review*, 37, 4 (1998): 281–98.

18 Maniruzzaman, 'Group Interests in Pakistani Politics, 1947–1958'; and Philip E. Jones, *The Pakistan People's Party: Rise to Power* (Karachi: Oxford University Press, 2003), p. 488.

19 Aasim S. Akhtar, Foqia S. Khan, and Shahrukh R. Khan, *Initiating Devolution for Service Delivery in Pakistan: Ignoring the Power Structure* (Karachi: Oxford University Press, 2007).

20 Maurice Duverger, *Political Parties: Their Organization and Activity in the Modern State* (London: Methuen, 1954).

21 Shahnawaz Pirzada, member from Nawabshah District, Provincial Assembly of West Pakistan Debates (PAWPD), 27 August 1958, p. 234, Punjab Assembly Library, Lahore (PAL).

22 In addition to being 'overdeveloped' relative to Pakistan's political parties and civil society (see Hamza Alavi, 'The State in Post-Colonial Societies'), the establishment also exhibited a clear Punjabi bias rooted in the preponderant position of Punjabis within the different organs of the state and armed forces. See Hamza Alavi, 'Pakistan and Islam: Ethnicity and Ideology', in Fred Halliday and Hamza Alavi (eds), *State and Ideology in the Middle East and Pakistan* (New York: Monthly Review Press, 1988). This 'Punjabization' of the Pakistani state from the very onset – for which see Yunas Samad, 'Pakistan or Punjabistan: Crisis of National Identity', *International Journal of Punjab Studies*, 2, 1 (1995): 23–42; G. Kudaisya and Tan T. Yong 'Punjab and the Making of Pakistan', in *The Aftermath of Partition in South Asia* (London: Routledge, 2000); Ian Talbot, 'The Punjabization of Pakistan: Myth or Reality?', in Christophe Jaffrelot (ed.), *Pakistan: Nationalism without a Nation* (London: Zed Books, 2002); and Tahir H. Naqvi, 'The Politics of Commensuration: The Violence of Partition and the Making of the Pakistani State', *Journal of Historical Sociology*, 20, 1–2 (2007): 44–71 – gave rise to ethno-national tensions within the country, as the other provinces fought against Punjabi dominance of the state. Bengal, in particular, constantly strove to secure a position for itself within the state that was commensurate with its demographic strength and importance. For its own part the establishment saw the challenge from the non-Punjabi provinces as an assault on its own power and would continually strive to reinforce its own position relative to them in the decades to come, with this ethnic tension becoming a powerful force inhibiting Pakistan's democratization. See Christophe Jaffrelot, 'India and Pakistan: Interpreting the Divergence of Two Political Trajectories', *Cambridge Review of International Affairs*, 15, 2 (2002): 251–67; and Katherine Adeney and Andrew Wyatt, 'Democracy in South Asia: Getting Beyond the Structure-Agency Dichotomy', *Political Studies*, 52, 1 (2004): 1–18.

23 See Charles H. Kennedy, 'Policy Formulation in Pakistan: Antecedents to Bhutto's Administrative Reforms', *The Journal of Commonwealth and Comparative Politics*, 20, 1 (1982): 42–56; and N. Islam, 'Colonial Legacy, Administrative Reform and Politics: Pakistan 1947–1987', *Public Administration and Development*, 9, 3 (1989): 271–85.

24  See Khalid Nadvi, 'Social Networks in Urban Punjab: A Case Study of the Sialkot Surgical Instrument Cluster', in S.M. Naseem and Khalid Nadvi (eds), *The Post-Colonial State and Social Transformation in India and Pakistan* (Karachi: Oxford University Press, 2002); and N. Islam, 'Sifarish, Sycophants, Power and Collectivism: Administrative Culture in Pakistan', *International Review of Administrative Sciences*, 70, 2 (2004): 311–30.
25  See Ayesha Jalal, 'The State and Political Privilege in Pakistan', in Myron Weiner and Ali Banuazizi (eds), *The Politics of Social Transformation in Afghanistan, Iran, and Pakistan* (Syracuse: Syracuse University Press, 1994); Ali Cheema and Asad Sayeed, 'Bureaucracy and Pro-Poor Change', *PIDE Working Papers*, No. 3, 2006; and Aasim S. Akhtar, 'Pakistan: Crisis of a Frontline State', *Journal of Contemporary Asia*, 40, 1 (2010): 105–22.
26  Clive Dewey, 'The Rural Roots of Pakistani Militarism', in Donald A. Low (ed.), *The Political Inheritance of Pakistan* (Basingstoke: Macmillan, 1991).
27  Craig Baxter, 'The People's Party vs. the Punjab "Feudalists"', in J.H. Korson (ed.), *Contemporary Problems of Pakistan* (Leiden: E.J. Brill, 1974).
28  Khalid B. Sayeed, 'The Breakdown of Pakistan's Political System', *International Journal*, 27, 3 (1972), p. 391.
29  M. Shahid Alam, 'Economics of Landed Interests: A Case Study of Pakistan', *Pakistan Economic and Social Review*, 12, 1 (1974): 12–26.
30  Pierre LaFrance, 'Political Parties in Pakistan: Role and Limitations', in Imran Ali, Jean-Luc Racine, and Soofia Mumtaz (eds), *Pakistan: Contours of State and Society* (Karachi: Oxford University Press, 2002).
31  According to the statistics provided on the website, two-thirds of the members in 2012 had family members who are, or were, part of the Punjab Assembly, the National Assembly, the military, and the bureaucracy. See www.pap.gov.pk/index.php/members/stats/en/19.
32  Saghir Ahmad, 'Peasant Classes in Pakistan', in Hari P. Sharma and Kathleen Gough (eds), *Imperialism and Revolution in South Asia* (New York: Monthly Review Press, 1973).
33  Ilhan Niaz, *The Culture of Power and Governance in Pakistan 1947–2008* (Karachi: Oxford University Press, 2010), pp. 245–9.
34  File No. 111/CF/55, 'Dismissal of Noon Ministry', Cabinet Secretariat, 1955, NDC.
35  File No. 17/CF/55, 'Allocation, Distribution, Sale, Lease of the Land in West Pakistan', 1955, Cabinet Secretariat, NDC.
36  File No. 17/CF/55, 'Allocation, Distribution, Sale, Lease of the Land in West Pakistan', 21 April 1955, Cabinet Secretariat, NDC.
37  File No. 17/CF/55, 'Allocation, Distribution, Sale, Lease of the Land in West Pakistan', p. 1, April 1955, Cabinet Secretariat, NDC.
38  File No. 17/CF/55, 'Allocation, Distribution, Sale, Lease of the Land in West Pakistan', p. 1, June 1955, Cabinet Secretariat, NDC.
39  File No. 17/CF/55, 'Allocation, Distribution, Sale, Lease of the Land in West Pakistan', 21 April 1955, Cabinet Secretariat, NDC.
40  Provincial Assembly of West Pakistan Debates (PAWPD), 6 April 1963, pp. 2263–5, PAL.
41  PAWPD, 1 May 1968, pp. 14–18.
42  Ibid., p. 50.
43  Ibid., p. 58.
44  Punjab Legislative Assembly Debates (PLAD), 28 July 1972, pp. 2188–92.
45  PLAD, 12 February 1975, pp. 180–207.
46  PLAD, 1 March 1952, p. 78.
47  PAWPD, 23 May 1968, pp. 4556–64.
48  PLAD, 26 July 1972, pp. 1833–5.
49  PLAD, 30 January 1973, pp. 1108–10.

50 PLAD, 28 June 1989, pp. 1609–17.
51 Nelson, *In the Shadow of the Shari'ah*, p. 178.
52 Muhammad U. Qazi, 'Computerisation of Land Records in Pakistan: A Comparative Analysis of Two Projects from a Human Security Perspective', Paper presented at Asia Pacific Development Information Project Conference, Bangkok, Thailand, 2006.
53 'Zulfiqar Ali Bhutto: Cases Regarding Irregularities in Declaring Landholdings and Tractors, 1968–69', Acc. No. S. 940, NDC. In a different, more contemporary context, Matthew Hull shows how villagers in the outskirts of Islamabad, as well as local officials, use the opaque and nebulous nature of official ownership records to defraud the government of money, and to initiate legal proceedings against rivals. Again, the ease with which local land records lend themselves to manipulation underscores the importance of local functionaries to the landed elite. Furthermore, as was discovered by Moir and Moir, district-level records on revenue are often difficult to locate and access, thus providing the local-level bureaucracy with a tremendous amount of discretion with regards to the use and manipulation of these records. See Matthew S. Hull, 'Rule by Records: The Expropriation of Land and the Misappropriation of Lists in Islamabad', *American Ethnologist*, 35, 4 (2008): 501–18; and M. Moir and Z. Moir, 'Old District Records in Pakistan', *Modern Asian Studies*, 24, 1 (1990): 195–204.
54 Shahid J. Burki, 'West Pakistan's Rural Works Program: A Study in Political and Administrative Response', *Middle East Journal*, 23, 3 (1969), pp. 327–9.
55 Ibid., p. 331.
56 Ibid., p. 337.
57 Mohammad Waseem, 'Local Power Structures and the Relevance of Rural Development Strategies: A Case Study of Pakistan', *Community Development Journal*, 17, 3 (1982), p. 230.
58 Shafqat, 'Democracy and Political Transformation in India', p. 216.
59 Cheema and Mohmand, 'State and Capital in Pakistan'.
60 Waseem, 'Local Power Structures', p. 233.
61 C.E. Gibbon, Anglo-Indian Member, 6 April 1948, West Punjab Legislative Assembly Debates (WPLAD), p. 487, PAL.
62 Nelson, *In the Shadow of the Shari'ah*.
63 The first round of land reform in Pakistan was initiated by Ayub Khan in 1959. The second round was initiated in 1972 by Zulfiqar Ali Bhutto using powers he possessed as Pakistan's first, and only, Civilian Martial Law Administrator.
64 Ibid.
65 See Sarfraz K. Qureshi, *Agricultural Pricing and Taxation in Pakistan* (Islamabad: Pakistan Institute of Development Economics, 1987), pp. 169–84; Muhammad M. Qureshi, *Fiscal Imperatives in Pakistan's Economic Development* (Lahore: Progressive Publishers, 1989), pp. 45–66; Mahmood H. Khan and Mohsin S. Khan, 'Taxing Agriculture in Pakistan', *IMF Paper on Policy Analysis and Assessment*, 1998; and Ishrat Husain, *Pakistan: The Economy of an Elitist State* (Karachi: Oxford University Press, 1999), pp. 43–126.
66 In the decade immediately after independence, agriculture comprised 60 per cent of Pakistan's GDP. This percentage has slowly decreased over time.
67 See Hamid, 'Suggested Approaches to Agricultural Taxation in West Pakistan', B.A. Azhar, 'Agricultural Taxation in West Pakistan', *Pakistan Economic and Social Review*, 11, 3: 288–315; and Khan and Khan, 'Taxing Agriculture in Pakistan'.
68 Qureshi, *Agricultural Pricing and Taxation in Pakistan*.
69 Hamza Alavi, 'The Rural Elite and Agricultural Development', in Robert D. Stevens, Hamza Alavi, and Peter J. Bertocci (eds), *Rural Development in Bangladesh and Pakistan* (Honolulu: University Press of Hawaii, 1976).
70 Akmal Hussain, *Strategic Issues in Pakistan's Economic Policy* (Lahore: Progressive Publishers, 1988).

71 Husain, *Pakistan: The Economy of an Elitist State*.
72 Azhar, 'Agricultural Taxation in West Pakistan'.
73 WPLAD, 2 April 1948, p. 429.
74 Ibid., pp. 429–30.
75 WPLAD, 6 April 1948, 467–9. Given that average per capita income in Pakistan at this point in time was barely Rs. 200/year, and that the land revenue per acre was roughly Rs.4 in 1959–60, Nurullah Ahmad was clearly speaking on behalf of the richest elements of the landed elite.
76 Ibid., pp. 470–1.
77 Ibid., pp. 472–3.
78 Ibid., pp. 486–7.
79 WPLAD, 6 April 1948, pp. 475–7.
80 According to Andrus and Mohammad, 5.28 million refugees had settled in the Punjab by 1951. In its efforts to support them, the Punjab government provided each refugee family with Rs.500 to use on any land they were allotted, a further Rs.70 to build a hut on such land, and a monthly allowance of Rs.35 until their first harvest was completed. The total cost of refugee rehabilitation was estimated to be about Rs.100 million by March 1951. See J. Russell Andrus and Azizali A. Mohammad, *The Economy of Pakistan* (Palo Alto, CA: Stanford University Press, 1958), pp. 451–64.
81 WPLAD, 15 March 1948, p. 3.
82 Ibid., p. 11.
83 WPLAD, 9 April 1948, pp. 555–7.
84 PLAD, 29 April 1952, pp. 117–18.
85 Ibid., pp. 118–19.
86 PLAD, 30 April 1952, pp. 123–4.
87 Ibid., pp. 135–6.
88 PLAD, 29 April 1952, pp. 120–1.
89 Ibid.
90 Ibid.
91 Ibid., p. 163.
92 PLAD, 30 April 1952, 140–3.
93 Ibid., pp. 151–9.
94 Ibid., p. 158.
95 Bhutto's tax proposals were introduced at the same time as his second round of land reforms and, like the latter, were shelved by the Zia government.
96 Khan and Khan, 'Taxing Agriculture in Pakistan'.
97 PLAD, 13 June 1997.
98 PLAD, 1 January 1997, pp. 62–3.
99 PLAD, 23 April 1998.

# 3 Factionalism and indiscipline in Pakistan's political party system

*Mariam Mufti*

Political competition has been understood in Pakistan as the interaction between two dominant political forces: a state elite comprising a military-bureaucratic oligarchy, and a political elite that comprises political parties and their leaders. However, attempts to understand this political competition have focused on variables pertaining to the military: that is, military intervention in politics; manipulation of the electoral process by the Inter-Services Intelligence (ISI); party-less governance during martial law regimes; and the persecution of political leaders. While I do not dispute these factors, scholarship on Pakistan through its overemphasis on the military has neglected to observe the political elite, which either through cooperation or through competition with the military, has come to be a viable contender for political power. It is also pertinent to question what set of circumstances led the army to intervene in politics, or what allows the army to claim that an intervention was necessitated by the failure of political leadership.

Political parties provide an important lens through which to examine the political system. They also function as fundamental conduits of political life as major agents of representation and institutions that order legislative life. For the voter, political parties provide critical information about the candidates and the programmatic agenda they stand for. For the politician, who is likely to be focused on the short term and his own personal interests, the political party is an institution which resolves a variety of coordination problems in pursuit of public office and state resources. Finally, political parties are essential to democratic governance because they serve as a bridge between the executive and the legislature and provide a critical mechanism to overcome gridlock. This is not to suggest that the function of political parties inevitably leads to democratic ends, but to argue that the prospect for democracy can be enhanced if strong and well-institutionalized political parties exist.

This chapter is an attempt to redress the gap in the literature on Pakistani politics by examining the party system. One of the most glaring features of party politics is the rampant factionalism and indiscipline manifested by party-switching and defections. Party indiscipline is not unique to Pakistan, but this particular weakness of the party system reveals much about political competition in the country. The inability of political parties to elicit credible commitment from party members inhibits the strengthening of political parties and consequently hampers the consolidation of democracy. In this chapter I have focused less on the debilitating consequences. Instead, I offer an explanation for party indiscipline that is rooted in the recruitment and selection process of the political elite by examining four political parties: the Pakistan People's Party (PPP), founded in 1967; the Pakistan Muslim League (PML), founded in 1949; the Muttahida Qaumi Movement (MQM), founded in 1997 (the MQM was originally created in 1978 as the All Pakistan Muhajir Student Organization); and the Awami National Party (ANP), founded in 1986. These four parties have been selected because they have had an average vote share of 76 per cent in the National Assembly and are, therefore, deemed representative of party politics in Pakistan.

## Lack of party discipline

Party discipline cannot be understood without considering the related concept of party cohesion. Ergun Ozbudan[1] is credited with having distinguished between cohesion and discipline. Cohesion is the extent to which party members are willing to work together toward the goals of the party. This willingness may be based on common ideological principles or even the anticipation of abiding by certain norms of legislative behaviour, whereas discipline is the extent to which party members obey the commands of party leaders and the ability of party leaders to induce recalcitrant members to act upon commands. In other words 'discipline is needed when cohesion fails'.[2]

When examining the practice of parliamentary governance, political scientists have paid considerable attention to party cohesion and discipline for two reasons: (1) maintaining a cohesive voting bloc is necessary for responsible party governance because it enables accountability of the executive to both legislature and voters; and (2) a majority voting bloc is a necessary condition for successfully passing legislation.[3]

There are three important points to make. First, political parties in Pakistan, notably the PPP and the PML, before they enter parliament, are weakly organized and not particularly cohesive because they are prone to factionalization and party-switching. Second, once in parliament, these parties appear to be reasonably unified in that legislators tend to vote according to the party line. Legislators seem to recognize that parliamentary cohesion is necessary for the survival of the government and a steady access to state resources. However, third, at the same time, numerous instances of defections and the formation of 'forward blocs' point to a lack of cohesion and discipline within the party in the legislative arena as well. This is because politicians motivated by a desire to access state resources for patronage may be driven to switch parties, defect, or factionalize if any of these actions improve their ability to retain free and easy access to resources.

## Party factionalism

Political parties in Pakistan, in particular the PPP and the PML, are prone to factionalization both inside and outside of parliament. In the aftermath of the bloodless coup by General Pervez Musharraf (b. 1943, President 2001–8), in October 1999, and the subsequent exile of the PML-N party leader Nawaz Sharif (b. 1949, Prime Minister 1990–3, 1997–9), a large number of members defected from the PML-N to form the PML-Q (Quaid). In the 2002 election, the PML-Q, with Musharraf's patronage, emerged as the strongest party, securing 118 seats, while the PML-N won only 18 seats in the National Assembly.[4] This was not the first time that the PML had factionalized. In the 1990s the splintering of the nine-party alliance, the Islami Jamhoori Ittehad (IJI), led to the emergence of the PML-N. Soon after this, a group of politicians who were against Nawaz Sharif's dominance and felt that he had wrongly wrested control of the party from ex-Prime Minister Muhammad Khan Junejo (1932–93, Prime Minister 1985–8) led to the emergence of the PML-J (Junejo) under the leadership of Hamid Nasir Chattha (b. 1944) of Gujranwala and Manzoor Wattoo, Chief Minister of the Punjab between September 1993 and September 1995, and very briefly in 1996 as well. Other factions of the PML included the PML-F (Functional) led by Pir Pagaro (1928–2012) and the PML-Z (Zia) led by Ijaz-ul-Haq (b. 1952), the son of General Zia-ul-Haq (1924–88, President 1978–88), who entered politics after his father's death. It is notable that each of these factions was led by an individual or group of individuals who were identified as political heavyweights in their own right. The PML splintered into factions time and again during its existence because senior party members were unable to accept the centralized control of the party by a single leader, in this case Nawaz Sharif.

Factionalism has also occurred when politicians felt their interests were not being met by the political party. This precipitated the decision to part ways with the party's leadership and to create their own faction. This not only hindered the electoral chances of the parent party, but was detrimental to the newly formed faction. However, factions formed in such a way often ally with independent candidates to swell their ranks and may enter seat adjustments or political alliances with the opposing political party. By aiding the opposing party, the party faction hopes to receive material benefits in the event the party eventually forms the government. The factionalization of the PPP in Khyber Pukhtunkhwa Province led by Aftab Ahmed Sherpao (b. 1944), an army major who retired early to enter politics in 1977 after the assassination in November 1967 of his elder brother Hayat Sherpao (1937–75), one of the co-founders of the Pakistan People's Party, at the request of one of the other co-founders of the PPP, Zulfiqar Ali Bhutto (1928–1979, President 1971–3, Prime Minister 1973–7), is an excellent illustration of this dynamic. Differences between Zulfiqar's daughter and political heir Benazir Bhutto (1953–2007, Prime Minister 1988–90, 1993–6) and Aftab Ahmed Sherpao (b. 1944) arose in the wake of the PPP's poor performance in the 1997 election. Sherpao, who had served as chief minister in Khyber Pukhtunkhwa twice, had earned the reputation for being a master of political manipulation. He had enough political acumen to cobble together a group of shrewd politicians with substantial financial resources to retain a power base for himself. However, he had served as the provincial leader of the PPP for nearly 22 years and he was unwilling to lose PPP voters as his main constituents.

Hence, in 2000, he founded the PPP (Sherpao). This faction eventually renamed itself the Qaumi Watan Party in October 2012 in order to distance itself from the PPP's politics. By following a strategy of winning over independents against whom the PPP never fielded candidates, Sherpao strengthened his own base while hurting the electoral chances of the PPP.

Another consequence of factions contesting an election as an independent party is that if it wins a significant number of seats it can end up holding the balance of power. Manzoor Wattoo split from the parent party to form the PML-J (Junejo group) to contest the election. He eventually succeeded in attaining the post of chief minister and became an important power-broker in the Punjab provincial assembly. In 1993, the PPP contested the election as part of an electoral alliance with the PML-J known as the Pakistan Democratic Alliance (PDA). As part of this alliance, the PPP ceded 38 provincial assembly seats in the Punjab to the PML-J. Of these 38 seats, the PML-J returned 18 candidates successfully to the assembly. However, the election in the Punjab was a close contest between the PPP (94 seats) and the PML-N (106 seats). The PML-J used its bargaining potential to leverage its position as a power broker. After much wheeling and dealing with the PPP, it was decided that the PML-J would appoint the chief minister, the deputy speaker of the assembly, and half of the ministers, but only if the ministry of home and services and general administration would be appointed by the PPP. At the time, Wattoo, who had coveted the post of chief minister, accepted this deal and ceded control of the two essential departments for the day-to-day administration of the government. In the meantime, he further consolidated his position by winning over independent members to increase the numbers of the PML-J. Using his strength in the Assembly, he succeeded in blackmailing the PPP into returning the home ministry and services and general administration department to him.[5]

Factionalization of political parties has also been seen in the formation of forward blocs to make or break governments. For example, in 2002 the 18 members from the PPP who defected to join the PML-Q first formed a forward bloc known as the PPP (Patriots).[6] Legislators who defect from their parties to form a forward bloc claim they have not left their party but are simply asserting their autonomy to vote against the party line in favour of the governing party.

In the 2008–13 administration a group of 51 PML-Q members under the leadership of Dr. Tahir Ali Javed[7] formed a forward bloc in the Punjab provincial assembly, called the 'Unified bloc'. This forward bloc allegedly supported the PML-N government in the Punjab while retaining its membership of the PML-Q. Constitutionally, an anti-defection clause may have been used by the PML-Q party head to disqualify these members on the charge of defection. But instead of doing this, the PML-Q's leadership decided to serve show-cause notices to the defecting members to try to solve the matter amicably. The PML-Q leadership defended itself saying that 'it does not want to disqualify all the dissidents in a single go and give them an opportunity to contest polls from the platform of PML-N'.[8] In response to being served show-cause notices, the forward bloc members claimed they could not be disqualified because the anti-defection law did not apply to forward blocs:

> We have not joined another political party ... and we did not vote for the PML-N in the election for the provincial chief minister. As citizens of Pakistan and as politicians, there is nothing wrong in supporting somebody through statements.[9]

Another example of factionalism over the question of party leadership emerged when this same forward bloc gave support to a number of parliamentarians and unelected politicians to form the PML-Likeminded group that sought an electoral alliance with the PML-N in 2013.

## Party-switching

Politicians have changed party allegiance between elections. It is interesting to observe that most cases of party-switching were incongruous from the ideological point of view, with politicians moving from one party to a rival party. This indicates that politicians are not interested in ideology or policy but only in what the political party can do for them. The ease of party-switching reflects an individual candidate's autonomy vis-à-vis the party organization.

What explains this frequent party-switching? A politician could consider switching parties: if denied a party ticket in favour of another candidate in the constituency; if the candidate has been expelled from the party on counts of misconduct; or if the candidate is displeased with the party on ticket-distribution or policy-making. Politicians may also switch parties because they believe they will benefit by changing parties, either because their career prospects will improve or if they feel their ideological predisposition may be better suited to the new party.

Politicians have switched parties because they want to ensure that the party they join is likely to form the government. This trend was especially obvious during the 1990s: the use of Article 58 section 2(b) of the constitution to dissolve governments led politicians to calculate whether the incumbent party was likely to make a political comeback after dissolution, and on that basis decide if it was best to switch parties. If politicians want to win at any cost, they are likely to calculate the extent to which a particular party would guarantee an electoral win. In this case, the candidate is likely to be more amenable to party switching and contesting an election on a different party ticket. In other words, politicians go shopping for party tickets and buy entry into provincial or national politics. Upon 'selecting' the party of their choice, they cede their right to speak on issues of national interest to the political party's leadership in return for complete autonomy in conducting the local affairs of their constituency and having open access to state patronage.

For example, in National Assembly 160 Sahiwal I constituency in east Punjab, Naurez Shakoor (b. 1950) followed in his father Chaudhry Abdul Shakoor's footsteps by contesting all five general elections held since 1988 on a PPP ticket and successfully making it to the National Assembly three times: 1988, 1993, and 2002. However, in 2002 he defected to the PML-Q as part of the PPP (Patriots) forward bloc. His long-standing opponent, Anwar-ul-Haq Ramay (who contested elections on an IJI ticket in 1988 and 1990; and a PML-N ticket in 1993 and 1997), also defected to the PML-Q. But in 2002 he finished a distant third to the PPP's Naurez Shakoor and the PML-N candidate, Syed Imran Ahmed Shah. In 2008, Shakoor easily got the PML-Q ticket; the PML-N gave the ticket to their previous candidate in 2002, and Anwar-ul-Haq Ramay was left with no option but to apply for a PPP ticket. He was given the ticket because the PPP also had no choice: they too had lost their erstwhile loyal candidate from the constituency.[10] This example illustrates that political parties often overlook loyalty as a criterion and give the ticket to the most competitive candidate. The only way the PPP could have contested Naurez Shakoor's candidacy from the PML-Q was to give the ticket to his archrival who was originally a Muslim League member.

## Defections

'Switching', 'defecting', or '*waka* [canoe]-hopping'[11] are terms used to describe the time when a candidate elected to legislative office as a member of one party changes to another while still serving in parliament. This should not be confused with 'floor-crossing', which refers merely to voting with the opposition. Such defections have been relatively common and have mostly gone unpunished despite an anti-defection clause written into the constitution. The anti-defection clause contained in Article 63 of the constitution states that a member of parliament may be disqualified on grounds of:

> i) resigning from a political party or joining another parliamentary party and
> ii) voting or abstaining from voting against the parliamentary party's whip in relation to the election of the prime minister or the chief minister or a vote of confidence, a constitutional amendment or a money bill.

This clause empowers the party head to decide defection cases and requires that the Election Commission confirm this decision. However, as a tool to encourage party discipline, the anti-defection law has proved to be ineffective. It has neither curbed the act of defection nor enhanced party discipline within the legislature.

Some major instances of defections during the 1990s were attempts to topple national and provincial governments. In 1993, Chief Minister Ghulam Haider Wyne's government in the Punjab was overthrown by Mazoor Wattoo's defection. In 1994, Chief Minister Sabir Shah's government in Khyber Pukhtunkhwa Province was removed by opposition leader Aftab Sherpao's efforts to win over defectors from other parties. The General Election of 2002 under Pervez Musharraf (b. 1943, President 2001–8) resulted in the PML-Q winning 118 seats in the National Assembly, falling short of attaining a majority, while the PPP won 81 seats. Only with the support of turncoats from the PPP did the PML-Q succeed in securing a majority to enable Prime Minister Zafarullah Khan Jamali (b. 1944, Prime Minister 2002–4) win a vote of confidence on 15 November 2002. Jamali won the vote with the help of 18 defectors from the PPP,[12] two legislators from the Islamist alliance the MMA, and two from the PML-N.[13]

In some instances legislators have been paid to switch parties – more commonly known as horse-trading, and used to refer to party defections. This is because defections often occur when politicians are promised material incentives in exchange for their allegiance in legislative voting, much the same way the jockey of one's opponent is bought off prior to a horse race to ensure victory. In 1989 Benazir Bhutto (1953–2007, Prime Minister 1988–90, 1993–6) herself was responsible for facilitating the defection of members belonging to opposition parties by offering them material incentives to defeat a no-confidence motion. The main opposition party from 1988 to 1990 was the IJI. It was supported by its erstwhile coalition partners, the PPP, the MQM, and the ANP, to form the Combined Opposition Parties. On 23 October 1989, the Combined Opposition Parties moved a notice for a no-confidence resolution claiming the support of 129 out of 135 members of the National Assembly. There were allegations that in order to defeat the no-confidence motion members of the opposition were physically prevented from attending the session. Also, more than 100 members of the PPP were taken to a remote location, Mingora in Swat District, so they were beyond the reach of the opposition.[14] Although there are numerous other claims, no hard evidence exists to prove these instances of horse-trading.

The ineffectiveness of the anti-defection law is apparent in that it has never been used to disqualify a member of parliament. Three scenarios explain why this law has not been applied: first, defection has been overlooked by the party leaders because they themselves stand to be implicated under the law;[15] second, notifications to the presiding officer of the assembly or to the Election Commission have not reached them in time;[16] or, third, the law has been in abeyance or had lapsed at the time the defection occurred.[17]

However, there were also times when the law was not in abeyance and the abandoned party leaders did not make use of the anti-defection law. There is no obvious answer to why this is the case. However, one could speculate that party leaders are complacent about defections – especially when they result in the formation of forward blocs. Precedence suggests that party factions merge and split with such ease that a defection from one party faction to another under the same party umbrella would not cause a dent in party strength. For example, shortly after Nawaz Sharif's dismissal in 1999, his factional rivals founded the PML-Q. In keeping with the tradition of opportunism, many members of the PML-N who were supporters of Nawaz Sharif defected to the PML-Q, whose rising fortunes were tied to support and patronage from the military regime. Nonetheless, these defectors were given PML-N party tickets in 2008. A second reason that party leaders have not disqualified party members is that they often stand to benefit from the defections. For example, if an opposition party were successful in prying enough members away from the governing party, leading to a no-confidence motion, all those who defected are still guaranteed reasonably good chances of re-election. Only two no-confidence motions have taken place at the national level and both have been defeated. However, it is not too much of a stretch to imagine a no-confidence motion being successful. Similarly, to form a government, the party with the largest number of seats could put together a coalition of parties to increase its numbers in the assembly. To do this, it would try to wrest members of the main opposition party away by offering incentives, such as ministries or funding for local developmental projects. Hence, politicians, although disciplined in legislative voting, may prove to be unreliable allies in times of political crises.

The above discussion has by no means exhaustively listed all instances of factionalism, party-switching, and defections as sitting members of the assembly. But it has served to show that political parties, in particular the PPP and the PML, are unable to elicit credible commitments and loyalty from their party members. But herein lies a paradox, because when it comes to passing legislation, political parties do appear to be cohesive voting blocs. Those party members who have been disloyal to their parties have also explained that voting on legislation of national importance is unlikely to disrupt structures of power in their constituency or harm the interests of the constituents at the local level. The same legislators say they would not consider voting against the party but would more likely abstain from the vote if they disagreed with the party line. Clearly this behaviour is not motivated by fear of repercussions that would occur as a result of indiscipline, but because legislators are cognizant of the fact that a steady flow of state resources can only be secured by being agreeable members of the governing party.[18]

To recap, Pakistan's larger political parties, the PPP and the PML, are undisciplined seen in the tendency of legislators to defect, factionalize, or form forward blocs. There is, therefore, a need for party leaders to enforce disciplinary measures and elicit loyalty from their party's legislators for two reasons: (1) dissent in the form of abstaining from voting or staging walk-outs can destabilize a political party in parliament, keeping legislation from being passed; and (2) dissent in the form of defections leads to the formation of forward blocs, party switching between elections, and party factions resulting in the toppling of governments. However, political parties have been unable to secure the loyalty of their members as is evidenced by party-switching during elections.

## Party-centric explanations for party indiscipline

The goal of an incumbent legislator is to get re-elected, therefore, the proximate aim is to get re-selected as a candidate or to secure access to the ballot. The critical issue, however, is not access to the ballot, but the ability to maximize electoral chances through affiliation with a party label. An incumbent could easily contest an election as an independent candidate, but the question is why a legislator seeks out a political party and how that political party might control access to the party label for prospective candidates.[19]

Since 1988, political competition has been dominated by the PPP and the PML as control of the government has alternated between these two parties. The ANP and the MQM are smaller parties that have been relevant in the party system as coalition partners at both the national and provincial levels. The PPP and the PML are large, catch-all party organizations that claim national representation by contesting elections all over Pakistan. The organizational apparatus of these parties is fragile, under-resourced, and not professionalized. The PPP and the PML exercise control over the party label in their traditional strongholds of the Sindh and the Punjab respectively. However, in a vast majority of constituencies, where party identification is low, the PPP and the PML have relied on a class of locally influential and charismatic leaders to mobilize voters by offering direct material incentives. The resulting clientelism makes these parties subservient to the local interests of politicians instead of forming their own policy programs. As a result, the PPP and the PML, who together capture on average 72 per cent of the seats in parliament, have been unable to elicit credible commitments toward party unity from a majority of their legislators. This lack of party discipline on account of their recruitment and selection policies renders them vulnerable to defections, party-switching, and party factionalization.

On the other hand, the MQM and the ANP are smaller political parties with relatively more disciplined and robust organizations because they contest elections from their ethnically defined geographical strongholds and are not burdened by the need to be representative nationally. The MQM and the ANP contest safe seats only where voters have strong partisan identification with the parties, and this sharply increases the importance of the party label. Party leaders successfully control the recruitment and candidate selection process by withholding nomination, thereby encouraging cohesive and disciplined behaviour from their candidates.

A parliamentary political system encourages political parties to calculate electoral success in terms of the number of seats won in the national and provincial assemblies. Hence the party ticket-distribution strategy is to field competitive candidates in as many constituencies as possible in order to increase the odds of winning a larger number of seats in the assemblies than its opponent. Political parties assess the strength of a candidate based on a host of criteria. Candidates should be able to demonstrate local influence through their kinship networks, factional affiliations, and the ability to provide patronage. Parties also look for charisma and the integrity of a candidate. Candidates who have been active supporters of the party and have demonstrated loyalty by adhering to party principles are likely to be given priority, although this is not a necessity. Finally, political parties look at the capability of the candidate to finance his or her own electoral campaign. The ranking of these criteria differs from party to party.[20] This reality is further complicated by three other variables. These are party organization, the nature of the constituency, and the party resource base.

## Party organization

Political parties have functioned as coalitions that field candidates for public office and are therefore 'aggregate potential winners and not potential interests'.[21] As a result, the pattern of political competition that has evolved among political parties is heavily invested in stimulating the mobilization of constituencies by offering patronage to those who support party candidates. Clientelism in politics has led to non-programmatic parties dependent on charismatic leaders to capture the hearts and minds of voters.

The PPP and the PML operate as catch-all parties claiming to be nationally representative of the Pakistani people. To keep this image alive, they rely on local, charismatic leaders to sustain the party's position instead of investing resources in a permanent organizational apparatus at the local level. The candidates selected invest their own resources (time, capital, personnel) to deliver the message of the political party to the constituents in exchange for the party ticket and access to public office. The relationship between the politician and the central party can vary enormously depending on how influential and indispensable the candidate is to the party.

In this sense, political parties are akin to franchise organizations with the politicians like individual franchises, operating 'autonomously and unhindered' in their own constituencies.[22] The party is dependent on the politician to advertise the party label, thereby increasing party identification instead of the politician being dependent on the right party ticket to win the election. Since the party does not finance the campaign either, politicians are beholden to their constituents and their own resources for re-election and can, therefore, switch to another franchise (party) without incurring any significant costs. As a result of this dynamic, the PPP and the PML are not cohesive party organizations.

In contrast, the MQM and the ANP have not factionalized and are relatively more cohesive than either the PPP or the PML. The MQM was, however, splintered into the MQM (Altaf) and the MQM (Haqiqi) in 1992, allegedly at the instigation of intelligence agencies prior to launching an armed operation against the party. The ANP has not factionalized either. However, this party has a historical legacy of being part of several mergers of leftist parties during the 1950s and 1960s.[23] The cohesiveness of these parties may simply be a function of their smaller size, but more significantly it could be because of the different strategies adopted to appeal to party supporters.

Another important aspect of party organization is that decision-making is a highly centralized process. The ANP, however, provides a noticeable exception, standing out as being the only political party to include a large representation of its local organization in the highest decision-making body of the party. In contrast to the ANP, the MQM has a very strong and rigid party structure demanding absolute loyalty from its members. On the surface, the process of decision-making in the MQM appears to be relatively less centralized as the body responsible for making decisions and coordinating and implementing the party's program is an elected body. Within the *Rabta* Committee, the Central Coordination Committee, all members besides the convener and the deputy have an equal say on policy matters. It is claimed that all decisions made by the committee are communicated through the sector organization to the unit organization and to the party members, and is open to feedback and suggestions. But this process is also highly centralized in its decision-making mechanisms, mainly because the committee may take its direction from the *Quaid-e-Tehrik* (Leader of the Movement), Altaf Hussain (b. 1953), the founder, in 1984, of the MQM who has been living in exile in England since 1992, and often relies on his input on policy and party reform decisions. Similarly, local organizations and their subcommittees abide by the decisions that are passed onto them by the *Rabta* Committee.

In the PML-N, Nawaz Sharif is known to consult his closest advisors on key policy and party-related decisions. He relies on two types of politicians: those who are close allies and those who form the inner circle, also known as the kitchen cabinet and referred to in the media as the *panj pyaaray* (the 'five favourites'). The meetings of the Central Working Committee are essentially held to inform other party members of the decisions already made instead of being a forum for deliberation and consultation. As a result of the president's dominance in the Central Working Committee, the Central Parliamentary Board, which does the candidate-selection and is constituted by the Central Working Committee, is really beholden to the party president.[24] A similar tendency towards centralization of power in the office of the party chairperson is seen in the PPP. Arguably, the PPP's greatest strength has been its strong charismatic leadership. Zulfiqar Ali Bhutto, his daughter Benazir Bhutto, and her husband, Asif Ali Zardari (b. 1955, President 2008–13), adopted a personal form of leadership that produced an 'informal hierarchy of access' to the party chairman, and this dynastic leadership was passed down to the third generation of the family in December 2007 when Benazir's and Zardari's son, the 19-year-old Bilawal Bhutto Zardari (b. 1988), was appointed chairman of the party. Party members who had direct personal access to the chairman constituted the 'central cell' and in turn acted as intermediaries between the party chairperson and other local party leaders, district networks, or special interest groups.[25]

The centralized nature of party organization has a bearing on the loyalty of party members in that it determines who within the party does the selection of candidates. If the key actors in the selectorate are located in the party organization, then the candidate will be beholden to either the national or the regional party executives. But if the key actors are located in the constituencies, then the candidate will be loyal to the voters, party supporters, and local party office-bearers.[26] The tendency is toward centralization in almost all matters of decision-making within the political parties. In all four cases studied, a small group comprising the party elite (also known as the parliamentary board), selects the candidates after receiving input from local party organizations which compile information on the applicants, the incumbent candidates, and the results of previous elections. Based on this information, the final decision on candidate selection is made.

In the PML, the PPP, and the MQM this decision is subject to the approval of the party leader who has the right to retain, revise, or annul the decision of the parliamentary board, making the process centralized and exclusive. The ANP is unique in that the decision is made by a provincial election board constituted by the provincial party that decides on candidates for both national and provincial assembly seats. This decision is not subject to the approval of the central party organization unless it is contrary to the party's overall electoral strategy. Intuitively then, we should expect party candidates to be loyal to the party in the case of the PPP, the PML, and the MQM. In the case of the ANP, the party candidates will be loyal to the provincial party organization. But we do not observe great party loyalty due to the nature of the constituency and the party resource base.

## Nature of the constituency

The nature of the constituency determines the kind of candidate who would be most suitable for the party. Here the main distinction is between safe and competitive seats. A constituency may be considered a safe seat if the political party is confident that regardless of the candidate selected, the party will win the seat by a safe margin. There are several ways by which a party can secure a large enough vote share to make a seat safe. First, voters may identify strongly with the party because of the party leader regardless of the party's policies and program. For instance, party workers of the PML-N have been known to say that 'if the party were to make an electric pole contest the election from Lahore, the pole would surely win'. This is because Lahore is the hometown of Nawaz Sharif, the PML-N leader. Second, a seat may be safe because the constituents identify strongly with the party and what it stands for. This level of party identification is often achieved through the maintenance of a strong party organization and the delivery of patronage. For example, the MQM's strong party organization and the delivery of patronage to constituents has led to a higher degree of party identification in a small number of seats in urban Sindh consistently won by the MQM with wide margins of victory. Third, a seat can be considered safe by a party because the candidate selected by the party continues to win. If the party can count on the loyalty of a particularly strong candidate, then the combination of the candidate's personal vote share and the party's vote share will make the seat safe. In a sense, these constituencies are more like 'safe candidates than safe seats'. In this case the strength of the candidate and his loyalty to the party determines how safe a seat is. Approximately a quarter of the seats were safe because of the candidate. These were seats from where the same candidate won any three consecutive elections held between 1988 and 1997. After delimitation in 2002 and the Musharraf regime's intentional weakening of the PML-N and the PPP, something like a third of the seats may be considered safe because of the candidate. These are seats where the same candidate won both the 2002 and the 2008 election.

A constituency may be competitive if more than one party has a significant vote share and the relevant parties can field strong candidates to contest the election. In a competitive seat, the party's vote share is not enough to win the seat, and the strength of the candidate can make the crucial difference. A candidate would be considered strong if he can mobilize the party vote, add to the party vote with his own personal vote bank, and sway the swing vote in his favour. In a competitive constituency a party may not rely on a strong candidate's loyalty. Also in a competitive constituency the party may not be able choose the same candidate from election to election. A party may be compelled to go with another candidate based on circumstances created prior to the election. These circumstances may vary with the formation of new electoral alliances and seat adjustments, and also the popularity of the candidate himself.

The choice of candidate may, therefore, vary based on whether a constituency is safe or competitive. If a constituency is safe because of high levels of party identification, a party will select a candidate who, by virtue of his affiliation with the party, can articulate party policy and mobilize the party vote. Such a candidate may rely on both his own resources and the party organization to conduct his electoral campaign. Most likely this candidate will be loyal to the party. But in a constituency which is safe because of the candidate and not the party, then the choice of candidate is predetermined. Such a candidate could potentially switch parties and still win the constituency. In a competitive constituency a party will attempt to select the strongest available candidate and not necessarily the most loyal one in order to increase its chances of winning.

The degree to which party support is dispersed or concentrated also affects the strategies employed in candidate selection. Political parties are aware that beyond selecting candidates, elections provide the opportunity to make a legitimate claim to national representation thereby increasing party identification. Only the PPP and the PML can claim to have succeeded in nationalizing electoral alignments in their favour.[27] To retain their claim to national representation, the PPP and the PML endeavour to contest elections from a maximum number of seats, even if their chances of winning are not high, because the next best alternative is to at least try to break the vote bank of their opponent. Both parties rely on their safe seats, which are geographically concentrated, the PPP in rural Sindh and southern Punjab, and the PML in northern and central Punjab. However, in constituencies that are more competitive both parties have a tendency to overlook party loyalty and instead prioritize the personal resources of a candidate, such as his financial capability and local influence. As a result candidates are aware of the leverage they can exercise on the party and they can switch parties at no cost to their chance of re-election.

In stark contrast, the MQM and the ANP, the two smaller regional political parties, are not geared toward the formation of single-party majority governments. These political parties are interested in maximizing their coalition potential with the larger mainstream parties by aiming to win a maximum number of seats in their geographical strongholds (in other words safe seats with high levels of party identification), the MQM in urban Sindh and the ANP in Khyber Puktunkhwa.[28] The MQM and the ANP contest elections from constituencies where voters identify strongly with their respective ideologies and policies, and as a result they prioritize those candidates who manifest a strong commitment to the party's program.

## Party resource base

Parties also consider their resources and the practicality of fielding candidates in a large number of constituencies. For instance, the smaller parties such as the ANP and the MQM are more likely to field candidates in constituencies where the party vote share is high instead of trying to field candidates nationally. Parties receive no financial support from the state and in the absence of public funding they have sought alternative sources of income such as membership fees, ticket-application fees, office-bearer subscriptions, and private donations.

Three out of the four parties examined, the PPP, the PML, and the ANP, demand ticket application fees. Additionally, these three parties select candidates that are able to finance their electoral campaigns, hence their candidates are likely to be locally influential and wealthy. In contrast, the MQM is the only political party that does not charge a ticket application fee and funds the electoral campaigns for all its candidates. Morgernstern and Siavelis observe that 'the path of money and the path of loyalty usually run parallel'.[29] When parties control the purse strings the loyalty of the candidate to the party is enhanced. This is true in the case of the MQM. However, when candidates raise their own money their loyalty is directed to the constituents who elect them. These candidates do not rely on the political parties to provide them with resources to win an election and can therefore afford to act autonomously from the party.

In summary, the indiscipline of party members, mainly in the PPP and the PML relative to the ANP and the MQM, is due to the differences in the candidate-selection process of the parties. Loyalty to the political party and adherence to the party platform have not been significant criteria for mainstream parties. The PPP and the PML have sought electables with local influence and resources to contest elections on their own. Only the MQM and the ANP consider loyalty and party affiliation in candidate selection because the party candidate needs to be able to mobilize partisan support in the constituency.

The MQM and the ANP contest elections from their ethnically defined, geographical strongholds, where voters have strong partisan identification. This sharply increases the importance of a crucial party prerogative: control over the party label. Here, party leaders can firmly control the candidate-selection process by withholding nomination, thereby encouraging cohesive and disciplined behaviour from candidates. The PPP and the PML similarly exercise control over the party label in their traditional strongholds. Both the PPP and the PML, like the MQM, exhibit centralized and exclusive candidate selection, but this does not always lead to candidates who are party loyalists. This is because levels of party identification in the constituencies contested by the PPP and the PML vary. Safe seats may very well produce party loyalists. But in a vast majority of the constituencies that are competitive, the candidate selection process and criteria for selection predominantly lead to the emergence of candidates who are likely to be more responsive and attentive to nonparty actors.

In order to get re-elected, legislators are not dependent on the party organization, but on their own personal resources and popularity. Neither the PPP nor the PML finance the electoral campaigns of its candidates and, therefore, both are likely to choose candidates who are either locally influential, extremely wealthy, or both. Such a candidate does not recognize the importance of a political label for his electoral success and can switch parties at no cost. The ANP also does not fund the election campaign of its candidates; but because selection of candidates is localized, successful candidates not only must demonstrate the ability to finance their own campaign, they must also have connections with the party's provincial organization. The above offers an institutional explanation rooted in candidate-selection processes for party indiscipline in Pakistan and offers an explanation for the volatility of politics in Pakistan.

## Notes

1. See his *Party Cohesion and in Western Democracies: A Crucial Analysis* (London: Sage, 1970).
2. Reuven Hazan, *Cohesion and Discipline in Legislatures* (New York: Routledge, 2006).
3. Shaun Bowler, David Farrell, and Richard S. Katz, *Party Discipline and Parliamentary Government* (Columbus: Ohio State University Press, 1999).
4. The weakened position of Nawaz Sharif within the PML-N after the coup is covered in Mubashir Zaidi, 'A Coup of Sorts', *The Herald* (August 2000): 59–62. The defection of PML-N members to form the PML-Q under the leadership of Mian Azhar is reported in Mubashir Zaidi, 'A Spooky Split', *The Herald* (December 2000): 35–9; Mubashir Zaidi, 'Déjà vu', *The Herald* (April 2001), pp. 44–6; and Azmat Abbas, 'Operation PML', *The Herald* (March 2001), pp. 48–9. For details on the coalition formed by the PML-Q, the PML-F, and the Millat Party to form the government after the election of 2002, see Idrees Bakhtiar, 'Battlefield Parliament', *The Herald* (December 2002).
5. See the coverage of how the dealings between the PPP and the PML-J were carried out in Aamer Ahmed Khan, 'The Best of Enemies', *The Herald* (January 1994): 118–19; 'There was an Inherent Defect in Our Understanding with the Junejo League', *The Herald* (February 1994): 49–51; and 'The Wattoo Coup', *The Herald* (March 1994): 57–8.
6. See Editorial, 'Forward Blocs in the Offing', *The Daily Times* (16 November 2002). Also see note 8.
7. See Rana Kashif, 'Dr Tahir Ali Javed Names PML-Q Forward Bloc President', *The Daily Times* (8 April 2009).
8. See Pakistan Election 2007–8. 'PML-Q to Serve Show Cause Notices to Dissidents', Lahore, 13 April 2009, at http://elections.com.pk/newsdetails.php?id=768.
9. Ibid.
10. See *The Herald* (February 2008): 134.
11. Sarah Miskin, 'Politicians Overboard: Jumping the Party Ship', Department of the Parliamentary Library, Australia, Research Paper No. 4, 2003.
12. PPP members who initially defected to form the forward bloc included Faisal Saleh Hayat, Rao Sikander Iqbal, Malik Zaheer Abbas, Raees Munir Ahmed, Khalid Lund, Dr Nisar, Nouraiz Shakoor, Tanweer Sayed, and Malik Amir. See Rana Qaiser, 'Faisal, Sikander Unveil 10 MNA Forward Bloc', *The Daily Times* (15 November 2002).
13. It was impossible to get voting records for each of these examples from the National Assembly of Pakistan. Votes of no-confidence and the election of the prime minister are actually counted. However, this information is strictly confidential and is accessible only to the Speaker of the House. Whatever information I have produced here has been gleaned from newspapers.
14. See *The Muslim*, Islamabad (28/29 October 1989). For more details on how exactly the horse trading occurred, see the cover story which appeared in *The Herald*: Zafar Abbas, 'Win Some Lose Some', *The Herald* (November 1989): 25–43.
15. For example, in 1989 Benazir Bhutto herself was responsible for facilitating the defection of members belonging to opposition parties.

the institutional balance of power between elected and non-elected institutions but during which the state structure was cast into an enduring, even rigid, mould.[4]

In understanding the history of the first decade, the accession and integration of the princely states, nine principalities from the erstwhile British Indian Empire, which formed more than half the land mass of western Pakistan, and mostly lay strategically on the borders of the country, has been woefully understudied. Except for the work of political scientist Wayne Wilcox (1932–74) in the 1960s no attempt has been made to study the pattern of accession and integration of the princely states in Pakistan, and its resultant effect on state formation. Since there were hardly any declassified archives in the 1960s and local information was scant and unreliable, the assessments reached by Wilcox have been at best tentative, though useful. A number of princely states, however, have received individual attention, such as Kalat, Bahawalpur, and Swat, though all of these studies have failed to contextualise the princely states in the larger picture and have treated them as peripheral areas with mainly nuisance value (except of course in Kalat where the general Baloch insurgency has overtaken the debate on the existence of a princely state as the initial cause of the revolt).

The aim of this chapter is to rehabilitate the integration of the princely states in the central narrative of Pakistan, and utilise the analysis of their constitutional integration to understand constitutional and structural problems of the state both in the past and today. Beginning from the period immediately after the nine princely states acceded, this chapter will primarily focus on the pattern of constitutional integration, the principles which underlay the policy of the government, and the results of such policies. The chapter will begin with an overview of the accession and integration process, the people involved, and a broad comparison with India. The next two sections will analyse the two major themes of integration: centralisation and the weakening of the princes, and distrust of democracy, to illustrate the effects of integration on the states as well as Pakistan. The final section will chart the merger of the states.

## Accession

The process of accession of the princely states was markedly different in India and Pakistan. Even before independence, the Indian National Congress, founded in 1885, and the All-India Muslim League, founded in 1906, had significantly different attitudes towards the princely states. As early as January 1946, Jawaharlal Nehru (1889–1964, Prime Minister 1947–64) was clear about the future of the states. He noted:

> it is inevitable that the vast majority of states which cannot possibly form economic units should be absorbed into neighbouring areas.... It is also not desirable that a number of small states should be grouped together to form a

larger state unit. There will be no history or tradition of unity about this – only artificial joining together of backward areas with no leaven to pull them up. Therefore, the union should be with provinces. The rulers of such small states may be given some kind of pension and may be further encouraged to serve in a different capacity if they are fit enough for it. Of the other states, which may be 15 to 20 in number and which will form autonomous units in the federation, the rulers can remain as constitutional heads under a democratic system of government.[5]

For the states which did not intend to join the future Indian Union, the Congress expected that some powers of paramountcy would transfer to them. Sardar Vallabhbhai Patel (1875–1950, Minister of Home Affairs 1947–9) stated in a major policy statement in July 1947:

In these cases, eventually a considerable measure of paramountcy will devolve upon the Central Government. Either specific agreements between such states and the Union will vest this authority in the Union, or the Union will be obliged to take over this authority by force, if necessary, since circumstances may emerge in which independent defence arrangements or external relations of an individual state will become incompatible with national policy and security.[6]

Thus, even before the transfer of power it was clear what fate the Congress contemplated for the states, and the States ministry under Patel and V.P. Menon (1893–1965) as his secretary, was actively wooing the states to accede to the future Indian dominion.

After accession the policy of the Government of India was soon clear: full integration and democratisation were the basic non-negotiable principles. Integration began, as explained by Menon in *The Integration of the Indian States*, with Orissa and Chattisgarh in December 1947. Menon himself acknowledged that unions and mergers were against the promises given to the states under the Instruments of Accession but still defended the *volte face*. He noted:

I pointed out to Sardar that the proposed merger of the states [with Orissa] was contrary to the assurances held out in his own statement of 5 July and in Lord Mountbatten's address to the Chamber of Princes on 25 July 1947. It was true that, at that time, we were anxious by the policy of accession on three subjects to preserve the integrity of the country, thus preventing the States from becoming so many 'Ulsters' in the body politic. Nevertheless, a guarantee once given could not be lightly set aside, unless it could be proved that there were overwhelming considerations which were demonstrably in the interests of the country.[7]

When Patel and Menon met the rulers of Orissa and Chattisgarh on 14 and 15 December 1947, they impressed upon them that if they did not agree to the merger they would lose all their power and authority very soon. Under the merger agreement they were being promised their personal property, succession, and other privileges. Patel further noted that

> if his advice were not listened to, the rulers, after being ousted by their people, would have in the end to come to Delhi, by which time things might have gone so far that he would no longer be in a position to help them.[8]

The rulers were also given a tight schedule of about 30 hours to consider all their options. Obviously, the only option which lay in front of them, as in August 1947, was to agree with the Government of India. None of the rulers were powerful enough to ward off a revolt, especially in circumstances where the rebels would have the clear support of the Indian administration. The rulers saw the writing on the wall and merged their states with Orissa in return for a privy purse. Patel defended his decision:

> In the world of today, where differences are fast shrinking and masses are being gradually brought into touch with latest administrative amenities, it is impossible to postpone for a day longer than necessary the introduction of measures which would make the people realise that their progress is also proceeding at least on the lines of their neighbouring areas.... Indeed in many of the States, with which I had to hold discussions during the last two days, large-scale unrest had already gripped the people.... In such circumstances ... there was no alternative to integration and democratisation.[9]

On the heels of the merger of Orissan princely states with Orissa and the Chattisgarh states with the Central Provinces, other mergers and unions were soon carried out. The policy of the Government of India was that save the larger viable states, all others should either merge with existing provinces, be created into centrally administered Chief Commissioner's provinces, or be joined together to form a union of states. With some medium-sized states, such as Baroda and Rampur, a transitional phase saw the takeover of the states by a Chief Commissioner for a few months, pending merger into adjoining provinces. By the end of the integration phase there were seven centrally administered areas under Chief Commissioners: Bilaspur, Kutch, Bhopal, Tripura, Manipur, Himachal Pradesh, and Vindhya Pradesh (converted to a Chief Commissioner's province on 1 January 1950). Five unions of states had also been formed through regional groupings. The Union of Saurasthra, inaugurated in February 1948, included all the states in the Kathiawar region; the Madhya Bharat Union created in May 1948 consisted of the states of Gwalior, Indore, and Malwa; Patiala and East Punjab States Union comprising of all Punjab states was established in July 1948; in May 1949 the new United State of Rajasthan was created after a three-staged process consisting of all the states within the Rajputana region; and in July 1949 the union of Travancore and Cochin was finalised. All the other states, except Hyderabad, Mysore, and Jammu and Kashmir, which retained their territorial integrity, were merged into neighbouring provinces. Shortly afterwards, all rulers signed supplementary Instruments of Accession to give legal cover to the changes, and also accepted the federal and concurrent lists according to the Government of India Act 1935.[10] Thus, at the end of the integration period the princes were constitutional rulers at best, and that, too, for only a few more years. The White Paper therefore gleefully noted:

> The policy of integration and democratisation, which the Government of India have applied to the States, constituted the only solution of the problem of the States, and the only method of fitting in the states in the new setup of India. This was, therefore, no emotional approach, any expansionist policy, nor power politics.[11]

On the other hand, the Muslim League had a *laissez faire* attitude towards the princely states. Unsure about several issues regarding the British Indian provinces, the Muslim League had little time to worry about them, especially since most Muslim princes were patrons of the Muslim League, unlike the Congress which was mostly hostile towards the princely cadre. Therefore, Governor-General Mohammad Ali Jinnah (1876–1948, Governor-General 1947–8) was content with giving maximum leeway to the princely states once paramountcy came to an end with the departure of the British. Reuter's noted the policy of Jinnah as:

> 'Constitutionally and logically the Indian states will be independent sovereign states on the termination of paramountcy and they will be free to decide for themselves any course they like to adopt.... It is open to the states to join the Hindustan constituent assembly or the Pakistan constituent assembly or decide to remain independent. In the last case they can either enter into such arrangement or relationship with Hindustan or Pakistan as they may choose....' He added that he was not of the opinion that the states were limited only to the option of joining one or other constituent assembly. 'In my opinion they are free to remain independent if they so desire. Neither the British government nor the British Parliament nor any other power or body can compel them to do anything contrary to their free will and accord....' he said.[12]

While the States Department section for the future Indian dominion was busy ensuring that the states acceded to India before 15 August 1947, the Pakistani section, headed by Sardar Abdur Rab Nishtar (1899–1958), was largely inactive. Complicating relations with the princes was the fact that Jinnah kept to himself the task of negotiating with any prince who wanted to accede to Pakistan. With his hands full with tasks associated with creating a new country, the issue of the states was a distant secondary problem for Jinnah for months.

By 15 August 1947 a very large percentage of the more than 600 princely states in India had acceded to the Indian dominion, but none to Pakistan. The first state to accede to Pakistan was a Kathiawar state, Junagadh, which was separated by hundreds of miles of Indian territory from west Pakistan and only had access by sea. Junagadh had primarily acceded to Pakistan because the ruler, Nawab Mohammad Mahabat Khanji III (1900–59, Nawab 1911–47), was a Muslim, and his Dewan (chief minister), Sir Shah Nawaz Bhutto (1888–1957) – a Muslim Leaguer – had convinced him to accede to Pakistan despite the fact that over 80 per cent of the states' population was Hindu. India did not react favourably to the 15 September 1947 accession and a blockade of Junagadh and a general uprising was organised under Samaldas Gandhi, a nephew of Mohandas Gandhi (1869–1948). By the end of October 1947, the economic, food, and security situation in Junagadh had deteriorated so much that the Nawab fled to Karachi, leaving the state in the hands of the Dewan who saw no option but to hand over the state administration to India by 9 November 1947. Pakistan protested the takeover by India but, as Spear noted, 'the case was so small and the non-juridical considerations so strong that even Pakistan contented itself with indignant protests'.[13]

Bahawalpur and Khairpur were two mid-ranking princely states in the Punjab and Sindh respectively. As both states lay on the border of India and Pakistan, they could have acceded to either country. However, since the rulers and the populations of both states were Muslim, it seems that India was not interested in these states. In 1947, Bahawalpur was ruled by Nawab Sadiq Abassi V (1904–67), and Khairpur was under a council of regency since the ruler, Mir George Ali Murad Khan (Mir 1947–55), who had acceded the throne only in July 1947 after his father was declared mentally unsound, was still a minor. Since the Nawab of Bahawalpur usually spent his summer holidays in England, the prime minister of the state (since April 1947), Mushtaq Ahmed Gurmani (1905–81) was pivotal in securing the states' accession to Pakistan which accepted on 5 October 1947.[14] With a minor ruler and a council of regency only installed in July 1947, Khairpur also easily acceded to Pakistan and its accession was accepted by Pakistan on 9 October 1947.

Adjacent to the North-West Frontier Province (renamed Khyber Pakhtunkhwa in 2010) were four small princely states: Chitral, Dir, Swat, and Amb, out of which only Chitral merited a hereditary salute of eleven guns. All states had only come under the influence of the Government of India in the last two decades of the nineteenth century and hence the imprint of the British government on these states was small. The states were mostly tribal, operated a subsistence economy, and their rulers lacked the regal paraphernalia associated with other states. The Mehtar (ruler) of Chitral was always a well-wisher of the Muslim League and Jinnah, and together with the prospect of repudiating a tenuous suzerainty of Kashmir, eagerly acceded to Pakistan on 6 November 1947. Jinnah, however, did not want to compromise his position that Kashmir, occupied by India, was Pakistani territory, and only accepted the accession in February 1948. The rulers of the states of Swat and Amb, both surrounded on all sides by Pakistani territory, were also eager to accede to Pakistan and had signed Instruments of Accession by end of 1947. Only the ruler of Dir state, Sir Shah Jahan Khan

(Nawab 1925–60), hesitated in joining Pakistan, especially since his state also lay on the border with Afghanistan. A dispatch from the United Kingdom High Commission for Pakistan succinctly described the process through which Dir came within the ambit of Pakistan:

> The Nawab of Dir, a more than usually conservative ruler, took fright at the provisions in the instrument of accession regarding defence and external relations, and refused formally to accede to Pakistan; he insisted that his relations with Pakistan should remain the same as those with the British Government previously, and the Pakistan Ministry of States and Frontier Regions have for the present acquiesced in this position.[15]

There were also two tiny states, Hunza and Nagar, which were under the suzerainty of Kashmir. With the alleged accession of Kashmir to India, both these states, together with the Gilgit region, rebelled against the Kashmir maharaja and acceded to Pakistan.[16] Since their legal state was never clear, however, Pakistan has still not formally incorporated them in its territory and they still remain outside the ambit of the constitution.

The state which gave the most trouble to the Government of Pakistan was the confederal state of Kalat. It was ruled by the Mir, Ahmed Yar Khan (Mir 1933–55), who had pretentions of keeping Kalat an independent state, along similar lines as the ill-fated decisions of Hyderabad and Travancore. He thought that due to his close friendship with Jinnah, he would be able to convince the Government of Pakistan of a friendship treaty instead of accession. The people of Kalat, especially the *sardars* (chiefs) and local notables, now constituted in the Lower House (*Dar-ul-Awam*) and Upper House (*Dar-ul-Umara*) in Kalat, were also vehemently against accession and recommended a treaty between two sovereign states. While it is impossible to go into the details of the whole negotiating process, it suffices to note that in the end Jinnah had to terminate his personal role in the process and turn over negotiations to the Ministry of Foreign Affairs in February 1948.[17] This led to the civil servants literally dismembering the state by recognising the feudatory states of Las Bela and Kharan, and the district of Mekran as independent states, which then immediately acceded to Pakistan. This move on 17 March 1948 left Kalat landlocked and with less than half its landmass. Further pressure on Ahmed Yar Khan, including false news on All-India Radio that Kalat wanted to join India, led him to sign the Instrument of Accession on 27 March 1948. This move immediately led his brother, Prince Abdul Karim, to raise the banner of revolt in July 1948, starting the first of the now five Baloch insurgencies.

In mid-1948 the government began the process of integrating the states into Pakistan (see Figure 4.1 for Pakistan after accession and before integration). However, the principles which guided the process in Pakistan were markedly different from those in India and have, as a result, bred a different result. For Pakistan, centralisation and the weakening of the ruling prince were far more important considerations than the development of democracy and representative institutions. As a result, the hands of the military and bureaucracy were further strengthened.

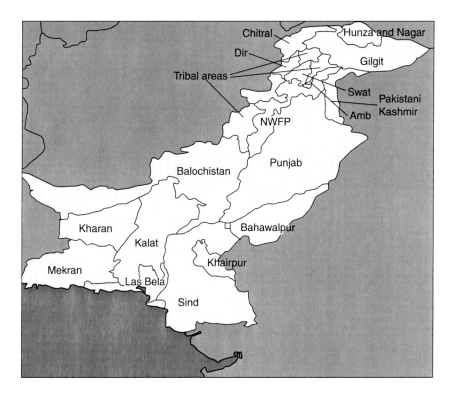

*Figure 4.1* West Pakistan in 1948.

## Centralisation and the emasculation of the princes

Soon after the process of accession finished, the government began to consolidate and centralise power in its own hands. The first move in this regard was to control the appointment of prime minister in the states and to integrate the states' forces. The appointment of Prime/Chief Ministers in the princely states had always been a matter of contention between the princes and the Political Department in the Government of India. Where the prince wanted a person whom he could trust and who would be subservient to his interests, the Political Department focused more on how far the minister would be friendly towards the Government of India, initiate reforms, and spearhead development. However, the instruments of accession signed by the states in 1947–8 did not allow the successor governments such influence. The government was acutely aware of the fact that if it did not have a decisive role in the appointment of ministers in the state, it could not ensure its general sway over the states. Very quickly a Supplementary Instrument of Accession was forced on the ruler of Bahawalpur on 1 October 1948, giving a decisive role to the central government in the appointment of the state's prime minister. The clause read:

> The Government of Pakistan may entrust to the Prime Minister of my State such duties relating to the administration of acceded subjects within the state as it may deem necessary. In the discharge of such duties the Prime Minister of my State shall be under the direct control of and responsible to the Government of Pakistan and shall carry out its directions issued to him from time to time.[18]

The Supplementary Instrument of Accession signed by Khairpur later on 1 February 1949 carried a crystallised version of what the government aimed at concerning the appointment of the Prime/Chief Ministers. It read: 'The Chief Minister of the State will be appointed by the Durbar with the previous consent and approval of the Government of Pakistan and the person so appointed shall not be removed without their prior consent.'[19] Thus, with the execution of these agreements, the Khairpur Durbar (still functioning in the name of the minor ruler), and the ruler of Bahawalpur, under pressure from the government, lost effective control.

The prospect of having a prime minister representing the central government as well as the ruler was fraught with problems from the outset and it was almost immediately clear in the negotiations over the appointment of a new premier for Bahawalpur in December 1948. As mentioned by the States Department Secretary, Shah, in the report on his visit to the Amir on 6 December 1948, the Amir wanted an Englishman of his choice as Prime Minister. The Amir wanted

> someone who would not rush things too much but go about his work in a steady and tactful manner and also bear in mind the dignity of the ruler as well as the interests of the people of the state.[20]

Shah, however, insisted that the nominee of the government, Col. Dring (who at that time was Chief Secretary to the Government of the North-West Frontier Province), be accepted by the Amir. Shah noted: 'I reassured His Highness … and said that Col. Dring fulfilled all the qualifications His Highness had in mind and had the advantage of his name being sponsored by the Prime Minister of Pakistan.'[21] In the end, the Amir accepted the suggestion of Shah, but with reservations and a promise of review within a year. The same attitude was also adopted regarding Khairpur when its Durbar began searching for a Chief Minister. As noted in a letter by Shah, the Khairpur Durbar wanted the services of a certain Mr. Williams as Chief Minister. However, Jinnah overruled the choice and instead suggested a member of the Pakistan Administrative Service, Khan Bahadur Mumtaz Kizilbash.[22]

Under the supplementary instrument of accession the Government had also taken over operative control of the state forces. The negotiations over the Bahawalpur army also clearly showed that it was impossible for a prime minister to represent the state and also be the political agent for the central government. Shah emphasised in his telegram to the Pakistani Prime Minister that he was not happy with the way in which Col. Dring had behaved during the negotiations with the Amir. He noted:

> As soon as I arrived here I informed Dring of my plans. I told him I would submit my appreciation of each question for your orders before I finalise it with His Highness. I still fail to understand why he was so anxious to rush me through everything in one afternoon, and why when he saw that I was going to tackle my task in my own way he took it upon himself to present me with a fait accompli and why he sent the ruler away on tour and himself proceeded to Karachi. All this must have caused him a very uneasy conscience because he had to tell lies in my face and accuse me of statements which he knew I had not made.... I request that Dring may be told that all negotiations will be conducted personally with the Ruler by me under your instructions.... He is quite capable of adapting himself to the conditions and a word from Prime Minister will put him in an wholesome state of mind. Unfortunately he has still not reconciled himself completely to the fact that the British rule has gone and that we mean to do our work in our own way. Should Dring threaten to resign or asks for reversion to Norwef [NWFP], I recommend that his request may be accepted because the situation in Bahawalpur does not permit any differences with the policy of the centre.[23]

Whatever the real intentions of Col. Dring, it was patent that he found it hard to represent both the Government of Pakistan and the Amir of Bahawalpur when Pakistan was trying to limit the authority of the Amir, and the Amir was desperately trying to shore it up.

As further reforms were initiated in Bahawalpur, especially those relating to the instituting of an electoral system, the policy of the government towards increased centralisation and emasculation of the prince continued. The Government of Bahawalpur Act 1952 made the state a federated unit of Pakistan, but also gave the prince wide-ranging powers, analogous to the provincial governors. However, almost immediately the Government of Pakistan asked the Amir to sign the Third Supplementary Instrument of Accession on 27 March 1952 in which the Amir agreed to

> appoint an experienced officer with the approval of the Governor General, as my Adviser to aid and advise me in the exercise of my powers and authority under the Government of Bahawalpur (Interim Constitution) Act 1952, as the constitutional Ruler of my State and in the discharge of my functions in respect of matters with respect to which I am charged with special responsibility ... and required to act in my discretion or in the exercise of my individual judgment.[24]

The Amir further agreed that

> should an occasion arise where I differ from the advice given to me on any matter by my Council of Ministers or my said Adviser, I shall seek the advice of the Government of Pakistan thereon and shall accept the advice as given.[25]

This instrument crystallised the policy of the Government of Pakistan towards the Amir, where even though he still technically held vast powers, he could now never act without the consent of his centrally appointed Adviser or in the case of a disagreement, the central government. Thus, the Adviser was in effect the proxy governor of Bahawalpur State and was to direct the Amir in his conduct on the lines agreed by the central government. The Amir was now a mere puppet and the centrally appointed Adviser the real master of Bahawalpur.

In Khairpur, democratic reforms did not even lead to an elected chief minister (even though Kizilbash did contest and win a seat), and the Government of Khairpur Act 1953 which made Khairpur a province, consolidated even further powers in the hands of the centrally appointed chief minister. Therefore, the chief minister in Khairpur also became the advisor to the Mir, and became even more powerful than his opposite number in Bahawalpur. The Mir, now vested with full powers after his eighteenth birthday in November 1951, was a mere ceremonial ruler with only theoretical powers.

In Kalat, since the Khan did not sign any supplementary instrument of Accession after his initial accession, the government had to exercise control through the Prime Minister, who, after the resignation of Nawabzada Aslam Khan, was Douglas Fell. As the Khan noted in his autobiography:

> A fortnight after the merger, on the 15th of April 1948, to be exact, the Agent to the Governor-General in Balochistan called upon me with an order of the Quaid-e-Azam, informing me that it was decided to maintain a status quo ante in Kalat. That the position of Kalat State would revert back to what it was during the preceding British rule! A Political Agent, an officer subordinate to the Agent to the Governor-General was appointed to look after the administration of the State and guide the Chief Minister in all internal affairs. Thus, my legal authority as the Khan-e-Azam came to an end on 15th April, 1948, and my connections with the affairs of Kalat were cut off; and within 20 hours of the Orders executed upon me, several of the ministers of Kalat Government were exiled or arrested.[26]

Despite the fact that Fell was now working under the guidance of the government, he was not a member of the Pakistani civil service and was still technically employed by the Khan. Within months, Fell was called 'disloyal' to the country and a campaign started to remove him from office. *Dawn* noted in its editorial:

> Neither the AGG nor the officials of the new Ministry which the Governor General has set up ... can deny that Kalat State continues to be the happy hunting ground of anti-Pakistan elements and that the activities of these elements have been on the increase.... It needs no great imagination to realise that these elements could not possibly be engaging in their anti-Pakistan activities without encouragement from responsible quarters within the state. The name which is widely and openly mentioned in this connection is that of Mr D Y Fell ... [who] seems to be going strong and snapping his fingers at Pakistan.[27]

The newspaper even quipped that such conditions would not be allowed to prevail in a state which had acceded to India, and noted:

> we deliberately draw this comparison because it is by no means pleasant to reflect that the wheels of the Pakistan Government move so slowly and grind not at all, even in the department which functions directly under the Quaid-e-Azam's guidance.[28]

With such vitriolic attacks against Fell in the media, the government took immediate action and appointed Khan Bahadur Mohammad Zarif Khan of the NWFP and Punjab Provincial Civil Service as Prime Minister of Kalat in late July 1948. Placed in a situation where he did not have the backing of either his *sardars* or the government, the Khan had no option but to accept the nomination. The government further thought it best to send the Khan as part of its United Nations delegation in 1948, so that the new Prime Minister could consolidate his control of state affairs. The Khan was also encouraged to tour various countries with the expectation that the longer he remained out of the state, the stronger the Prime Minister could become and that the Khan might even acquiesce to becoming a constitutional ruler.

Besides the difficulties in dealing with the Khan of Kalat, by accepting Kharan, Las Bela, and Mekran as separate states, the government had created for itself a new set of problems. Not only was the Khan of Kalat unhappy about this situation, the rulers of these states were adamant in asserting their authority and hence were proving to be difficult for the Assistant/Additional Political Agents (APAs) to handle. For example, when the government restricted the powers of the Nawab of Mekran, large-scale protests began for the restoration of his powers, creating a law and order problem for the APA.[29]

All four Baloch states were small, impoverished, backward, and sparsely populated. These factors meant that only a joint approach to reform was workable for the states, as they did not have the ability to support separate constitutional structures. In February 1951, the Agent to the Governor General (AGG) Aminuddin noted:

> I feel that some caution is indicated in approaching the problem of drafting constitutions to pave the way for reforms in the States of Las Bela, Kharan and Mekran. The economy of the first and last is shortly to be profoundly disturbed by the taking over of the Customs Posts and control of the coast by the Central Government and by the general abolition of 'Sung.' It is hoped that generous compensation offered for the former and the substitution of true octroi for the latter, will open the way for an elected assembly of sorts and some form of local bodies respectively.... I can, at present, see no future for Kharan; the State can barely afford her existing ridiculously cheap system of administration and, until some way is found of making the desert pay increased dividends, cannot contemplate the cost of any reforms. Progress has so far passed Kharan by almost entirely, and the State in many ways resembles an Arab Shaikhdom of the Middle Ages.[30]

Thus, from the perspective of the government there was hopelessly little which could be done to reform the Baloch states, except Kalat to an extent, under the prevailing conditions. A plausible solution to the Baloch states' problems was, however, to return somewhat to their status before accession, that is, when they were all treated as one. After all, the government knew that it had only recognised Las Bela and Kharan as separate states to put pressure on the Khan, and Mekran was simply a figment of legal imagination. Therefore, a solution could be found if all the four states were brought together in some sort of a union of states. As early as March 1948, Nawabzada Aslam Khan, the Prime Minister of Kalat, had suggested the creation of a Baloch States Union as the 'only way the states and tribes can be saved from disintegration'.[31] As a result, in January 1952 the idea of a Balochistan States Union was mooted, first to the Khan of Kalat and then the other rulers.[32] Later, the rulers signed a covenant in April 1952 establishing 'a united state comprising the territories of our respective states with a common executive, legislature and judiciary'. Under the covenant, the executive government of the state would be carried out by a Chief Adviser, also known as the Wazir-i-Azam (Great Minister), who would be appointed by the Council of Rulers comprising the four rulers, with the Khan of Kalat as the president of the Council of Rulers during his lifetime, and given the title of Khan-i-Azam (Great Khan). The Wazir-i-Azam would be approved by the government and could not be dismissed without its concurrence. Also, no cabinet ministers could be appointed or dismissed without approval of the government.[33] Subsequently, Agha Abdul Hamid, who had been Private Secretary to Liaquat Ali Khan (1895–1951, Prime Minister 1947–51) and Prime Minister of Kalat since March 1951, was appointed as the first Prime Minister of the Balochistan States Union (BSU), keeping the new union firmly under the control of the central government.[34]

The policy of the government remained the same in the Frontier states except that here the realities on the ground and the firm loyalty of the rulers, with the exception of Dir, prevented any dramatic integration until very late. The states minister, Dr Hussain, succinctly noted the policy of the government:

> We have dealings with one single individual who looks after law and order and who practically does exactly the same thing in the states which all the maliks do in the tribal regions. So here at the moment we are not thinking in terms of establishing a parliamentary system of government on western lines.[35]

Regarding Dir, its position on the border with Afghanistan, and the distrusting nature of the Nawab, prevented any further development of its relations with the centre, and relations with the state were governed by the original instrument of accession until the 1960s.

Out of the four Frontier states, Chitral was the first where conditions allowed the Government of Pakistan to exercise greater influence than the original instrument of accession permitted. On 6 January 1949, the Mehtar (ruler) of Chitral,

Muzzafar-ul-Mulk (r. 1943–9) died, resulting in his young son, Saif-ur-Rehman (r. 1949–55), becoming Mehtar.[36] Owing to the young age and inexperience of the Mehtar and the continual intrigue of some of his family members, the Government of Pakistan thought it best that the Mehtar be sent away on 'training' and the state run by a Board of Administration presided over by an APA. The Malakand PA noted:

> His Highness is young and easily misled. He is not able to govern as he should. He has little aptitude for making correct decisions. He has to rely on advice which is not always reliable. His uncles appear to be either actively working against his authority, or intriguing amongst themselves.... The present Ruler appears to be helpless. One remedy appears to be the appointment of an able APA with powers to control the affairs of Chitral through a Council appointed by Government.[37]

In November 1949, the Mehtar agreed to the above proposal and promulgated a *Farman* (edict) establishing a Board of Administration under an APA and proceeded for training in Lahore.[38]

Regarding the other Frontier states, the ruler of Swat was so loyal that democratic reforms were only introduced late in 1954, but that too under the firm control of the Wali (ruler). In Amb too, the loyalty of the Nawab prevented actual change for a long time until a revolt of the people forced the hands of the government. Dir, as mentioned earlier, remained a complete autocracy until the Nawab was forcibly removed in 1967.

This piecemeal constitutional integration of the states meant that all the states were at different levels of legal integration. While Bahawalpur and Khairpur achieved provincial status which lasted until 1955, others did not, but remained much longer. Therefore, when a new constitution came into force in March 1956, only the former subjects of Bahawalpur and Khairpur achieved the same status as the rest of Pakistani citizens; the subjects of the BSU, the Frontier states, and Hunza and Nagar did not enjoy the same rights and privileges as other citizens. This factor alone, and especially the fact that to date the people of Hunza and Nagar remain outside the ambit of the constitution, has adversely affected the consolidation of the country and prevented the development of a common sense of citizenship and identity.

## Distrust of democracy

The policy of the Government of Pakistan towards democratisation in the states was firmly gradualism. The states were thought of as not 'ready' for responsible government and, therefore, such measures had to be phased in. Also, the government did not want to lose control over the states in case an independent ministry were elected which would compromise the security-centric approach of the centre.

Following the establishment of local municipal bodies (with universal franchise) under the 8 November 1948 *Farman*[39] of the Amir of Bahawalpur, further pressure was exerted on the Amir to initiate more reforms, and an agreement was signed between the Amir and the secretary of the ministry for states on 19 January 1949 which charted the future of the state. Under the agreement, the Amir agreed to assume the position of a 'Constitutional Ruler', with 'the responsibility for the executive administration of the State ... with the Prime Minister'.[40] Following the agreement, further democratic reforms were announced on 8 March, which were later codified in the Government of Bahawalpur Act 1949. This Act created a *Majlis* (assembly) composed of 25 members with 16 chosen by the elected representatives of local bodies from among themselves, two ex-officio members, and seven nominated by the ruler.[41] Under the Act, the ruler still appointed the Prime Minister from outside the *Majlis* and could dissolve the legislature without giving a reason. Only two ministers in the cabinet were to be members of the *Majlis* and held the portfolio of 'Transferred subjects', that is, 'local self-government, medical and public health, education, agriculture, civil veterinary, cooperative societies, stores and stationary ... forests and gardens'.[42] The actual powers of the *Majlis* were extremely restricted. The *Majlis* could make laws concerning the transferred subjects, but they were subject to the veto of the Prime Minister. It could discuss the reserved subjects, but only with prior consent of the Prime Minister. The Prime Minister could also override the *Majlis* and promulgate any laws he thought were 'essential for the safety, tranquillity or other interest of the State or part thereof'.[43] In effect therefore the main result of the Act was that the ruler became more or less a constitutional ruler and the Prime Minister became the executive head of government. The assembly was there to advise and give the semblance of democratic government, but ultimate control lay with the Prime Minster, who was now appointed only after the approval of the Government of Pakistan. The ruler's powers were extremely curtailed and his only consolation was that all 'executive action of the Government ... [was] in the name of the Ruler'[44] and that *Majlis*' members had to swear allegiance to him.

Similarly, in Khairpur, as soon as the Supplementary Instrument of Accession was signed in February 1949, the Government of Pakistan began to create plans for reforms along the same lines as Bahawalpur. The result was the Government of Khairpur Act 1949 which created an assembly of fifteen members which was to work in conjunction with the Chief Minister.[45] However, just like the Bahawalpur Act, in Khairpur the government appointed the Chief Minister who could veto or himself promulgate laws. In the absence of a ruling prince (as Mir George Ali Murad Talpur was still a minor) it was relatively easy for the government to push through these changes, especially since the Chief Minister, Mumtaz Kizilbash, was already their appointee. It was significant, however, that even though the Act related to internal government, it was mainly formulated, scrutinised, and approved by the government and the Khairpur Durbar was merely asked to promulgate it.[46]

In Kalat, after the Khan of Kalat returned from his tours abroad in 1949, he tried in vain to recall his two houses of parliament, the now dormant *Dar-ul Awam* and *Dar-ul Umara*. The government was perturbed by such plans and thwarted them immediately. The states ministry report noted that:

these houses are a creation of His Highness. Dar-ul-Umara was an attempt to bring the semi-Independent Sardars of Kalat State firmly under the control of the Khan and to wean them from their loyalty to the Agent to the Governor-General, while Dar-ul-Awam was a body of Congress-minded individuals whom the Khan used to keep his own sardars under control and to stop the British Government interfering too much in the internal affairs of the State.... Under the Hon'able the Prime Minister's orders instructions were issued to Agent to the Governor General to ask His Highness to explain the necessity of calling these Houses at this juncture and to defer their summoning till he has thrashed out with the Government of Pakistan the future constitution of his State.[47]

While accurate about the composition of the houses, the report was flawed in that it characterised the lower house as existing to prevent the interference of the British, since both the houses of parliament were only called in the first instance after the lapse of paramountcy. Moreover, they were broadly representative of the people in the states – no less than the advisory councils established in the Frontier states. In any case, the government foresaw political turmoil in case the houses met and so strongly advised the Khan against convening them. Shah noted: 'our experience of the Khan has been that whenever he decides to create mischief, he summons his Upper and Lower Houses.... I advise against allowing him to start meddling with politicians by summoning the Houses of Legislature.'[48] As a result, the houses never met again.

The creation of the BSU in 1952 signalled that political activity might be allowed in the princely states. Under its interim constitution, the Union was to have a legislature of twenty-eight elected and twelve nominated members. With the expectation of elections, political activity picked up and the former members of the Kalat State National Party (the largest party) under the leadership of Ghaus Bakhsh Bizenjo (c. 1917–89) created the BSU Muslim League.[49] Initially, the BSU constitution allowed for universal adult franchise. However, in September 1953, the government of the Union proposed to amend the constitution to allow only men to vote, a move the government approved.[50] This amendment was a clear sign that even though the government wanted to see some democratic reform in the Baloch states, it did not want the introduction of democracy to initiate any radical change in the social and political structure of the states. Adult males, especially in the *jirga* (assembly) system, were the decision makers, and the new constitution now envisaged the same. No consideration whatsoever was given to the equal status of women and their individual and political rights under the new constitution – and it seemed that no one cared either. However, the voter lists and the general preparations for the elections never materialised and in June 1955 the BSU merged with Balochistan and then with One Unit in October 1955.

In the Frontier states the government of Chitral was already under the control of the APA and the government was not willing to loosen its control over this strategic state. However, incessant protests by the people led to the return of the

Mehtar in April 1953 and the promulgation of the Government of Chitral Act 1953 under which the APA became the Wazir of the state with all executive power vested in him. Under the Act, the Wazir or Chief Adviser was the chair of an Advisory Council composed of ten members, half of whom were to be elected.[51] Later, however, on 12 October 1954, the Mehtar died in a plane crash and was succeeded by his four and a half year-old son, Saif-ul-Mulk Nasir. The young age of the new ruler mandated that a regent be appointed by the central government who was the PA Malakand, meaning that government officials now held supreme power in the state.[52]

A similar pattern was followed in Amb where a revolt in the state against the Nawab necessitated some reform. The resulting Government of Amb Act 1953 provided for a Wazir and a council of four advisers, two nominated by the Nawab and two elected. The Wazir would be appointed with the approval of the Governor-General and the Nawab would follow his advice on matters of state. The constitution also provided for elections to the Council, for which only male residents of the state were eligible to vote.[53] Hence, the centrally appointed Wazir was now the main authority in the state and the Nawab was to follow his advice on all matters relating to state affairs.

The relations of Swat State with the central government developed very differently when compared to the other Frontier states. Swat was by far the most developed and progressive state on the Frontier and its Wali, Miangul Jehanzeb (1908–87, Wali 1949–69), who had taken over in 1949 after the abdication of his father, was very loyal to Pakistan.[54] As a result, the government wanted to strengthen his rule, rather than weaken it. Nevertheless, reforms in adjoining states put pressure on the government to press for the federation of Swat with Pakistan. Accordingly, Swat became the last state on the Frontier to federate through the signing of the Supplementary Instrument of Accession by the Wali on 12 February 1954. In the following Government of Swat (Interim Constitution) Act 1954, however, no Adviser or Wazir was imposed upon the Wali and he was left alone at the helm of an Advisory Council of twenty-five, of whom fifteen were to be elected.[55] *Dawn* clearly saw the wool this Act had pulled over the eyes of the people of Swat as it only further consolidated the power of the Wali, now with the official blessing of the government. In a scathing editorial it noted:

> the Council is only advisory and can only advise on matters on which the Wali is pleased to refer to it. Even then, since the Wali will be the President of the Council, he will be in the position of advising himself on matters chosen by himself.[56]

Quite obviously, the government was not prepared to permit democratic reforms to weaken the control of a progressive and loyal ruler.

Here, too, the different degrees to which a democratic system was introduced in the states created political and structural problems for the consolidation of the country. In contrast, by 1951 India – all princely states included – was participating in the first nationwide general elections on the principles of 'one person, one vote' and representative government, while in Pakistan only Khairpur and Bahawalpur even achieved universal adult franchise, and no state realised full responsible government. This ambivalent attitude towards an electoral system took root in the formative first decade of Pakistan and has lasted to the present, especially in the former states, unsure about even the democratic system. As the states were never allowed to experience full democratic governments, the people were never actually able to grasp the nature of responsible government and therefore did not develop any strong ideological leanings towards democracy. Concerns over security and control kept trumping democracy then and, it seems, even now.

## Merger

By the end of 1954 only Bahawalpur had some semblance of democratic government amongst the states, but even there an all-powerful advisor was keeping watch. The Khairpur Chief Minister was still not required to be elected (though Kizilbash did get elected), Chitral was under the firm control of the APA as Wazir and Regent, Amb had a centrally appointed advisor, and the elections promised in the BSU never materialised. Only in Swat did the ruler, owing to his progressive and loyal views, escape direct central control and became his own advisor, and in Dir the ruler simply refused to change anything. Relations with the states of Hunza and Nagar were frozen due to the Kashmir dispute, and they were governed by the rulers working under the Political Agent in Gilgit.

While the states were being integrated in various ways, a strong disagreement arose over the future democratic setup. For its first nine years of existence Pakistan was governed under an adapted form of the Government of India Act of 1935 mainly because the eastern and western wings of the country could not agree on the question of representation. The saga of this nine-year-long process is too long to be narrated here, but suffice it to note that in the end a formula was devised under which the numerical majority of East Bengal would be equalled by a united West Pakistan in the legislature and an elaborate procedure outlined how laws were to be passed with the concurrence of a majority of legislators from both wings.

As murmurings began to be heard of the creation of a unified West Pakistan, the fate of the princely states also became important. The Khan of Kalat immediately reacted to the news, especially of the BSU being merged into the Chief Commissioner's province of Balochistan, and wrote a lengthy memorandum to the Government of Pakistan protested such a move.[57] The opposition to the merger led the government to allow the BSU to be designated a 'Special Area' under the proposed constitution, which would shield it from legislation without the consent of the Governor and President. Paragraph 132C of the amended report of the Basic Principles Committee (BPC) now read that the BSU was to merge with the new Governor's province of Balochistan but since 'these areas have no representation in the provincial legislatures, the provincial legislatures will not be competent to extend their laws in these areas'.[58] Thus, except for the legal amalgamation of the BSU with Balochistan, no steps were taken to actually democratise the areas of the BSU and integrate them into the province. Seeing the writing on the wall, the BSU rulers finally agreed to the merger of their states with Balochistan and signed a Merger Agreement to this effect on 1 January 1955. Subsequently, on 14 October, the BSU was disbanded and reorganised into divisions and districts.

The rumours of the amalgamation of the BSU with Balochistan in early 1954 also led to other states becoming concerned about their future status. Khairpur especially was worried that it might be merged with Sindh. In order to pre-empt such a move, the Khairpur Assembly passed a unanimous resolution on 25 May 1954 arguing against the change of status:

> The Government and people of Khairpur State have heard with concern vague rumours of a suggestion to merge the Khairpur State in the province of Sindh ... such rumours have created serious apprehensions in the minds of the Government and the people of Khairpur about their future.[59]

However, by the middle of 1954 the central government had set its mind on the creation of a unified West Pakistan and would not listen to any opposition to the plan, either from the states or even the provinces. On 7 November 1954 the Sindh ministry under Pirzada Abdus Sattar declared its opposition to the One Unit scheme and Sattar was summarily dismissed within twenty-four hours on account of maladministration. Mohammad Ayub Khuhro (1901–80, Chief Minister 1947–8, 1951, 1954–5) was appointed in his place and given the task of making the provincial assembly agree to the One Unit plan.[60] Similarly, the Sardar Abdul Rashid (1906–95) ministry, which commenced on 23 April 1953 in the NWFP, was dismissed on 18 July 1955 and replaced by the pro-One Unit Sardar Bahadur Khan (1908–75) (who had been appointed Chief Commissioner of Balochistan in November 1954) to bring about support for the One Unit scheme in the provincial assembly.[61]

With the summary dismissal of provincial ministries which opposed the unification of west Pakistan, the states had little chance of survival. On 1 November 1954 the Amir of Bahawalpur was summoned to Karachi by the Governor-General and by the next day it had been announced that the Amir had dismissed the elected ministry of Hasan Mahmud (1922–86) and had assumed full ruling powers under section 74 of the interim constitution of Bahawalpur.[62] Seeing the treatment of Bahawalpur and subsequently the Sindh ministry, the Khairpur Assembly realised that it had no option but to accept the merger and so passed a resolution in favour of unification on 10 November 1954.[63]

With support for One Unit finally gathered, the central government made the rulers of the BSU, Khairpur, and Bahawalpur sign Merger Agreements which *inter alia* wiped out their states and abolished their status as sovereign rulers. The Amir of Bahawalpur was the first to sign a Merger Agreement on 17 December 1954, followed by the Mir of Khairpur three days later on 20 December and the BSU rulers on 1 January 1955 (see Figure 4.2 for Pakistan after the mergers). All rulers also received hefty privy purses as *quid pro quo* for them agreeing to merge their states. The privy purse, which was free of all taxes, for the Khan of Kalat was fixed at Rs.650,000; the Nawab of Mekran secured Rs.225,000; the Jam of Las Bela's was Rs.200,000 and the Nawab of Kharan received Rs.70,000 annually. The privy purses for the Amir of Bahawalpur and Mir of Khairpur were set at Rs.3,200,000 and Rs.1,000,000 respectively. These purses not only saddled the government with additional non-development expenditure but effectively served to 'buy out' the opposition of the princes to the deeply unpopular mergers.

The four Frontier states, as well as Hunza and Nagar, survived the formal establishment of One Unit on 14 October 1955. Under the establishment of the West Pakistan Act 1955, the Frontier states were designated as 'Special/Tribal Areas', and left untouched. Hunza and Nagar, on the other hand, formed a part of Gilgit Agency and since the government considered the whole of Gilgit Agency to be part of the state of Jammu and Kashmir, these states were not even mentioned in the Act.

The main reason why the central government did not merge the Frontier states, it seems, was the continual propaganda of Afghanistan against the merger. As noted by Wayne Wilcox, 'Radio Kabul analysed the plan as a conspiracy to put the Pathan under the heel of the Punjabis',[64] and there was resentment in the region

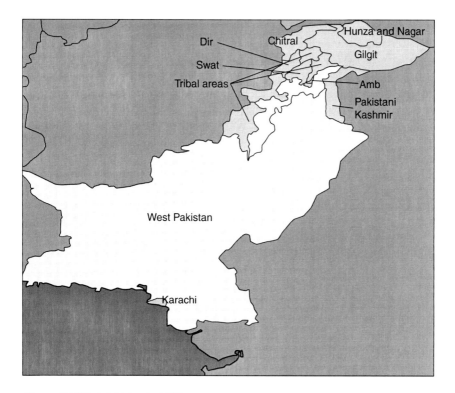

*Figure 4.2* West Pakistan in 1955.

against the plan. Furthermore, the appointment of Major General Iskander Mirza (1899–1969) as states minister in October 1954 meant that there was now an experienced Frontier man at the helm of affairs and so the threat of Afghan propaganda was taken seriously. As late as 1962, the political authorities in the Frontier states were wary of giving any impression that the government was planning to take over or merge the states. On the question of the extension of Pakistani law in the agency, the Malakand PA noted: 'the extension of laws is likely to create the impression that it is a prelude to a complete takeover of the administration by the government. This is an impression, which we must avoid to create.'[65]

The Frontier states were finally merged through the promulgation of the Dir, Chitral, and Swat (Administration) Regulation of 1969 under General Yahya Khan (1917–80, President 1969–71), which removed the rulers from their role in the administration of the states. While the Regulation did not technically 'merge' the states, the takeover of the administration by the government meant that effectively the states had been extinguished and merged with the country. The states of Hunza and Nagar remained a separate entity until 1973, when Zulifqar Ali Bhutto (1928–79, President 1971–3, Prime Minister 1973–7) merged them fully with Gilgit Agency, which still remained separate. (See Figure 4.3 for map of Pakistan in 1973.)

The paramount principles which underlay the integration of the princely states are still in force, and are giving rise to several structural and political problems such as insurgency, low development, weak political institutions, and the pre-eminence of the military and bureaucracy. Therefore, as compared to India, where integration and democratisation swiftly followed accession, Pakistan has lagged behind in state consolidation and development due to such lop-sided policies.

In several ways, the policies of the government towards the states were a continuation of old Political Department policies under the British Raj. The Pakistan government wanted to recreate the doctrine of paramountcy in its relations with the states and did not care much about democratic reform and national integration. The existence of several officers from the Indian Political Service, such as Sir Ambrose Dundas (1899–1973), who served as Chief Commissioner of Balochistan (1947–8) and then as Governor of the NWFP (1948–9), Cecil A.V. Savidge who was AGG and Chief Commissioner in Balochistan from 1948 to 1949, Nawab Mahbub Ali Khan who was Political Agent in Malakand, Major General Iskandar Mirza who was Defence Secretary and later Governor-General and Prime Minister, and Col. A.S.B. Shah who was secretary of the States and Frontier Regions ministry, meant that 'old hands' had a lot of influence and sway. As a result, beyond the re-establishment of paramountcy, which ensured firm central control, the government remained scarcely interested in anything else. A US Embassy report attested to the powers of the civil servants in the states:

> Pakistan Government policy toward the states has been in the hands of a group of permanent civil servants concentrated in the Ministry of States and Frontier Regions who have tended to carry on the traditions by which Britain dealt with the states in the past.[66]

*Constructing the state* 97

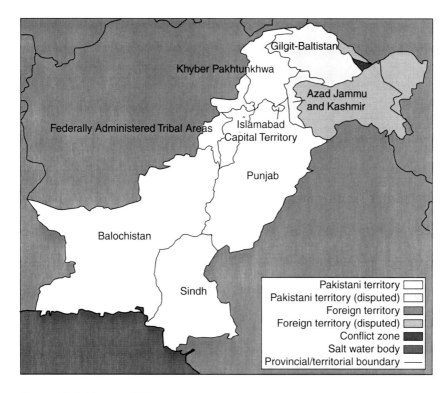

*Figure 4.3* Pakistan in 1973.

With security the overarching concern, the central government only wanted to consolidate its control over the states, mainly at the cost of the ruler. In all states, except Dir and Swat, powerful advisors ran the government. In no state was the advisor elected or answerable to an assembly or advisory council; the post was filled by and answerable only to the government. This factor led the government to enforce the policy of 'gradualism' in the states, something it held in common with the erstwhile British Government of India. Democracy could be tolerated but only when the government in the states was subservient to the central government. Just as the framing of the constitution was being postponed from one year to the next, the introduction of full democracy was continuously pushed forward. Liaquat Ali Khan explained: 'with sympathy and firmness we will be able to bring the states to the same level of democracy as Pakistan by the time the new constitution was ready.'[67] But this gradualism was not without its supporters. *Dawn* strongly supported this stance in an editorial: 'Most of these states are without even that elementary grounding in procedures and affairs which is essential to an intelligent casting of votes. Democracy without political education has all the potentialities of chaos.'[68]

The illiberal attitude of the Government of Pakistan where the people of the princely states were denied the right to chose their own representative and be ruled by them was not lost on the members of the Pakistan Constituent Assembly. In the debate on 6 January 1950, Liaquat Ali Khan defended the decision of the government to allow the rulers to nominate their representatives to the Assembly. He said: 'Would the world applaud you if you marched your forces into the states?... Some other country had done it, but it was wrong.'[69] In response, *Dawn* noted:

> The criticism was led by Sardar Shaukat Hayat Khan [1915–98] who charged that the States Negotiating Committee's report was a 'betrayal of the revolution' and a 'betrayal of the principles for which we fought,' and asked that the people of the States should be given the right to elect their representatives. Mian Iftikharuddin [1907–62] was the other staunch critic who hurled volley of abuses on the rulers of the states.... He said that it was a mistake to negotiate with them. 'By doing so we accepted the principle of people being properties.'... With sarcasm he told the House: 'You are Government of India to build our State in a new way.... Let us tell the world that Pakistan is a really progressive, revolutionary, and democratic state.' He urged the House to 'do away with the despots with the stroke of the pen.'[70]

The dissenting members went to the heart of the issue: if the government were devoted, as it had repeatedly proclaimed, to bring the states to the same level as the provinces, then why were they not prepared to follow India's example and pension off the princes and fully integrate their states?

The pattern of constitutional integration of the princely states still has its effects. The strengthening of the bureaucracy and military in Balochistan still means that these institutions carry a lot of sway and influence in the province, which has led to several Baloch insurgencies, with one still ongoing. Similarly the deliberate denial of the right to vote in the Baloch and Frontier states meant that even in the general elections in Pakistan in May 2013, women were barred from voting in a number of places in the former states.[71] The erstwhile princely states formed more than half of the landmass of the then-western Pakistan, and therefore the pre-eminence of the military and bureaucracy in formulating and controlling policy in these states meant that these institutions were already in control of a large part of Pakistan, well before the ascendency of the military under General Ayub Khan in the late 1950s. The ambivalent attitude of the government towards democracy still plagues Pakistan and the continuation of democracy in the country still remains fraught with challenges.

## Notes

1 James Chiriyankandath, 'Colonialism and Post-Colonial Development', in Peter Burnell, Vicky Randall, and Lise Rakner, (eds), *Politics in the Developing World* (Oxford: Oxford University Press, 2008), p. 47.
2 Sir Hilary Synott, *Transforming Pakistan: Ways out of Instability* (Abingdon: Routledge, 2009), p. 14.

3 Ibid., p. 15.
4 Ayesha Jalal, *The State of Martial Rule: The Origins of Pakistan's Political Economy of Defence* (Cambridge: Cambridge University Press, 1990), p. 3.
5 Nehru's address to the All India States People's Congress, *Hindustan Times*, 1 January, 1946, L/PS/13/1826, India Office Records (IOR).
6 Statement of Sardar Patel on the Indian States, 5 July 1947, L/PS/13/1827, IOR.
7 V.P. Menon, *The Story of the Integration of the Indian States* (New York: Longmans, 1956), pp. 159–60.
8 Quoted in ibid., p. 164.
9 See P.N. Chopra (ed.), *The Collected Works of Sardar Vallabhbhai Patel*, Vol. 12 (Delhi: Konark Publishers, 2008), p. 257.
10 For details, see Ministry of States, *White Paper on Indian States* (Delhi: Manager of Publications, 1950), pp. 38–58.
11 Ibid., p. 145.
12 Reuters quoting Jinnah, 17 June 1947, L/PS/13/1827, IOR.
13 Percival Spear, *The Oxford History of India* (Delhi: Oxford University Press, 1994), p. 427.
14 Lewis to Marshall, 11 January 1949, Political Reports 1949, Box 16, MLR UD3064A, United States National Archives (USNA).
15 UK High Commission Dispatch No. 303 (198) 31.5.1949, L/PS/12/3284, IOR.
16 For details, see Yaqoob Khan Bangash, 'Three forgotten Accessions: Gilgit, Hunza and Nagar', *Journal of Imperial and Commonwealth History*, 38, 1 (2010): 117–43.
17 For details, see Yaqoob Khan Bangash, *Subjects to Citizens: Accession and Integration of the Princely States of Pakistan* (Karachi: Oxford University Press, 2013), Chapter 3.
18 Government of Pakistan, *Instruments of Accession and Schedules of States Acceding to Pakistan, presented by the Honourable the Minister for States and Frontier Regions to the Constituent Assembly (Legislature) on February 14, 1949* (Karachi: Governor-General's Press and Publications, 1949), p. 7.
19 Ibid., p. 11.
20 Report of Shah to Prime Minister, 13 December 1948, 10 (5) PMS/49, National Documentation Centre (NDC).
21 Ibid.
22 Shah to Mohammad Ali, Secretary General, Government of Pakistan, 13 July 1948, 10 (5) PMS/49, NDC.
23 Shah to Prime Minister, 2 January 1949, ibid.
24 Third Supplementary Instrument of Accession, Para. 2, 67/CF/52, NDC.
25 Para. 3 in ibid.
26 Ahmed Yar Khan, *Inside Balochistan: Political Autobiography of Khan-e-Azam Mir Ahmed Yar Khan Baluch, Ex-ruler of Kalat State* (Quetta: 1975), pp. 163–4.
27 *Dawn* editorial, 15 July 1948.
28 Ibid.
29 Martin Axmann, *Back to the Future: The Khanate of Kalat and the Genesis of Baluch Nationalism, 1915–55* (Karachi: Oxford University Press, 2009), pp. 240–57.
30 AGG Balochistan to Shah, 26 February 1951, 367-S/49, 1949 Vol. 2, BN 27, Balochistan Secretariat Archives (BSA).
31 Aslam to AGG Balochistan, 23 March 1948, 9.369-S/1948 Vol. 1, BN 26, BSA.
32 Fortnightly Summary No. 2, 17/CF/52, NDC.
33 See Covenant entered into by Rulers of Kalat, Mekran, Las Bela and Kharan for the formation of BSU, 11 April 1952, General File (States), States Ministry.
34 Fortnightly Summary No. 8, 17/CF/52, NDC.
35 Government of Pakistan, *Constituent Assembly of Pakistan Debates* (Karachi: Government Printing Press, 1947–56), 21 March 1951, pp. 531–3.

36 For details, see File No. 54 S.Sts. I Vol. V, North West Frontier Province Archives (NWFPA).
37 Note by PA Malakand, 14 March 1949, File No. 347, NWFPA.
38 Fortnightly Summary No. 21, 264/CF/49 Vol. III, NDC.
39 See Government of Bahawalpur, *Extraordinary Gazette* notification, 8 November 1948, Bahawalpur Central Library.
40 Agreement between the Nawab of Bahawalpur and the Government of Pakistan, Karachi, 19 January 1949, General File (States), States Ministry.
41 Government of Bahawalpur Act 1949, part II, 1, (a), (b), (c), Bahawalpur Central Library.
42 Ibid., part III.
43 Ibid., part IV.
44 Ibid., part V.
45 Press Note, Chief Minister's Office, Khairpur, 17 August 1949, Khairpur Durbar Archives.
46 See Fortnightly Report of States Ministry from April to October 1949, 264/CF/49, NDC.
47 Fortnightly Report No. 15, 264/CF/49, NDC.
48 Cited in A.B. Awan, *Balochistan: Historical and Political Processes* (London: New Century Publishers, 1985), p. 214.
49 Fortnightly Report No. 3, 33/CF/53 Vol. XI, NDC.
50 Fortnightly Report No. 18, ibid.
51 For details, see the text of the Act and Supplementary Instrument of Accession, 89/CF/53, NDC.
52 Fortnightly Report Nos. 20 and 21, 8/CF/54 Vol. 16, NDC.
53 For more details, see KW 175 S.Sts., NWFPA.
54 In his inauguration speech Jehanzeb had noted: 'We form part of Pakistan without which we cannot exist.' *Dawn*, 14 December 1949, p. 8.
55 See Government of Swat (Interim Constitution) Act 1954, 3/CF/54, NDC.
56 Quoted in Fortnightly Report, 25 February 1954, DO35/5327, UKNA.
57 Text of the letter in Gul Khan Naseer, *Tarikh-e-Balochistan* (Quetta: Kalat Publishers, 2009), pp. 596–601.
58 Government of Pakistan, *Constituent Assembly of Pakistan Debates* (Karachi: Government Printing Press, 1947–56), Prime Minister's Speech, 20 September 1954, p. 454.
59 Memorandum Basic Principles Committee, 1, Khairpur Durbar Archives.
60 *Dawn*, 9 November 1954, p. 1.
61 Hildreth to State Department, 19 July 1955, Box 50, MLR UD3064A, USNA.
62 *Dawn*, 3 November 1954, p. 1.
63 *Dawn*, 11 November 1954, p. 1.
64 W.A. Wilcox, *Pakistan: The Consolidation of a Nation* (New York: Columbia University Press, 1966), p. 184.
65 PA to CPD, 13 February 1962, 703, NWFPA.
66 Survey of the Pakistan States, 28 May 1951, Box 34, MLR UD3064A, USNA.
67 *Dawn*, 7 January 1950, p. 1.
68 *Dawn*, 10 January 1950, p. 5.
69 *Dawn*, 7 January 1950, p. 1.
70 Ibid.
71 See, for example, Zahir Shah Sherazi, 'Agreement Surfaces Barring Women from Polling in Lower Dir', *Dawn*, 14 May 2013, accessed 14 May 2013, http://dawn.com/2013/05/14/agreement-surfaces-barring-women-from-polling-in-lower-dir.

# 5 Identity politics and nation-building in Pakistan
## The case of Sindhi nationalism

*Sarah Ansari*

An undoubted feature of political life in the Pakistani province of Sindh since independence has been the growth in support for, often competing, so-called ethnic nationalisms. Apart from the emergence of a *muhajir* political identity among the Urdu-speaking inhabitants of the province's towns and cities from the 1980s onwards, the province has witnessed a challenge posed by Sindhi nationalism (like its Bengali and Baluchi counterparts) to the ideological premises on which the state of Pakistan has been based since (or before) 1947. Sindhi nationalism for many people seemed first to hit the headlines in the early 1970s, when, in the wake of Bangladesh's secession, there appeared to be an apparent hardening of the Sindhi nationalist stance. This shift has led some commentators to suggest that it was only once they had been inspired by Bengali nationalism that Sindhi nationalist politicians such as G.M. Syed (1904–95) retrospectively located the roots of their postcolonial discontent in the pre-independence era. In other words, they read history backwards.

However, as this chapter explores, a clear Sindhi sense of identity and sentiment had without question surfaced much earlier, and this played an important role in laying the basis for developments from the 1970s onwards. Events prior to independence were then reinforced by events following Partition, whose cumulative effect was to add weight to Sindhi claims of disadvantage, whether political, economic, or cultural. As a recently published study in Pakistan also argues, the articulation of Sindhi (ethno-)nationalism in the second half of the twentieth century, as much as it represents a response to changes taking place within Sindh during this period, also points to continuities that link post-1947 political trends in the province to their pre-1947 forerunners.[1] Even before independence, there was already awareness of, and debate about, the need to protect Sindhi interests in the face of perceived interference and domination by 'outsider' communities – a theme that has underpinned Sindhi nationalist rhetoric in more recent decades.

One of the main 'historical' factors fuelling the politicisation of a Sindhi identity is the way in which the region, from more or less the time that it was annexed by the British, was administered. Initially Sindh (after just a few years as a separate entity) was attached to the Presidency of Bombay, before it achieved a kind of 'independence' in 1936 when it became a separate province in its own right. With the creation of Pakistan, Sindh remained a separate province (albeit at the 'cost' of losing Karachi to the Federal Centre) until 1955 when it then became part of the One Unit of West Pakistan established that year as a counterbalance to the more populous East Pakistan.[2] By the early 1970s, Sindh's separate status was restored but, by then, with the secession of East Pakistan, and the dominance of the Punjab within what remained of Pakistan consequently further enhanced, the stage was set for Sindhi resentment at the new *status quo* that threatened local, Sindhi, interests. This history in effect helped to reinforce perceptions among groups of politicised Sindhis that their interests have been repeatedly, and persistently, sacrificed to those of others, whether before or after independence, and hence reinforced a politicised sense of Sindhi identity. In many ways, therefore, Sindhi nationalism has been characterised as a 'sons of the soil' movement, with language often, but not always, the key marker of identity.

The following sections accordingly explore the factors involved in the emergence of Sindhi nationalist sentiment both before and after the creation of Pakistan, in order to approach this phenomenon from a deliberately historical perspective. In particular, the broad sweep deployed here emphasises the importance of acknowledging the historical context alongside more contemporary developments when assessing how and why Sindhi nationalism has proved itself to be such an enduring, if less well-known outside the region, feature of the political landscape in this part of South Asia.

## Colonial past

At least some of the roots of Sindhi nationalist sentiment undoubtedly go back to the early years of British rule. The annexation of Sindh by the British in 1843 ushered in a period that eventually witnessed the arrival of growing numbers of settlers from the Punjab in particular. Changes in the socio-economic framework of the region that followed the consolidation of British control sharpened the issue of so-called ethnic identity, albeit now drawn up along British-constructed provincial lines. British rule had a far-reaching impact on Sindh, as it did elsewhere in the subcontinent. New revenue laws, new civil laws, and new government education policies, among other things, all helped to change the complexion of Sindhi society. British policy in Sindh arguably had two main objectives: the consolidation of British rule, and the creation in Sindh of a market for British goods and a source of raw materials as well as revenues. Thus, Sindh, from a British point of view, was useful – first, as the route to the heartland of northern India and, second, as a region with economic potential once the appropriate kind of infrastructure had been set in place.

The conquest of the Punjab in 1849, which followed not long after Sindh's own annexation, had an effect on the relative importance of Sindh in British eyes. One consequence was that officials raised the suggestion that Sindh be absorbed into the Punjab, rather than continue its recently established administrative relationship with distant Bombay Presidency. Sindh, sharing the Indus

Valley with its northern Punjabi neighbour, was regarded by some British officials as the latter's natural outlet and, as a result, the significance of Sindhi to the internal security of the empire increased. In February 1856 Dalhousie proposed elevating Punjab from a 'Chief Commissionership' to the status of a province with its own Lt. Governor and Sindh included within his jurisdiction. There was opposition to this on financial grounds from London, but events of 1857–8 delayed any decision and, although the proposal was revived in 1858 with the idea of producing a fourth Presidency, it failed to materialise.[3] The problems of a mismatch between Sindh and the rest of Bombay Presidency, however, continued to surface from time to time – in particular Sindh's relative isolation from the centre of provincial power led to complaints there that it was neglected in comparison with other parts of the Presidency. And so again periodically the possibility of linking Sindh with the Punjab was raised. In the 1880s, for instance, such plans were rejected, not so much out of any desire to protect Sindhi interests but because, from a British point of view, Sindh provided an excellent training ground for Bombay officials before they were transferred elsewhere. In passing, mention was also made of the fact that the Sindhis themselves – *waderos* and *zamindars* (Muslims) and *amils* (Hindus) – would dislike being 'annexed' by the Punjab, which was the way that they would see the shift.[4] When the debate again resurfaced before the First World War, feelings in Sindh were reported as being strongly opposed to any transfer to the Punjab.[5] Hence, by the early twentieth century, there is clear evidence of Sindhi perceptions of the Punjab being clouded by a sense of resentment, something that officials did not fail to notice.

A large part of the reason for this feeling was related to the second of those two British priorities mentioned earlier: profit. British profitability in the region largely depended on Sindh undergoing important structural changes to bring its largely agricultural economy into line with British requirements, and this set in motion a sequence of developments that directly encouraged increasing numbers of people from the Punjab to settle lower down the Indus Valley. Sindh was steadily drawn over the second half of the nineteenth century into producing cash crops often destined for far-flung export markets. This shift in emphasis was facilitated by the introduction of new, supposedly improved, irrigation systems that regulated more precisely the enormous potential of the river Indus. In many ways, the British set about taming the river at the same time as they metaphorically 'tamed' those living along its banks. For instance, in the 1890s, the British began the Jamrao Canal project which was completed ahead of schedule in 1900.[6]

But such schemes had to be profitable. Local British officials tended towards a rather low opinion of the 'quality' and 'reliability' of the work of Sindhi agriculturalists. Sindhi *zamindars* and *haris*, for all their apparent eagerness to make the most of the new opportunities that improvements to the province's irrigation system offered them, were often described as 'lazy' in official correspondence when compared with their apparently more hard-working, skilled northern – Punjabi – counterparts, and, hence, the British readiness to import Punjabis to carry out this work. While precise figures are hard to come by, records point to large numbers of these economic migrants arriving in the province between 1891 and 1901, and this continued thereafter, with a further pronounced inflow of Punjabi-speakers in the 1920s and 1930s coinciding with the next stage in the extension of Sindh's irrigation system.[7] The construction of the Sukkur Barrage was an enormous undertaking and cost many crores of rupees. It also brought with it severe financial headaches for the authorities, which agonised about how to ensure the scheme's profitability. In the end they concluded that economic viability depended on the sizeable influx of 'more industrious' and 'more skilled' cultivators from further north. As the Barrage moved slowly towards its completion in the early 1930s, officials also commented on the increasing apprehension among Sindhi landlords of an impending 'invasion' of Punjabi peasant proprietors. The same officials were very clear that Sindhis were not going to like any great influx of people from the Punjab, but this was 'inevitable if the Barrage [was] to be paid for'.[8]

It is not surprising, against this backdrop, that, when pressure to establish Sindh as a separate administrative entity in its own right eventually surfaced in the early twentieth century, the campaign from the outset emphasised Sindh's distinct identity. At Congress's annual session of 1913 that was held in Karachi, for instance, demands were made for separation on the grounds of Sindh's distinctive cultural and geographical character, though because the motion at this stage was proposed by a prominent Sindhi Hindu it probably reflected the desire on the part of Sindh's commercial community (largely Hindu) to extricate itself from having to compete with much more powerful Bombay business interests.[9] By the interwar period, however, the arguments were becoming more communal, reflecting the increase in this kind of tension that was taking place in various parts of British India by this time. Sindh, in comparison with other parts of the subcontinent, undoubtedly maintained a better-than-average, 'cleaner', record as far as being tainted by communalism was concerned. However, that debate in the region could not avoid being drawn into wider subcontinental developments was illustrated by the way in which the separation of Sindh was discussed and advocated by those in favour and those against in the late 1920s. Now members of Sindh's various Muslim elites perceived in 'separation' a strategy by which to promote and safeguard their own, locally based, interests. An informal organisation, the Sind Azad Conference, was formed in 1932 to bring together the landed 'aristocracy' and the emergent Muslim middle classes, the two groups who felt their position to be most fragile. The communal tensions that subsequently coloured the campaign stemmed precisely from the way in which local Muslims identified Hindus with 'Bombay' as opposed to 'Sindh': the latter were cast as representative of an outside force whose interests appeared inimical to those of the majority of Sindhi Muslims.

Under these circumstances, Sindh's small but still relatively sizeable, and certainly very influential, Hindu community now on the whole rejected separation, arguing that it did not add up in terms of financial viability, though it is likely that the community was acutely conscious of how far its position would be weakened once it lost the security of the balance of numbers provided by the Presidency's large Hindu majority. British officials in Bombay recognised that separation would be something of a financial relief for the Presidency as a whole, but they also felt nervous at the prospect of 'losing' Sindh, for with it would go the usually cooperative votes of Sindhi representatives on the province's Legislative Council. The central authorities in Delhi were equally wary at the prospect of Sindh becoming a so-called deficit province as a result of the huge debts generated by the construction of the Sukkur Barrage. But following discussions at the London Round Table Conference in the early 1930s, and two official investigations into the financial aspects of separation, the decision in favour of an autonomous Sindh was announced at the end of 1932. Actual separation took place in 1936.

It is important to note that the issue by now had also been taken up successfully at the all-India level by the Muslim League and, hence, in the process had become a political as well as a communal bargaining counter. As a result, the separation of Sindh needs to be seen as the product of longer-term tensions created by the British joining together, in a fairly arbitrary and artificial way, regions that were ethnically and culturally quite distinct from each other, against the more immediate backdrop of the growth of communalised politics in the subcontinent during the interwar years. Importantly, the campaign demonstrated a growing belief among at least some Sindhis that Sindh, together with its Muslim majority, possessed its own particular regional identity, which, in the view of those pressing for separation, had suffered as a result of association with Bombay.[10]

As was the case in relation to the provincial separation campaign, at first the 'outsiders' were seen as local Hindus, but after 1936 resentment also came to be articulated in relation to the growing number of Muslim settlers who were drawn to the province from places such as the Punjab by its attractive agricultural conditions and the lure of government employment. This later hostility was increasingly presented in the form of a distinction drawn between 'Sindhis' and 'non-Sindhis', and was highlighted in the decade that preceded independence by discussion over the employment of non-Sindhis in the newly created provincial services. Time, for instance, was spent in the new Sindh Legislative Assembly debating the definition of a 'native of Sindh' in relation to the eligibility of non-Sindhis to be selected for government jobs. Questions were often raised about the recruitment of non-Sindhis into the services when Sindhis were themselves available for the jobs. For some of the politicians involved in these debates, the suggestion of a qualifying criterion of three years residence in Sindh was not sufficient: instead, they insisted on a prospective employee being someone 'who is born and resides in Sind'. Such a restriction, it was felt, would not only prevent outsiders from coming in, but also, in the short term at least, very often applying to the children of such people born elsewhere.[11] Initially, the calls for restricting opportunities for outsiders to work in Sindh were applied widely to people from other parts of Bombay Presidency including present-day Gujarat and Maharashtra, as well as places further away such as Madras. However, as time passed, it emerged that the Punjab was the main focus for this sentiment.[12] The issue finally entered the political debate of the mid-1940s more directly when G.M. Syed (the eventual 'Godfather' of Sindhi nationalism), following his expulsion from the Muslim League in January 1946, argued in favour of Sindh becoming a sovereign nation in its own right. Indeed, his group of supporters were vehemently opposed to the province having anything to do with the Punjab in particular: in their minds, Sindhis would never 'buckle down' under Punjabi dominance.[13]

Thus, even before independence had actually taken place, there were signs of potential trouble ahead. Despite their apparently enthusiastic support for the notion of Pakistan, many Sindhi Muslims were already suspicious about what exactly their province's place would be in the new, envisaged, state. For instance, a fair degree of bitterness was aroused by the end of July 1947 in relation to the question of Sindh's representation in both the Pakistan Constituent Assembly (PCA) and the Cabinet. Containing a population of only around 4.5 million out of a total projected Pakistani population of approximately 70 million, Sindh had been allocated just four of the PCA's 69 members.[14] Many Sindhis, however, viewed this share as far too low, particularly bearing in mind, as they saw it, their province's crucial role in kick-starting the Pakistan movement. Whether or not the claim of Karachi's *Daily Gazette* that 'Sind's demand for parity of representation with other provinces constituting the Dominion of Pakistan [had] already become a popular cry in the remotest villages' should be regarded as journalistic exaggeration, apprehension existed among politicised Sindhi Muslims at this time.[15] Similarly, the prospect of a single seat in the Cabinet, which was later adjudged to have been 'taken away' when the overall number of Cabinet ministers was reduced from nine to seven, confirmed many doubts about the new, forthcoming, inter-provincial power-sharing arrangements.[16] Newspaper articles of the time thus reflected a widespread concern that Sindh would be swamped by an inflow of people from other parts of the new state, which would result in the province's interests being reduced to 'an insignificant position'.[17]

## Postcolonial present

It was against this backdrop that Sindhi nationalist sentiment took more institutional form in the post-1947 period, fuelled by a combination of four main 'ingredients': hence, as Das argues, overlapping demographic, economic, cultural, and political factors must be taken into account when seeking to understand how and why Sindhi nationalism developed in the new state of Pakistan.[18]

Demographically, this sentiment was affected by the huge influx of refugees from India and migrants from other parts of what had become Pakistan. Apart from the hundreds of thousands of Urdu-speakers (around 20 per cent of the province's population by the mid-1950s), the continued long-term migration of Punjabi-speakers to different parts of the province caused grave misgivings in certain circles about the growing numbers of other people in Sindh. By the early

1980s, over 50 per cent of the inhabitants of the city of Karachi were Urdu-speaking with over 13 per cent Punjabi speakers. In rural areas, during the Ayub period, the allocation of lands to non-Sindhis, and Punjabis in particular, accelerated. In economic terms, there seemed to be, to many Sindhis, a process of deprivation taking place, with frustration at developments both in urban and rural sectors of the economy, and complaints of 'a calculated perpetuation of regional inequalities'. Third, Sindhis also experienced what many regarded as attempts on the part of the central Pakistani government to undermine Sindh's cultural identity. In particular they saw their language – Sindhi – being challenged by the country's national language, Urdu. 'Urduisation' policies seemed to confirm the threats posed to Sindhi culture, and its second-class status in official eyes. Such has been the extent of the damage inflicted that some commentators have spoken in terms of a 'cultural genocide' having been perpetrated by the federal authorities. Finally, there has been the political dimension. Political decisions right from the early years of Pakistan's existence helped to reinforce Sindhi perceptions that they were on the losing end of the new arrangements as these unfolded after 1947. Sindh's loss of Karachi in 1948 when the city became federal territory, the introduction of One Unit in 1955, martial law in 1958, all appeared in many Sindhi eyes as proof of the extent of outsider ambitions.[19]

The catalogue of grievances steadily grew, ranging from a Sindhi tendency to attribute what few incidents of communal violence that had taken place in Sindh to the presence of Punjabis, to (perhaps understandable) resentment at Sindh being saddled with a Punjabi governor from time to time, to the 'usual tolerant contempt' which they perceived Punjabis (but also Urdu-speakers) exhibited whenever issues connected with Sindh arose. At an official level, there were complaints that Sindh was unfairly treated by the central authorities, for example in the allocation of loans for development projects, as compared with other provinces, especially the Punjab. Sindhi politicians called on 'new Sindhis' (as post-1947 settlers in Sind were often labelled at the time) to assimilate themselves as quickly as possible into the rest of the population 'for they could not expect discrimination in their favour against "old Sindhis"'. In various ways, how power was distributed – what seemed like the growing possession of it by non-Sindhis and its perceived loss by Sindhis – prevented, during the decades following independence, the kind of meaningful blurring of identities that might have produced a working composite alternative in the region.

It is important to explore in greater detail some of the developments taking place during those early years. Once 14 August 1947 had actually passed, and the traffic of 'refugees' between Pakistan and India had begun in earnest, the impact of the demographic upheaval and the contractions involved in it hit Sindhis with force. On the one hand, Sindhi Muslim politicians could hardly fail to be supportive of refugees arriving from India, bearing in mind the prevailing political climate. On the other hand, though, they did not wish to lose those non-Muslim Sindhis who were intent on leaving. Fears were expressed about the long-term consequences of so many of these Sindhis being replaced by outsiders who had a far less proven degree of attachment to the province. Thus, during the later months of 1947 a discernable shift took place in the way that the Sindh provincial ministry, headed by M.A. Khuhro (1901–80, Chief Minister 1947–8, 1951, 1954–5) viewed its responsibilities to these two sets of refugees. It moved to an apparently more conciliatory position vis-à-vis departing non-Muslims while, at the same time, adopting a more confrontational stance towards the central Pakistani authorities over the issue of refugees entering the province. As Khuhro and his colleagues took steps to retard the outflow of non-Muslims, the central government recognised that his ministry's stance was increasingly coming into conflict with its own desire to admit the maximum possible number of Muslim refugees into the province so as to relieve the pressure that was mounting in the Punjab. A special committee was set up to examine the whole issue of refugee resettlement in Sindh, but almost immediately Khuhro announced that his ministry had reached a number of important decisions concerning the treatment of refugees: namely, their numbers would be limited and any 'excess persons' would be removed from the city of Karachi in particular. Pro-refugee newspapers, not surprisingly, condemned the 'provincialism' of the Sindhi authorities, while the Sindh Muslim Students Federation reiterated its call for a 'Sindh for Sindhis'.[20]

Sindhi 'fears' about the province's relationship with the rest of Pakistan were further reinforced during this period by the separation of Karachi from the rest of Sindh that was proposed by the central government early in 1948. Sindhi politicians complained bitterly that their province stood to be robbed – effectively beheaded – and the Sindh Muslim League Council condemned the move.[21] To a large extent, Sindh's financial future, as a small province with limited resources, depended on how adequately the centre would compensate it for the loss of the city and its port income, but this was something that a large number of Sindhi politicians did not believe was being satisfactorily addressed. Eventually, however, in May 1948 the Constituent Assembly voted through the necessary resolution to make Karachi the country's permanent capital as well as a federally administered area.[22]

This 'battle for Karachi', with its negative fall-out as far as centre-province relations were concerned, took place at the same time as another issue gained momentum that would complicate, and sour, centre-province relations, namely, whether and if so how to absorb the large number of 'overspill' refugees from the Punjab into the Sindhi countryside. By January 1948 there were still some 900,000 refugees in camps in the Punjab, including some quarter of a million living in the open air. Relocating some of them to Sindh seemed like an obvious solution, particularly since the vast majority of refugees already there had headed for towns and cities, apparently leaving space in the countryside for more. Action, despite the bitterness of the cold season, was delayed by the initial reluctance of the refugees themselves to be uprooted again so soon. Many of them opposed the prospect of reassembling into foot convoys to start the lengthy journey southwards. The move was also delayed, though, by the reluctance of Khuhro's ministry to accept more than 100,000 newcomers, around half of what the central government expected Sindh to take.[23] Khuhro as a consequence was blamed for stirring up hatred for refugees among 'the public of Sindh', and the Minister for Refugee Rehabilitation warned against the 'virus of provincialism' that, he argued, went against both the teachings of Islam and the principles on which Pakistan had been fought, and which would destroy the very foundations of the newly born state if it were allowed to operate unchecked.[24]

By April 1948 conditions in the Punjab camps had deteriorated further, with outbreaks of cholera increasing tension there. The Punjab's provincial authorities seemed unable to deal with the potential consequences of this, and so the central authorities stepped in to oblige other provinces, such as Sindh, to take a greater share of the migrants involved. Khuhro was now no longer in charge, and so the central authorities were confident that they could rely instead on the new Sindhi premier, Pir Illahi Baksh, who had undertaken to follow a path of greater cooperation with the centre, to deliver the goods. Even so, the prime minister, Liaquat Ali Khan (1895–1951, Prime Minister 1947–51), hammered the message home in his speeches at this time when he repeatedly highlighted the need to 'replace provincialism by a spirit of Islamic unity, sacrifice and discipline ... and loyalty to [in other words, cooperation with] the new Government of Pakistan'.[25] All the same, the Sindh government was reluctant to get the convoys moving, fully conscious of the negative response that they would provoke.

By late August, the central government could afford to wait no longer. Tension in the Punjabi camps had started to run dangerously high. So on 27 August it declared a state of emergency, giving itself the authority to resettle large numbers of refugees in Sindh – 200,000 rather than the 100,000 previously discussed limit; 6,000 refugees a day were subsequently despatched to Sindh. Their arrival there unfortunately coincided with the aftermath of serious floods that was already adding to the number of homeless people locally and handicapping agricultural production, together with an upsurge in malaria cases with which the local authorities were already finding it hard to cope.

The Sindh government accordingly found itself in an uncomfortable predicament. Serious refugee discontent in the Punjab had demonstrated clearly the importance of securing the goodwill of newcomers if only to avoid any repetition of that instability in Sindh. Yet effective rehabilitation on such a massive scale was an extremely costly business and the Sindh government regarded the Rs.10 lakhs (Rs.1 million) offered by the central government as inadequate financial assistance. Accordingly, the official reaction in Sindh was mixed, even without Khuhro at the helm. By the end of October the Punjab camps had been cleared, although there remained apparently many refugees scattered in villages who were supposed to be resettled in Sindh. Eventually more than 200,000 were transferred, but the costs in terms of 'ethnic harmony' were high. Tensions between the various communities in Sindh increased, with refugee spokesmen critical of the lack of official support, and Sindhi tenant farmers clashing with refugees who represented competition for agricultural resources. Newspapers of the period regularly included reports of incidents, which ranged from physical confrontations between cultivators to fairly violent verbal reactions to the decisions of the central authorities that affected Sindh.[26]

Disagreements between centre and province over refugee rehabilitation continued in Sindh from the late 1940s well into the 1950s. Even the eventual seepage back to the Punjab of a proportion of the overspill refugees managed to generate ill-feeling: by the middle of 1949 some 30,000–40,000 had returned north, citing problems concerning the allotment of land as well as the poor state of relations between themselves and local people. The fact that many took with them the *taccavi* funds that they had been loaned, however, was seized upon by the Sindhi press, which regarded this as a serious financial loss inflicted on the resources of the province. Clashes between locals and newcomers were a feature of the time, to the extent that the Central Minister for Refugees and Rehabilitation at the time, Khwaja Shahabuddin (1898–1977), called on the press to make a greater effort to promote better relations between refugees and Sindhis. Indeed, it was decided that the press would deliberately play down reports of any clashes and avoid sensational headlines. At the same time, the central government distributed a free fortnightly journal, *Nai Zindagi* (New Life) that aimed to educate refugees in the new way of life they were to lead in the province as well as to help local people to understand their new neighbours better.[27] In the early 1950s, the issue dragged on, thanks to fresh waves of migrants who arrived from India during this period. Sindh once again found itself with overflowing refugee camps, and the responsibility for financing the maintenance of these refugees was effectively tossed like a 'hot potato' between the two sets of authorities. The provincial government, for instance, maintained that a substantial deficit in its budget precluded it from bearing any additional expenditure, while the central government argued adamantly that the cost of this maintenance had to be shared equally. Interestingly, there is more evidence, by this stage, of refugees blaming both sets of authorities for trying to evade their respective responsibilities for dealing with the crisis.[28]

As these developments indicate, Partition-related migration thus played a key part in establishing a particular pattern of relations between the province and the centre that was characterised by bouts of tension and simmering disagreement from Pakistan's earliest days. This tension was further increased by subsequent political developments, not least the introduction of One Unit, which has to be seen as an attempt not only to deal with difficulties in the political relationship between East and West Pakistan but also as an attempt to paper over cracks within the country's fragmented western wing, cracks that had been widened in part by issues such as the refugee problem. What is ironic, but perhaps not so strange when one considers the extremely factional nature of Sindhi provincial politics, is that the centre secured the support of the Sindh Legislative Assembly for One Unit thanks to the efforts of Khuhro, who by then was once more the Sindhi premier.[29] In the eyes of his critics, the former champion of Sindh's interests immediately after Partition had become the chief culprit responsible for its loss of independent provincial status.

However Khuhro, for many, was no Sindhi nationalist. Rather, Sindhi nationalism – in its organised form, as opposed to 'popular' sentiment or manipulated politicking – was epitomised for virtually the whole of the second half of the twentieth century by the stand taken by the well-known Sindhi politician, G.M. Syed, who having become disillusioned with the Muslim League before Partition joined the Sind Awami Party in 1950. In September 1953, the Sindh Legislative Assembly debated the issue of Centre-Sindh relations. Leader of the opposition Syed took the opportunity to argue that Sindh constituted a distinct nationality and deserved equal treatment with 'other nationalities' in Pakistan. He accordingly criticised the Centre for what he regarded as its paternalistic attitude towards the province. The same year Syed consolidated Sindhi nationalist groups to form the Sindh Awami Mahaz (SAM), spurred on by the likelihood of One Unit (and hence, from a Sindhi perspective, the reinforcement of Punjabi dominance) looming.[30] The programme of the SAM, later renamed the 'Sindh United Front', called for the recognition of the de facto existence of separate nationalities in Pakistan. It demanded full provincial autonomy, leaving only defence, foreign affairs, and currency with the centre, and also insisted on the re-merger of Karachi with Sindh. It was the first party to oppose the One Unit scheme, eventually introduced in 1955 (it had been talked about from as early as 1948), and together with other regional parties formed the anti-One Unit Pakistan National Party. In the mid-1960s, Syed renamed his front 'Jiye Sind', thus providing Sindhi ethno-nationalism with a somewhat sharper focus, even though it still represented an umbrella organisation, covering a wide spectrum of interests from cultural forums to leftist political bodies.

However, two decades further on, in 1972, the stakes were raised when G.M. Syed established the 'Jiye Sindh Mahaz', which, via its student wing ('Jiye Sindh Student Federation' – JSSF), developed strong support in the province's campuses and educational institutions. Disillusioned by attempts to work within Pakistan's political system, and undoubtedly emboldened by recent events in East Pakistan that had resulted in the emergence of Bangladesh, its primary aim was now to achieve the independence of Sindh from Pakistan. The movement, which demanded the creation of a 'Sindhu Desh' (or 'Sindhi Nation' – Land of the River Indus), enjoyed a reasonably strong base of support in rural areas, as well as among students and the fast-emerging Sindhi middle classes. Sindhu Desh's fundamental demands[31] included the following:

- Recognition of the principles of secularism, socialism, democracy, and nationalism.
- Redistribution of agricultural land from non-Sindhis to Sindhis.
- Control of trade, commerce, banks, insurance, and government agencies by Sindhi-speakers and people settled permanently in Sindh.
- Checking of immigration to Sindh and expulsion of all those resisting absorption into Sindhi society.
- Quotas for Sindhis in government jobs.
- Recognition of Sindhi as the sole national and official language and the cancellation of citizenship for those having no knowledge of the language.

Other stipulations covered:

- Prohibition of the institutions of pirdom and tribal headmanship.
- Guaranteed strict legal separation between religion and state.
- Nationalisation of all means of production.
- Provision of a greater role for women in public life on a footing of equality with men.
- Promotion of friendship with India and the Soviet Union, among other states.

Of course, 1972 was the year when the Sindh legislature, under the Chief Ministership of Mumtaz Ali Bhutto (b. 1933, Chief Minister 1972–3), enacted the Teaching, Promotion and Use of Sindhi Language Bill which accorded Sindhi the status of the province's sole official language, with both Sindhi and Urdu compulsory subjects for students from class IV to class XII, and hence the politics of this period were very much tied up with language issues (that contributed to the eventual emergence of a so-called *muhajir* ethnicity in the towns and cities of the province too). Karachi was restored as the capital of Sindh and many lower and middle-level jobs in the government were made available to Sindhis. Government employees in Sindh of whatever 'ethnic' background were now required to learn Sindhi within a stipulated period. To undo the under-representation of Sindhis in provincial education and civil service, a new quota system was also introduced that extended to educational and professional institutions. The nationalisation of major industrial concerns also meant the expansion of ethnic quota system as jobs which were previously in the private sector were subject now to the quota system.[32]

Urdu-speakers in cities such as Karachi and Hyderabad protested vehemently in defence of their linguistic interests and took to the streets, and the province witnessed language riots in July of that year, during which Jiye Sindh Mahaz activists made bonfires of Urdu newspapers and defiled pictures of the national – Urdu-writing – poet, Iqbal. *Sindh Sujag Jathas* (Sindh Awakening Squads) were formed to carry the message of Jiye Sindh to the rural areas. Parallels were frequently drawn between Sindh's position and the recent events in East Bengal that had resulted in the drama of Bangladesh's bitterly fought secession. To quote a later (1989) interview with Syed himself:

> The reason was the continuous struggle to get the rights of Sindhis accepted by the authorities. When they were neglected, we went on escalating our demands.... We said Sindhis were a separate nation. We insisted that we have a separate culture. We were not given proper rights. So we demanded the right of self-determination. So from the idea of Jiye Sindh, we have reached the conclusion that without the breaking up of Pakistan and the formation of Sindh as an independent country and a member of the United Nations, no other solution is possible.[33]

However, Syed's organisations were not the sole spokespeople for Sindhi interests and rights. Alongside the Jiye Sindh Mahaz were organisations such as Rasool Bux Paleejo's 'Sindh Awami Tehreek' but, unlike Syed who was prepared to postpone socio-economic reconstruction until political change had taken place, Paleejo combined arguing for greater Sindhi autonomy with land reform, and therefore proposed a more radical interpretation of the nationalist message.

Sindhi (ethno-)nationalist sentiment was boosted still further by the political developments of the late 1970s and 1980s. Another military coup that brought General Zia-ul-Haq (1924–88, President 1977–88) to power in 1977 reinforced perceptions of Punjabi-*Muhajir* dominance, and turned Zulfikar Ali Bhutto (1928–79, President 1971–3, Prime Minister 1973–7) into a martyr for many living in the province. Added to this were the preferential quotas in favour of Punjabis and Pathans that were introduced within the central bureaucracy during this period. Many Sindhis recognised that the new regime promised little in terms of tangible gains for them, and hence the province-wide support for the Movement for the Restoration of Democracy (MRD) that gripped rural areas in 1983 under the Pakistan People's Party's (PPP) banner of demanding national elections be held as per the 1973 constitution. As many as 45,000 troops were mobilised by the military authorities and up to 600 protesters died over subsequent months, with large numbers of 'political prisoners' held in the province's jails. Army camps for Punjabi soldiers were described by critics as 'colonial outposts in defence of distant interests'. Sindhi nationalist organisations were driven underground. It is important to note that G.M. Syed himself (he was under house arrest from 1973 to 1987) distanced himself from the MRD on grounds that it was intended to reinstate the Bhutto 'dynasty' rather than advance Sindh's cause per se. But, with or without Syed's endorsement, the MRD period helped to reinforce the perception among many Sindhis that their province could not fare well in Pakistan as it was then constituted.[34]

The 'fate' of Sindhi nationalism since the 1970s, however, has without doubt also been complicated by the role of the Pakistan Peoples Party (PPP) in Pakistani political life. An all-Pakistan party that only comes to power when it can gain sufficient support in the Punjab, it is nonetheless closely associated with the province, thanks to the Sindhi origins of its national leaders, first Zulfikar Ali Bhutto, more recently his daughter Benazir (1953–2007, Prime Minister 1988–90, 1993–6) and Asif Ali Zadari (b. 1955, President 2008–13). Indeed, electoral support for the PPP among Sindhi voters seems to have made it hard for Sindhi nationalist parties to attain the level of support among voters for which they aim in all-important 'hard' numerical terms. But this should not detract from the fact that there is an underlying sympathy among many Sindhis for organisations that they regard are challenging what appears to be the 'second-class status' of the province, its inhabitants, its language, and its culture, in present-day Pakistan. Electoral support for Sindhi nationalist parties may well have been greater without the PPP 'distracting' voters from more clear-cut, nationalist, alternatives. And periodic alliances between the PPP and *Muhajir* parties such as the MQM have alienated a certain amount of support, such as from Benazir Bhutto in the late 1980s. As we all know, the late 1980s and early 1990s witnessed high levels of ethnic tension and violence, not just involving Sindhis and *Muhajirs* but also Punjabis and Pathans, in cities such as Karachi and Hyderabad. This polarisation led to a huge number of deaths, with parts of the province becoming virtual no-go areas.

G.M. Syed lived to a very ripe old age. In January 1992, his eighty-ninth birthday was celebrated in Karachi's Nishtar Park. At that rally, around 7,000 Jeay Sindh activists waved party flags and chanted along the following lines: 'G.M. Syed is our leader, Sindhu Desh is our destiny.' Work by one of Sindh's leading nationalist poets, Shaikh Ayaz, was recited with passion. Suggestions that a separate province be created for *Muhajirs* out of southern Sindh received short shrift. While the central government clamped down hard, Sindhi nationalists made political capital out of the strong-arm tactics pursued by the authorities – G.M. Syed himself was placed back under house arrest where, despite the coming to power of a PPP government in 1993, he died in 1995.[35]

Recent years have seen the picture become even more complicated, with alliances and the breaking of alliances, further intervention in Pakistan's political life by the military, and the current return to civilian democracy. After a PPP-led federal government once again in power (and an MQM led coalition in control of Karachi), but with the Muslim League return to power in June 2013 Sindhi nationalism faces the challenge of working out where it fits into the political environment both at a provincial and at a national level. At present, it appears fragmented and, thus, on the back foot. Syed's Jiye Sind movement is split – his grandson, Jalal Shah, recently resurrected his father's Sindh United Front party of the early 1950s. Other organisations have emerged. The Sindh Democratic Forum is one such example. Drawing on a constituency of support from among the Sindhi-speaking educated and urbanised middle classes, it is a self-styled civil society pressure group which, for instance, spoke out vehemently against PPP-MQM attempts to form a government of 'consensus' in Sindh in 2008.[36] Indeed, much Sindhi nationalist rhetoric today now focuses on the environmental damage being done to the province by the long-term consequences of irrigation schemes and development projects alike. 'Green issues', which mobilise rural Sindhis in defence of precious local resources, may be deflecting attention away from more traditional political grievances. Sindhi nationalist sentiment therefore has become a more complex phenomenon in recent years.

Sindhi nationalism in the decades since independence has clearly had much in common with other 'sons of the soil' movements that have emerged in different parts of South Asia in the post-independence era. In this respect, it forms part of a wider pattern of ethno-nationalist responses to the changing circumstances of these years. As political scientists have emphasised, the ethnic conflict that has become particularly prevalent since the 1980s contradicts commonly shared assumptions that ethnicity, like religion, was something which belonged to an earlier stage of transition, something that, in effect, was bound to disappear as societies were reconfigured into 'modern' nation-states. Clearly the case of Sindhi nationalism, like other so-called ethnic nationalisms of the late twentieth century, has not followed this model of supposed 'progress'. Rather, incomplete processes of modernisation and state-building, as witnessed in Pakistan, have produced circumstances that have encouraged the emergence, rather than the submergence, of political movements coalescing around ethnic identities and concerns. The 'tight fit' between country and nation that the West thought that it could bequeath to other parts of the world at the time of independence has proved elusive for many states.

The relationship of ethnicity with politics, of course, fluctuates – its appeal as a marker of political identity, as many case studies testify, does not remain constant, but is determined to a great extent by levels of material well-being and security (the all-important 'feel good factor') that members of a particular community collectively enjoy. In the case of Sindhi nationalism, there is one aspect that makes it stand out a little from the crowd – that is, the way in which it crosses the relatively new national borders that were drawn up thanks to Partition. Unlike the majority of the subcontinent's other ethno-nationalisms, the migration of Sindhi Hindus to what had become India in 1947 means that there exists a constituency of support for Sindhi nationalist rhetoric outside Pakistan but which regards just as fondly as its Pakistani counterparts the province's distinctive cultural and language heritage. The worldwide diasporic Sindhi community also plays its part in keeping attention focused on things Sindhi. And even if Sindhi nationalist organisations do not make the impact that they would desire in electoral terms, as a cultural phenomenon Sindhi nationalist sentiment has undeniably a well-entrenched place in the life of this part of Pakistan.

## Notes

1 Tanvir Ahmad Tahir, *Political Dynamics of Sindh 1947–1977* (Karachi: University of Karachi, Pakistan Study Centre, 2010).
2 Ian Talbot, *Pakistan: A Modern History* (London: Hurst, 1998), pp. 126–7.
3 Sahib Khan Channo, 'The Movement for the Separation of Sind from the Bombay Presidency, 1847–1937', PhD Dissertation, University of Sind, 1983, p. 34.
4 Letter No. 70, 30 March 1888, MSS EUR E 243/51, IOR, British Library.
5 See Channo, 'The Movement for the Separation of Sind from the Bombay Presidency, 1847–1937'.
6 While undoubtedly the Jamrao Canal system was the most ambitious project undertaken by the British thus far in Sindh, Cheesman has pointed out how in practice it damaged the workings of other canals, which in turn reduced the full impact of the scheme. See David Cheesman, *Landed Power and Rural Indebtedness in Colonial Sind 1865–1901* (London: Curzon Press, 1997), p. 32.
7 The increase in people with a Punjabi background can be gleaned from the census reports of the period. Between 1891 and 1901 Sindh's rural population rose by over 850,000, and while some of this increase can be attributed to incorrect classifications in the 1891 census, a large part related to the development of irrigation resources and the arrival of people from the north. Judging from later census reports, a large proportion of those people who were born outside Sindh hailed from the Punjab, and their numbers grew from the 1920s onwards, see Government of India, *Census of India*, Vol. 2, 1921.
8 Sir Leslie Wilson to Lord Birkenhead, 11 February 1925, MSS EUR D 703/14, pp. 17–18, IOR, British Library.

9 Muhammd Irfan, 'A Brief History of the Movement of the Separation of Sind', *Al Wahid* (Karachi), Special No. 1 (April 1936), p. 52.
10 Hamida Khuhro, *Documents on the Separation of Sind from the Bombay Presidency* (Islamabad: Islamic University, 1982).
11 *The Sind Legislative Assembly Debates*, Official Report, 2, 8 (11 August 1937).
12 Ian Talbot, *Provincial Politics and the Pakistan Movement: The Growth of the Muslim League in North-West and North-East India, 1937–47* (Karachi: Oxford University Press, 1988), p. 55.
13 Sarah Ansari, *Life after Partition: Migration, Community and Strife in Sindh, 1947–1962* (Karachi: Oxford University Press, 2005), pp. 37–9.
14 Despatch 61, 29 July 1947, 845.00/7–2947, United States National Archives.
15 *Daily Gazette* (Karachi), 5 August 1947, cited in Despatch 77, 8 August 1947, 845F.01/8–847, United States National Archives.
16 Despatch 77, 8 August 1947, 845F.01/8–847, United States National Archives.
17 'Sind's Place in Pakistan', *Daily Gazette* (Karachi), 8 August 1947.
18 Suranjan Das, *Kashmir and Sindh: Nation-Building, Ethnicity and Regional Politics in South Asia* (London: Anthem Press, 2001), pp. 103–73.
19 See Das, *Kashmir and Sindh*, pp. 103–73, for more detailed discussion.
20 See Ansari, *Life after Partition*, Chapter 3, pp. 46–73.
21 *Dawn* (Karachi), 10 February 1948.
22 UK High Commission Opdom 42, 20–26 May 1948, L/WS/1/1599, IOR, British Library. For further discussion of the separation of Karachi from M.A. Khuhro's perspective, see H. Khuhro, *M.A. Khuhro: A Life of Courage in Politics* (Karachi: Oxford University Press, 1999), Chapter 18.
23 Sarah Ansari, 'Partition, Migration and Refugees: Responses to the Arrival of *Muhajir*s in Sind during 1947–48', *South Asia*, 17, Special Issue (1995), pp. 95–108.
24 *Dawn* (Karachi), 24 February 1948.
25 UK High Commission Opdom 46 (June 1948), L/WS/1/1599, IOR, British Library.
26 UK High Commission Opdom 88, 29 October–4 November 1948, L/WS/1/1599, IOR, British Library.
27 'Third Year of Refugee Problem', Despatch 295, NND 842909, United States National Archives.
28 See Ansari, *Life After Partition*, Chapter 4.
29 Review, 2–15 December 1954, DO 35/5322, UK National Archives.
30 Sobho Gianchandani explained this transition in an interview with *Newsline*:

> Bhutto had wanted to join the Awami Party. G.M. Syed told me a joke regarding this: 'One day, Bhutto came to my residence and said, "Shah Sahib, I want to join your party." Jokingly, I said to him, "Do you know ours is a party of rebels?" Bhutto replied, I know. Comrade Hyder Bux Jatoi interrupted us and asked Bhutto "Have you taken your father's permission? A Khan Bahadur's son cannot become a member of a rebel party." Bhutto shouted back, "Revolution is not the monopoly of Hyder Bux Jatoi! I am also a revolutionary." Hyder Bux Jatoi persisted. Bhutto spoke to Shah Nawaz Bhutto via telephone. Meanwhile, Iskander Mirza contacted Shah Nawaz Bhutto and told him, "I have planned a great career for your son Zulfiqar, tell him not to join the rebels." Consequently, the next day Bhutto came and submitted his resignation, saying he didn't want to be a rebel. "I told you so," shouted Hyder Bux Jatoi.'
> http://iaoj.wordpress.com/2011/01/13/g-m-syed/#more-10799 (accessed 30 October 2012)

31 G.M. Syed's *A Nation in Chains*, first published in 1974, encapsulated this thesis for a separate homeland for Sindhis by presenting the social, political, economical, and philosophical arguments in support of the formation of 'Sindhudesh'. See www.

sindhudesh.com/gmsyed/nation/saeen-book5.htm (accessed 30 October 2012). These aims were then later restated in Syed's 1985 *A Case for Sindhu Desh*, in which he called for the creation of a separate Sindhu Desh.
32 Talbot, *Pakistan*, pp. 220–1.
33 See *Dawn*, 9 December 2009, www.safhr.org/index.php?option=com_content&view=article&id=73&Itemid=374&limitstart=18 (accessed 30 October 2012).
34 Talbot, *Pakistan*, pp. 252–4.
35 See Das, *Kashmir and Sindh*, pp. 103–73.
36 'SDF Policy Statement on PPP-MQM Talks', posted 29 February 2008, http://groups.yahoo.com/group/Writers_Forum/message/32185 (accessed 30 October 2012).

# 6 Understanding the insurgency in Balochistan[1]

*Yunas Samad*

The management and incorporation of ethno-national identities in Pakistan is a problem that has been highly challenging in Balochistan. The state was merged into the federation to become its largest province with the smallest population and it has been the site of periodic resistance and overt conflict over the last 60 years. With the killing of Akbar Bugti[2] in 2006 by the military, the province became politically polarised and has descended into a new cycle of bombings, abductions, and murders. This has rekindled separatist demands, alienated the majority of the Baloch political leadership from the centre, and the rebellion has resulted in a major security operation, which is raising serious questions around human rights. Pitting the security forces against the Baloch people threatens to derail major development projects and increase instability in the country as a whole. The contours of the insurgency, however, are different from previous rebellions in the province such as those of the 1970s, which were triggered by the dismissal of the inter-ethnic coalition represented by National Awami Party. While the conflict then was Baloch centred, led mainly by the Marri tribe, it was primarily between the rebels and the army. This time it is a broader Baloch rebellion that is spread throughout the province, with increasing hostility to Pukhtun and Punjabi residents and sectarian violence entering the equation. This chapter will only consider the Baloch dimension of the conflict, as it is the main driver of the conflict.

Akbar Bugti repeatedly quarrelled with Islamabad over provincial autonomy, construction of Gwadar Port and the terms on which Balochistan's mineral wealth, in particular gas, was extracted. The Bugti tribes' importance is amplified by their location as the inhospitable, barren and hilly Bugti district is home to the largest gas fields in Pakistan and the Sui Gas plant supplies nearly 40 per cent of Pakistan's gas production. However despite the area's mineral wealth the Bugti district is the most impoverished locality in Pakistan.[3] With these tensions simmering in the background, since 2000 there have been attempts by the ruling party to consult with the Baloch leadership, and Pervez Musharraf, President of Pakistan from June 2001 until August 2008, relented and sent senior members of the Pakistan Muslim League to negotiate with Akbar Bugti. As a result, Senator Mushahid Hussain, Chairman of the Senate Sub-Committee on Balochistan, was able to produce a number of recommendations on various contentious issues that concerned the province.

However, events on the ground overtook the Senate Sub-Committee recommendations. In December 2005 there were a series of rocket attacks on the security forces. Musharraf was targeted and the Inspector General of the Frontier Corps, Major General Shujaat Zamir Dar, and Divisional Inspector, General Brigadier Salim Nawaz, were both injured in Kohlu. Taking the attack personally, Musharraf rejected any political compromise and turned to Military Intelligence who advised him to crush the opposition. On 27 August 2006 Akbar Bugti was killed in his hideout in the Bambore Mountains along with 60 people. Originally Musharraf claimed that he was tracked by his satellite phone and bombed from the air. Later the story was changed and it was claimed that commandos from the Special Services Group pounded a cave in which he had been hiding, resulting in the 79-year-old invalid being killed by rubble. The body was buried in a sealed coffin and no family member was allowed to see or verify the body at the funeral.[4] The army justified the use of force in the name of the 'War on Terror', with Western allies turning a blind eye as Musharraf had been mirroring their own tactics of targeted killings and renditions. Many defenders of human rights considered this action to be an extra-judicial execution[5] and it caused outrage among the Pakistani political class. They unanimously opposed the killing, and it created a furore in Balochistan and fanned the fires of the insurgency, which expanded from attacks and bombings of government installations and pipelines, to attacks against Punjabi settlers and the security agencies.[6]

Again, a military solution was being employed for a political problem in Balochistan. In the Marri Bugti areas, the army launched major security operations resulting in 200,000 Internally Displaced Persons of which 20,000–30,000 took refuge in Afghanistan.[7] The security establishment – led by Military Intelligence, along with Inter-Services Intelligence, the Intelligence Bureau, and supported by the Frontier Corps, police, levies, and death squads – attempted to brutally crush the insurgency and operated a campaign of abductions and detentions, as well as torture and extra-judicial executions. The modus operandi appears to be that individuals are rounded up by the security agencies and held in secret detention centres located on cantonments.[8] In effect, they 'disappear' and in some case their dead bodies are later found dumped by the roadside. Collaborating with the security forces were vigilante groups. The disappearances and 'kill and dump' cases tarnished the image of the intelligence agencies: as an alternative strategy they formed armed militias to abduct and kill activists who demanded independence. The Tehreek-e-Nefaz-e-Aman Balochistan is alleged to be the armed wing of the United Front of Balochistan, a political party headed by the brother of the former chief minister, Siraj Raisani.[9]

The exact number of disappearances conducted by the security forces in the province is contested and precise figures are not known. Baloch nationalists claim that the figure runs into the thousands whereas the Balochistan provincial authorities on a number of occasions have cited the figure of 1,000 enforced disappearances. The Federal Interior Ministry states that 1,102 Baloch were abducted and disappeared during General Musharraf's presidency that ended in August 2008. The Human Rights Commission of Pakistan verified 169 cases in the period 2005 to January 2011 and Human Rights Watch identified 49 cases in the period 2009–10.[10] The Centre for Research and Security Studies, an independent non-profit think tank in Islamabad, examined data from various sources, collated it longitudinally, and inferred that there was a significant increase in disappearances from 2010 and that there was a noticeable spike in disappearances in 2011. Disappearances continued into 2013 and 18 missing persons cases were reported to the Human Rights Commission of Pakistan. However many others refused to report their missing relatives fearing that they would be killed. The Supreme Court had taken *suo moto* action after the discovery of around 100 bodies in shallow graves in Khuzdar. It is believed that these may be the remains of missing people who had been killed while in detention. These cases coupled with the discovery of dead bodies, indicate that the situation has not improved.[11] Most disappearances occurred in Quetta, Dera Bugti, Gwadar, and Karachi. There are, however, cases recorded of disappearance of ethnic Baloch in localities where there are concentrations of Baloch people, in particular northern Sindh and Dera Ghazi Khan in the Punjab.[12]

Many of those taken into custody have been killed and bodies bearing evidence of torture and extrajudicial killing have been discovered. The most publicised disappearances and extrajudicial killings were those of Ghulam Mohammad Baloch, Chairman of Baloch Nationalist Movement and General Secretary of the Baloch National Front, Lala Munir Baloch, also of the Baloch National Movement, and Sher Mohammad Baloch of the Baloch Republican Party. Their hooded, tortured, and bullet-ridden bodies were found several days after the intelligence agencies abducted them from their lawyer's office in a courthouse in Turbat. Students are significant in Balochistan politics given the underdeveloped nature of the Baloch middle class. Student leaders and supporters, particularly members of the Baloch Students Organisation, have been targeted and either arrested on campuses and disappeared or simply abducted by the security forces.[13] Since mid-2010, Human Rights Watch have reported 70 bodies of those who had disappeared and between December 2010 and January 2011, a further 22 bodies were found of ethnic Baloch who had been abducted. Amnesty International for the period October 2010 to September 2011 has noted that 249 Baloch activists have disappeared or been murdered, many in 'kill and dump' operations.[14] Different government agencies or government-supported groups are operating a 'kill and dump' policy with impunity. As one official stated to an abductee,

> Even if the president or chief justice tells us to release you, we won't. We can torture you, or kill you, or keep you for years at our will. It is only the Army chief and the [intelligence] chief that we obey.[15]

The Supreme Court reopened inquiry cases into disappearance in 2009, and in May 2010 formed a Commission of Inquiry on Enforced Disappearances headed by a retired justice of the Supreme Court. The Commission was charged with preparing a comprehensive list of the disappeared, collecting evidence and testimony on missing persons, recommending procedures for tracing missing persons, and providing compensation for victims. It was not, however, given powers to file criminal charges. Baloch activists boycotted the Commission because it refused to register the majority of disappearances. The Commission submitted its report to the Supreme Court, which has not released the document. However, it claimed that 290 disappeared persons were traced of which 78 had been recovered from the custody of the various intelligence agencies. The Federal Ministry of the Interior established a new Commission of Inquiry in March 2011 to trace the remaining 136 victims, fix responsibility for their disappearances, and register First Information Reports against individuals. Families have submitted cases to the Commission but were not aware of any action taken by it. The Chair of the Commission, Justice Fayyaz Ahmed, observed that the 'government appears to be helpless before the spy agencies'.[16] These comments appeared to be confirmed by Aslam Raisani, the Chief Minister of Balochistan, who admitted to the Human Rights Commission that the provincial government had no control over the security agencies and that the intelligence agencies along with the Frontier Corps were running a parallel government in the province.[17] It is alleged that even the then President, Asif Zardari, admitted to Baloch leaders that he had no control over army operations in the province.[18]

As the narrative shows the conflict has been brutal, bloody and with complete disregard of human rights norms. There are a number of perspectives that have been used to explain the conflict: the Pakistani 'Establishment' (i.e. government and military leadership) have been quick to argue that this is the result of external intervention in combination with tribal leaders' resistance to social change. However, there are other arguments that need to be considered such as the resource driven conflict theory, the role of transnationalism and diaspora, and the failure to manage difference by not allowing federalism to function effectively. This chapter will assess each of the different approaches and evaluate them attempting to identify the principal cause for the present conflict. This is not to suggest that there may not be multiple factors but to identify which holds primary purchase/sway in triggering the present conflict.

## Resistance to social change

There is an Establishment perspective that argues that the *sardari* (tribal) system and culture is the main reason behind the crisis in Balochistan. Shah[19] and Hasnat[20] reflect this and view the internal politics of the sardari system of Balochistan as the main reason behind region's problems. They consider separatism to be fuelled by the inflated authority of the *sardars*, who resist the expansion of educational opportunities, and development, which is seen as a threat to the authority of the tribal leaders, combined with foreign intervention. Dunne[21] also looks at the relevance of the Baloch chiefs to their political problems and the cultural divide between Baloch and Punjabis and how this has been used by the *sardars* to deflect Baloch criticism from themselves.

There are several themes in this argument that need to be considered, first is the way that the Pakistani state has managed the *sardari* system, how the system is changing, and finally how inter-tribal rivalries map onto pro- and anti-government positions. Balochistan is divided into 'A' and 'B' areas. 'A' areas cover the cities and towns and are regulated by the Army, the Coast Guard, the Navy, the police, and the Frontier Corps. This direct system of control is found elsewhere in Pakistan with the exception that the Army and paramilitary forces play a more important role due the history of unrest in the province. The rural areas are classified as 'B' areas and are policed by Levies recruited from the local population and under the auspices of the local *sardar*. Levies are a form of community policing functioning within the parameters of the customs and traditions of the tribes. Their strength is that the community assists them in the prevention and detection of crime. However, they can also become a nucleus around which *sardars* exert their domination over the locality, a force in inter-tribal rivalry, or, in extreme cases, a nucleus around which to lead an uprising.[22] Thus there have been attempts to eliminate the 'B' areas by introducing direct state control and reducing the authority of the *sardars*. For example, Zulfikhar Bhutto's Pakistan People's Party (PPP) government in 1976 passed the Sardari Abolition Ordinance[23] and General Musharraf in 2006 convened the Qaumi Bugti Jirga, which was designed to specifically abolish the *sardari* system of the Bugti tribe and to replace it with the District Commissioner structure.[24] More recently the Balochistan package aspires to eliminating 'B' areas.[25]

However the Establishment's position has been riddled with political expediency and inconsistency. In the 1970s revolt Akbar Bugti sided with the authorities and was briefly governor of the province, while Ghous Bux Bizenjo, Ataullah Khan Mengal, and Khair Bux Marri were incarcerated. The abolition of the *sardari* system was selectively applied to the opponents of the regime while the supporters were excluded from its remit. Similarly Musharraf's reform was only designed to punish Bugti tribesmen who supported the revolt and was not applied to pro-government Bugti tribesmen or other areas where *sardars* remained loyal to the regime highlighting the political nature of this approach and the inconsistent way it has been applied.

The tribal system, where it exists in Balochistan, is different from the system among Pukhtuns in that the latter is a more devolved structure and the former more hierarchical and bounded by the tribal chief at the apex. Furthermore the *sardari* system is of varying influence in different regions of Balochistan and undergoing social change. There are a number of anthropological studies examining cultural and social norms, tribal structures, and their interaction with modernity. Scholz's[26] study examines the relationship between nomadism and colonialism in the nineteenth century and investigates the impact of social change on tribal society in its encounter with modernity. Matheson[27] investigated a similar theme in relation to the impact of modernity on the Bugti tribe with the discovery of natural gas in Sui. More recently, Titus[28] has investigated the adaptation and social change of tribal structures in the face of modernisation. He shows how urbanisation is leading to the emergence of a middle class and how tribal identities and structures are undergoing social change and how all this impacts on intra-ethnic relations within Balochistan.

Tribal structures are going through a rapid transformation, more so in some areas, such as on the Makran coast, where they were weak initially. According to the Human Rights Commission of Pakistan, restricting the democratic process and the failure to implement provincial autonomy inhibits the process of social change and reinforces the tribal system despite people's unhappiness with it.[29]

The relationship between tribal structures and the present insurgency is complex as the unrest is mapped on to inter-tribal and political rivalries. There are around 60 tribes in Balochistan but the insurgency mainly involves three of the larger tribes, Bugti, Marri, and Mengal. Areas where the rebellion is significant are the Marri-Bugti area, where the tribal structure is strong and led by tribesmen, the cities of Quetta and Khuzdar, the Lasbela District in the southeast of Balochistan, Lyari Town in Karachi, and on the Makran coast, where the *sardari* system is weaker and led by an emergent middle class.[30]

When political parties in Balochistan are examined there is no correlation between separatists and tribal structures. The typology of Baloch political parties, all dominated by *sardars*, is spread between mainstream Pakistani parties such as the two factions of the Muslim League, the PPP, those parties demanding greater autonomy, such as the Balochistan National Party (Mengal), the National Party, the Jamhoori Wattan Party, and the Baloch National Front (an alliance of eight political parties demanding independence). The alliance includes the Baloch National Movement, the Balochistan Student Organisation-Azad, and the Balochistan Republican Party. *Sardars* are present across the political spectrum and the former chief minister, Muhammad Aslam Khan Raisani, and the governor, Zulfikar Ali Magsi (both members of the PPP who were removed from office in 2013), are tribal chiefs as are most of the elected representatives in the Balochistan Provincial Assembly. Tribal chiefs dominate the provincial administrations and collaborate with the Federal government. Furthermore, they are involved in the vigilante groups that are alleged to be behind many of the extrajudicial executions of Baloch nationalists. The Tehreek-e-Nefaz-e-Aman Balochistan, for example, is purported to be the armed wing of the United Front of Balochistan, a political party headed by the brother of the former chief minister, Siraj Raisani, and Shafiq Mengal leads the Baloch Musla Defai Tanzeem, which has been implicated in sectarian attacks on Hazara Shias. Both organisations have been linked to vigilante squads that abduct and kill activists who demand independence.[31] So while they remain tied to and bound by the *sardari* tribal structure, their political orientations are varied and underpinned by pragmatism rather than ideology. In summary, blaming the insurgency on the tribal system is not a convincing explanation but clearly it plays a subordinate role as *sardars* are a pervasive feature of Baloch society.

## External intervention

The realist perspective, which sees the international system through the prism of nation states,[32] is dominant within the security Establishment and claims that the insurgency is supported by external intervention. This is usually in conjunction with the earlier hypothesis on the role of the tribal system. There are a number of possible candidates for this external involvement. India is the primary suspect, but suspicion also falls on Afghanistan, Iran, and the USA. There are a number of political differences between Pakistan and Afghanistan. The Durand Line, for example, is not accepted by Kabul as the border between the two countries, and when Pakistan gained independence in 1947 it raised the Pukhtunistan issue where it was proposed that all the Pukhtun tribes on both sides of the Durand Line would be united in an independent Pukhtunistan state. Kabul was an ally of Pakistan's archenemy, India, and throughout the 1970s Baloch insurgency, Afghanistan provided training camps for Baloch militants.[33]

In the present insurgency, Bugti and Marri refugees have sought sanctuary in Afghanistan and insurgents launch attacks from Afghanistan across the porous border. President Musharraf lobbied the USA for assistance claiming that 200 Bugtis wanted by Islamabad were in Afghanistan, with the most prominent being Brahamdagh Bugti, the grandson of Akbar Bugti. Brahamdagh Bugti heads the separatist Baloch Republican Party and allegedly its militant wing, the Baloch Republican Army, and remained in Kabul for four years from 2006 and was accused by the authorities in Pakistan of being responsible for attacks against Punjabi settlers in Balochistan, government installations, and the Pakistan armed forces. Brahamdagh Bugti's presence in Kabul strained relations between the two countries and forced the USA and its allies to intervene. The President of Afghanistan, Hamid Karzai (elected in October 2004), negotiated with Washington for an alternate sanctuary to be found in the West, to which, in principle, Islamabad was agreeable. Brahamdagh Bugti finally left Afghanistan for exile in Switzerland in late October 2010, ostensibly on an Indian passport; the Pakistani authorities, however, are contesting his application for asylum.[34] In March 2012 the Government of Balochistan, in a conciliatory move, withdrew 28 cases registered against Brahamdagh Bugti in Dera Bugti and Sui for carrying out anti-Pakistan activities from Afghanistan with the support of India. Similar cases against Hyrbyair Marri, alleged leader of the Balochistan Liberation Army, and others were also withdrawn. However, the nationalists refuse to enter into a dialogue with the authorities until the disappeared persons are recovered and extrajudicial executions investigated.[35]

Delhi's influence was notable in Afghanistan until the Soviet invasion of the country on Christmas Eve in 1979. Islamabad's support for the Afghan resistance eventually resulted in the defeat of the Soviet Union but it was also the termination, however temporary, of Delhi's sway in the country. Pakistan, during the course of the intervention, formulated the policy of strategic depth whereby a compliant and pro-Pakistani regime in Kabul was the reward for supporting the intervention against the Soviets.[36] The US-led intervention in October 2001, Operation Enduring Freedom, premised on the light footprint strategy meant that they required the manpower of the Northern Alliance in conjunction with US air power to defeat the Taliban. The Northern Alliance's takeover of Kabul, however, meant the return of Indian influence to Afghanistan and a major policy reversal for Pakistan. Viewed from this lens, the Pakistan Army sees its interest closely tied with that of the

Pukhtun groups hostile to the Karzai regime: the Taliban, as well as Hekmatyar's and Haqqani's factions. They see these groups as important allies in neutralising Delhi's increasing influence in their own backyard.[37]

In spite of Pakistani objections, New Delhi has become one of the largest donors to Afghanistan with US$1.2 billion given in reconstruction aid for a wide range of activities including the building of roads and schools, to the construction of dams, power transmission lines, and the parliament building in which nearly 3,000 Indian workers are engaged.[38] This has been followed up by an Indo-Afghanistan security agreement whereby India would expand the limited training programme for Afghani Army and police officers, with an immediate cohort of 150 army officers sent to India to receive training at an Indian military establishment.[39] Critically for Pakistan, India has been collaborating with Iran in the construction of the Chabahar port, a direct competitor to Gwadar Port, and it has built a Delram-Zanraj link road connecting the Iranian border with the main road between the cities of Herat, Kandahar, and Kabul. On the Iranian side, it links with a route to the port of Chabahar and this gives Afghanistan a route to the Persian Gulf that bypasses Pakistan. The road was constructed by the Borders Road Organisation, which is staffed with a mixture of Border Roads Engineering Service officers from the General Reserve Engineer Force, the work force, under the Ministry of Surface Transport and officers from the Corps of Engineers of the Indian Army. The Indo-Tibetan police force was secreted into the Borders Road Organisation to offer protection from Taliban attacks.[40]

Pakistan has made a number of direct accusations of Indian meddling in Balochistan's affairs. At the Sharm el-Sheik meeting between Indian Prime Minister, Manmohan Singh, and the Pakistani Prime Minister, Yousaf Reza Gilani, in 2009 it was alleged that a dossier was presented containing photographs of Brahamdagh Bugti meeting Indian agents in Kabul and meeting officials in India, and that the Indian consulate at Kandahar was organising and funding the Baloch Republican Army and the Balochistan Liberation Army. As Alok Banasal points out, funding the Baloch insurgents with as little as only US$2 million per month can pin down three to five Pakistani army divisions making it a tempting prospect for India. Pakistan also threatened to bring the media's attention to three Indian nationals arrested for their involvement with Baloch militants. Further accusations were made that Baitullah Mehsud's Tehreek-e-Taliban was receiving support from bases in Afghanistan.[41] However these allegations have not been publically substantiated or the dossier made public. Reluctantly Manmohan Singh agreed to Balochistan being added to the agenda at the Sharm el-Sheik meeting. US State Department documents suggest that Balochistan as an agenda item was only accepted by India at the meeting under US pressure, and this enabled Islamabad to be more relaxed in discussing terrorism with New Delhi, thus allowing the dialogue between the two countries to continue. It allowed them to equate Pakistan's ISI with India's RAW, the Research and Analysis Wing, or external intelligence agency, and to counter India's concerns over Mumbai with Pakistan's concerns over Balochistan.[42] Thus, for Pakistan, it was able to finesse India's diplomatic posturing without the need for Pakistan producing any concrete evidence. The debate on foreign involvement has recently been revived when Akhtar Mengal of the Balochistan National Party (Mengal) who returned from self-imposed exile to fight the 2013 elections repeated the claim that foreign forces are involved in the conflict in Balochistan. This reiterates the military Establishment perspective, blaming India for fomenting violence in the province by at least providing money to the Baloch rebels.[43]

Pakistan has accused both the USA and the UK of being involved in Balochistan's affairs. Abdul Basit, a Foreign Ministry spokesman, suggested that there was evidence that weapons used by Baloch insurgents are of NATO origin,[44] but this is not surprising as the Taliban are also using NATO weapons, which they procured from the black market. The other evidence is that rather than prosecuting Baloch leaders in exile, they have been granted asylum status. President Musharraf did, however, convince the UK and US authorities to declare the Baloch Liberation Front a terrorist organisation. His regime also attempted in 2007 to unsuccessfully extradite Mehran Baloch, the Baloch representative to the UN Human Rights Council, and it accused Hyrbyair Marri and Faiz Baloch of acts of terrorism. Hyrbyair Marri and Faiz Baloch were eventually brought to trial in the UK in 2008 but they were subsequently acquitted of all charges. Only after the acquittal did the UK authorities grant them refugee status.[45] Some analysts argue that the rebellion has the support of the USA. There are claims that US defence contractors, with the aid of Afghan guides and interpreters, are 'shifting loads of money from Afghanistan to Balochistan'. The USA is unhappy that Gwadar will provide the Chinese access to the Gulf uncomfortably close to the US Naval Forces Central Command and US Fifth Fleet in Bahrain.[46] While there is some evidence of the USA supporting militants in Iranian Balochistan, there is no serious analysis of this possible angle in the Balochistan conflict in Pakistan, other than conspiracy theories, which see the rebellion as a grand US plan to break up Muslim countries.[47] Contemporary concerns with the crisis in Balochistan intersect and conflate with the international obsession with Al Qaeda and the Taliban and the supposed instability of a nuclear state, Pakistan.[48]

When the external intervention argument is evaluated there is circumstantial evidence of Afghan (by providing sanctuary) and Indian (offering financial support) involvement in Balochistan. This is not really surprising given Pakistan's support for the Taliban and Kashmiri militants and poor relations with those two countries. However, to suggest that this is the primary cause for the crisis in the province would be overstating it. At most these powers are simply exploiting an opportunity created by inept handling of the situation by the Pakistani security Establishment. As for the UK and US role this is an even weaker hypothesis, which perhaps could be indicative of blowback from support for Iranian Baloch dissidents.

## Resource conflict thesis

Collier and Hoeffler's comprehensive study of civil wars suggest that a high proportion of primary commodities in national exports significantly increases the risk of a conflict. An abundance of resources can cause conflict, and influence its onset and duration.[49] Balochistan's total contribution to Pakistan's economy has been constant, around 4 per cent of GDP, but the province supplies around 40 per cent of the country's energy needs.[50] Grare,[51] Wirsing,[52] and Niazi[53] emphasise the resource-driven conflict approach, arguing that expropriation of natural resources, marginalisation, and dispossession are crucial factors.[54] Baloch antagonism with the centre was heightened by the fact that exploitation of natural resources, such as Sui natural gas, failed to benefit the local population. Discovered in the 1950s, Sui is the heart of gas production in Balochistan; overall 38 per cent of the country's gas production comes from Balochistan. However, in terms of distribution, only 6 per cent of Balochistan has access to gas and it is not available in Sibi, the closest town to the Sui gas fields. Furthermore, the cruel irony was that Balochistan received only a tiny fraction of the financial benefits.[55]

The federal government has devoted a lot of its resources to the exploitation of the large copper reserves in Balochistan, as a result of which copper production has increased from 10,000 in 2002–3 to almost four million metric tonnes in 2004–5.[56] The biggest copper and gold mining project in Balochistan is the Saindak Copper Gold Project in Chagai, the largest district of Pakistan, located in northern Balochistan. The project, led by Saindak Metals Limited (SML), comes under the jurisdiction of the Federal Ministry of Petroleum and Natural Resources. In 2002, the SML agreed on a 10-year joint venture with the Chinese Metallurgical Construction Company.[57] A second major copper-gold mining project is in the Rekodiq area, which is also in Chagai district. This is a joint venture between the Government of Balochistan, Antofagasta of Chile, and Barrick Gold of Canada on a 25:37.5:37.5 partnership. This project aims to tap the estimated two billion tonnes of copper and 20 million ounces of gold reserves in Balochistan.[58] The whole project has enraged the local population as they see little benefit accruing to them. The result has been that mineral exploitation has been bogged down in the courts as the Balochistan provincial government challenged the original licence granted to the company[59] and the Supreme Court in January 2013 declared the Rekodiq agreement null and void.[60]

Balochistan is also a transit and transport route for gas pipelines. The US$4 billion Iran–Pakistan–India gas pipeline, with an approximate length of 3,000 km and a capacity of 1.1–3.4 billion cubic feet per day, is planned to pass through Balochistan.[61] The proposed 1,700 km Turkmenistan–Pakistan gas pipeline and the 1,650 km Qatar–Pakistan gas pipeline also passes through Balochistan.[62] Accordingly, besides energy production, the province is strategically placed for transportation of energy to the power hungry metropolises of Pakistan. The Iran–Pakistan pipeline for the transportation of gas, which is not now going to include India, is going ahead in spite of opposition from the USA. The pipeline from Iran would traverse Balochistan, enter the Punjab at Multan, and go on to Lahore in the north, and Karachi to the south. Furthermore, Iran will also supply Pakistan electricity, as the country is desperate for energy. However, besides Pakistan's financial precariousness acting as an impediment to the completion of this project, it is dependent on the security situation in Balochistan and on Washington's determination to enforce the embargo against Tehran. The Turkmenistan pipeline, favoured by the White House, would cross Afghanistan, enter Balochistan, and cross the Punjab from Multan to Lahore before entering India. This pipeline, however, is not only dependent on stability in Balochistan but also in Afghanistan.[63] Without peace in these two places it remains, in more senses than one, a pipe dream.

The port of Gwadar similarly enters into the equation as it provides China with access to the Persian Gulf and it allows Islamabad to be less dependent on Karachi, which is strategically vulnerable. However, poor infrastructure development means that the port cannot effectively service either the Afghan or the Chinese demand and, in the latter case, a Karakorum-Gwadar link would only be worthwhile if Pakistan was an access point for the larger and more lucrative Indian market. The deep sea Pak-Qatari pipeline is anticipated to reach Gwadar on the Balochistan coast where Beijing has already invested heavily in a port and a military base. The Chinese want to move the gas along the Indus River by a land route across the Karakorum Highway via a 'white oil pipeline' and feed its energy grid. China has accelerated its effort in this direction after its earlier interest in joining the Iran–Pakistan–India gas pipeline and the Turkmenistan–Afghanistan–Pakistan (TAP) gas pipeline diminished. While the first pipeline is bogged down due to global politics, Beijing is not too keen on the TAP line for security reasons.[64]

Unlike conflicts elsewhere, resources are not directly feeding the conflict, such as is the case with blood diamonds in Liberia or oil in the Niger delta.[65] Resources are not a motive and opportunity for violent conflict. However they are an important driver that underpins the discontent among the Baloch. At present resources are mainly hypothetical, as extraction has yet to take place, and the Baloch concern is that outsiders will reap the benefits at the expense of locals as the case of Sui gas. Energy, access to it, and mineral wealth, is encouraging discontent, informs the context underpinning the insurgency and has the potential of becoming an important variable by providing an opportunity for international rivalry to conflate with internal discontent, giving the conflict a regional and global dimension. Resources can potentially be an important variable in the conflict but at present there does not seem to be evidence to support this as they are more hypothetical in nature. This could change if and when extraction takes place.

## Transnationalism and diaspora

There are two scholarly discourses on the flow of people: transnationalism and diaspora, which have divergent trajectories and yet intersect. The categories have considerable similarities but important differences. The commonality between the two is communication and the transformative impact it has in the formation of the global village. Transnationalism refers to human interaction and communication over vast distance becoming routinised and natural for groups of actors operating within globally integrated sectors.⁶⁶ The interpersonal connectedness of transnational individuals overlaps, or perhaps is replaced by, inter-communal and inter-organisational connectedness and networks across borders. Theories of transnationalism focus on modes of communication, the pressures from the home country, and the flows of remittances. Diasporas are groups, unlike transnationals who are individuals, who have used technological innovation to go global. The classical examples cited in the literature such as the Jews and Armenians⁶⁷ are highly assimilated and their vestiges of difference may only be totemic, but they can symbolically position themselves to mobilise for a collective cause that feeds into and enables the performance of diasporas as a vehicle for long distance nationalism.⁶⁸

A conservative estimate of the worldwide Baloch population is around nine million with the largest concentration found in Pakistan (around seven million). There are just over one million in Iran, under half a million in Afghanistan and Oman, and approximately 36,000 in Turkmenistan.⁶⁹ The porous borders between Iran, Pakistan, and Afghanistan means that many Baloch move freely across them and many have Pakistani identity cards. A substantial population is established in Oman and comprise just over 20 per cent of the country's settled population: this figure excludes temporary workers. There are smaller groups in Bahrain and Dubai. Baloch presence in the Gulf dates back to the sixteenth and seventeenth centuries; in 1784 the Omani ruling family sought refuge in Gwadar, with permission from the Khan of Kalat, and the port and region became Omani territory but in 1958 Pakistan purchased the territory and port of Gwadar. Omani sovereignty over parts of the Makran coast facilitated the movement of Baloch to search for work and settlement in Oman. Consequently many of them settled in Oman and are concentrated alongside the al-Batina coast, which stretches along the Gulf of Oman from Muscat to the United Arab Emirates as well as pockets scattered elsewhere. There are Baloch quarters in both Muscat and Muttrah.⁷⁰

Baloch have a long history of serving in Gulf armies. The first modern army unit in Oman formed in 1921 was entirely Baloch and there was steady demand for them during the Dhofar insurgency (1965–75). Most Baloch are from Pakistan but there are some Iranian Baloch who arrived in the 1950s and 1960s when the Shah of Iran exerted his authority over the region. Some of these arrivals were recruited into Sultan of Oman's para-military force. Today in Oman 40 per cent of the army is of eastern Baloch origin and they have a significant presence in the Bahraini police force. Several Baloch have served as ministers in the Oman government, others have become prominent merchants and even commanded the air force. In Dubai the former head of the intelligence service was Major General Sharafuddin Sharaf who hailed from western Balochistan.⁷¹

According to the Collier-Hoeffler Model, a second source of finance for rebellions and insurgencies are diasporas and the bigger the diasporas the more the likelihood they would fund rebellions. The study found that statistically switching the size of a country's diaspora from the smallest found in the study to the largest, resulted in a six fold increase in the chance of a civil war.⁷² Homeland politics among the Baloch diaspora is difficult to detect, as the right of political expression is non-existent in the Gulf States and Pakistan is applying pressure so that the Gulf States do not become a haven for Baloch dissidents. There is also pressure from within the Baloch community not to engage in activities that create diplomatic problems and hurt the interests of Baloch diaspora in the Gulf. Baloch maintain kinship relations and active ties with their towns and villages back home on the Makran coast but these ties are stronger for the first and second generation Baloch who still maintain the language and cultural norms. There are approximately 5,000 people living in the Wadi Hattat suburb of Muscat City who belong to Gwadar and there are biweekly flights between Gwadar and Muscat. The residents include noted Baloch nationalist poets like Abdul Majid Gwadari – the author of Baloch national anthem Ma Chuken Balochaani! (We are the sons of Baloch!) – and the late Gulam Hussain Shohaz. More generally, a significant proportion of Omani Baloch and other Baloch residents in the Gulf Region sympathise with and support the cause of Baloch nationalism because the Makran Division has been one of the important centres of an emergent Baloch middle class and nationalist awakening.[73] Thus members of the Baloch diaspora, naturally concerned by recent developments, are angered by the brutalities committed by the Pakistan Army and its supporters. For example, a Baloch major from Muscat, a retiree from the Oman army, was quoted in the press saying 'Pakistani army soldiers are like beasts and cannibals.'[74]

The transnational processes, the triangular circuit of Federally Administered Tribal Areas (FATA)/Helmand, Karachi, and the Gulf (mainly Dubai), used by the Taliban have been replicated by the Baloch. Probably the most infamous examples are Khalid Sheikh Mohammed (architect of 9/11) and Ramzi Yousef (perpetrator of the 1993 World Trade Centre bombing and a co-conspirator in the Bojinka plot), both Baloch Gulf residents and affiliates of Osama bin Laden.[75] For secular nationalist Baloch, like the Taliban, a major source of funding is from the trade in narcotics. Baloch criminal networks also traffic people along with contraband goods. Some Baloch groups were named in a Central Intelligence Agency (1992) document revealing heroin trafficking in Pakistan during the 1990s. It is generally accepted by diplomatic sources that it is this nexus of criminality that is being tapped by Baloch militants to fund the insurgency (anonymous diplomatic source, interview, 15 July 2012). The money is laundered in Dubai and combined with money raised from the Baloch diaspora where sentiments are running high at the atrocities being committed against the Baloch. Again, due to the absence of legal and overt political activity in the Gulf States, it not possible to identify the financial resources that are being collected and transferred to the insurgents. However, like the Taliban, drug money and money raised from other sources is transferred electronically through the informal Hawala network, or through the secretive formal banking system based in Dubai, or simply carried by courier.[76]

The funding network intersects with transnational arms-dealing circuits. The Baloch are buying weapons from Afghan narcotic traffickers who are selling armaments obtained from multiple sources to the Taliban. There is no evidence that the Baloch nationalists are collaborating with either the Taliban or

Al Qaeda.⁷⁷ While there is an indigenous weapon-making industry in Darra Adam Khel and other areas in Khyber Pukthunkhwa, most militants prefer to use reliable foreign-made weaponry. There is also stock left over from the Afghan intervention, available for a price, but it is supplemented by a number of other sources. The unregulated free market in Dubai is not only a major source of funding but also of weapon procurement. Another important source is armaments provided by the Pentagon for the Afghan army which have ended up on the black market. The Taliban and Baloch militants can source this pool of illicit weaponry without difficulty. This diversion of NATO weaponry to the black market forms the basis of Pakistan's accusation that the USA and the UK are supporting Baloch militants.⁷⁸ As one can see, the Baloch militants are also tapping the same networks that are providing arms for the Taliban insurgency.

While diasporic support is often covert and surreptitious in the Gulf, the activities of Baloch exiles in Europe and America are very much in the open. These transnational activists in the UK, the USA, Norway, and Sweden are very visible. Exiles from Iran and Pakistan in Europe and America are collaborating in lobbying the UN in Geneva and New York, the European Union as well individual governments. They are constructing a common Baloch political identity, and using the media to communicate their views. Baloch websites, with servers located outside Pakistan and Iran, document disappearances, claim extrajudicial executions, publish statements by separatist leaders and general news on Baluchistan in an attempt to challenge the narrative produced by Islamabad and Tehran and present an alternative history and cultural memory. As a result, Internet service providers, on the instructions of the authorities, block these in both Pakistan and Iran. Nonetheless, this diasporic activity caused so much concern in Pakistan that President Musharraf persuaded the British and American governments to declare the Baloch Liberation Front a terrorist organisation. In 2007 his regime also attempted to extradite Mehran Baloch and accused Hyrbyair Marri and Faiz Baloch of terrorism.⁷⁹

An important focus of the exiled leadership, Khan of Kalat, Hyrbyair Marri and Brahamdagh Bugti, is the development of a unified platform whereby the different Baloch groups from Pakistan as well as Iranian Baloch can come together with a single voice. To this end there are discussions, bogged down in personal rivalry, on developing a constitution, which would eventually lead to the formation of a government in exile. The bringing together of Iranian and Pakistani groups as well as different groups within Pakistan is something which has been encouraged by Republican Congressman Dana Rohrabacher, Chair of the US House of Representatives Committee on Foreign Affairs Subcommittee on Europe, Eurasia and Emerging Threats. Rohrabacher is hostile to Pakistan because of its alleged support for the Taliban and believes a unified Baloch opposition would be something that could persuade Congress to view the region in a different light.⁸⁰ To the alarm of the Pakistani authorities, Baloch activists in exile were able to persuade Rohrabacher to convene a congressional hearing in February 2012 on the situation in Balochistan.⁸¹ At this hearing, Baloch activists raised the possibility of an independent Balochistan. The plan was presented to the

USA as a package whereby Iran and Pakistan would be broken up and Gwadar would be handed to the USA as a facility for the US fleet. This is a minority view in Congress, and is more an attempt to embarrass Pakistan, but such developments have caused considerable concern within the security Establishment in Pakistan and exacerbate their concerns about exile activity abroad.

Washington's nightmare scenario for Pakistan is that instability would lead to Al Qaeda getting access to nuclear weapons. These concerns restrain it from intervening and certainly make the scenario of breaking up the country to form an independent Balochistan highly unlikely.[82] However, there is a remote possibility that conflict with Iran could lead to regime change, and the formation of an autonomous and de facto independent western Balochistan along the lines of Kurdistan in Iraq. This scenario would cause a serious setback for Islamabad, as it would provide a safe haven for Baloch militants.

Diaspora and transnational activity are playing a role in mobilising support and funding for the separatists. They are sourcing finance through narcotics and procuring weapons from drug traffickers. They are using the well-established regional networks of finance, narcotics, and money laundering used by the Taliban for their own agenda. In the Gulf States where they are established as diasporic populations they are providing financial support, although due to the non-democratic environment this is not verifiable. The most visible activity is by exiles based in the West who have attempted to promote their cause, unify the opposition, unsuccessfully, and to lobby governments. They have been supported by some Congressmen who are hostile to Pakistan and given a platform where they attempted to sell an independent Balochistan as a vehicle promoting US interest in the region. Diasporic activity is providing oxygen for the nationalists and transnational circuits are being used raise funding and source weapons. Thus, they are a variable in understanding the insurgency but not necessarily causal factors.

## Managing difference: federalism

Managing difference has been a major concern for most nation states, and various strategies have been employed, ranging from eliminating difference to recognition of cultural difference. McGarry and O'Leary[83] identified eight distinct approaches to ethnic conflict regulation that are not necessarily applied in discrete and distinct fashion but are usually found in combinations, both sequentially and simultaneously. Four of the grand stratagems involving the elimination of difference are genocide, ethnic cleansing, secession and Partition, or political homogenisation (ranging from integration to assimilation), while the other four strategies involve the management of difference through hegemonic control, arbitration, federation or autonomy, and consociation.

Hegemonic control, however, has been the most common method by which historically segmented societies are stabilised.[84] Authoritarian or imperial regimes manage cultural difference through elite co-option and coercive domination. Ethnic divisions, both latent and active, particularly in periods of rapid modernisation, were suppressed. Control was hegemonic if explicitly violent ethnic challenges to state power were at an unacceptable high human cost. Hegemonic control accordingly was a system where ethnic challenges to state power were unthinkable or unworkable for subordinate communities. Regulators overturn ethnic difference in a partial manner on behalf of the dominant nationality, what O'Leary[85] calls the Staatsvolk. To do this the dominant group needs to be organised, which in a liberal democracy means the monopolisation of state institutions and the disenfranchisement of minorities. Hegemonic control in authoritarian regimes did not necessarily depend on the support of the largest ethnic groups but rather on the control of the coercive apparatus by an ethnic group, and there are many examples of ethnic minorities' control of the security forces and the police allowing them to sustain hegemonic control.[86]

Federations tend to emerge out of multi-ethnic colonies, where administrative elites have an interest in sustaining the federation which is usually justified in terms of large economic markets and greater security. Federalism can be a successful mechanism for managing difference if the constituting units mirror ethnic divisions and combine with positive discrimination of disfranchised groups as in the case of India.[87] In formal constitutional terms, the official mechanism for regulating ethnic difference in Pakistan is federalism, which with the Eighteenth Amendment has gone through significant modification moving towards consociationalism. As a system for regulating ethnic conflict it can be successful if the boundaries between ethnic communities match the units of the federation; which is not the case in Pakistan as most of the provinces have a mix of ethnic groups.

Despite Pakistan being a federation, hegemonic control became the main system of ethnic regulation. Authoritarian regimes controlled multiple cultures through coercive domination and elite co-option. However hegemonic control is only possible if the Staatsvolk control the institutions of state power. The key institutions were the military and bureaucracy with the former being more important under military rule, which covers most of Pakistan's history. This phenomenon has been called the Punjabisation of Pakistan. Punjabisation is not simply about the numerical domination of Punjabis in Pakistan but the conflation of ethnicity with institutional domination through an over-concentration of the Punjabi service class in key state institutions and in particular its predominance in the armed forces.[88] The army is the biggest employer in the country, acts as a development agency encouraging strategic industries, is the largest landholder in the country, and generates a relatively sophisticated pool of labour. The military-industrial complex is another important sector that is extremely influential in Pakistan.[89] However the Punjabi service class had to form coalitions to dominate these key institutions. Up to the emergence of Bangladesh the military-bureaucratic oligarchy was dominated by coalition of Punjabis and Mohajirs (migrants from India). With the Soviet intervention in Afghanistan there was a realignment of the forces in the military-bureaucratic oligarchy reflecting the increased influence of Pukhtuns, which was at the expense of Mohajirs.[90] Today Punjabis dominate the Staatsvolk in coalition with Pukhtuns and to a lesser degree Mohajirs.

Balochistan's history from accession to date, in spite of the changing political context, is littered with examples of co-option and coercion. When Mir Ahmed Yar Khan dithered over acceding to the Baloch-Brauhi confederacy to Pakistan in 1947 the centre's response was to initiate processes that would coerce the state to join Pakistan. By recognising the feudatory states of Las Bela, Kharan, and the district of Mekran as independent states, which promptly merged with Pakistan, the State of Kalat became land locked and reduced to a fraction of its size. Thus Ahmed Yar Khan was forced to sign the instrument of accession on 27 March 1948, which immediately led to the brother of the Khan, Prince Abdul Karim raising the banner of revolt in July 1948, starting the first of the Baloch insurgencies.[91] In the 1970s Zulfikar Bhutto similarly used coercion and co-option in dealing with the National Awami Party coalition in Balochistan and he dismissed Ataullah Mengal's provincial government on trumped up charges and precipitated a rebellion led by Ataullah Mengal and Khair Bux Marri who retreated into Afghanistan. Akbar Bugti was co-opted as governor of the province but he resigned after a short period because of the coercive tactics used to pacify the province. The heavy-handed approach politicised the Baloch and intensified separatist feelings.[92]

Today there are a number of local concerns that coalesce in the present dispute – the issue of development, the share of revenue from energy and mineral resources extracted from the province, and the construction of the port of Gwadar. While initially it appeared that the Balochistan problem is about resources, the construction of Gwadar presents a much more serious threat of difference being eliminated by assimilation. Assimilation is a stratagem used by states to eliminate ethnic difference.[93] The migration of several million people to the port city would turn the Baloch into a minority population, which is why Baloch politicians argued for a 12-year suspension of voting rights for new migrants to the province.[94] However, the security Establishment had very little patience with the Baloch nationalists and rapidly moved from negotiations to coercion with military operations in the Marri–Bugti areas, allowing the agencies to run a province-wide 'kill and dump' policy and mobilise pro-government *sardars*, some with sectarian affiliation, to run a vigilante campaign against suspected nationalists that has spiralled out of control into sectarian violence against Hazara Shias.[95]

To explain the impatience of the security Establishment, groups that are excluded from key institutions found their grievances are not dealt sympathetically with the military resorting to force very quickly. Compare, for example, the differences in the centre's handling of the Waziristan dispute with the Balochistan dispute. In contrast to Washington which looks at the tribal areas from a 'War on Terror'/Islamic militancy perspective, Islamabad has a more nuanced view primarily as a number of senior officers hail from the region which is why they proposed negotiations in preference to launching military campaigns in FATA.[96] Furthermore the army has opposed suggestions that local levies be abolished as in the case of Balochistan,[97] and the dozen or so assassination attempts against Musharraf were not taken personally as in the case of Balochistan.[98] In contrast, Baloch grievances were treated more harshly through assimilation strategies linked to development or dealt with coercive strategies, because as a disenfranchised minority they had no access to the centres of power in the armed forces. This group is not represented in the senior ranks of the military-bureaucratic oligarchy particularly in the crucial institution, the army, which explains why the move to coercion was so quick. Because Baloch are not part of the Staatsvolk, hegemonic control becomes the preferred option for ethnic regulation in Balochistan. The present conflict is part of a historical pattern of how political discontent has been dealt with in the province. Hegemonic control has been the preferred way that difference has been managed suggesting that it is the causal factor that intersects with other variables in the intensification of this conflict. It provides the context where other elements can amplify the conflict and the resistance of Baloch nationalists.

However there has been an attempt to move away from hegemonic control and deal with the problem of difference within the context of federalism. With the election of a PPP administration in 2008 and the swearing in of Asif Ali Zardari as President on 9 September, the government again attempted to deal with the issue politically. It did so on two levels: one, it instituted constitutional reforms that dealt with provincial rights on an all-Pakistan level; and, two, it introduced measures that directly dealt with the crisis in Balochistan. The Eighteenth Amendment of the Constitution in 2010 was a positive step forward, as it made parliament supreme, reduced the power of the centre to intervene in provincial affairs, and renamed the North-West Frontier Province as Khyber Pukhtunkhwa. The concurrent list was abolished, and the Government increased the provinces' say in some subjects in the Federal List by widening the purview of the Council of Common Interests. Greater power was invested in the provincial assemblies: the power of the governor of the provinces to declare emergencies and extend ordinances was curtailed and required the approval of the provincial assemblies.

Plans for granting greater autonomy to the provinces were designed to address grievances from smaller provinces, in particular Balochistan. Federating units were made joint- and co-equal-partners with the centre for mineral and oil and gas deposits in the provinces and parliament was empowered to legislate laws that redressed provincial under-representation in the services of Pakistan. Furthermore, the federal government had to consult the relevant provincial government in any decision to build a hydroelectric power station. The Council of Common Interests, a quasi-executive body to manage centre-province issues, which had been ineffective under Musharraf, was expanded, apparently strengthened, and required to report regularly to Parliament. The National Finance Commission Award moved away from distribution of revenues on the criteria of population to a multi-criteria formulation based on underdevelopment, revenue collection and generation, and inverse population density. The centre's share of revenue was considerably reduced and provinces now could raise loans on the domestic and international markets.[99] Along with the Eighteenth Amendment, Yousaf Gilani's administration introduced the Balochistan Package, Aghaaz-e-Huqook Balochistan,[100] and together they should have addressed the grievances of the province. This political initiative also had the support of the main opposition party the Muslim League (N) which was ready to throw the weight of the Punjab behind a settlement of the conflict. Furthermore there was an attempt to win over the Baloch leadership in exile, the Khan of Kalat was the focus of this attempt, but the initiative failed to develop traction due to the trust deficit.[101]

Although it was seen as a step in the right direction, the Baloch response was sceptical. Militants declared a unilateral ceasefire and demanded that military operations cease, those detained be released, and that an investigation into extra-judicial executions be held. However it had no impact on the ground as the army was out of control, and the cease-fire broke down.[102] Neither the federal nor the provincial government has been able to rein in the army and deal with the problem through negotiation. In 2013 Nawaz Sharif's Muslim League won the general elections and he supported Abdul Malik Baloch becoming chief minister and leading a coalition provincial government. The chief minister, who is not a *sardar* and hails from the Makran coast and whose political pedigree includes belonging to the National Awami Party, continues the political dialogue initiated by his predecessor with Baloch nationalists. However he has conceded that he has been unable to make much headway on the issues of disappearances, and extrajudicial executions continue. The Chief Minister of Balochistan Dr Abdul Malik Baloch's lack of success in recovering the disappeared and halting the extra-judicial executions led him to turn to political strategy to resolve these issues. He raised the issue of disappearances and extra-judicial executions with the All-Party Conference in order to develop a political consensus across the political spectrum but he met only partial success.[103] While the APC and the government endorsed negotiations with the insurgents the Baloch crisis became entangled with the government's approach to Islamic terrorism and the legislation designed to deal with it. He also supported the long march organised by Mama Qadeer from the NGO Voice of Missing Baloch Persons, and the families of the missing persons walked first from Quetta to Karachi and then another 700 miles from Karachi to Islamabad in search for justice.[104] On 28 February 2014 the historic long march ended in Islamabad and the participants presented a memorandum to the UN demanding the UN to investigate the target killings, enforced disappearances, and alleged involvement of agencies in heinous crimes; and a UN fact-finding mission to investigate mass graves, which should include DNA tests to identify bodies. The offices of the European Union and the US Embassy also met the marchers but the absence of representatives' from Nawaz Sharif government was noticeable. The refusal of the Prime Minister to meet the long marchers illustrates that this government does not want to enrage the military and intelligence agencies that are autonomous in their actions.[105]

The United Nations Working Group on Enforced and Involuntary Disappearances (WGEID) published its report on Pakistan, following its visit to the country in September 2012. The report expressed concern at the continuing practice of enforced disappearances and made a series of recommendations to the government. The WGEID urged Pakistan to ratify the International Convention for the Protection of All Persons from Enforced Disappearance (Convention on

Enforced Disappearance). Instead of ratifying the convention the government sought to undermine an attempt by the Supreme Court to apply the principles enshrined in the convention. In a commendable judgement passed in the Muhabat Shah case in December 2013, the Supreme Court had held that the Convention on Enforced Disappearance was applicable in Pakistan, as it was inextricably linked with the right to life guaranteed by its Constitution, also recognised by the International Covenant on Civil and Political Rights (ICCPR), which Pakistan ratified in 2010. It also held that this obligated Pakistan to bring perpetrators of enforced disappearance to account. The government, however, challenged the ruling, arguing that as Pakistan has not ratified the convention, the Supreme Court could not apply it in Pakistan and filed for a review of the judgement, asking the court to delete remarks implicating the security agencies in enforced disappearances as such findings could demoralise the troops.[106]

The WGEID also recommended that the crime of enforced disappearance be included in the criminal code in line with the definition given in the convention. Instead the authorities introduced the Protection of Pakistan Ordinance, in October 2013 to assist it in the fight against Islamic militancy. However it has a negative affect on the issue of abductions and extra-judicial executions in Balochistan. Section 9 of the Protection of Pakistan Ordinance allows the government to withhold information regarding the location of detainees, as well as their place and grounds of detention, for any reasonable cause. It seeks to place detainees beyond the protection of the law, and denies them legal personality, which is absolutely prohibited under the International Covenant on Civil and Political Rights and general principles of the rule of law. It effectively legalises the practice of enforced disappearance. Furthermore, the Protection of Pakistan Ordinance also grants blanket immunity to state agents for acts done in good faith and provides that any person detained before the ordinance came into force shall be deemed to have been detained pursuant to the ordinance, undermining the progress made in the last few years by the superior courts of Pakistan to bring perpetrators of enforced disappearance to account. It is likely to entrench the already pervasive impunity enjoyed by the security forces, particularly related to human rights violations.[107]

The Asian Legal Resource Centre made a written submission to the Working Group on Enforced Disappearances of the United Nations to intervene in order to stop the disappearances and the accompanying brutality, describing the Baloch disappearance as the largest number of enforced disappearances in the world. Recommending that the appropriate response from the Working Group, as well as other UN agencies, should be to engage with the government of Pakistan, providing advice and technical assistance in order that the government may decisively intervene to stop the on-going practice of enforced disappearances. The ALRC also called on the international human rights community to prioritise the problem and to take appropriate action with the government of Pakistan and the relevant United Nations agencies.[108]

The government instead reacting to Islamic terrorism introduced harsher legislation giving the military even greater powers. In response to the Peshawar school massacre of December 2014 the government launched the National

Action Plan empowering military courts to try militants and reintroduced the death penalty that had been suspended.[109] It is not clear at this stage how this will impact on the Baloch crisis but the fear is that it will inadvertently snare the Baloch insurgency within its remit and aggravate the crisis.[110]

Examining the different perspectives on the Balochistan issue strongly suggests that the main driver for the insurgency in Pakistan is due to poor management of difference, which then feeds into distribution and control of resources. Baloch history shows that the pattern of ethnic regulation has been a combination of co-option and coercion and today's crisis is the result of the continuation of this strategy. Baloch objections and concerns to the assimilationist implications of Gwadar development plan and to mineral extraction and energy projects that would have little benefit for the Baloch people were ignored. First, because legitimate avenues to express dissent were not available as key features of federalism had been suspended and, second, because they are disenfranchised from the Staatsvolk where key decisions were being made. In this period the army, where Baloch influence is negligible, was the main forum for decision-making. It also explains how from negotiations the military moved rapidly to coercion and a brutal campaign to eliminate dissent. While there seems to be a strong emotional appeal for independence, it is, for many, political posturing[111] that is sustained by the brutality of the operations against the nationalists. The Eighteenth Amendment and the Balochistan Package have the possibility of resolving the crisis by engaging with all the sensitive issues raised by Baloch dissidents and introducing a degree of consociationalism. Only time will tell whether the move away for hegemonic control will be successful and that managing difference would be through consociationalism within a reformed federal system. However, the inability of any civilian government to control the army, which is determined to crush the opposition, has scuttled these attempts. Dialogue and compromise is still the only realistic option, but this only has a chance if the detainees are released, and there is an investigation into the extrajudicial killings. However, the Pakistan governments' attempts to deal with Islamic terrorism through the Protection of Pakistan Ordinance and the National Action Plan, inadvertently, are undermining attempts to resolve the insurgency through political means. The jeopardy for Pakistan is that international human right agencies are taking increasing interest and may intervene in the future in a manner that will embarrass the government.

As for the *sardars* they are divided by personal rivalries that are mapped on to pro-government and anti-government positions. There are only three tribal leaders involved in the revolt, and parts of Balochistan, where there are no *sardars*, are very active in mobilising against the centre. There appears to be some evidence to suggest external intervention, but Pakistan's claim of the degree of Indian involvement is unproven. There does seem to be some evidence to suggest that Delhi is providing resources and given Pakistan's difficult relationship with its eastern neighbour, it is not easy to completely discount India or Afghanistan fishing in troubled waters. However external intervention, with or without the support of tribal leaders, is not a strong argument for explaining the present crisis.

The resource argument has some mileage, not in that it is responsible for funding the insurgency, but that it accentuates the sense of deprivation and the exploitation of the province. Clearly, if the numerous pipelines that are being planned are built, then there must be some settlement of the conflict and a relative degree of security before large corporations are prepared to make the sizeable investments required to operate in Balochistan. As yet, there is no evidence to suggest that strategic rivalry between the USA, China, India, Iran, or any other state, is feeding into instability in the region. The Baloch diaspora and transnationals are, in different ways, involved. Due to the fact that political activity is banned in the Gulf States, diasporic support there is surreptitious and underground. In many ways, the transnational circuits linking Quetta, Karachi, and Dubai parallel the Taliban's circuits used to fund and sustain the conflict against NATO in Afghanistan. In the Baloch case, narcotics trafficking are a key resource generator used to purchase weapons from the same black market pool accessed by the Taliban, Al Qaeda, and common criminals. However, Baloch exiles in Europe and America collaborate with their Iranian counterparts to form joint positions on media dissemination and lobbying. The hearing by a fairly minor US Congressional committee on Balochistan in 2012 came as a shock to Islamabad and highlighted the effectiveness of this tactic.

## Notes

1. Yunas Samad, 'Understanding the Insurgency in Balochistan', first appeared in *Commonwealth and Comparative Politics*, 52, 2 (2014): 293–320, Taylor & Francis Ltd, www.tandfonline.com, reprinted by permission of the publisher.
2. The Oxford-educated Nawab Akbar Khan Bugti was the *tumandar* (head) of the Bugti tribe and served as Minster of State (Interior) in Feroz Khan Noon's Cabinet in 1958. He was briefly appointed Governor of Balochistan in 1974, re-emerging in the 1988 elections leading the Baloch National Alliance to become Chief Minister of the province from 1988 to 1990. He subsequently formed the Jamhoori Watan Party in 1990 which became the largest Baloch party. Bugti was a National Assembly member in 1993 and 1997.
3. Yunas Samad, *The Pakistan–US Conundrum: Jihadists, the Military and the People, the Struggle for Control* (London: Hurst, 2011), pp. 225–6.
4. A. Rashid, 1 September 2006. 'Rebel Killing Raises Stakes in Pakistan'. *BBC News*. Retrieved 6 November 2013, from http://news.bbc.co.uk/1/hi/world/south_asia/5290966.stm; S. Nawaz, *Crossed Swords: Pakistan, its Army, and the Wars Within* (Karachi: Oxford University Press, 2009), p. 550.
5. Asian Human Rights Commission. A Statement by the Asian Human Rights Commission, Pakistan: UN Human Rights Council must Respond to the Bombing in Baluchistan, 28 August 2006; Human Rights Commission of Pakistan, *Pushed to the Wall: Report of the HRCP Fact-Finding Mission to Balochistan (5–11 October 2009)* (Lahore: Human Rights Commission of Pakistan, 2009), pp. 13–14 and 23; Rashid, 'Rebel Killing Raises Stakes in Pakistan'.
6. Samad, *The Pakistan–US Conundrum*, p. 228.
7. US State Department. 07ISLAMABAD2782, Peter Bodde, Boucher visits Balochistan. Embassy Islamabad, 22 June 2007. Retrieved 25 July 2012, from http://wikileaks.org/cable/2007/06/07ISLAMABAD2782.html#.
8. Human Rights Watch, 2011, 'We can Torture, Kill, or Keep you for Years'. Enforced Disappearances by Pakistan Security Forces in Balochistan. Retrieved 2 May 2012, from www.hrw.org/sites/default/files/reports/pakistan0711WebInside.pdf.

9. Asian Human Rights Commission, 2012. 'Pakistan: Army Creates an Organization to Kill Intellectuals and Activists in Balochistan, in the Name of Peace'. Retrieved 2 May 2012, from www.humanrights.asia/news/ahrc-news/AHRC-STM-005–2012.
10. Human Rights Watch, 'We can Torture, Kill, or Keep you for Years'.
11. 'Chief Justice takes suo notice of Khuzdar mass graves', News International (1 February 2014). Retrieved 11 February 2014, from www.thenews.com.pk/article136318 ChiefJusticetakessuonoticeofKhuzdarmassgraves. Human Rights Commission of Pakistan, State of Human Rights in 2013 (Lahore, Human Rights Commission of Pakistan, 2014).
12. Centre for Research and Security Studies, *Balochistan's Maze of Violence* (Islamabad: Centre for Research and Security Studies, 2011); Human Rights Watch, 'We can Torture, Kill, or Keep you for Years'.
13. Ibid.
14. Ibid.; T. Kumar, Testimony by Amnesty International on Human Rights in Balochistan to the Committee on Foreign Affairs, United States House of Representatives. T. Kumar – House Committee on Foreign Affairs. Retrieved 2 May 2012, from *T. Kumar – House Committee* on *Foreign Affairs*, http//:foreignaffairs.house.gov/.../HHRG-112-FA-WState-TKumar-201202.
15. Cited in Human Rights Watch, 'We can Torture, Kill, or Keep you for Years', p. 1.
16. Human Rights Watch, 'We can Torture, Kill, or Keep you for Years'.
17. Centre for Research and Security Studies, *Balochistan's Maze of Violence*.
18. Anonymous Baloch activist, interview (10 February 2012).
19. A.H. Shah, 'The Volatile Situation in Baluchistan – Options to Bring it into Streamline', M.A. Thesis (Monterey, CA: Naval Postgraduate School, 2007).
20. S.F. Hasnat, *Global Security Watch – Pakistan* (Santa Barbara, CA: Praeger, 2011), pp. 83–7, 100, 107, and 114.
21. J.S. Dunne, *Crisis in Balochistan: A Historical Analysis of the Baluch Nationalist Movement in Pakistan* (Monterey, CA: Naval Postgraduate School, 2006), pp. 65–8.
22. S. Baloch, 2012. Retrieved 2 May 2012, from www.thenews.com.pk/Todays News-9–99303-The-real-Balochistan. 'Balochistan govt decides to quash cases against Brahamdagh'. *Dawn* (16 March 2012). Retrieved 16 March 2012, from http://dawn.com/2012/03/16/balochistan-govt-decides-to-quash-cases-against-brahamdagh.
23. S.H. Panhwar, (n.d.). 'Sardari System Abolished by Prime Minister Zulfikar Ali Bhutto in 1976. A Historical Document'. Retrieved 18 July 2013, from www.pppusa.org/Acrobat/Sardari_System.pdf.
24. 'Editorial: Abolishing Sardari System or Baloch Nationalism?' *Daily Times* (26 August 2006). Retrieved 18 July 2013, from www.dailytimes.com.pk/default.asp?page=2006%5C08%5C26%5Cstory_26–8–2006_pg3_1.
25. Human Rights Commission of Pakistan, *Balochistan: Blinkered Slide into Chaos* (Lahore: Human Rights Commission of Pakistan, 2011).
26. F. Scholz, *Nomadism and Colonialism: A Hundred Years of Baluchistan 1872–1972*, H. Van Skyhawk, Trans. (Oxford: Oxford University Press, 2002).
27. S. Matheson, *The Tigers of Baluchistan* (Karachi: Oxford University Press, 2009).
28. P. Titus, *Marginality and Modernity: Ethnicity and Change in Post-Colonial Balochistan* (Karachi: Oxford University Press, 1997).
29. Human Rights Commission of Pakistan, *Conflict in Balochistan: Report of HRC Fact-Finding Mission, December 2005–January 2006* (Lahore: Human Rights Commission of Pakistan, 2006).
30. Ibid.
31. Asian Human Rights Commission. 'Pakistan: Army Creates an Organization to Kill Intellectuals and Activists in Balochistan, in the Name of Peace'; A. Mustikhan, 2 January 2012. 'Some Baloch Happy over Bomb Attack on "I.S.I. Safe-House" in Quetta'. Retrieved from www.examiner.com/article/some-baloch-happy-over-bomb-attack-on-i-s-i-safehouse-quetta.

32 H. Bull, *The Anarchical Society: A Study of Order in World Politics* (New York: Columbia University Press, 1977); B. Buzan, *People, States and Fear: National Security Problems in International Relations*, 2nd Revised Edition (New York: Prentice Hall, 1991).
33 T.M. Breseeg, *Baloch Nationalism: Its Origins and Development* (Karachi: Royal Book Co., 2004), p. 353.
34 B.S. Syed, 'Pakistan Seeks Bramdagh's Extradition', *Dawn* (11 September 2011). Retrieved 11 September 2011, from http://dawn.com/2011/09/11/pakistan-seeks-bramdaghs-extradition; USSD, 2009c.
35 'Balochistan Govt Decides to Quash Cases against Brahamdagh', *Dawn* (16 March 2012). Retrieved 16 March 2012, from http://dawn.com/2012/03/16/balochistan-govt-decides-to-quash-cases-against-brahamdagh.
36 National Commission on Terrorist Attacks upon the United States, 2004. '9/11 Commission Report: Final Report of the National Commission on Terrorist Attacks upon the United States'. Washington, DC. Retrieved from www.9–11commission.gov/report/911Report.pdf.
37 Samad, *The Pakistan–US Conundrum*, p. 87.
38 J. Bajoria, 'India-Afghanistan Relations. Council on Foreign Relations' (2009). Retrieved 24 February 2014, from www.cfr.org/india/india-afghanistan-relations/p17474#p2.
39 DefenceNow, 7 October 2011. 'India Decides to Train Afghanistan's Army and Signs other Bilateral Agreements with Afghanistan'. Retrieved 7 October 2011, from www.defencenow.com/news/322/india-decides-to-train-afghanistans-army-and-signs-other-bilateral-agreements-with-afghanistan.htmlpage=2006%5C08%5C26%5Cstory_26–8–2006_pg3_1.
40 C. Fair, *India in Afghanistan and Beyond: Opportunities and Constraints* (New York: Century Foundation, 2010).
41 A. Bansal, 'Balochistan: Continuing Violence and its Implications', *Strategic Analysis*, 30, 1 (2006): 46–63; S. Mazari, 'Balochistan and the "Great Power Games"', *The News International* (2 February 2005); H. Mir, 2009. 'Pakistan has Proof of "3 Indian Kasabs" in Baluchistan'. Rediff.com. Retrieved from http://news.rediff.com/report/2009/jul/28/hamid-mir-on-the-real-reason-why-india-agreed-to-discuss-baluchistan.htm; D. Qayyum, 2009. 'ISI Summons RAW Chief over Terrorism in Pakistan', 22 July 2009. Retrieved 22 July 2009, from http://pakistankakhudahafiz.wordpress.com/tag/christine-fair. Senate Sub-Committee on Balochistan. (n.d.). Final report headed by Senator Mushahid Hussain Sayed.
42 US State Department, 2010. 10NEWDELHI387, 'Uzra Zeya, more on Feb. 25 Indo-Pak talks: "No breakdown but no breakthrough"', 25 February 2010. Retrieved from http://wikileaks.org/cable/2010/02/10NEWDELHI387.html#.
43 'Editorial: Mengal's Stance', *The News International* (12 July 2013). Retrieved 25 July 2013, from www.thenews.com.pk/Todays-News-8–189429-Mengals-stance. Government of Balochistan. Mines and Minerals Department (Presentation). Retrieved 28 December 2006, from www.balochistan.gov.pk.
44 A. James, 2012. 'Foreign Policy Magazine Laura Rozen and Christine Fair of Rand Corp. Confirmed that India (RAW) were Neck Deep in Supporting Terrorists (TTP) against Pakistan'. Retrieved 28 July 2012, from www.fourwinds10.net/siterun_data/government/war/afghan_war/pakistan_war/news.php?q=1337959875; US State Department, 2009. 09ISLAMABAD1840, Pakistan Media Reaction. Embassy Islamabad, 7 August 2009. Retrieved 25 July 2009, from http://wikileaks.org/cable/2009/08/09ISLAMABAD1840.html# USSD, 2009b.
45 Samad, *The Pakistan–US Conundrum*, p. 225.
46 T. Saeedi, S. Pyatakov, A. Nasimzadeh, Q. Jan, S.M. Kasi, R. Kival, and M. Davidson, 'Pakistan: Unveiling the Mystery of Balochistan Insurgency – Part One', *News Central Asia* (18 July 2011). Retrieved 26 July 2013, from http://newscentralasia.

net/2011/07/18/archive-material-pakistan-unveiling-the-mysteryof-balochistan-insurgency-part-one.
47 S. Mazari, 'Balochistan and the "Great Power Games"', *The News International* (2 February 2005).
48 A. Bansal, *Balochistan in Turmoil: Pakistan at the Crossroads* (New Delhi: Manas, 2010); BBC News, 'Lonely Burial for Baloch Leader', (1 September 2006). Retrieved 6 November 2013, from http://news.bbc.co.uk/1/hi/5304594.stm.
49 P. Collier, A. Hoeffler, and N. Sambanis, 'The Collier-Hoeffler Model of Civil War Onset and the Case Study Project Research Design', in P. Collier and N. Sambanis (eds), *Understanding Civil War: Evidence and Analysis, Africa* (Washington, DC: The World Bank, 2005), Vol. 1, p. 13.
50 H. Gazdar, *Balochistan Economic Report, Background Paper on Social Structures and Migration* (Karachi: Collective for Social Science Research, 2007).
51 F. Grare, *The Resurgence of Baluch Nationalism* (Washington, DC: Carnegie Endowment for International Peace, Carnegie Papers, No. 65, January 2006).
52 R. Wirsing, *Baloch Nationalism and the Geopolitics of Energy Resources: The Changing Context of Separatism in Pakistan* (Carlisle, PA: Strategic Studies Institute, U.S. Army War College, 2008).
53 T. Niazi, 'Globalization, Resource Conflicts and Social Violence in South Asia', *International Journal of Contemporary Sociology*, 5, 1 (2008): 184–208.
54 Gazdar, *Balochistan Economic Report*.
55 Samad, *The Pakistan–US Conundrum*, p. 225.
56 M. Stanley, E. Koryukin, and L. Maraboli, 'Balochistan Economic Report – Mining Sector Development' (Presentation) (The World Bank Group, 2006).
57 Gazdar, *Balochistan Economic Report*, p. 6; Government of Balochistan, Mines and Minerals Department (Presentation).
58 Gazdar, *Balochistan Economic Report*, p. 6; World Bank, *Pakistan: Balochistan Economic Report from Periphery to Core, Volume II: Full Report* (Report No. 40345-PK) (Washington, DC: The World Bank, 2008), p. 41. Retrieved from https://openknowledge.worldbank.org/handle/10986/8094.
59 Z. Bhutta, 2012. 'Pakistan Should Think about Reko Diq Carefully', *The Express Tribune*. Retrieved 29 June 2012, from http://tribune.com.pk/story/400703/pakistan-shouldthink-about-reko-diq-carefully-thomson.
60 'Supreme Court Declares Reko Diq Agreement Void', *Dawn* (13 January 2013). Retrieved 22 February 2013, from http://dawn.com/2013/01/07/supreme-courtdeclares-reko-diq-agreement-unlawful.
61 D. Temple, *The Iran–Pakistan–India Pipeline: The Intersection of Energy and Politics* (New Delhi: The Institute of Peace and Conflict Studies, 2007).
62 Gazdar, *Balochistan Economic Report*.
63 A. Cohen, L. Curtis, and O. Graham, 2008. 'The Proposed Iran–Pakistan–India Gas Pipeline: An Unacceptable Risk to Regional Security' (No. 2139). The Heritage Foundation. Retrieved from www.heritage.org/research/reports/2008/05/the-proposed-iran-pakistan-india-gas-pipeline-an-unacceptable-risk-to-regional-security; World Bank, *Pakistan: Balochistan Economic Report from Periphery to Core*, pp. 96–97.
64 Chinapage.com (n.d.), 'Proposed Qatar-Pakistan Gas Pipeline'. Retrieved 25 July 2012, from www.chinapage.com/transportation/pipeline/pipeline-qatar.html; World Bank, 2008, pp. 67–71).
65 Amnesty International, n.d. 'Conflict Diamonds: Did Someone Die for that Diamond?' Retrieved 6 November 2013, from www.amnestyusa.org/ourwork/issues/business-and-human-rights/oil-gas-and-mining-industries/conflict-diamonds; A. Ikelegbe, 'The Economy of Conflict in the Oil Rich Niger Delta Region of Nigeria', *Nordic Journal of African Studies*, 14, 2 (2005): 208–34.

66 A. Appadurai, 'Disjuncture and Difference in the Global Cultural Economy'. In M. Featherstone (ed.), *Global Culture: Nationalism, Globalization and Modernity* (London: Sage, 1990), pp. 295–310.
67 R. Brubaker, 'The "diaspora" diaspora', *Ethnic and Racial Studies*, 28, 1 (2005): 1–19; Bull, *The Anarchical Society*.
68 P. Werbner, 'Theorising Complex Diasporas: Purity and Hybridity in the South Asian Public Sphere in Britain', *Journal of Ethnic and Migration Studies*, 30, 5 (2004): 895–911.
69 Joshua Project. (n.d.) 'The Baloch'. Retrieved 15 July 2012, from www.joshuaproject.net/people-profile.php.
70 J.E. Peterson, 'Oman's Diverse Society: Northern Oman', *Middle East Journal*, 8 (2004): 31–51.
71 Mustikhan, 'Gulf Baloch Army Officers Say Paki Soldiers are Cannibals'; Peterson, 'Oman's Diverse Society: Northern Oman'.
72 Collier, Hoeffler, and Sambanis, 'The Collier–Hoeffler Model of Civil War Onset and the Case Study Project Research Design', p. 13.
73 H. Jamali, 'Shorelines of Memory, Sediments of History: Britain, Oman and the Shifting Geographies of Trade on the Mekran Coast'. Paper presented at the 46th Annual Meeting of the Middle East Studies Association, Denver, CO (17–20 November 2012); Interview with H. Jamali, anthropologist who has conducted fieldwork in Oman and has completed a PhD thesis on Gwadar (2 August 2013).
74 Mustikhan, 'Gulf Baloch Army Officers say Paki Soldiers are Cannibals'.
75 S. Reeve, *The New Jackals – Ramzi Yousef, Osama Bin Laden and the Future of Terrorism* (London: Andre Deutsch, 1999); Samad, *The Pakistan–US Conundrum*, p. 52.
76 United States State Department, 2009, Pakistan Media Reaction. Embassy Islamabad; United States State Department, 2010.10ABUDHABI33, UAE FM Discusses Taliban Financial Flows and Reintegration with Amb. Holbrooke and Treasury A/S Cohen, 25 January 2010. Retrieved 5 August 2013, from http://wikileaks.org/cable/2010/01/10ABUDHABI33.html.
77 US State Department, 2006. Islamabad 017547, Peter Bodde, 'Balochistan (6): The Nationalist Insurgency', Embassy Islamabad, 4 September. Retrieved 2 May 2012, from http://wikileaks.org/cable/2006/09/06ISLAMABAD17547.html#.
78 'Scraping the Barrel, the Trade in Surplus Ammunition', *Small Arms Survey*, Issue Brief, 2 (April 2011); United States State Department, 2009. 09ISLAMABAD1840, Pakistan Media Reaction: 7 August 2009. Retrieved 5 August 2013, from http://wikileaks.org/cable/2009/08/09ISLAMABAD 1840.html.
79 Samad, *The Pakistan–US Conundrum*.
80 Participant observation, 2012–13.
81 'US Bill Seeks Balochistan Sovereignty', *Dawn* (18 February 2012).
82 Samad, *The Pakistan–US Conundrum*.
83 J. McGarry and B. O'Leary, *The Politics of Ethnic Regulation: Case Studies of Protracted Ethnic Conflicts* (London: Routledge, 1993).
84 I. Lustick, 'Stability in Deeply Divided Societies: Consociationalism Versus Control', *World Politics*, 36, 31 (April 1979): 325–44; McGarry and O'Leary, *The Politics of Ethnic Regulation*.
85 McGarry and O'Leary, *The Politics of Ethnic Regulation*, p. 39; B. O'Leary, 'Introduction'. In B. O'Leary, I. Lustick, and T. Callaghy (eds), *Right-Sizing the State: The Politics of Moving Borders* (Oxford: Oxford University Press, 2001), pp. 1–14.
86 McGarry and O'Leary, *The Politics of Ethnic Regulation*; O'Leary, 'Introduction'.
87 G. Pandey and Y. Samad (eds), *Faultines of Nationhood* (New Delhi: Roli, 2007), pp. 67–138.
88 Y. Samad, 'Pakistan or Punjabistan: Crisis of National Identity', *International Journal of Punjab Studies*, 2, 1 (1995): 23–42; Y. Samad, 'Minority Rights to

Majoritarian Discourse'. In Pandey and Samad, *Faultines of Nationhood*, pp. 67–138; Ian Talbot, 'The Punjabization of Pakistan: Myth or Reality?' In C. Jaffrelot (ed.), *Pakistan – Nationalism without a Nation?* (New Delhi: Manohar, 2002), pp. 51–62.
89. A. Siddiqa, *Military Inc.: Inside Pakistan's Military Economy* (London: Pluto, 2007).
90. Y. Samad, 'In and Out of Power but not Down and Out: Mohajir Identity Politics'. In Jaffrelot, *Pakistan – Nationalism Without a Nation?*, pp. 63–83; Samad, 'Minority Rights to Majoritarian Discourse; and Samad, *The Pakistan–US Conundrum*.
91. M. Axmann, *Back to the Future: The Khanate of Kalat and the Genesis of Baluch Nationalism, 1915–55* (Karachi: Oxford University Press, 2009); Y.K. Bangash, *Subjects to Citizens: Accession and Integration of the Princely States of Pakistan* (Karachi: Oxford University Press, 2013), Chapter 3.
92. S. Harrison, *In Afghanistan's Shadow* (New York: Carnegie Endowment for International Peace, 1981).
93. McGarry and O'Leary, *The Politics of Ethnic Regulation*.
94. Samad, *The Pakistan–US Conundrum*, p. 225.
95. Asian Human Rights Commission, 2012. 'Pakistan: Army Creates an Organization to Kill Intellectuals and Activists in Balochistan, in the Name of Peace'; Human Rights Watch, 'We Can Torture, Kill or Keep you for Years'.
96. Samad, *The Pakistan–US Conundrum*, p. 222.
97. S. Baloch, 'The Real Balochistan', *The News*. Retrieved 2 May 2012, from www.thenews.co.pk/Today's-news-9–99303-The-real-Balochistan.
98. Samad, *The Pakistan–US Conundrum*, pp. 66 and 85.
99. Government of Pakistan, *Amendment XVIII of the Constitution of Pakistan* (Islamabad: Government of Pakistan, 2010).
100. Government of Pakistan. *Aghaaz-e-Huqook Balochistan* (Islamabad: Government of Pakistan, 2009).
101. Q. Butt, 'Balochistan Conundrum: Khan of Kalat's Return is a Distant Possibility', *Express Tribune*, (26 May 2013). Retrieved 27 February 2015, http://tribune.com.pk/story/554511/balochistan-conundrum-khan-of-kalats-return-is-a-distant-possibility.
102. US State Department, 2006. 06ISLAMABAD5596, Ryan Crocker, 'Government's Charm Offensive Leaves many Baloch unimpressed'. Embassy Islamabad, 3 April 2006. Retrieved 25 July 2012, from http://wikileaks.org/cable/2006/04/06ISLAMABAD5596.html#; United States State Department, 2008. 08ISLAMABAD3533, Anne W. Patterson, 'Zardari Reaches out to Balochistan'. Embassy Islamabad, 10 November 2008. Retrieved 25 July 2012, from http://wikileaks.org/cable/2008/11/08ISLAMABAD3533.html#; United States State Department, 09ISLAMABAD42, Anne W. Patterson, Pakistan Political Roundup. Embassy Islamabad, 8 January, 2009. Retrieved 25 July, 2012, from http://wikileaks.org/cable/2009/01/09ISLAMABAD42.html#.
103. 'Malik Plans APC on Balochistan Issue', *Dawn* (19 October 2013). Retrieved 6 November 2013, from http://dawn.com/news/1050518/malik-plans-apc-on-balochistan-issue.
104. 'VBMP long march reaches DG Khan today', *The Nation* (26 January 2014). Retrieved 11 February 2014, from www.nation.com.pk/national/26-Jan-2014/vbmp-long-march-reaches-dg-khan-today. 'Truck "marches" into long marchers in Okara; 2 hurt', *The Nation* (9 February 2014). Retrieved 11 February 2014, from www.nation.com.pk/national/09-Feb-2014/truck-marches-into-long-marchers-in-okara-2-hurt.
105. 'Pakistan: The government ignores the historical long march for the recovery of disappeared persons, Asian Human Rights Commission' (4 March 2014). Retrieved 5 March 2014, from www.humanrights.asia/news/ahrcnews/AHRCSTM0392014.

106 'Pakistan: Disappearances no end in sight', Asian Human Rights Commission (5 March 2014) Retrieved 5 March 2014, from www.humanrights.asia/opinions/columns/AHRCETC0062014.
107 Protection of Pakistan Ordinance, Ordinance IX 2013 (31 October 2013), Retrieved 5 March 2014, from www.na.gov.pk/uploads/documents/1383819468951.pdf. 'Pakistan: Disappearances no end in sight', Asian Human Rights Commission (5 March 2014). Retrieved 5 March 2014 www.humanrights.asia/opinions/columns/AHRCETC0062014.
108 Pakistan: Disappearances, A written submission to the UN Human Rights Council by the Asian Legal Resource Centre (28 February 2014) *Human Rights Council, Twenty fifth session, Agenda Item 4, General Debate*, Retrieved 5 March 2014, from www.alrc.net/doc/mainfile.php/hrc25/787.
109 Mateen Haider, 'Military courts part of National Action Plan: PM Nawaz', *Dawn* (30 December 2014). Retrieved 28 February 2015, from www.dawn.com/news/1154046.
110 Mian Abrar, 'Are we children of a lesser God?' *Pakistan Today* (24 January 2015). Retrieved 28 February 2015, from www.pakistantoday.com.pk/2015/01/24/featured/are-we-children-of-a-lesser-god.
111 US State Department, 2006. Islamabad 16994, Peter Bodde, Balochistan (4): Who's who – the Baloch tribes. Embassy Islamabad, 29 August 2006. Retrieved 15 November 2013, from http://wikileaks.org/cable/2006/08/06ISLAMABAD16994.html.

# 7 A sublime, yet disputed, object of political ideology?

Sufism in Pakistan at the crossroads

*Alix Philippon*

Pakistan was created in 1947 in the name of Islam and was thus branded, way before the Iranian revolution, as the 'paradigm of Islamic revivalism'.[1] But far from being a social monolith, Islamic revivalism covers a wide spectrum of ideologies and practices.[2] As Katherine Ewing rightly points out in the case of Pakistan, Islam was actually a 'sublime object of ideology'[3] that succeeded in mobilizing a population for the sake of a nationalist enterprise, yet 'it functioned in political discourse (though not, of course, in the lives of individual Muslims), as virtually an empty signifier'.[4] The omnipresence of the Islamic reference on the Pakistani political scene as well as the fight for the monopoly of its interpretation have indeed generated a 'fragmentation of authority'[5] and thus a struggle between multiple actors appropriating religious symbols to define 'real Islam'. In Pakistan as elsewhere in the Muslim world, this 'Muslim symbolic politics'[6] has been the arena of intense debates on the traditions, values, and ideals constituting Islam and has implied 'the competition and contest over both the interpretation of symbols and control of the institutions, formal and informal, that produce and sustain them'.[7] This 'struggle for the real', that is to say these attempts to impose a conception of the world, institutionalize it and thus influence the ways in which people are to behave,[8] has implied in the political field a constant redefinition of the 'we', where it comes from and where it goes,[9] in the normative language of Islam.

As a major resource of Islamic language, Sufism is a major component of identity politics in Pakistan and is used by groups as well as individuals to negotiate and articulate their identity, often in highly inconsistent ways. It has often been tapped as a political resource and instrumentalized as a legitimizing tool by both state and non-state actors. Generally speaking, it has played a major role in the ideological debates on the place of Islam in Pakistani state and society. According to American anthropologist Clifford Geertz (1926–2006), the function of ideology is to provide authoritative concepts to help in making sense of politics, and to produce images through which it can be grasped. Ideology, just like religion, is a 'cultural system' creating meaning and shaping political life. It is the 'apologetic dimension of culture' that is concerned with the establishment and defence of belief and value models,[10] the matrix for the creation of a collective consciousness.[11] As the complex dialectics between Islam and politics unfolded in Pakistan, Sufism acted as a foil as well as a source of inspiration for contradictory ideological discourses whether reformist, modernist, secularist, traditionalist, or nationalist. As the contested 'mystical' aspect of faith, it has indeed become part of the 'ideologization of Islam', and its definition has become increasingly the *locus* of arguments within the public sphere.

As a matter of fact, Sufism, like Islam, is not a static universe of meaning and action. On the contrary, it can be analysed as a 'tradition' with which all the actors active in the political arena can never quite distance themselves in their political discourse and practices. According to Belgian political theorist Chantal Mouffe (b. 1943),[12] tradition is all about 'language games' and practices that allow individuals to constitute themselves as subjects but also allow the political community to constitute itself through the reinvention of the meanings encapsulated in this tradition. It allows politics to be conceived as the creation of new uses of its key terms, in order to render possible new 'forms of life'. Hence, it is not easy to define Sufism, or Islam for that matter, without falling into essentialism. Delineating it only as the mystical trend within Islam does not enable one to understand the more social and political dimensions of this diverse phenomenon. Given the 'polyphonic'[13] heritage and the great hermeneutic plasticity of Sufism, it seems best here to use the word in a descriptive way to avoid getting trapped in one ideological discourse or another.

As a matter of fact, Sufism is a highly ambiguous signifier, an Islamic 'discursive tradition'[14] which most players active in the political arena can never quite manage to supersede. From the reformist Muhammed Iqbal (1877–1938),[15] who reinterpreted Sufism in a dynamic idiom to inspire the new Muslim community, to the latest political endeavours of the state-sponsored National Sufi Council, not to mention the doctrinal struggles between the different religious sects like the Deobandis[16] and the Barelvis,[17] Sufism emerges as a relevant symbol to analyse the never ending ideological debate on the identity of a country caught in controversial political contexts, especially since 2001 and the beginning of the so-called 'War on Terror' in which Pakistan has played an ambiguous role as a front-line state. The universe of Sufism, deeply embedded in Pakistan's ethos, became the natural ally of power and an ideological weapon of 'mass seduction'. Indeed, Pakistan is today pointed out as one of the most dynamic hotbeds of international 'jihadism' and of extremist activities of all kinds. In this tense political context, Sufism has been brandished more than ever as an ideological alternative to the most radical versions of Islamic faith.

On the basis of many years of fieldwork in Pakistan during which I conducted dozens of interviews and undertook numerous participative observations, I intend to analyse the social and political underpinnings of the various narratives that Sufism has inspired, especially since 9/11, to the different actors mobilized in Pakistan's political arena, and more specifically to the powers that be. I will start with a general overview of the long-standing contest the very category of Sufism has been confronted with in history, and will focus more specifically on Muhammad Iqbal's reformulation of Sufism in his attempt to build Muslim nationalism in India. I will then analyse how Iqbal's point of view has influenced the way post-colonial Pakistan has dealt with this issue by intervening directly in the definition of what Sufism entails through the regulation of the mystical sphere. I then pay attention to the master narrative 'Sufi Islam versus radical Islam' celebrated in the frame of the 'War on Terror' and institutionalized in various initiatives, notably the National Sufi Council. I will then show how and by whom this master narrative is contested in the public sphere, before concluding on the latest ironic twist in the official promotion of Sufism: when empowering Barelvi groups to fight radical Islam might have actually ended up in the very radicalization of Sufi Islam.

## Sufism: a concept in an ideological contest

In the process of the 'objectification of Muslim consciousness'[18] through which believers hailing from all social backgrounds started wondering about fundamental issues pertaining to religious practice and to the definition of religion, Islam 'has become a self-contained system that its believers can describe, characterize and distinguish from other belief systems'.[19] This is not to say that self-consciousness was merely absent from previous eras, but it has gradually intensified with the advent of modernity. Ever since this awakening which gave rise to various movements of reformism, Sufism has played an *ambivalent* role in Islamic revivalism. A rhetoric of decline, decadence, and at times, downright condemnation, dominated the public discourse on 'Sufism', and particularly on the system of meanings and practices centred around shrines, *pirs*[20] and their much criticized descendants called *gaddi nashins*, whose sanctity had been naturalized in popular culture. In this historical process, Sufism has come under successive attacks of Wahhabism, reformism, and lately Islamism, and has gradually been objectified as a new category. Sufism and reformism have indeed been constructed as dichotomous, in Muslim discourses as well as in the academic world.[21] The criticisms addressed to Sufism have remained quite the same since the thirteenth-fourteenth-century theologian Ibn Taimiyya (1263–1328) and have been relentlessly reiterated from one reformism to another: it is usually condemned as associationism (*shirk*), for it allows veneration of saints and the Prophet Muhammad (c. 570–632) and comes into contradiction with the principle of the unity of God (*tauhid*). The practices associated with it are also branded as innovations (*bidat*), unknown in the time of the Prophet. Sufis have also been condemned for their so-called apolitical position, and thought of as being unable to take an active part in society.

For the past 10 to 15 years, the interactions between Sufism and its supposed challengers have increasingly become the focus of a growing number of scholars.[22] As a matter of fact, not one of the great figures of Islamic reform throughout history, and especially since the eighteenth century, has constructed his own thought without being inspired by the Sufi tradition at one level or the other. In the subcontinent, from Sheikh Ahmed Sirhindi (1564–1624) to Shah Wali Allah (1702–62), from Syed Ahmad Barelvi (1856–1921) to the Deobandis, from the Barelvis to Muhammad Iqbal, most of the celebrated religious reformers relied on the Sufi tradition, though they held different views of what it entails. The distinction between 'scripturalist Sufism' and a 'deviant' version of the latter has often been highlighted. Sufi orders have also often been called on to fuel other forms of mobilizations, including Islamism. Hassan Al Banna (1906–49), the founder of the Egyptian Muslim Brotherhood, Abu Ala Maududi (1903–79), the founder of the Pakistani Jamaat-i Islami (Islamic Party), and Sheikh Abdessalam Yassine (1929–2012), the founder of the Moroccan al Adl wal Ihsan (Justice and Spirituality), were all initiated into Sufism, before coming to establish an arm's length relationship with the latter in an ambivalent way. If they went on being influenced both by the organizational model of the brotherhood and by the conception of the leader (*amir*) as a charismatic figure, they did not wish to be identified with 'traditional' Sufism and were very critical of its more 'popular' aspects such as the cult of the saints.

## Incorporating 'the higher Sufism of Islam'[23] into a national ideology

The author that best exemplifies this ambivalent approach to Sufism in the subcontinent is the poet and philosopher Muhammad Iqbal who, in the 1930s, started defining his idea of Muslim nationalism. His contribution to the formation of the Indian Muslims' collective consciousness seems unequalled.[24] In his eyes, the reform of Islam must have socio-political aims: his goals were to restore the dynamism of Islam, and to exhume its original truths in order to reconstruct the great Islamic concepts and reconnect them with their initial universality. Even though, in his youth, Iqbal appears almost embarrassed by the mystical content of his own heritage, influenced perhaps by European Orientalist attitudes,[25] he later on tried to redefine the role of Sufism in the modern world in order to achieve his reformist and modernist mission. He advocated self-development against self-renunciation and, against the indifference to the socio-political process, he promoted a type of personality actively involved in the progress of Islam as a social polity and in the reconstruction of society according to Islamic principles. It is mainly in his philosophical doctrine of the ego (*khudi*), borrowed from the Sufi tradition but reformulated in a radically new way, that he tries to offer a new frame of reference to Muslim national identity both for the individual as well as for the collective Muslim 'self'.[26] In his eyes, there is no need for an intercession between God and man, as man can benefit directly from the blessed embrace of the divinity.[27] Iqbal affixes a contemporary seal to old Sufi ideas in order to orientate the Muslim community towards a grand political destiny. Obviously, this great modernist thinker holds derogative views of 'pirism', that is to say the ascendancy of rural *pirs* over the ignorant masses. In this sense, Iqbal was very much attuned to the Orientalist conceptions about institutional Sufism prevailing in his time and that were to dominate academic studies on the topic in the 1960s and 1970s. He does not hesitate in denouncing the incapacity of contemporary Sufi representatives to receive inspiration from modernity.[28]

Iqbal's audacious intellectual experimentations aiming at reconciling Sufism and modernity were popularized in the *Secrets of the Self*,[29] a philosophical poem published in Lahore in 1915. In classical Sufi doctrine, the individual self is insignificant when confronted by the absolute Being, and its goal is to extinguish itself (*fana*) in the divine. For Iqbal, on the contrary, the limited self is central to existence. It should not dissolve its identity but intensify it in an assertive and creative endeavour of self-assumption which is the ideal of the perfect humanity in Islam.[30] Critical of the so-called Sufi quietism which weakened Muslims and hastened their never-ending decadence, Iqbal presents the model of the free man in the guise of a strong personality who is involved in the world and imprints his desires on it. He despises the fatalistic mentality of the masses and portrays a man daring to negotiate with his destiny instead of submitting to its pre-ordained patterns.[31] Indeed, the fascination of latter-day Sufis for 'other worldly concerns' and their nihilistic concentration in this imaginary realm are indicators of Muslim decline. Instead of confronting the burning issues of their time with vitality, the 'prophets of decadence' get lost in other worldly mysticism. It is the prevalence of this symptom in the most brilliant minds of Islam that has led to the neglect of one of the most important aspects of religion, that of a 'social polity'. Iqbal deplores this waste and deems it the main cause of the mediocre political leadership found in Islam and of the rigidity of Islamic law (*sharia*), resulting in ignorant populations simply imitating schools of jurisprudence.[32] The spirit of 'Muslim democracy' has thus always been enslaved by a sort of a 'spiritual aristocracy' claiming an authority and a power which is out of reach for the ordinary Muslim. It is hardly surprising that, in the *Reconstruction of Religious Thought in Islam*, Iqbal's main references are the great reformist thinkers who, though they were involved in Sufism, have also been very critical of its more popular versions: Ibn Taymiyya (1263–1328), who claimed the freedom of *ijtihad* and inspired the Wahhabi movement considered to be the first expressions of modern Islam;[33] Abd al-Wahhab (1703–92), the great puritan reformer;[34] Shaykh Ahmad Sirhindi (1564–1624), a great religious genius of the seventeenth century,[35] and a great reformer of Islamic Sufism;[36] Shah Waliullah, who felt the necessity of a new spirit in Islam[37] and was the last great theologian of Islam;[38] and Jamal al-Din Al-Afghani (1838–97), the *salafi* thinker who knew how vast the task of reforming Islam was. All these Islamic role models share a similar type of 'prophetic consciousness'.[39] Whereas the mystic does not want to return from his unitary experience with God, the prophet is able to convert this religious transformative experience into a creative and pragmatic skill.[40] For Iqbal, the quality of religious and mystical experience must be felt in its effective objectification in this world.

Many authors have highlighted Iqbal's inconsistency as his thoughts are impregnated by the norms and symbols of Sufism, and yet often prone to anti-Sufi views or to even deny the esoteric aspect of faith. These contradictions were to mark Pakistani public discourses on Sufism. Though he was initiated in the Qadiri order, Iqbal considers the contemporary expressions of institutionalized Sufism to have been corrupted and to be unable to assist Muslims on their way to progress. 'There are no more goods of Islamic conduct in the shops of the

Sufis.'[41] Iqbal operates a conscious return to his own roots through the prism of modernity. And the way in which he integrated Sufism into his intellectual project of the reconstruction of religious thought had strong bearings on the way Sufism was perceived and defined in the post-colonial Pakistani state.

> The linkage of pirs with the 'tradition' pole of the tradition-modernity axis – with its associated labels of ignorance, superstition, weakness, and gullibility – has persisted in contemporary Pakistani discourse. But not all of Sufism succumbed to this designation.... One of the consequences of labelling *pirs* antithetical to the project of modernity was a bifurcation of Sufism itself, so that for many Pakistanis today, the practices associated with *pirs* are seen as something that has no relationship to Sufism.[42]

In contemporary Pakistan, the living *pir* figure has a very derogatory connotation, detached from the Sufism once thought of as a prestigious but now decadent mystical tradition. As a form of leadership and authority, the *pir* still is this ambivalent *locus* of construction, deconstruction, and negotiation of Muslim identity and of the right Islamic practice. *Piri-muridi*, the relationship between a spiritual master and his disciple, is viewed by many modernists as 'authoritarian' in nature and as structuring the hierarchies of local culture and politics hence against the democratic ethos promoted both by 'Islam' and by the new post-colonial state.

When Pakistan was created, the *gaddi nishins*, and more specifically the *pir zamindars*, that is, those among them who were landlords, emerged as the dominant social class, along with other feudal lords with whom they had contracted alliances or marriages. As Sufis, feudal lords, and politicians, these powerful leaders with a composite authority appear today to be some of the main players in Pakistan's local power structure. However, they have not entered the political scene as a social class, but have been active in all the parties, often jumping from one to the other. Thanks to their disciples, most prominent *pirs* possess a 'spiritual constituency' potentially convertible into a vote bank. If the adequacy between the spiritual and the political allegiance is not always complete, since some disciples might not vote according to their *pirs'* wish, the latter, whether they are politicians or not, enjoy a great ability to mobilize the masses. Each election is an exercise in clientelist practices involving disciples/citizens and *pirs*/notables. One understands better what is politically at stake in the institution of shrines and *piri-muridi*, and why the Pakistani state wanted to legally regulate the mystical sphere.

## An ambiguous politicization of Sufi shrines

The judge Javaid Iqbal (b. 1924), following the footsteps of his illustrious reformist father Muhammad Iqbal who did not consider contemporary *pirs* as potential vectors for Islamic modernization, deplored as early as the 1950s in his *Ideology of Pakistan*[43] the decadence and corruption plaguing Sufi orders. The path to 'progress' was only thought possible once these alternative centres of power had been harnessed by the authorities and their powerful religious appeal channelled into allegiance to the state. As influential religious and political actors, living *pirs* were delegitimized in modernizing discourses. It is against the beliefs, practices, and leaders associated with this 'traditional' social order that the Ministry of Religious Endowments (*awqaf*) was created in Pakistan in 1959 under the regime of the modernist president and military dictator Ayub Khan (1907–74, President 1958–69). Shrines, thought to be remains of a backward social order, had to become catalysts of modernization and the authority of the *pirs* was meant to be curbed thanks to the nationalization of shrines.[44]

Since then, every successive Pakistani ruler has tried to redefine Sufism and the *pirs*, and instrumentalize them for his or her own political benefit.[45] If the redefinition of Sufi saints undertaken by Ayub emphasized their role as social reformers, under Pervez Musharraf (b. 1943, President 2001–8) they were envisaged more for their role as promoters of peace and tolerance. If, under Zulfiqar Ali Bhutto (1928–79, President 1971–3, Prime Minister 1973–7), the great patron saint of Lahore was presented as the precursor of 'Islamic socialism',[46] he became under Musharraf the symbol of intercommunal harmony, which Pakistan needs for progress.[47] Indeed, since 2001 and the beginning of the 'War on Terror', Sufism and the saints gradually became the symbols of the fight undertaken by the government against creeping 'talibanization', deemed to threaten the very fabric of the nation. The ideologization of Sufism has, since 2005, led many shrines to be attacked in retaliation by radical militants who consider the cult of the saints mere heresy. Conversely, these Sufi saints have been once again been officially redefined as metaphors of the ideal Pakistani nation and of the 'true' Islam in the name of which the country was created. They are the indigenous identity hallmarks embodying the positive values that Pakistanis are exhorted to emulate to become truly who they are. During his trips to Sindh or Punjab, Musharraf exhorted the populations of this 'land of Sufi saints' to 'promote tolerance, liberalism and a moderate culture in order to eliminate the destructive forces of extremism' and to pray 'to protect the country against the misdeeds of extremists and fanatics who are trying to damage it'.[48] This discourse endows past Sufi saints (and their shrines which prolong their moral reign) with an Islamic authority as they embody an ethical order and social values that make sense in Sindh and the Punjab. These saints are perceived by society and projected by the powers that be as symbols who have to be exalted to defeat the extremists' designs.

The commemoration of the death of the saints (*'urs*), are also used by the government and its administration to promote and popularize the philosophy and poetry of the great Sufis. On the occasion of the 264th *'urs* of the Sindhi saint Hazrat Shah Abdul Latif Bhitai (1689–1752) in January 2008, Sindh's secretary for Tourism and Culture Shams Jafrani asked the Pakistan Broadcasting Corporation to launch a 'Bhit Shah radio' in order to cover the religious celebrations live. Three books dedicated to the work of the saint and Sindhi culture were also launched, and a literary conference and a cultural show were organized. In 2006, the Sindhi minister for Tourism and Culture Qamar Mansoor, announced that a 'Shah Latif day' would be observed in all the headquarters of the districts by the Department of Culture to disseminate the message of love and tolerance of the great poet.[49] Sufi shrines are thus secularized by being turned into cultural centres and, as places of huge communal gatherings, have become platforms for the state to relay its ideology to the masses and, by showing allegiance to the saints, find a source of Islamic legitimacy for its own authority. For instance, during the *'urs*[50] of Pir Hazrat Abdul Kareem (1848–1936) in June 2007, numerous high-ranking officials supported the stance of the government on 'religious extremism': Punjab Governor Khalid Maqbool (b. 1948) praised the government for 'countering the pessimistic attitude of anti-Islamic forces', adding that Islam is a 'religion of peace promoting respect' and that it 'categorically negates extremism and intolerance'. He hailed Musharraf for 'presenting Islam's true position before the world' and commended the *gaddi nashin* for 'his efforts to create unity among Muslims'. The railways federal minister Shaikh Rashid Ahmed (b. 1950) said 'evil powers were actively engaged in subversive activities to destabilize the country's integrity' but added that the Holy Prophet and the Sufi saints' blessings would 'shower on Pakistan'.[51] In his official speeches during these *'urs*, the *awqaf* minister Sahibzada Saeedul Hassan Shah tried to disseminate the same message to the pilgrims. For example, at the *'urs* of Shah Jamal (1588–1671) in Lahore in April 2007, after inaugurating the festival by laying a *chaddar* (piece of cloth) on the tomb of the saint and reciting the first verse of the Qur'an (*fatiha*), the minister said that his teachings had helped the promotion of Islam in the subcontinent, that he had presented the 'true face of religion' to the world, and that his shrine was a 'source of guidance' (and 'amusement!') for everyone. He encouraged the devotees and the 'clerics' to play their part in maintaining interreligious harmony, tolerance, and dialogue at the grassroots level and he claimed the shrines were the best places to bring about 'social change'.[52]

If the social change expected by the *awqaf* ministry at its inception during Ayub's time involved the transformation from a 'traditional' to a modern 'cosmology', the change expected today concerns the propagation of Sufi ideals to fight extremism. Indeed, many in Pakistan deplore the fact that 'Sufi Islam', which constitutes the matrix of the subcontinent's Muslim identity, has been gradually eclipsed by more 'fundamentalist' versions of Islamic faith averse to the mystical tendencies of Islam. Interviewed during the *'urs* of Shah Jamal in April 2007, many devotees denounced the increasing trend of 'talibanization' in the country, contrasting it to the teachings of Sufi saints.[53] Hence, the state remains politically and symbolically dependent on these traditional institutions which it initially aimed at reforming, but which still continue to act as symbolic reservoirs and political resources for the powers that be.

## The master narrative 'Sufi Islam versus radical Islam' in the War on Terror

Pervez Musharraf was not the first Pakistani leader to have manipulated Sufi symbols for political ends. This has been a constant endeavour and started even before the creation of Pakistan in 1947. However, the extreme tensions that

Pakistan has been subjected to since 9/11, and especially since the beginning of the military action in the tribal areas in 2004, constitute a major political and cultural crisis, the matrix of a vigorous ideological reformulation of Sufism. It was indeed erected, or even reified, as an 'Islam of peace and love', and promoted as an integral part of Musharraf's 'enlightened moderation' and of the 'soft face of Pakistan'. This new paradigm[54] of enlightened moderation aimed at promoting to Pakistanis as well as Westerners a tolerant, open, and progressive image of Pakistan and of the version of Islam which is practiced on its soil. It was all about engaging once again in the old symbolic struggle on the nature of Islam in the name of which the country had been created, but also to impose a new image of Islam in the West and restore foreign investors' confidence. The recourse to Sufism was also an attempt at justifying the principles and actions of enlightened moderation on the basis of references hailing from the Islamic heritage of Pakistan.

Since the beginning of the 'War on Terror', the number of initiatives aimed at promoting Sufism (festivals, conferences, shows, and TV programmes), often financed by the government, has proliferated. The entrepreneurs of such initiatives mostly belong to the Westernized, cosmopolitan, and liberal fringe and are inscribed in common networks of sociability. Many have been co-opted by the government or support it unconditionally. Indeed, the support of the liberal bourgeoisie to the 'enlightened' general was a widespread phenomenon[55] before Musharraf's popularity plummeted from 2007 onwards due to the judicial crisis, which shook the country in the wake of the sacking of the Chief Justice of the Supreme Court, Iftikhar Chaudhry (b. 1948), in November 2007 (he was reinstated on 22 March 2009 and served until 11 December 2013), and the earlier Red Mosque crisis of July. A striking homogeneity is to be found in the discourse among this class. For Sarwat Ali, a musicologist and a professor at the National College of the Arts (NCA), Sufism, which served in the past to humanize religion in the sense of tolerance, inclusiveness, and love, has become an empty tradition, a soul-less convention within the existing religio-political groups. It is better observed among democratic and secular actors.[56] For Khaled Ahmed (b. 1943), a well-known political journalist, Sufism and Barelvis represent, according to him, a more tolerant and eclectic form of Islam than the one promoted by anti-Sufi Islamist parties, and could only regain their lost influence if a leader such as Musharraf succeeded in the long term in implementing secularization.[57] For Ayeda Naqvi, a journalist and a teacher at the Lahore American School who is also the disciple of the Chishtiyya, one of the four main Sufi orders in the subcontinent, the Sufi philosophy, universalism, and inclusion are the way out of current problems, not the exclusive purity of the Islamists.[58] Soroush Irfani, a Sufi intellectual and professor at NCA and former researcher at the Institute of Strategic Studies in Islamabad, feels optimistic about the future thanks to the reorientation adopted by Musharraf to build a new identity by returning to Sufism. He feels that when the president calls on the saints of the country to counter extremism, he is more sincere than Benazir Bhutto (1953–2007, Prime Minister 1988–90, 1993–6) was when she visited Sufi shrines in the 1990s. It is more significant and urgent than ever in the current context.[59]

Indeed, one of the most decisive variables of the ideologization of Sufism seems to be the rise of Islamist groups generally contesting the legitimacy of the government. This is not only true of Pakistan. In Morocco, the monopolization of power by King Hassan II (1929–99, r. 1961–99) both as the political and the spiritual leader of the faithful had relegated Sufis to the position of rivals for the king and they were only referred to in a discreet manner. Today, Muhammad VI (b. 1963, r. 1999–) 'advocates a religious practise tinged with tolerance to counter the rise of fanaticism'[60] and favours a spectacular return in strength of the brotherhood whereas they had been marginalized by his father. According to political analyst Muhammad Tozy (b. 1956), one of the ways in which the state intervenes in the religious field is through the defence of a Moroccan Sufism.[61] The way the West vilifies political Islam in all its forms, coupled with the legitimizing strategies of Muslim regimes confronted with Islamist opposition (at least prior to the Arab spring beginning in December 2010), have generated an imperative to find and promote another more 'politically correct' and socially legitimate expression of Islamic tradition. That is precisely the case of Sufism, which, furthermore, can boast of an artistic heritage allowing better communication with the West. The Sufi potential for dialogue between cultures and civilizations is indeed constantly highlighted.

This ideology of 'good Sufism versus bad Islamism' tends to anesthetize the reality of power struggles and to ignore the socio-political dynamics of sectarian radicalization in Pakistan and elsewhere. The Taliban insurgency is understood above all as a religious phenomenon. This interpretation aims at opposing and reifying the 'Sufi' and 'extremist' expressions of Islam. Consequently, Sufism is interpreted as a solution to extremism in all its forms. The definition that is made of Sufism is operated in reaction against an implicit definition of 'extremism' as a 'violent and sectarian' Islam. In this perspective, Sufism is systematically presented as an 'Islam of peace, love, tolerance' and subsequently acquires a 'secular' and 'universalist' dimension. While being invoked as an endogenous identity reference linked to the past, it however manifests deep dynamics of reinvention, 'cultural extraversion' and 'transfer of meaning'.[62] This recourse to Sufism among the political or cultural elite corresponds to a 'fabrication of authenticity', to a 'process of cultural elaboration in the ideological and sensitive realms'.[63] As the ideologization of Islam since the nineteenth century can testify, arguments in favour of a 'tradition' are constructed and defended once its legitimacy has been questioned. This recourse to Sufism does not constitute a return to a naive traditionalism but rather to an 'ideological re-traditionalization'.[64]

As a matter of fact, in this master narrative, the history of Sufism is often reinvented in order to erase, wittingly or unwillingly, all the elements which might go beyond the bounds of this ideological mould. That reinvention is not necessarily strategic. Many actors deem it impossible for Sufis to be politically active or involved in the military, and they simply ignore the historical evidence of such profane activities carried out by many Sufi orders. Moreover, Sufism is overwhelmingly culturalized, that is to say its value is enhanced in many different cultural products. In order to elevate Sufi music and poetry as pillars of national identity, a massive diffusion policy has been undertaken to spread the poetry of Punjabi and Sindhi saintly poets who are celebrated in editorial activities and in CDs, the production of TV or radio programmes, and the organization of Sufi music festivals. In 2006, four classical works of Punjabi poetry were translated into Urdu and published, including the work of the *chishti* Baba Fariduddin Masood Ganj-i Shakar (1188–1280), Sultan Bahu (1631–97), Bulleh Shah (1680–1758), often compared to Jalaluddin Rumi (1207–73), and who remains the most popular Punjabi poet, and Waris Shah (1730–90), the author of the legendary epic *Heer*, the most quoted work of the Sufi Punjabi *corpus*.[65] The trend of Sufi music is also noticeable in the rock scene.[66] The ideologization of Sufism encompasses a strong marketing dimension.

## The institutionalization of 'Sufi ideology'

Consistent with this vision, Muhammad Iqbal's grandson, the famous socialite and musical producer Youssaf Salahuddin (b. 1951), has been the advocate of a version of Sufism defined as the 'liberal', 'tolerant', and almost 'secular' trend of Islam. His idea of a National Sufi Council aimed at promoting Sufi music, poetry, and philosophy was swiftly appropriated in 2006 by the powers that be, willing to inject a specific religious referent to Musharraf's 'enlightened moderation' and to counter extremism. In September 2006, Youssaf met Musharraf to put forward his concept of a Sufi Council and Musharraf gave him *carte blanche* to form a think tank of 30 people aimed at rethinking programming at the state television station, PTV. Youssaf wished to transform the connotation of 'Westernization' attached to 'enlightened moderation' into a non-conservative endogenous modernization.

> People think that the enlightened moderation is an attempt at westernizing them. And mullahs[67] also say that. Everything that the government does, mullahs say 'The Americans tell us what to do.' But we used the same means the mullahs use. They try to do politics with religion and so do we. I don't think we should try to culturally change this religious society. People wouldn't accept it and it would play against the government. It doesn't mean we want to become conservative. Not at all. But we want to keep our own identity, like any other nation.[68]

The NSC was composed of Musharraf as its chief patron, the leader of the then-ruling Pakistan Muslim League (Q), Chaudhry Shujaat Hussain (b. 1946), as its chairman (who was given a turban at the Punjab House in Islamabad by Pir Sarwar Chishti, the *pir* of the Indian shrine of Ajmer, in a symbolic bid to promote himself as a 'Sufi'), as well as other high-profile politicians and intellectuals: the Chief Minister of Baluchistan Jam Mohammad Yussuf (1954–2013); the Chief executive of Dawn press group, Hameed Haroon; and an ex-senator and ex-federal minister for NWFP and Northern Areas, Abbas Sarfaraz; as well as the president of the Senate committee for foreign relations and general secretary of the party in power, Mushahid Hussain, who declared in 2006 during the launching ceremony of the Rumi Forum aimed at spreading the teachings of the great mystic poet, 'the mystic literature of Islam is a source of inspiration and following its universal values of love, peace, harmony and tolerance can bridge the gap between East and West'.[69] Meanwhile, the Pakistan Army was attacking the 'insurgents' in Waziristan (2004) and in the Swat valley (2007). Obviously, military action was considered at the time as a more efficient means of eliminating terrorism in the short term than Sufism. Geertz has observed similar dynamics in Indonesia where, while the president and his entourage were mostly absorbed in the 'creation and recreation of mysticism', the army was busy fighting competing claims to leadership as all the insurgencies and protests arising because mysticism had failed to achieve its expected results.[70]

The National Sufi Council was launched by Musharraf in a grand ceremony in the historic heart of Lahore at the occasion of Iqbal's birthday in November 2006. This event was a great get-together of the indigenous elite and diplomatic circles. The same month, an international conference called 'Sufism, the Way to Peace' was organized by the Punjab Institute of Language, Art and Culture (PILAC) under the direction of the Chief Minister of the province, Chaudhry Pervaiz Elahi (b. 1945). The same 'Sufi ideology' of love and peace was promoted to combat the expressions of 'mullah Islam'. The Punjab secretary for culture stated that,

> the Sufi culture and teachings have always been a part of our rural scene.... All our folk culture is based on Sufi teachings. That is why people of these areas, especially the rural ones, are more secular, or if I want to use another word, more tolerant. This wave of extremism, this radicalism, has never existed before today. It has gradually come about because of the domination of extremists in our society who have indoctrinated people and made them more radical, less tolerant of other religions and sects.... There was a necessity to revive, or at least recall to our people what our culture and our system were in the past. That is why we think the renewal of Sufism is a necessity.... The extremists are a minority. The majority of Pakistanis are Barelvis. They believe in shrines, in Sufis and in their tolerant teachings and message. The others are Shias and Deobandis. All the extremism we can witness today, Al Qaeda, the Taliban, all of them are Deobandis.[71]

American officials in Pakistan showed a keen interest in all these manifestations. Generally speaking, Sufism has become the new Islamic horse Western powers are betting on.

Other activities monitored by the NSC were the creation of a calendar distributed in the whole administration with pictures taken at Pakistani shrines by an American photographer. In collaboration with the Turk-Pak Council, the NSC also organized a tour of whirling dervishes in all the great cities of the country, including Islamabad where the Prime Minister Shaukat Aziz (b. 1949, Prime Minister 2004–7) was invited to be the chief guest. The *sama* of the *mevlevis* is traditionally a prayer. However, the performances organized by the NSC resembled folkloric shows.[72] The whole poetic work of the saint Shah Abdul Latif Bhitai was recorded by famous singer Abida Parveen (b. 1954) and *qawwali*[73] songs composed by Nusrat Fateh Ali Khan's (1948–97) uncle and father were recorded in their homage. Music is indeed a prominent component of this proverbial 'tolerance' associated with Sufism. Youssaf is aware that Sufism has a great market and symbolic value in the eyes of mystic-hungry Westerners. 'Basically I have always thought that in today's world where every culture is being promoted by governments, the things that Pakistan can sell are Sufi music and Sufism!'[74]

The promotion of the arts and the promotion of Sufism are thus inscribed on the same political agenda and were instruments of legitimization for Musharraf. The general always had the ambition to present himself as a true democrat and an enlightened liberal to the Westernized fringe of the Pakistani population and to his Western interlocutors. Hence, the Musharraf administration seized the opportunity to promote festivals of Sufi music. As early as February 2005 the cultural organization Rafi Peer Theatre Workshop (RPTW) was approached by Musharraf to celebrate the 'soft face of Pakistan'. Later that year, in November, Musharraf was the chief guest of the annual World Performing Arts Festival organized by RPTW. The international media widely reported on the event, like Robin Denselow's article published in the *Guardian* of 2 December 2005 and entitled, 'Sufi's Choice: In Pakistan, One Festival is Defying Islamic Hardliners – but Delighting the President'. The first international festival of Sufi music was organized in April 2006 by RPTW in Lahore, then in Karachi and in Multan the following year in collaboration with the government of Sindh. It was a resounding success.

This Sufi ideology is shared by many Sufi actors and orders in Pakistan and abroad who have undertaken similar initiatives. In April 2006, the two representatives of Sufi Order International[75] in Lahore, then in empathy with Musharraf's doctrine of 'enlightened moderation', organized an international Sufi conference in collaboration with RPTW's music festival. Entitled 'Universalism and Islam', it wished to address the 'war within Islam between those who take religion hostage ... and those who believe in a religion of peace and tolerance'. In March 2006, an international conference organized by SAARC[76] in Delhi projected Sufism as nothing less than the 'panacea' to the turmoil in the region and as a voice for 'democratic secularism'. We could multiply many times over examples of such attempts at brandishing Sufism as a symbol of reaction against 'fundamentalism', 'extremism', and 'terrorism', all used as synonyms.

However, many Sufi and political actors, as well as journalists and intellectuals, criticized the Sufi venture of the government as the latest effort of a long series to manipulate the symbols of Sufism in order to paint the military dictatorship in mystical colours. Others denounced it as bid to use a 'sweetened' Sufism as a neo-colonialist tool, giving a harmless content to Islam acceptable to Western powers. 'Sufis are being projected as subservient goodie-goodie Muslims', says a civil servant who helped organize PILAC's conference.

## A contested master narrative?

As a matter of fact, the state does not hold a monopoly on the interpretation of Sufism. For this heavily charged signifier encompasses doctrines, forms of organization as well as practices performed by actors belonging to the whole of the political spectrum, including the Islamist opposition. The 'party of *pirs*', the Barelvi Jamiyyat-e Ulama-e Pakistan founded in 1948 to protect its interpretation of Islam and take part in the political process mainly as a pressure group, defends the traditional leadership and practices of Sufi shrines. Despite historical doctrinal struggles with its more reformist counterparts such as the Deobandis or the Jama'at-e Islami, it joined the religious alliance of the Islamist Muttahida Majlis-e Amal (United Action Front) (MMA), the third parliamentary force in Pakistan after the 2002 elections, alongside parties whose position on Sufism and *pirs* ranges from partial acceptance to complete rejection. Far from being quietist and opposed to violence, the leader of the JUP from 1973 to 2003, the *alim* and Sufi *sheikh* Shah Ahmed Nurani (1926–2003), even urged his followers in 2002 to wage a *jihad* against allied forces in Afghanistan. One Barelvi sectarian outfit turned political party, the Sunni Tehreek (ST), is even famous for having recourse to radical modes of action to forward its religious and political agenda. Its official aim is to defend 'practically' the Barelvi sect. It is a group that was placed under surveillance a few years ago in the context of the 'War on Terror'. It is involved in urban guerrilla warfare in Karachi both against so-called 'Wahhabi' groups and against the secular *Mohajir* party, the Muttahida Qaumi Movement, an organization which is perceived by the ST as the invisible hand behind the bomb attack that killed its whole leadership in February 2006, along with 60 other people. Its founder, Salim Qadri, who was killed in 2001, was not educated in a Barelvi mosque and was not a religious scholar. The three successive leaders of the ST, Salim Qadri, Abbas Qadri, and Serwat Qadri, were businessmen and were disciples of the leader of the Barelvi Dawat-e Islami, Ilyas Qadri (b. 1950). Hence, they all belong to the Qadiriyya Sufi Order.

In order to designate such groups, like Barelvis, claiming Sufism and Sufi identity as a register for Islamist mobilization, I have coined the concept '*Sufislamism*'. Besides enabling an enhanced analysis of the various interactions between Sufism and Islamism, this concept may also improve our understanding of the highly fissile politicization of the doctrinal fractures among Islamists, thus helping to chart the deep waters of identity politics, especially those of what seem relevant to be called 'intra-Sunni sectarianism'. Sufism has taken on an ideological dimension amongst new organizations formalizing their doctrinal difference in order to transform their specific religious identity into a political resource and a sectarian position. Some expressions of Sufislamism in Pakistan clearly clash head on with the master narrative defending the idea that all Sufis and Barelvis[77] are peaceful and quietist.

According to a leader of the JUP, this promotion of Sufism equals the promotion of a new Islam: 'Do you know who the president of the NSC is? Youssaf Salahuddin!! Do you realize? They are doing that to alter Islamic values.

Promote Sufism ... but that is not Sufism!!'[78] For others, this attempt at politicizing Sufism can only fail, for the interpretation that is made of it is erroneous:

> Sufism has become Washington's agenda. They think Sufism will take people away from violent struggles, that it will liberalize them, modernize them, but it is not so. Sufism will only bring you closer to Islam. It will make you more fundamentalist,[79]

says a disciple of the Sufi order *Naqshbandiyya Owaisia*. This Deobandi order counts thousands of disciples across Pakistan and in the diaspora who are taught a quiet '*zhikr*[80] of the heart' and an intricate system of numerous meditative stages. Its *sheikh*, Maulana Akram Awan (b. 1934), launched in the 1990s a political wing to its Sufi order, a radical pressure group called Tanzeem-ul Ikhwan which is very popular in the Army and has links with numerous sectarian and jihadist outfits. Its ideology is to implement Islam on one's own being before implementing it at state level. And if the *sheikh* does defend in one of his speeches the idea that Islam is 'the religion of love', he adds 'If Mr. Bush continues with his policy of slaying innocent children, bombing elderly civilians, dishonouring women, backing Israel to destroy homes and habitations, then he should ask himself, who has ever earned love with tyranny?'[81]

Belonging to a Sufi order and indulging in Sufi practices under the guidance of a *sheikh* does not presuppose any given position in the political arena or in the ideological spectrum. As a matter of fact, *pirs* can be found in all Pakistani parties. Some even head their own, like Ajmal Qadri, head of a Sufi order and leader of a faction of the Deobandi Jamiyyat-e Ulama-e Islam (JUI) close to sectarian and jihadist outfits; or the Pir of Pagaro (1928–2012), who headed for a few decades his own faction of the semi-secular Pakistan Muslim League and was renowned for his support to the military establishment and for the devotion of his disciples, who were ready to die for him. As a matter of fact, the hegemonic 'Sufi Islam versus mullah Islam' narrative appears as one ideology among others once confronted with the complexity of social, religious, and political forces in Pakistan.

## Empowering Sufi Barelvis to fight radical Islam or radicalizing Sufi Islam?

The Barelvi Sunni Tehreek is not exactly what one might objectively call a 'moderate' Sufi group. However, in May 2009 the Foreign Minister, the hereditary *pir* from Multan Shah Mehmud Qureshi (b. 1956), officially announced during the '*urs* of the Sufi saint Shah Rukn-e Alam the mobilization of the Barelvis against the 'talibanization' of the country.[82] Several meetings organized by the government had already taken place with the leaders of the ST and other Barelvi groups to encourage them to take the lead in a social movement against the insurgents of the Swat valley,[83] the Taliban Movement of Pakistan (Tehreek-e Taliban Pakistan)[84] and suspected of being close to al-Qaeda. The militants wanted to impose a judicial system founded on Islamic law. The day following Qureshi's speech, the first demonstration of Sunni Tehreek in Peshawar took place, which was then followed by the launching of 'Save Pakistan' campaign by Barelvi forces, just before a Barelvi party alliance was formed, the Sunni Ittehad Council.

If the rhetorical and doctrinal conflicts between contending sectarian groups in the Indian subcontinent could be interpreted in the nineteenth century less as a sign of the division of the Muslim community than as 'a substantial homogeneity among Muslims',[85] a different interpretation seems necessary today. The doctrinal conflicts among Barelvis, Deobandis, and Ahl-e Hadith[86] are indeed not new. But their scope has gradually broadened and has given way to mobilizations on the basis of religious identities that have endorsed a political function. Their very existence threatened by the Taliban phenomenon, influenced by Deobandi doctrine, and inimical to popular Sufism, Barelvi leaders have tried to organize themselves into a common platform to promote their views. The Taliban insurrection in the north has allowed the convergence of Barelvi sectarian interests and those of the government and of the military establishment. As a matter of fact, the radical militants have not only targeted official figures and institutions but also Sufi leaders and shrines. Therefore, the Barelvi presence in the public sphere has increased. The different groups of the movement have organized many conferences and demonstrations aiming both at denouncing the 'talibanization' of Pakistan and at reasserting the role of Sufis in the promotion of an Islam of 'peace, love, and tolerance'. In March 2009, a conference gathered 300 Sufis from across Pakistan at the headquarters of Minhaj-ul Quran (MUQ) in Lahore to try to elaborate measures to fight those actors who wanted to 'discredit the peaceful message of the Sufis' and wanted to promote 'anti-mysticism ideologies'.[87] In May 2009, the MUQ organized yet another convention for the 'protection of Pakistan' (*Tahaffuz-e Pakistan*) in which more than 200 Barelvi Sufis and scholars participated. They adopted a highly informative communiqué highlighting the positions of Barelvi representatives about the most recent developments in the 'War on Terror'. They once again emphasized the 'key role' of Sufis in 'the construction of a peaceful society', in the promotion of 'peace and harmony' and more generally in the propagation of Islam throughout history. Sufi shrines have been celebrated as 'cultural symbols' whose recent profanation by pro-Taliban groups is only the expression of 'un-Islamic actions'. The 'violations' of the Constitution carried out by these groups have also been condemned in the harshest terms, as well as their attacks on girls' schools. According to the communiqué, gaining knowledge is compulsory for every Muslim without any gender discrimination. Islam guarantees the 'respect and dignity' of women and their 'practical role' in society. Suicide attacks are also strictly forbidden in Islam and are likened to 'barbarian acts'. Taliban practices, such as declaring war on the Army, the security forces, and the police, or eliminating the voices of opposition, were also condemned.

However, as we have seen in the case of the Sunni Tehreek, Barelvi actors are not all as tolerant and peaceful as they would wish to be seen in the current context. The latest developments of the 'War on Terror' have indeed intensified intra-Sunni sectarianism and clearly manifested the Barelvi potential for radicalization. Indeed, it was a member of a Barelvi neo-Sufi order who killed Salman Taseer (1944–2011), the Governor of the Punjab, in January 2011. Taseer wanted to amend the law on blasphemy, which imposes the death penalty for any offence against the Prophet Muhammad, who is venerated by Barelvis. Taseer's killer, Mumtaz Qadri, is now considered a hero, a clear sign that the current radicalization of Pakistani society is not only to be blamed on the Taliban, but paradoxically also on what some might perhaps call an over-zealous interpretation of certain basic Sufi tenets. During a conference in Lahore on 'the protection of the prestige of the Prophet', Barelvi leaders warned the supporters of the deceased Salman Taseer that a Mumtaz Qadri would be at every corner of the country to stop such displays of solidarity. 'Don't associate Mumtaz with any terrorist group, they said. He is a true lover of the Holy Prophet (pbuh).'[88]

## Notes

1 I am most grateful to Patrick Hutchinson for helping me edit the original version of this chapter. It appeared as 'A Sublime Yet Disputed, Object of Political Ideology? Sufism in Pakistan at the Crossroads', *Commonwealth and Comparative Politics*, 52, 2 (2014): 271–92, Taylor & Francis Ltd, www.tandfonline.com, reprinted by permission of the publisher. John Esposito, 'Preface', in Anita M. Weiss (ed.), *Islamic Reassertion in Pakistan: The Application of Islamic Laws in a Modern State* (Lahore: Vanguard, 1987), p. ix.
2 Michael Gilsenan, *Connaissance de l'islam* (Paris: Karthala, 2001), p. 198.
3 Slavoj Žižek quoted in Katherine Ewing, *Arguing Sainthood: Modernity, Psychoanalysis, and Islam* (Durham, NC: Duke University Press, 1997), p. 67.
4 Ibid., p. 66.
5 Dale Eickelman and James Piscatori, *Muslim Politics* (Princeton, NJ: Princeton University Press, 1996), p. 59.
6 Ibid., p. 5.
7 Clifford Geertz quoted in Eickelman and Piscatori, *Muslim Politics*.
8 Clifford Geertz, *The Interpretation of Cultures* (New York: Basic Books, 1973), p. 316.
9 Ibid., p. 320.
10 Ibid., p. 231.
11 Ibid., p. 220.
12 Chantal Mouffe, *Le Politique et ses Enjeux: Pour une Démocratie Plurielle* (Paris: La Découverte, 1994), p. 39.
13 Martin Van Bruinessen and Julia Day Howell (ed.), *Islam and the 'Modern' in Islam* (London, I.B. Tauris, 2007), p. 4.
14 Talal Asad quoted in Muhammad Qasim Zaman, *The Ulama in Contemporary Islam, Custodians of Change* (Karachi: Oxford University Press, 2002), p. 5.
15 A poet and a philosopher, he is considered the main creator of the idea of Pakistan and as the spiritual father of the country.
16 The Biggest Sunni school of *ulama* in Pakistan originating in nineteenth-century India and whose members follow the Sufi tradition but are very critical of the cult of the saints, unlike Barelvis.
17 Religious movement in South Asia originating in nineteenth-century India and whose members venerate Sufi saints and shrines.

18 Eickelman and Piscatori, *Muslim Politics*, p. 38.
19 Ibid.
20 In the academic literature on South Asian Islam, different definitions are given for this term, all evolving around Sufi tradition: a religious leader, a spiritual leader, a Sufi master who has disciples (*murids*), a guide and a professor of Sufism, the descendant of a Sufi saint, or even the politico-religious leader of a tribe, as *pirs* are often political leaders and Sufi orders are often structured on segments of the population (tribes, clans etc.).
21

> The Sufi tradition is a movement of devotion and divine rapture focusing on spiritual experiences. It represents a particular creative and liberal dimension of Islam characterised by practiced tolerance, humanism, peace, and the accommodation of differences.... It can be generally recognised as a 'softer' alternative to the authoritarian voices of formal scriptural religion and of Islamist movements.
> (Jürgen Wasim Frembgen, *The Friends of God: Sufi Saints in Islam* (Karachi, Oxford University Press, 2007), Preface)

22 Julian Johansen, Sufism and Islamic Reform in Egypt: The Battle for Islamic Tradition (Oxford: Clarendon Press, 1996).
23 Muhammad Iqbal, *The Reconstruction of Religious Thought in Islam* (Lahore: Sh. Muhammad Ashraf, 1975, orig. 1930), p. 88.
24 Hafeez Malik (ed.), *Iqbal, Poet-Philosopher of Pakistan* (Lahore: Iqbal Academy, 2005), p. xi.
25 Elizabeth Sirriyeh, *Sufis and Anti-Sufis* (Richmond, Surrey: Curzon Press, 1999), p. 126.
26 Ibid., p. xii.
27 Iqbal, *The Reconstruction of Religious Thought in Islam*, p. 88.
28 Ibid., p. xxi.
29 Mohammad Iqbal, *Les Secrets du Soi, les Mystères du Non-moi* (Paris: Albin Michel, 1989).
30 Ibid., pp. 51–2.
31 Ibid., p. 77.
32 Mohammad *Iqbal, The Reconstruction of Religious Thought in Islam*, pp. 119–20.
33 Ibid., p. 121.
34 Ibid.
35 Ibid., p. 152.
36 Ibid., p. 153.
37 Ibid., p. 78.
38 Ibid., p. 97.
39 Ibid., p. 99.
40 Ibid., p. 100.
41 Annemarie Schimmel, *Gabriel's Wing* (Lahore: Iqbal Academy Pakistan, 2003), p. 370.
42 Ewing, *Arguing Sainthood*, p. 68.
43 Javaid Iqbal, *Ideology of Pakistan* (Lahore: Sang-e-Meel Publications, 2005, orig. 1959).
44 See Jamal Malik, *Colonization of Islam: Dissolution of Traditional Institutions in Pakistan* (Lahore: Vanguard, 1996); and Katherine Ewing, *Arguing Sainthood*, pp. 70–90.
45 Katherine Ewing, 'The Politics of Sufism: Redefining the Saints of Pakistan', in Akbar Ahmed (ed.), *Pakistan: The Social Sciences Perspective* (Karachi: Oxford University Press, 1990).
46 Ibid., p. 261.
47 Khwaja Naseer, 'Data's Urs Still Presses Message of Tolerance', *Daily Times* (21 March 2006).

48 Nadeem Shah, 'Musharraf Urges Nation to Reject Fanatics', *The News on Sunday* (27 February 2005).
49 'Three Books will be Launched to Mark Shah Latif's Urs', *Dawn* (15 November 2007).
50 The commemoration of the death anniversary of Sufi saints which has given way to annual popular festivals at Sufi shrines.
51 Quotations from 'Islam Rejects Extremism, Intolerance: Maqbool', *Daily Times* (9 June 2007).
52 'Baba Shah Jamal's Urs Kicks Off', *Daily Times* (22 April 2007).
53 'Followers of Shah Jamal Denounce Extremism', *Daily Times* (22 April 2007).
54 See Gilles Bocquérat and Nazir Hussain, *Enlightened Moderation: Relevance of a New Paradigm in the Face of Radical Islam*, unpublished document.
55 Bocquérat and Hussain observed that 85 per cent of the scholars, intellectuals, journalists, analysts, and politicians they interviewed in the course of their research believed in the sincerity and authenticity with which Musharraf promoted his enlightened moderation but that it was above all destined for Western consumption. Ibid., p. 21.
56 Interview with the author, Lahore (February 2005).
57 Ibid.
58 Ibid.
59 Ibid.
60 Thierry Oberlé, 'Mohamed VI Réorganise l'Islam Marocain', *Le Figaro* (4 July 2006).
61 Ibid.
62 Jean-François Bayart, *L'illusion Identitaire* (Paris: Fayard, 1996), p. 80.
63 Ibid., p. 90.
64 Geertz, *The Interpretation of Cultures*, p. 219.
65 Humair Ishtiaq, 'A New Lease of Life, Books and Authors', *Dawn* (30 April 2006).
66 For example, Junoon, which is the most famous Pakistani band of the 1990s and split up into Ali Zafar and Salman Ahmed, or the instrumental band Overload including traditional percussionist musicians from the shrine of Shah Jamal in Lahore. Salman Ahmed founded a web site called Sufi rock. The concept designates a fusion of traditional Sufi music and rock music. Sufism is not defined as a religion but as a state of mind present in all religions. www.isufirock.com.
67 'Mullah' is a derogatory term generally used in Pakistan to designate the Islamic clergy, and notably the least educated ones.
68 Interview with the author, Islamabad (February 2007).
69 '2007, the Year of Rumi', *Daily Times* (12 December 2006).
70 See Geertz, *The Interpretation of Cultures*, pp. 227–8.
71 Interview with the author, Lahore (December 2006).
72 Observations of the author, Lahore (February 2007).
73 Musical and poetical mode formalized by the *chishti* Sufi and scholar Amir Khusrau (1253–1325) in the thirteenth and fourteenth centuries on the basis of different musical traditions in order to attract Hindus to Islam.
74 Interview with the author, Islamabad (April 2008).
75 A New Age offshoot of the Chishtiyya initially designed for Westerners but that recently came back to where it originally came from, the Indian subcontinent.
76 South Asian Association of Regional Cooperation.
77 See the interview with Khaled Ahmed and the Punjab ministry for culture.
78 Interview with Ali Noor, general information secretary of JUP, Lahore (April 2007).
79 Interview with the author, Lahore (December 2006).
80 Mystical practice consisting of repeating divine names.
81 Speeches of Akram Awan can be found on the internet site of the order, 'Islam, the Religion of Love', www.owaisiah.com.

82 'We will not Surrender to Forces Harming Pakistan's Interests, says Qureishi', *The News* (4 May 2009).
83 Interview with Rasul Bakhsh Rais, professor of political science at Lahore University of Management Sciences, Islamabad (July 2009).
84 The genesis of this movement goes back to 2003 when the first intrusions of the Pakistan Army in the tribal areas took place to hunt for Afghan Taliban and al-Qâ'ida militants. But it was in 2007 that the movement really came to light as an identifiable entity under the leadership of Beitullah Mehsud (*c*.1974–2009). The radical circles in Pakistan seem to be comprised of dozens of more or less autonomous groups (Pashtuns, Punjabi, and foreign militants) but they share common strategic, financial, or even ideological interests.
85 Barbara Daly Metcalf, *Islamic Revival in British India: Deoband, 1860–1900* (Princeton, NJ: Princeton University Press, 1982), p. 358.
86 Reformist and elitist religious movement originating in nineteenth-century India which does not recognize the legitimacy of the juridical schools is very critical of Sufism and is often branded 'Wahhabi'.
87 www.minhaj.org/en.php?tid=7741.
88 Rana Tanveer, 'Taseer Murder: Sunni Ittehad Warns against Protests', *International Herald Tribune* (10 January 2010).

# 8 The rise of militancy among Pakistani Barelvis
## The case of the Sunni Tehrik

*Mujeeb Ahmad*

On 25 March 2012, in the *Azad Pakistan Kanfarans* (independent Pakistan Conference) held at Lahore, the *Sunni Tehrik* (Sunni Movement; ST) announced its transformation into a national political party under the name of *Pakistan Sunni Tehrik* (Pakistan Sunni Movement; PST). This announcement was welcomed by the major national political parties including Barelvi religio-political parties. The PST was the first-ever political party of the Barelvis to use the word Sunni after the short-lived party of the same name, later renamed *Pakistan Sunni Parti*, (Pakistan Sunni Party) in October 1972, by its founder-president Mian Abdul Rashid (1915–91).[1] This chapter examines the formation and working of the ST/PST, its turn to militancy, and its encounter with religious and political opponents.

### Schism within South Asian Sunnis

In South Asia the majority of Sunni Muslims are Hanafis (followers of Hanafi jurisprudence). Among the Sunni Hanafi Muslims, the Barelvis and the Deobandis are the most important sects. Both of them are staunch followers of the *Fiqh-i-Hanafi* (Hanafi jurisprudence), the oldest and most popular law school in Islam dating back to the eighth century. However, Barelvi-Deobandi doctrinal differences are deep-rooted. The greatest dispute is on the figure of the Prophet Muhammad (c.570–632). The Barelvis believe there could never be another person like him. They also have high regard for the *sufia* (Sufi way) of different Sufi orders. As a result, the Islam preached and practiced by the Barelvis is known as 'popular', 'folk-oriented', '*sufi*-inspired', or 'shrine-based' Islam. Deobandis denounce Barelvis for focusing strongly on the Prophet believing him, instead, to be part of Allah's *nur* (God's light), on his being present and observant, having knowledge of what is hidden, and invoking his powers of mediation and intercession, and having faith in the veneration of saints, seeing them as a dilution of the Oneness of Allah, and thus consider Barelvis to be polytheists. The Deobandi *ulama* are also critical of a number of popular religious practices to which the Barelvis adhere.[2]

Maulana Ahmad Raza Khan Barelvi (1856–1921) in his *fatwa* (legal opinion) entitled *Hussamul Haramain 'ala Munhir al-kufir wa al-Muin* (The Sword of the

*Haramain* at the Throat of Kafirs [unbelievers] and Falsehood) declared leading Deobandi *ulama* (scholars), Maulanas Rashid Ahmad Gangohi (1829–1905), Muhammad Qasim Nanowtawi (1832–80), Khalil Ahmad Ambethwi (1852–1927), and Muhammad Ashraf 'Ali Thanawi (1863–1943), to be infidels. He stated that their beliefs were similar, in one way or another, to the Wahhabis. This *fatwa* was endorsed by leading Barelvi *ulama*[3] and caused enormous resentment among Deobandis. They countered with their own *fatwa* receiving endorsements in turn from the *ulama-i-Hijaz* (*ulama* of the Hijaz, or Arabia), Syria, and Egypt, as well as by South Asian *ulama*.[4]

In the 1940s a solid majority of the Barelvis were supporters of the Pakistan Movement and played a supporting role in its final phase (1940–7), mostly under the banner of the All-India Sunni Conference which had been founded in 1925. The majority of Deobandis, on the other hand, under the auspices of the *Jam'iyyat-i-ulama-i-Hind* (Organization of Scholars of India; JUH), founded in 1919, were against the creation of a Muslim nation state in South Asia in the name of Islam.[5] The driving force for the Barelvis to play an active role was the hope that the new state of Pakistan would be based on the teachings and practices of Islam. After the creation of Pakistan in August 1947, however, they faulted the government for failing to live up to their expectations.

Until 1970 Barelvis did not pay much heed to electoral and parliamentary politics as they lacked an effective and disciplined countrywide organization. On the other hand, the Deobandis had practical experience of politics going back to the late 1930s. The JUH, for example, contested the 1936–7 and 1945–6 elections. Until 1972 the Barelvis had no representation in the constituent assemblies of Pakistan, whereas the Deobandis had their representatives even in the first Constituent Assembly. Both Barelvis and Deobandis, however, influenced the constitution-making process, especially its Islamic character. The *ulama* of both groups sought to impose a constitution and polity in the light of their own interpretation and understanding of Islam.

The social structure of Pakistan has been profoundly influenced and shaped by popular Islam. The vast majority of people are steeped in traditional religious modes of thought and action. A solid majority, particularly those living in rural areas, have very strong affiliations with different *sufi* orders and shrines. Grass-roots level celebrations of *Miladul Nabi* (Prophet's birthday), *mahafil-i-na't* (public recitations), *a'ras* (anniversaries), and other religious ceremonies, as well as social service groups, are expanding the reach of popular Islam. Barelvi *madaris* (schools) and *khanqahs* (Sufi shrines), religio-political and social organizations, institutions, academies, *tariqat* (Sufi way or path), the issuing of talismans, print, electronic media, the internet, and even mobile phones are playing a role in spreading it further. The broad acceptance of this Islam is due to the fact that it seems to meet a need felt by the people in their daily existence.

In national politics, the Deobandis are more influential than the Barelvis. The Barelvis failed to get a political mandate from the masses although it would not be correct to ignore and underestimate their socio-political importance. The *pirs* (saints) and *ulama* have remained the symbols of this dominant religious and cultural tradition. On the other hand, conservative *ulama* have remained committed to breaking the nexus between the masses and popular Islam and replacing it with a 'purer' Islam.

The Barelvi *Jam'iyyat-i-ulama-i-Pakistan* (Society of Pakistan Scholars; JUP), founded in 1948, and the Deobandi *Jam'iyyat-i-ulama-i-Islam* (Society of Islamic Scholars; JUI), founded three years earlier in 1945, both furthered the implementation of the *Hanafi* School of Law. The JUP and JUI, however, differ on certain policies. The JUP is more insistent in demanding the enforcement of the *Fiqh-i-Hanafi* as they support the implementation of the *Fatawa-i-alamgiriyah* (Alamgir's laws), a 30-volume codified law book compiled by the seventeenth-century Indian *ulama* at the behest of Mughal Emperor Aurangzeb, also known as Alamgir (1618–1707, Emperor 1658–1707). In national politics the Barelvi *ulama* campaign for the enforcement of the *Nizam-i-Mustafah* (*Fiqh-i-Hanafi*) (the system of Muhammad according to Hanafi jurisprudence). The JUI, on the other hand, stands for the enforcement of the *Nizam-i-Shari'at* (*Fiqh-i-Hanafi*) (Sharia system according to Hanafi jurispruence) and it has political and emotional attachments with the JUH.[6]

The JUP and the JUI both contested the 1970 elections as separate parties. They both won seven National Assembly seats. The JUP won four seats in the Punjab and seven in Sindh, while the JUI won four seats in the North-West Frontier Province (NWFP) (since 2010 Khyber Pakhtunkhwa) and one in Balochistan. It was able to form coalition governments in these provinces with the National Awami Party (National People's Party), founded in Dacca in 1957. Mufti Mahmud (1919–80), then president of his own faction of the JUI, was elected chief minister of the NWFP in May 1972. This JUI success was felt very keenly by the Barelvis, especially when Mahmud launched a programme of Islamization under the supervision of a board of Deobandi *ulama*. Although he remained in office only nine months, the JUP issued a paper criticizing his government and blaming him for victimizing Barelvis.[7]

## The formation of the Sunni Tehrik

When the military regime of General Muhammad Zia-ul-Haq (1924–88, President 1977–88) in October 1979 banned all political parties, religio-political parties were shocked for they had launched the *Nizam-i-Mustafah*[8] (order of the Prophet Muhammad) mass movement of March to July 1977 in protest against the alleged rigging of the 1977 general elections by Prime Minister Zulfiqar Ali Bhutto (1928–1979, President 1971–3, Prime Minister 1973–7). These, they believed, paved the way for the military take-over. Even though the the military junta claimed a religious basis for its rule, the JUP, unlike the JUI and the *Jama'at-i-Islami* (Islamic Society; JI), founded in 1941, decided not to cooperate with the Martial Law Regime.[9] However, intra-party conflicts broke out in the JUP and a few dissenters sided with Zia. Some Barelvi *ulama*, in the hope of Islamization, joined the *Majlis-i-Shura* (consultative council) in December 1981 and accepted some senior posts in the Council of Islamic Ideology, created in

1973, the Central *Ruet-e-Hilal* Committee (central committee of the sighting of the crescent moon), the Federal Shari'at Court, formed in 1980, and the Shari'at Appellate Bench of the Supreme Court of Pakistan. The JUP expelled all its members who supported Zia.[10] After political parties were banned the JUP became politically dormant. However, the party continued to function in the religious realm under the new name of the *Tehrik-i-Nizam-i-Mustafah* (Movement of the System of Muhammad).

Young middle-class Barelvis, for their part, wanted to play a leading role in the new socio-political and religious order established by Zia. As a result, Barelvi *ulama* formed organizations which represented alternative platforms to the JUP's. Dr Muhammad Tahirul Qadri (b. 1951) founded the *Idarah-i-Minhajjul Qur'an* (institute of the way of the Qur'an) in 1981 at Lahore.[11] He vowed to struggle for the enforcement of an Islamic system in Pakistan calling it the '*Mustaffawi* Revolution' (revolution of Muhammad). Later, in May 1989, he formed a broad-based political party having a moderate and non-sectarian approach, *Pakistan Awami Tehrik* (Pakistan People's Movement). Furthermore, the *Istakam-i-Pakistan Kounsal* (Council for the stability of Pakistan) was also organized in April 1981. It consisted of a dissenting group of Barelvi *ulama* and former JUP workers mainly from Karachi and Hyderabad, the stronghold of the JUP. This group, led by a former JUP member of the Sind Assembly, Zahurul Hassan Bhopali (1946–82), wanted to work with Martial Law authorities. A *tablighi* (evangelical) and faith-based organization of the Barelvis was also established in September 1981, *Da'wat-i-Islami* (Islamic preaching; DI).[12] In July 1987, one faction of the *Jama'at-i-Ahl-i-Sunnat Pakistan* (party of the Pakistani followers of Muslim practice), founded in 1956, headed by Sahibzadah Muhammad Fazl-i-Karim (1954–2013) also announced its participation in electoral politics.[13]

Muhammad Salim Qadri (1960–2001), the founder of the ST, was a *murid* (follower) of Maulana Muhammad Ilyas Qadri (b. 1950), *amir* (chief) of the DI. Qadri remained an active member of the DI for more than nine years but broke from it for its nonpolitical and passive attitude towards Barelvi issues. Before organizing the ST, he was an active member of the JUP in Karachi. In April 1990 he formed his own organization, ST, to defend Barelvi mosques, shrines, and interests against take-overs and intimidation by rival religious groups, particularly the Deobandis. The formation of the ST was also 'an attempt at stymieing the Deobandi onslaught'[14] on Barelvis. According to one estimate, more than 20 mosques had been taken over by the ST by October 1997.[15] Among his followers, Qadri was known as *Gernail-i-Ahl-i-Sunnat* (general of the followers of Muslim practice).[16]

His support came from *muhajir* (immigrant) youths who could no longer stomach the occupation of Barelvi mosques and *awqaf* (endowments) by Deobandis. Citing government patronage of the Deobandis, the ST violently battled with the Deobandis for control of mosques and shrines, particularly in Karachi.[17] The ST also vehemently opposed giving important religious posts to Deobandis in different government offices and the appointment of Deobandi *ulama* in mosques adjacent to a shrine. Its Lahore chapter publicly declared its opposition to the appointment of another Deobandi *alim* (scholar) as *imam* (leader of prayers) and *khatib* (person who delivers the Friday sermon) of the historic *Badshahi* Mosque (completed in Lahore in 1673) after the death of Maulana 'Abdul Qadir Azad (1939–2003) in 2003.[18]

## The assassination of Salim Qadri

Salim Qadri had been on a hit-list since 1994 and along with five other people was assassinated in Karachi on 18 May 2001. The law and order situation of Karachi and Hyderabad rapidly deteriorated as his followers rioted and protests were also held in other areas of the country.[19] The national press reported that the *Mutahidda Qaumi Movementi* (United National Movement; MQM), founded in 1997, formerly the *Muhajir Qaumi Movement* (Immigrant National Movement) created in 1978, may have been involved in the killings, but the ST blamed its religious rivals, the *Sipah-i-Sahabah Pakistan* (Pakistan Corps of the Prophet's Companions; SSP), founded in 1985, and *Jaish-i-Muhammad* (Army of Muhammad), founded in 2000, for the killing and registered a First Information Report against these groups.[20] The MQM and the SSP strongly denied any involvement.

The ST, for the first time ever, issued a countrywide call for a 'curfew in protest' against the arrest of their workers and the alleged failure of the government to apprehend Qadri's killers. It took effect in Karachi from the morning of 28 May 2001 and brought the city to a standstill. In retaliation, the Karachi Police besieged the central office of the ST, known as *Markaz-i-Ahl-i-Sunnat* (centre of the followers of Muslim practice) for four days, arrested more than 300 ST activists, and found a large quantity of illegal weapons for which the leadership of the ST was charged under the Anti-Terrorist Act of August 1997.[21]

## The Nishtar Park incident

Nishtar Park is one of the main parks of Karachi and the favourite venue for public meetings. The Barelvis and the Shi'as also hold religious gatherings there. From 1973, the traditional *milad* (Prophet's birthday) processions in Karachi end at Nishtar Park and after the *maghrib* (evening) prayer hold a grand *Miladul Nabi Kanfarans* (birth of the Prophet conference). On 11 April 2006 a conference was taking place when a bomb exploded under the main stage. Almost seventy people – all of its political leaders, including the president, Muhammad Abbas Qadri (1968–2006),[22] prominent Barelvi *ulama*, and workers – were killed.[23] As a result, riots broke out in the surrounding areas and public and private buildings were set ablaze including those of the paramilitary forces. Thousands mourned at the funeral prayer of the ST leaders, including prominent Barelvi *ulama* and *masha'ikh* (Sufi leaders), led by Mufti Munibur Rahman (b. 1945), a leading Barelvi *alim* (scholar). The Army was called out to assist the police and the Rangers maintain law and order, while the Sindh government announced a three-day mourning period when all educational institutions were closed. The city came to a standstill. Barelvis in other parts of the country joined in and held ceremonies to memorialize the atrocity and honour the dead.[24]

After the Nishtar Park incident, the religio-political landscape of Karachi changed dramatically. The ST was destroyed as a party.[25] Unlike the killing of Salim Qadri, the ST, bizarrely, accused the MQM of being behind the blast. The latter denied any involvement. The allegation may have been a reflection of its growing political rivalry with the MQM. The national press, on the other hand, blamed an offshoot of the SSP, the *Lashkar-i-Jhangvi* (Army of Jhangvi), founded in 1996.[26] The ST issued a seven-day ultimatum for the arrest of the culprits and demanded the dismissal of the Sindh Government and Governor, Dr 'Ishratul Abad Khan (b. 1963), a nominee of the MQM.[27] The Nishtar Park bombing case is still pending in one of the five Sindh Anti-Terrorist Courts. The inordinate delay in the disposal of the case is, *inter alia*, due to the reluctance of the complainant to pursue it. Muhammad Altaf Qadri registered a First Incident Report (FIR) and four people were arrested in mid-2007, only one of whom was tried, and acquitted, by the Court for 'lack of evidence'.[28]

Besides engaging in armed clashes with religious and political opponents, in July 1998 ST workers were also involved in a clash with the supporters of the *Anjuman-i-Sarfaroushan-i-Islam Pakistan* (Pakistan association of people who sacrifice for Islam) on the eve of the *Miladul Nabi* procession in Karachi. The *Anjuman* was formed by Riaz Ahmad Goharshahi (1941–2001), a Barelvi by birth, who was declared a heretic by the Barelvi *ulama* due to his 'deviant belief and practices'.[29] The ST was suspected of killing Maulana Abdul Wahid Qadri, chief of his own faction of the ST on 18 July 1998 in Karachi.[30] It was also held responsible by the national press for the killing of a prominent Deobandi *alim*, Maulana Muhammad Yusuf Ludhianawi (1932–2000), in May 2000 at Karachi, and two *Ahl-i-Hadith ulama*, Dr Ghulam Murtaza Malik (1941–2002) and Attaur Rahman Saqib (1960–2002), in May 2002 in Lahore.[31] The ST/PST also supports Mumtaz Qadri (b. 1985), the murderer of Salman Tasir (1944–2011), governor of the Punjab. On 1 October 2011 Qadri was sentenced to death for the crime but the sentence has yet to be carried out. The ST/PST, and other Barelvi religio-political parties and groups, is demanding his unconditional release.

The occasional and targeted killing of ST workers, especially in Karachi, police raids on the *Markaz-i-Ahl-i-Sunnat*, and the arrests of its workers is a fact of ST life.[32] The leaders and workers of the ST have been booked on a number of cases under different sections of the Pakistan Penal Code, but not a single case has been tried. On their part it is a routine matter for the ST to display weapons at rallies.[33] In January 2001, it was put on a government watch-list, but in March 2013 it was dropped from the list due to its 'good record'.[34]

The ST is very anxious to preserve the Sunni identity of the Barelvis. They believe that Barelvis are being deprived of their rights and their socio-political status. While addressing *Fikr-i-Ahl-i-Sunnat Kanfarans* (thought of followers of Muslim practice conference) in Lahore, Qadri rationalized ST's stance towards other religious groups as, according to him, they are occupying and using the income of dozens of Barelvi *awqaf* and mosques to the tune of millions of rupees.³⁵ For Shahid Ghuri, a prominent ST figure,

> our 'militancy' is for self-defense. Our opponents are armed and they used [weapons] to attack and capture our mosques and *awqaf* and kill our workers, so, we have to counter them and we are bound to retaliate in the same way.³⁶

In a meeting of all religio-political parties held on 13 January 2001 at Islamabad under the auspices of the Federal Ministry of the Interior, Qadri held the view that the prevailing militancy was due to groups exploiting the cause of the Kashmir *jihad*. After collecting donations in the name of the *jihad*, they bought weapons which are being used against the Barelvis to take over their mosques and *awqaf*. At the end of his statement, he rationalized his existing defense strategy, saying it was designed to counter militancy.³⁷

The ST joined the *Sunni Ittihad Kounsal* (Sunni Unity Council; SIK), an alliance of eight Barelvi parties and pressure groups formed in May 2009 to wage a joint struggle against the Talibanization of the country. Barelvis are staunch opponents of the Taliban as they claim that the Deobandi-oriented Taliban are responsible for bomb blasts at different shrines and the killing of several Barelvi *ulama* and *masha'ikh*, particularly Dr Muhammad Sarfaraz Na'imi (1948–2009) in June 2009 at Lahore. Just two days before his assassination, he had issued a *fatwa* against suicide attacks. The Barelvis perceive the Taliban to be a great threat because they experienced direct and pre-planned strikes against them in March 2005 when the shrine of Pir Rakhil Shah situated in Jhal Magsi district, Balochistan was attacked.³⁸ The ST believes its ongoing rivalry with the Deobandis could be ended by banning all the blasphemous literature produced by their *ulama*. It believes that respect for and safeguarding the rights of Barelvis must be guaranteed.³⁹

## Clashes over mosques

The Barelvi-Deobandi conflict took the form of a direct confrontation over the management of *awqaf* in the Punjab between March and May 1984.⁴⁰ The Deobandis fully enjoyed the support of the Zia regime (1977–88), especially during the Afghan War against the Soviet Union (1979–89). Zia unprecedentedly also favoured the preaching of the *Tablighi Jama'at* (society for the spreading of the faith), founded in 1926, in the Pakistan Army.⁴¹ Numerous Deobandi *madaris* were established during that time and they worked as a nursery for the Taliban. The Taliban also linked themselves with Deobandi *ulama*. The first ever ST 'martyr' was Abdus Salam who was killed in March 1992 at Karachi in a dispute over the administration of a mosque, Nur Masjid,⁴² constructed in 1947. In October 2010 the mosque was fortified and well-guarded. Until 1990 it was under the control of the Barelvis. Later, *Ahl-i-Sunnat wal Jama'at* (the new name for the SSP) took over the mosque but it was believed the ST would ultimately reclaim it.⁴³ On 5 October 2010, Mawlawi Amin, who led prayers at the mosque, was shot dead. The ST was blamed for his murder and Deobandis announced a strike on 7 October. On the same evening, the shrine of the patron saint of Sindh, Abdullah Shah Ghazi (720–73), near Clifton, a suburb of Karachi, was rocked by two suicide blasts killing nine people.⁴⁴

The ST immediately blamed the Deobandis and their allies for the blast. It claimed the Ghazi blasts were 'attacks of revenge' for Amin's murder and demanded the government 'free' Nur Masjid from the 'clutches of the terrorists'.⁴⁵ The ST also blamed Deobandis for attacking the shrines of the famous saints, Shaykh 'Ali bin 'Uthman Hajwairi (1009–72) alias Data Ganj Bakhsh, on 1 July 2010 at Lahore, and Baba Fariduddin Mas'ud Ganj Shakkar (1173/4–1265), on 25 October 2010 at Pakpattan. In these attacks more than 100 people were killed.⁴⁶

In July 2010 the ST and Deobandis attacked each other with sticks, metal bars, and guns on the premises of Nur Mosque. The bloody battle which started on the night of *Shabb-i-Mi'raj* (night of the nocturnal journey) left at least a dozen people injured, including one with a gunshot wound. The authorities arrested more than 20 Deobandis and sealed the mosque for several days. The Deobandis complained that despite the 'fact' that ST activists had started the fight, none of their people were apprehended. They went on to accuse the ST of instigating the violence.⁴⁷ Nur Masjid is now under the 'control' of the Deobandis although after *isha* (night-time prayers) and Friday prayers, Barelvis are welcomed.⁴⁸

The dispute over Nur Mosque is tied in with the history of the ST, which made its first show of strength on 18 December 1992 when it organized a huge rally at M.A. Jinnah Road in Karachi to put pressure on the administration to hand over the mosque to the ST. Dozens of people were injured and several vehicles were burnt. As a result, the government closed down the mosque in 1996. Similarly, a dispute occurred over a mosque in Lahore and there was an open clash between the ST and Deobandis in July 2010.⁴⁹

There have been innumerable clashes over the possession of mosques all over the country and they remain unsolved for years on end. Both sides present a long list of mosques and *madaris* which they claim have either been taken over or sealed by the government because of disputes over their ownersip. The ST claims the problem dates back to the Zia regime when hundreds of Barelvi mosques and *madaris* across the country were forcibly taken over by Deobandis.⁵⁰ The ST believe the disputed mosques should either be handed over to them or sealed until the issue of ownership is resolved. Leaders of both sides claim they are living under the threat of death.⁵¹ It was also observed in the national press that the failure of local administrations to settle local sectarian disputes, particularly in Karachi, has given undue importance to the ST.⁵²

## The ST/PST and the MQM

Differences between the ST and the MQM developed after July 2000 when, according to press reports, the ST leadership refused to accommodate and give shelter to MQM activists, to collect religious donations on its behalf, and to wage a war against jihadist organizations.[53] The collection of extortion and protection money is another important reason for their differences. They were exacerbated when the ST decided to jump into the electoral arena and contest the local bodies' elections in Sindh in 2005. According to the ST leadership, its winning candidates were tortured and killed, while several candidates were compelled to withdraw from the contest.[54] Maulana Abdul Karim Naqshbandi, who was contesting the election for *nazim* (chief elected official) of the Union Council-2, Lyari Town, Karachi, was the most prominent among those who were killed. He was gunned down on 13 August 2005.[55]

The All-Parties Peace Conference, convened by the ST on 24 June 2005 in Karachi, expressed its sympathies with ST demands for, *inter alia*, the holding of free and fair elections to local bodies in Sindh.[56] The ST announced the suspension of all its activities in Karachi in protest at the Sindh government's failure to stop the killing of its workers.[57] After the Nishtar Park incident, it presented a detailed memorandum to the government of Pakistan citing atrocities and tyrannies the MQM committed and a list of its workers and leaders gunned down.[58]

## Faith-based politics: the Pakistan Sunni Tehrik

In February 2009 the ST announced the creation of the *Pakistan Inqilabi Tehrik* (Pakistan Revolutionary Party; PIK) as its political wing. The president of the ST, Engineer Sarwat Ijaz Qadri (b. 1961), believed that people were estranged from the socio-political system and vowed to introduce a new political culture based on the principles of the city state of Medina established by the Prophet Muhammad in or after 622. Qadri believed that other religio-political parties had used Barelvis for their own vested interests and pledged to work for the good of the country.[59] He criticized the forcible implementation of militants' interpretation of the *Shari'at* in Swat, while at the same time he condemned all terrorist activities perpetrated in the name of Islam, and vowed to support all law enforcement agencies in keeping the writ of the state.[60] The background to the creation of the new party was that the ST had contested national and provincial elections in 2002 and elections for the Jammu and Kashmir Legislative Assembly in July 2006 but performed so poorly it failed to win a single seat, leading it to boycott the 2008 General Elections. As a result it created the new party. It also established a student wing, the Pakistan Islamic Student Federation. A women's wing of the ST had already been established.

The PST left the PIK in December 2012 as, according to Qadri, it failed to achieve its goals.[61] So the PST with a 'Table Lamp' as its electoral symbol, contested the May 2013 General Elections with the hope of emerging as a large pressure group. Although the election campaign was conducted freely, the PST, like the PIK, the JUP, and the JI boycotted the polls in Karachi citing irregularities and rigging. Qadri demanded a revote under the supervision of the Army.[62] The PST had once again failed to get a mandate from Barelvis as, according to

PST leaders, it failed to motivate and unite them on one electoral platform and to publicise its manifesto.⁶³

The manifesto of the PST called for drastic changes in the *status quo* of the religio-political and socio-economic system and pledged to transform the country into an Islamic welfare state and a free, sovereign, and prosperous country. It also promised to eradicate the menace of terrorism and vowed to have an independent and non-aligned foreign policy. In order to undermine what it said was the monopoly of Christians and Jews in global politics, the PST would work for the formation of a Muslim Commonwealth and free trade and favourable business practices among Muslim countries.⁶⁴

## Ahl-i-Sunnat Khidmat Committee

In spite of its specific religio-political stance, the ST/PST is also active in the social sector. The Ahl-i-Sunnat Khidmat Committee (followers of Muslim practice service committee; ASKC) is the main welfare organization of the ST/PST and provides help to people after natural disasters, drought, and when suffering from hunger. It was established in 1990 by Qadri and its network covers most of the country. It established a hospital in Karachi, provides an ambulance service, and establishes free medical camps and blood banks. It also provides food to needy people during the month of Ramadan and arranges a dowry for poor and orphan girls. It constructs mosques, *madaris*, and schools in poor areas.⁶⁵ The major source of its income is in the form of donations and *zakat* (alms), *sadqat* (charity) including *sadaqah-i-fitr* (charity at the end of Ramadan), and selling the hides of sacrificial animals on *'id-i-qurban* (feast held at the end of the pilgrimage to Mecca). As these skins are valuable, clashes occur as different groups try to steal them. In December 2006, the ASKC claimed its camps in Karachi were raided by the MQM and its skins were stolen.⁶⁶

Although no official statistics on the demographical strength of religious communities is available, as the census does not provide any data on religious communities and sects, it is believed that Barelvis are in the majority. Due to political polarization and their leadership crises, they do not perform well in national politics but they are, however, still relevant and influential in the national socio-political milieu.

The ST stands for the safeguarding of Barelvi beliefs, mosques, *awqaf*, and rights, which they claim is under severe threat from the increasing socio-political influence of the Deobandis and other groups. The moral support given to the *jihadists* by most of the Deobandi *ulama* is also a matter of great concern. The ST, like other Barelvi organizations, fears that as the Deobandis stand for their own 'reformist' and 'puritan' interpretation of Islam, so, like the Shi'as, Barelvis are also the target of their *jihad* against 'non-Muslims'.⁶⁷

The Barelvis as a community are against the use of force. They did not have organized and trained militant groups. So, they were not in a position to counter the onslaught of the Deobandis. Only the ST vowed to defend Barelvi interests through 'defensive militancy'. In its early phase, it 'succeeded' by getting back possession of mosques and shrines. Before the emergence of the ST, no Barelvi organization had ever indulged in organized sectarian violence and militancy.[68] However, the ST is unique in the sense that it does not share the Afghan *jihad* experience of other militant groups.[69] For making its voice more effective, the ST transformed itself into a political party, the PST.

The ST/PST claimed that as Barelvis are in a solid majority, and as they had also joined in the struggle to create Pakistan, they should get their due share and representation in all spheres of public life. They should also get maximum coverage in print and electronic media and their contribution in the creation of Pakistan acknowledged in the national curriculum.[70] In its clashes with its opponents, especially the Deobandis, it uses highly derogatory and inflammatory language. It frequently chants emotional slogans and reads provocative poems at its meetings. Although the PST has replaced the ST, its ideology, leadership, and methodology is still dominant. This may hamper its transformation as it will be very difficult for the PST to rid itself of the stain of its violent past. The 'good' thing about ST militancy is that it is fully indigenous and it does not have any international connections. Its turn to 'militancy' was only to counter the militancy of other religious groups with whom it has incompatible doctrinal differences. Further, although one can find passive antagonism against various policies of Western countries, the ST/PST is not at war with Western powers.

## Notes

1 Mian 'Abdul Rashid, *Ta'ruf: Pakistan Sunni Parti* (Lahore: Pakistan Sunni Parti, 1972), pp. 2–5. In July 1991, *Pakistan Sunni Ittihad* was formed in order to forge unity among the different Barelvi religious groups. For details, see monthly *Mah-i-Taiybah* (Sialkot), August 1991, pp. 47–8 and October 1991, pp. 16, and 46.
2 For details, see Muhammad Sharif-ul-Haq Amjadi, *Sunni Deobandi Ikhtalafat ka Munsifanah Ja'izah* (Ghosi: Da'rah al-Barakat, n.d.); Muhammad Ilyas Gumman, *Firqah-i-Barelviyyat Pak wa Hind ka Tehqiqi Ja'izah* (Sargodha: Maktabah-i-Ahl-i-Sunnah wa al-Jama'ah, 2012); and Mujeeb Ahmad, 'Schism within South Asian Sunnis: Emergence of the Barelvis and Deobandis', paper presented in a Research Workshop at CERI Sciences Po, Paris, France on 17 October 2011.
3 Ahmad Rida Khan Barelvi, *Hussamul Haramain 'ala Munhir al-kufir wa al-Muin*, trans. Iqbal Ahmad Faruqi (Lahore: Maktabah-i-Nabwiyyah, 1998), pp. 3–10; Hashmat Ali Khan (ed.), *as-Sawaruzmul Hindiyah* (Sahiwal: Maktabah-i-Faridiyah, n.d.); and Usha Sanyal, 'Are Wahhabis Kafirs? Ahmad Riza Khan Barelvi and His *Sword of the Haramayn*', in Muhammad Khalid Masud, Brinkley Messick and David S. Powers (eds), *Islamic Legal Interpretation: Muftis and Their Fatwas* (Cambridge, MA: Harvard University Press, 1996), 206.
4 Barbara Daly Metcalf, *Islamic Revival in British India: Deoband, 1860–1900* (Princeton, NJ: Princeton University Press, 1982), p. 310. Maulana Khalil Ahmad Ambethwi in refutation of this *fatwa*, in November 1907, gave a *fatwa* which was published in a book. In his *fatwa*, endorsed by the prominent Deobandi *alim*, Maulana Ambethwi, while denouncing the Wahhabis, argued that the beliefs of Deobandi *ulama* are in accordance with the *Fiqh-i-Hanafi* and the *Ahl-i-Sunnat wa Jama'at*. Khalil Ahmad Ambethwi, *'aqa'id-i-ulama-i-Deoband* (Karachi: Muhammad Sa'id and Sons, n.d.).
5 For details, see Ziya-ul-Hasan Faruqi, *The Deoband School and the Demand for Pakistan* (Lahore: Progressive Books, n.d.).

6 Mumtaz Ahmad, 'Madrasa Reforms and Perspectives: Islamic Tertiary Education in Pakistan', *The National Bureau of Asian Research, NBR Project Report, April 2009*, p. 24.
7 Mujeeb Ahmad, *Jam'iyyat 'Ulama-i-Pakistan: 1948–1979* (Islamabad: National Institute of Historical and Cultural Research, 1993), p. 119. A White Paper was also issued by the Federal Government about Mufti Mahmud's administration.
8 The term *Nizam-i-Mustafah* was used during the movement mainly by the JUP. With this nomenclature, the Barelvis claimed that facet of Islam which centralized the position of the Prophet Muhammad. For the role of the JUP in the movement, see Mujeeb, *Jam'iyyat 'Ulama-i-Pakistan*, pp. 136–43; Diya'ul Rahman Faruqi (ed.), *Tehrik-i-Nizam-i-Mustafah* (Faisalabad: Idarah Isha'at-i-al-Ma'rif, 1977); and weekly *Ufaq* (Karachi), *Tehrik-i-Nizam-i-Mustafah Nambar* (11–24 June 1978).
9 Mujeeb, *Jam'iyyat 'Ulama-i-Pakistan*, pp. 146–8.
10 *Ufaq*, 29 July–11 August 1981, pp. 8–9.
11 For the introduction of the *Idarah-i-Minhajjul Qur'an*, see Muhammad Tahirul Qadri, *Tehrik-i-Minhajjul Qur'an (Afkar wa Hidaiyat)* (Lahore: Minhajjul Qur'an Publications, 1996); and Muhammad Rafiq, *Tehrik-i-Minhajjul Qur'an kay ibtadai' pandrah sal* (Lahore: Minhajjul Qur'an Publications, 1998).
12 For details about the DI, see Mujeeb Ahmad, 'Conservative in Belief, Modern in Techniques. *Da'wat-i-Islami*: A Revivalist Movement of the Barelvis', *Journal of South Asian and Middle Eastern Studies*, 34, 2 (Winter 2011): 68–86; and Thomas K. Gugler, *Mission Medina: Da'wat-e Islami und Tabligi Gama'at* (Wurzburg: Ergon-Verlag, 2011).
13 *Jama'at-i-Ahl-i-Sunnat Pakistan ka Tarikhi Faisalah aur us ka Pasmanzar* (Lahore: Markazi Jama'at-i-Ahl-i-Sunnat Pakistan, n.d.), p. 2.
14 S.V.R. Nasr, 'The Rise of Sunni Militancy in Pakistan: The Changing Role of Islamism and the Ulama in Society and Politics', *Modern Asian Studies*, 34, 1 (February 2000), p. 176.
15 *Akhbar-i-Ahl-i-Sunnat* (Lahore), October/November 1997, p. 10. It was reported in the national press that prior to May 2010, 27 Barelvi mosques were captured by Deobandi militants in Multan and its suburbs. Mujahid Husain, *Panjabi Taliban* (Lahore: Sanjh Publications, 2011), pp. 278–9.
16 Sayyid Muhammad Zainulabidin Shah Rashidi, *Anwar-i-ulama-i-Ahl-i-Sunnat Sindh* (Lahore: Zawiyah Publishers, 2006), pp. 306–7.
17 *Pakistan: Karachi's Madrasas and Violent Extremism*, International Crisis Group Policy Report, 29 March 2007, Islamabad/Brussels, p. 11.
18 Personal Interview with Muhammad Shahid Ghuri, 17 March 2007, at *Markaz-i-Ahl-i-Sunnat*, Karachi.
19 *Nida-i-Ahl-i-Sunnat* (Lahore), June 2001, pp. 45–6 and *Dawn* (Karachi), 29 May 2001. On 19 May the Punjab Police in Lahore clashed with workers of the ST and other Barelvi parties protesting the Karachi incident. While chasing some of the protesters, the Lahore Police entered the premises of the shrine of Data Ganj Bakhsh, an action which was strongly condemned by Barelvis who portrayed it as a sacrilege committed against the shrine. On 28 June, a large group of Barelvi *ulama* and *Masha'ikh*, along with their followers, visited the shrine as a mark of respect. The Barelvis' countrywide protest against the shrine incident was so strong that the President of Pakistan, General Pervez Musharraf (b. 1943, President 2001–8), had to visit the shrine on 5 July and as a mark of respect presented a wreath and offered a prayer. *Nida-i-Ahl-i-Sunnat*, June 2001, pp. 61–3 and *Fateh* (Karachi), June 2001, p. 71.
20 *Fateh*, June 2001, pp. 11 and 98; and *Sunni Tarjuman* (Karachi), July 2001, pp. 4, 25–6, 43, and December 2001/January 2002, p. 16. *Sipah-i-Sahabah Pakistan* and *Jaish-i-Muhammad* were banned by the government in January 2002.
21 *Wajud* (Karachi), 30 May–12 June 2001, p. 25; and *Dawn* (Karachi), 28 May 2001.
22 Abbas Qadri, the most popular president of the ST is known as *Amir Shuhada'-i-Milad*.

23 Among those who were killed in the incident were Hafiz Muhammad Taqi (1948–2006) a prominent leader of the JUP; Sayyid Muhammad Faridul Hasnain Kazimi of Khawajahabad Sharif, Mianwali; Muhammad Hanif Billu, president of the *Tehrik-i-'Awam-i-Ahl-i-Sunnat* (April 1979); Mufti Mukhtar Ahmad Qadri of *Darul 'ulum Amjadiyah*, Karachi (1948); and Pir Muhammad Pairil Naqshbandi (1980–2006), Secretary General of the *Anjuman-i-Talaba'-i-Islam* (January 1968).
24 *Dawn* (Karachi), 14 April 2006.
25 *Mustafai' News* (Karachi), April 2009, p. 11.
26 *Dawn* (Islamabad), 14 January 2014. *Lashkar-i-Jhangwi* was banned by the government in August 2001.
27 *Sunni Tarjuman*, May/June 2006, p. 19; and *Nida-i-Millat* (Lahore), 20–6 April 2006, pp. 6–7.
28 *Dawn* (Islamabad), 14 January 2014.
29 *Dawn* (Karachi), 17 July 1998. For the differences between Barelvis and the *Anjuman-i-Sarfaroushan-i-Islam Pakistan*, see Abu Daw'ud Muhammad Sadiq, *Khatarah ka Alarm* (Gujranwala: Maktabah Rida-i-Mustafah, n.d.); and *Fitnah-i-Gohariyah* (Karachi: Jam'iyyat Isha'at-i-Ahl-i-Sunnat, n.d.).
30 *Dawn* (Karachi), 19 July 1998. Maulana Abdul Wahid Qadri, due to organizational differences, formed his own faction. Shahid Ghuri denied any involvement of the ST/PST in his murder. Personal Interview with Muhammad Shahid Ghuri at *Markaz-i-Ahl-i-Sunnat*, 25 October 2013, Karachi.
31 *Pakistan: Karachi's Madrasas and Violent Extremism*, p. 26; and *Daily Times* (Lahore), 23 November 2004.
32 Maulana Khurram Qadri, member of the *Sunni Tehrik ulama Board*, was killed in Lahore on 3 May 2013. *Nawa-i-Waqt* (Rawalpindi/Islamabad), 4 May 2013.
33 *Herald* (Karachi), August 2010, p. 46.
34 *Nawa-i-Waqt* (Rawalpindi/Islamabad), 16 March 2013.
35 *Rida-i-Mustafah* (Gujranwala), November 1993, pp. 23–4; June 1994, p. 23; and June 1995, p. 17; and *Mujallah Sunni Tarjuman* (Karachi), June/August 1999, pp. 49 and 51–2.
36 Personal Interview with Muhammad Shahid Ghuri, 17 March 2007, at *Markaz-i-Ahl-i-Sunnat*, Karachi. See also *Afkar-i-Rida* (Mumbai), January/March 1999, pp. 70–1. However, after the assassination of Salim Qadri, the ST stands for 'like-for-like' revenge killings. *Sunni Tarjuman*, July 2001, p. 2.
37 *Sunni Tarjuman*, January/February 2001, pp. 13–14.
38 Mujahid, *Panjabi Taliban*, pp. 267 and 269.
39 Muhammad Salim Qadri, ed. *Akhar yah jang kiyun?* (Karachi: Sunni Tehrik, n.d.), pp. 2–3; and *Nida-i-Millat*, 20–26 April 2006, p. 8.
40 Ian Talbot, 'Religion and Violence: The Historical Context for Conflict in Pakistan', p. 160, in John R. Hinnells and Richard King (eds), *Religion and Violence in South Asia: Theory and Practice* (London: Routledge, 2007).
41 Husain Haqqani, *Pakistan between Mosque and Military* (Washington, D.C.: Carnegie Endowment for International Peace, 2005), pp. 151 and 292–3; and Anatol Lieven, 'Military Exceptionalism in Pakistan', *Survival*, 53, 4 (2011), p. 64.
42 *Sunni Tarjuman*, December 2001/January 2002, p. 4.
43 *Ahl-i-Sunnat wal Jama'at* was banned by the government in February 2012.
44 *Nawa-i-Waqt* (Karachi), 8 October 2010.
45 *Dawn* (Karachi), 8 October 2010.
46 Mujahid, *Panjabi Taliban*, p. 267.
47 *Herald* (Karachi), August 2010, p. 45; and *The Express Tribune* (Karachi), 18 October 2010.
48 Personal Interview with Muhammad Shahid Ghuri, 25 October 2013, at *Markaz-i-Ahl-i-Sunnat*, Karachi.
49 *Herald* (Karachi), August 2010, pp. 44–5.

50 *The Express Tribune* (Karachi), 18 October 2010.
51 Ibid.
52 *Dawn* (Karachi), 18 November 2012.
53 *Nida-i-Ahl-i-Sunnat*, June 2001, pp. 47–8.
54 *Nida-i-Millat*, 20–26 April 2006, p. 10.
55 *Jang* (Karachi), 14 August 2005.
56 *The Nation* (Karachi), 25 June 2005.
57 *Awam* (Karachi), 28 August 2005.
58 *His Honourable Responsible Higher Authorities Islamic Republic Of Pakistan. Immediate Action against the Terrorist/Killer of Mutthada Qumi Movement (MQM), regarding Martyr at Nishtar Park Karachi (12 R.A.W) and Others.*
59 *Mustafai' News*, April 2009, p. 10.
60 http://en.wikipedia.org/wiki/Sunni_Tehreek, accessed 30 May 2012.
61 *Nawa-i-Waqt* (Karachi), 13 December 2012. However, according to Shahid Ghuri, the leadership of SIK followed the policy of estrangement towards the ST/PST, the largest component party. Personal Interview with Muhammad Shahid Ghuri, 25 October 2013, at *Markaz-i-Ahl-i-Sunnat*, Karachi.
62 *Dawn* (Karachi), 18 May 2013.
63 Personal Interviews with Muhammad Shahid Ghuri and Shadab Raza Naqshbandi president of the Punjab PST, 25 October 2013, at *Markaz-i-Ahl-i-Sunnat*, Karachi.
64 *Mansur: Pakistan Sunni Tehrik* (Karachi: Pakistan Sunni Tehrik, n.d.), pp. 1–4.
65 *Brochure Ahle Sunnat Khidmat Committee (Trust) 2004*, pp. 1–9.
66 *Sunni Tarjuman*, February 2007, pp. 5, 19, and 28.
67 Under the immense influence of the Taliban, the militant Deobandi groups are, since 1994 (the year the Taliban emerged in Afghanistan), of the view that to establish a 'real' Islamic state in Pakistan they need to purge the Barelvis and Shi'as. Mariam Abou Zahab, 'The Regional Dimension of Sectarian Conflicts in Pakistan', in Christophe Jaffrelot (ed.), *Pakistan: Nationalism without a Nation?* (New Delhi: Manohar, 2004), p. 123.
68 However, almost all Barelvi organizations are directly or indirectly involved in the *Jihad-i-Kashmir*. For details, see Mujeeb Ahmad, 'Tehrik-i-Azadi-i-Jammun wa Kashmir: 'ulama'-i-Ahl-i-Sunnat wa Jama'at ka Mu'aqif aur kirdar', *Mujallah Tarikh wa Thiqafat-i-Pakistan*, 10, 1 (April 1999/September 1999): 59–81; and Sushant Sareen, 'Islamic Terrorism: The Pakistan Factor', *SAPRA India Bulletin*, September 2001, p. 21.
69 *Pakistan: Karachi's Madrasas and Violent Extremism*, p. 11.
70 *Nida-i-Millat*, 9–15 February 2012, pp. 34–5.

# 9 Pakistan's religious *Others*
## Reflections on the minority discourse on Christians in the Punjab

*Tahir Kamran and Navtej K. Purewal*

The position of minorities has been a continuing theme in Pakistan's social and political history. While the 'core of Pakistan as a nation was defined by religion alone',[1] it would be naïve to view the outcomes of religious mobilisation in the creation of post-colonial Pakistan solely from the perspective of the dominant narrative of Muslim political mobilisation. Minority discourse contains elements of both the dominant narrative of nationalism (with its notion of protecting a Muslim minority out of the postcolonial configuration of South Asia) as well as the idea of creating a minority status for religious *Others* within subsequent and contemporary Pakistan. The majority/minority dichotomy is embedded in the state's discourse on national belonging. However, the status and stigma associated with minorities in contemporary Pakistan captures the denial and official disciplining of social and religious diversity which finds a cover in the language and discourse on minorities for the cause of solidifying an otherwise fractured and fraught national identity. This chapter explores the impact which the official streamlining of identity through the religious question has had upon the discourse of minorities. The religious question is one which has sought to construct a monolithic image of the state through the greatest common factor in state-aligned Sunni Islam which has then gone forth to label *deviant others* in order to construct and depict a malleable and obedient national public.

The erection of a distinct minority discourse represents a state-driven agenda to undermine difference rather than to recognise it by reifying a majoritarian approach towards national culture. The implications of this minority discourse is examined in how the state has utilised a bounded sense of nation and religion as a means of disciplining and creating a malleable, governable populace unchallenged by religious diversity. Christians in Pakistan occupy a minority position which is arguably proximate in terms of being 'people of the book,' and thus nominally protected, while also being socially stigmatised as deviant through social structure, low caste associations, and the continual threat of allegations of blasphemy.[2]

The discourse and status of minorities can best be understood as a foundational theme to the framing of the politics of power and legitimacy. In order to chart out this foundational frame, we explore how the categorical status of minorities has experienced a shift from being *proximate others* to being *deviant others*. In doing so, we highlight how the evolving discourse on minorities has shifted over time from showing the state's rhetorical attention to the protection of the rights of minorities under Governor-General Mohammad Ali Jinnah (1876–1948, Governor-General 1947–8) and his moral leadership to one which generates stigma against minority status, notably through the various phases of Islamisation and provincial challenges to state authority. We use the provincial example of the Punjab to highlight the positionality of the Christian 'minority'. The tensions that exist between both the politics of identification and the politics of stigma highlight the state's utilisation of minority *otherness* to establish its moral authority upon nationalism and its own sovereignty.

## Majoritarianism and its minorities in Pakistan

Minorities have been largely missed out from scholarly attention in the episteme of the creation of Pakistan. Apart from a few studies and reports which have made minorities their focus,[3] minorities have remained at the margins of historical and contemporary enquiries. Rather than being viewed as part of the creation of the state or as actors in the development of its social and economic polity, non-Muslims have been relegated as existing outside of political history and development.

American sociologist Louis Wirth's denotation in 1945 of a 'minority group' casts the term away from a numerical sense of presence towards a sense of a marker of social, political, and economic power. In his sense, minority groups refer to 'groups of people who, because of their physical or cultural characteristics, are singled out ... for differential and unequal treatment, and who therefore regard themselves as objects of collective discrimination'.[4] Wirth's analysis of minority status was firmly positioned within an assimilationist frame in which minority status is given to groups who suffer discrimination, prejudice, and victimization. This discussion subsequently, as in the case of the Civil Rights Movement in the United States, puts the responsibility for discrimination with the majority or dominant culture. From the onset, minority-majority power relations in Pakistan have been at the behest of the state's machinations in the creation of a cohesive religious majority. While the US context has shown that minority status has enabled a moral power in which claims and grievances against discrimination are recognised and viewed as legitimate, the Pakistan case shows us that the moral power around minority status has remained within the state's hands. However, as this chapter highlights, when minority status shifts from being one of *proximate otherness* (electoral existence as religious categories through separate electorates) to *deviant otherness* (objects of allegations of blasphemy), the moral power of minorities disappears or is compromised by a majoritarian view of otherness which becomes stigmatised. This is highlighted in the Islamisation process in Pakistan which has rendered minority status as a stigmatised position. This is the position Christians occupy.

The status of religious minorities has brought to the fore the position which 'non-Muslims' hold within an on-going hegemonising nationalist discourse on religion and the state. The conceptualisation of religious minorities has been central to notions of national cohesion and identity since the state's inception in 1947. The stigma associated with who is identified as a minority, and who is not part of the majority, identifies the Muslim majority as the organising principle of national cohesion. The 1998 census approximation that 97 per cent of Pakistan's religious make-up is Muslim highlights the dominant status which the category represents through the state's mechanism of identification.

The state's tools of religious categorisation conceal a heterogeneous social fabric which is indicative of the deviant status that minority status represents. Behind this majoritarian Muslim category it is possible to argue that, on the one hand, diversity is celebrated in terms of region and ethnicity while, on the other hand, the religious question has closed down the space for identification through the labelling of that which is legitimate and that which is not.

Turning our lens onto the Punjab, not commonly cited in the history of the All-India Muslim League, which was founded in Dacca in 1906, is the fact that three Christians were elected to the Punjab Legislative Assembly in 1945–6 who subsequently voted for Pakistan. Father J. Saldanha (b. 1936), the Archbishop of Lahore (2001–11), considered that contribution, if not 'decisive,' at least 'a small sincere contribution' on the part of the Christians.[5] Their leaders recorded their statements before the Punjab Boundary Commission, comprising Justice Din Muhammad, Sir Zafarullah Khan (1893–1985), and Sardar Baldev Singh (1902–61) and requested that 'the Christian population may be counted as part of Pakistan'.[6] Cecil Chaudhry reveals: 'He [S.P. Singha] told Jinnah that three out of four Christian members would vote for Pakistan. The resolution in the Punjab was passed by a margin of two votes. I believe that Christians created Pakistan.'[7] When a journalist asked Singha as to why Christians lent support to the Muslim League, he said:

> Muslims were a minority community of the sub-continent at that time and with the creation of Pakistan, they became the majority. The Muslims would remember the problems faced as a minority and would not perpetuate the same fate for other minorities.[8]

From the onset, the Pakistan movement drew upon the terms of colonial religious categorisation in order to present its case for representing a political voice for the Muslim minority within unified pre-1947 India. The concept and rhetorical notion of the *minority* within a religiously demarcated populace was born out of the Muslim League's campaign to address the tenuous and uncertain position which Muslims occupied as a minority. With the colonial backdrop of separate electorates, Hindu majoritarianism, within an increasingly religiously defined electorate and the Indian National Congress' unflinching commitment to 'secularism,' the Pakistan movement emerged as a voice of concern over the rights and the position of minorities within an independent India. The Lahore Resolution of 23 March 1940 represented an initial demand for Muslim independent states within British India but later came to be interpreted and utilised as a symbol for the Pakistan movement's argument for a separate more coherently denoted nation.

Christians are also notably present in the episteme of Partition, and not merely as minorities swept by the wave of refugees and violence but of agency and humanitarian contribution. During the initial phase of its existence, the newly founded state faced a demographic upheaval arising from Partition in which an estimated 7.5 million refugees migrated to Pakistan. A majority of them were consigned to refugee camps in Lahore and other transit points where there was a dire shortage of food, shelter, and water. Christians formed a notable source of charitable activity at this time, and 'in 1947, about 70 to 75% of the paramedical staff in the hospitals were Christians'[9] Victor Azriah states, while shedding light on the contribution of Christians in helping out migrants, 'Its classical example stays alive in our history when the Hostel of F.C. College, which was closed at that time, had been converted into full fledge hospital known as United Christian Hospital.'[10] Further, Christian educational institutions provided shelter to many homeless refugees in the wake of the mass migration of 1947. Christian women also rendered commendable service in aiding refugees, many of whom worked with the Red Cross to facilitate migration from India to Pakistan.[11]

The 1947 official creation of the state, therefore, was an expression of the aspirations for Muslim nationhood, which found itself having to state its own approach towards 'other' minorities, with Muslim political identity now being the hegemonic rather than a minority or marginal identity. The religious question became paramount due to the religious discourse around which the Pakistan movement had mobilised itself. The Lahore Resolution, in this sense, was meant to voice an assurance to non-Muslims that their minority position would not be in conflict with citizenship. The contradictions around the position of religion and the state and the recognition of minorities within a nation founded on the idea of defending minorities (within a unified India) began to emerge immediately. On 11 August 1947 at the brink of national formation, Mohammad Ali Jinnah, as the first Governor-General of Pakistan, stated in his historic speech to the Constituent Assembly:

> You are free, you are free to go to your temples, you are free to go to your mosques or to any other place of worship in this State of Pakistan. You may belong to any religion or caste or creed – that has nothing to do with the business of the State.... We are starting with this fundamental principle that we are all citizens and equal citizens of one State.

Indeed, the notion of 'freedom' which Jinnah invoked in this address was meant to assure those groups not included within the umbrella of Muslim political identity that religious freedoms of worship and belonging would be protected by the state's recognition of equal citizenship. It might be argued that this statement was little more than a symbolic, defensive gesture towards secularist critics of the Pakistan movement. However, the sentiments behind this initial statement would gradually be eroded through the Islamisation processes which would, in effect, create an Islamic ethos of the legal functioning of the state while continuing to uphold minority rights as an unattainable aim.

Jinnah's successors, while paying lip service to plurality and the protection of minority rights, became the agents of an increasingly religiously oriented monolithic nationalism, choosing to abandon the vision of an eclectic ethos of the territories and populace of Pakistan in 1947. The Objectives Resolution, which was introduced on 7 March 1949 to curb representation of non-Muslims, was passed after only five days on 12 March, in which Christians had no representation at all and which East Bengali Hindus comprised the largest group of minority representatives. The Objectives Resolution was the beginning of a long process of an erosion of minority rights and representation which would lead to stigmatisation.

After the passing of the Objectives Resolution, a number of committees and sub-committees were formed by the Constituent Assembly 'to work out the details of the Constitution on the principles as laid down in the Objectives Resolution'.[12] The most important among these was the Basic Principles Committee (BPC) which presented its interim report in 1950; it ascribed the Objectives Resolution a directive principle for all state policy. Even more significantly, the BPC also constituted a special committee, the *Talimaat-i-Islamia* (Islamic Scholars), which consisted of *ulama* (religious scholars) to 'advise on matters arising out of the Objectives Resolution'.[13] Thus, rather than asserting religious and social plurality, a unilateralist vision was advocated. The 'interim report' presented by the BPC evoked a scathing response in East Bengal leading to the withdrawal of the report. It was revised to address some of the Bengali grievances before being presented again before the Constituent Assembly on 22 December 1952.[14] Its main features were equality of all citizens before the law, the prohibiting of discrimination on grounds of religion, race, caste, and induction in the services of every qualified citizen irrespective of the religion to which he or she adhered. Furthermore, minorities were not barred from providing religious instruction to their children. Subsequently, these fundamental rights became part of the 1956 constitution. Minorities were also accorded 'Freedom of conscience and the right to profess, practice, and propagate religion, subject to public order and morality, were guaranteed'.[15]

However, one of the recommendations of the BPC report was that only a Muslim was entitled to be the head of the state. Minority representatives expressed discontent with this as they felt they had been relegated to the status of second-class citizens 'by virtue of being inferior to the Muslims'.[16] Another disconcerting feature of the BPC was the proposal to set up special boards by the governor-general and the provincial governors respectively comprising *ulama* well-versed in Islamic jurisprudence. Those boards would be empowered to scrutinise all laws in light of the injunctions of the *Qur'an* and the *Sunnah*. This amounted to entrusting the *ulama* boards with veto power over legislative bodies. Religious clerics, in that case, would 'monopolize the interpretation of the principles of the Quran and the Sunnah on behalf of the whole nation'.[17]

It was not until 1956 that Pakistan eventually received its first constitution, nine years after its inception. The preamble of the 1956 Constitution was identical to the Objectives Resolution passed by the first Constituent Assembly. Pakistan was designated an Islamic Republic. However, Article 18 provided minorities the right of religious freedom as it maintained: 'Every citizen shall have the right to profess, practice and propagate his religion, and every religious denomination and every sect thereof shall have the right to establish, maintain and manage its religious institutions.'

A Commission was subsequently set up by President Muhammad Ayub Khan (1907–74, President 1958–69) which circulated a questionnaire in 1962 to ascertain public response regarding the nature of the electorate: 55.1 per cent of the respondents favoured a joint electorate as opposed to separate electorates. The Commission, however, recommended separate electorates for voting for president as its members were not sure of the loyalty of Hindus. Ayub, contrary to the recommendation of the Commission, settled for a joint electorate for all communities which was considered a radical departure from existing practice.[18] The principle of a joint electorate was adhered to in the subsequent 1973 Constitution, despite the fact that after the separation of East Pakistan in 1971, religious minorities had been reduced to a mere 5 per cent of the total population. The Zulfiqar Ali Bhutto (1928–79, President 1971–3, Prime Minister 1973–7) government reserved six seats for minorities in the National Assembly whereas five seats were set aside for them in the Punjab.[19] That system ensured that minorities 'had a better sense of participation but were far from being treated with equality'[20] although much needed to be done in this regard.

The impetus to move toward separate electorates came after the 1970 and 1977 elections in which minorities mostly voted for the Pakistan People's Party (PPP), founded in 1967, under a joint electorate which gave rightist/religious parties sufficient reason to demand separate electorates. General Zia-ul-Haq (1924–88, President 1978–88) during his period of office between 1977 and 1988, announced local body elections in 1979 in the face of an imminent PPP electoral victory under the joint electorate system. Thus, political expediency left no other option for Zia but to rescind joint electorates in which Articles 51 and 106 were amended by Parliament in 1985 to force through the change.[21]

Separate electorates had long been denounced by human rights activists, election observers, and intellectuals, describing them as out of place with the United Nations Charter of Human Rights. After the institution of separate electorates, minority representatives were faced with a dilemma. Either they had to stay away from such an electoral system totally disenfranchising themselves or they were to accept 'enforced segregation'. Bishop Alexander John Malik (b. 1944) of Lahore called them 'apartheid electorates' that caused division. He, therefore, abstained from voting during Zia's regime.[22] Ironically, in the post-Zia era of the elected governments of Benazir Bhutto (1953–2007, Prime Minister 1988–90, 1993–6) and Nawaz Sharif (b. 1949, Prime Minister 1990–3, 1997–9) between 1988 and 1999 and three interim governments in between the dismissal of those governments 'consistently shied away from annulling the separate electorate law'.[23]

With the exception of a few individuals almost all minorities and minority leaders disapproved of separate electorates. Most of the Christian leaders, however, resented the fact that separate electorates were being thrust on them against their will. In that dispensation, constituencies for the minority contestants comprised several districts and, in some cases, even provinces. Christian candidates, in most cases belonging to the Punjab, were obliged to take their campaign up to Karachi, in a bid to appeal to their voters,[24] resulting in a fracturing of the electorate along religious lines.

There were, however, those who supported this law with the argument that it would ensure greater representation for minorities. Here it would not be out of place to recount that some Christian leaders such as Emmanuel Zafar, H.L Hayat, Gulzar Chuhan, Isac Sosheel, Aziz Hamdam, Walter Z. Haq, and Prof. Salamat Akhter from the Christian party, the Pakistan Massih League, protested the creation of joint electorates when the 1970 elections were announced.[25] Failing to forge a consensus, the League was divided into two factions over the issue. In the following elections, the League fielded 33 candidates for national and provincial assemblies, with 'spectacles' as the party insignia, but all of them lost very badly. A splinter group, the Azad Pakistan Massih League, persisted with its struggle against joint electorates under Joshua Fazal Din. Those espousing separate electorates aspired to have such a system whereby their separate identity would ensure the creation of their own political parties, the allocation of national and provincial assembly seats in proportion to their population, and the demarcation of constituencies to reflect the Christian population.[26] The separate electorates introduced by Zia met practically none of their aspirations.

The minority discourse on Christians has thus been shaped by the move towards separate electorates. However, another part of this discourse is also the Islamisation of the state. Despite becoming an Islamic republic in 1956, the state does not fully enforce *sharia* law and therefore characterises a state which stands on an Islamic national identity but falls short of enforcing *sharia* law. However, this has meant that this ambiguity cedes power to the state. The right to declare Muslim majoritarianism is anchored in the state's legitimising power while its accompanying minority discourse is utilised as and when majoritarianism is becoming weakened for electoral processes, as in the example of Zia.

## Blasphemy and the stigma of religious difference

Attempts by minority groups to maintain collective moral power for claims of discrimination have shown that minority status itself has come to denote a stigmatised position in contemporary Pakistan. This stigma was most firmly established in the 1960s and 1970s when mass conversion of untouchable, low-caste populations to Christianity took place. Within a short period of time, untouchables went from being 'people of no religion' to 'people of the book'. This was in response to the two India-Pakistan wars of the time (1965 and 1971) in which the syncretic and un-Islamic practices of these communities, who had previously been viewed as socially low in the hierarchy and thus politically insignificant, came under attack as 'traitors' and Indian sympathisers. The *Ad Dharmi* tradition of untouchables in the Punjab, as Ram[27] notes, was unique in the province in that it pertained more to prejudice and discrimination than pollution. The Ad Dharm movement of the 1920s, which had a significant presence, emerged as a voice for these people 'of no religion' in which they voiced an untouchable political assertion which did not align with the other categories of religion but constituted a concerted attempt to unite the various *dalit*/untouchable groups under one umbrella.[28] Thus, the presence post-1947 of 'people of no religion' in the Punjab was merely a continuation of the pre-Partition social make-up and milieu. However, the two India–Pakistan wars mustered a strong sense of competing nationalism and jingoism which pushed the religious question even further, particularly around the border areas between India and Pakistan. Seeking protection from being labelled Hindu or Indian, untouchables sought refuge within the minority label by becoming Christian, which offered an escape from accusations that they were *enemy others* (Hindu, Indian) and were people of 'the book'.

The very social composition which had allowed for a pre-1947 religious ambiguity for untouchables into the 1960s had now ceased to exist by the state's insistence that ambiguity be eradicated. While this can be seen as an outright rejection of Jinnah's declaration cited earlier about the protection of minority rights, it is the 1973 declaration of the Ahmadi community to be non-Muslim which resulted in the closure of the minority discourse as a protective mechanism for those seeking recognition of discrimination. This was a significant turning point in how an amorphous terrain of religious practice and identification suddenly became streamlined through the dichotomous Muslim versus non-Muslim categorisation. However, behind this was the backdrop of blasphemy laws which provided the legal justification for the creation of a minority, simultaneously labelling them as a stigmatised group. Beginning in 1974 Pakistan's National Assembly under Zulfiqar Ali Bhutto classified Ahmadis as non-Muslims. The most influential moves towards Islamisation, however, began in 1979 by Zia who introduced an Islamic reform programme in which penal measures were introduced based on Islamic principles, thus taking the 1974 Ordinance to another level. In 1984 the Ahmadi community were banned from performing religious ceremonies under Ordinance XX, the Anti-Islamic Activities of the Ahmadis (Prohibition and Punishment) Ordinance, 1984. Article 298-C states:

> any person of the Qadiani group or the Lahori group (who call themselves Ahmadis or by any other name), who directly or indirectly, poses himself as Muslim, or calls, or refers to his faith as Islam, shall be punished with imprisonment.

Immediately, the Ahmadi community became a deviant group with no recourse to defend themselves from within a minority discourse. Derided by an aggressive majoritarianism, claims to victimhood were denied the Ahmadis through the state's excluding definition of Muslimness, resulting in their expulsion from both the majority and their claims as a minority.[29]

Thus, minority status became a tool for the state to both legitimise its arbitration of religious identity as well as to stigmatise deviant *otherness*. The cases of

Christians and Ahmadis show this arbitration in practice in a two-pronged manner, with Ahmadis being depicted as deviant others and Christians continually attempting to be deemed *proximate* rather than *deviant* with the threat of 'blasphemy' continually hindering this transformation. In the case of the Ahmadis, the labelling of Ahmadi identity as 'non-Muslim' meant their religious practices and beliefs were deemed blasphemous, thus making their minority status uninhabitable. Ahmadis who continued to assert their Muslimness during the 1970s and 1980s faced violence and ostracisation, forcing Ahmadi identity to go underground amidst potential threats from populist sentiments mobilised by state propaganda. Also, during the 1960s and 1970s, Christians became a stigmatised minority due to their caste associations. Christian identity became synonymous with 'untouchable' or *chuhra* and thus stigmatized less for its religious connotations and more as a social signifier of caste and status.[30] While Christians are stigmatised in caste and pollution terms, for Ahmadis it is in terms of religious belief and a Sunni-centred vision of Islam in the shaping of a majoritarian Muslim nation. Both of these processes of othering within a minority discourse eroded the protective space of minority status by making it pariah – whether deviant or proximate – which, in both the cases of Christians and Ahmadis, further affirms that minority discourse is essential as a means of constructing and upholding a dominant Muslim identity.

In most blasphemy cases the accused is found guilty. This is due to a key *lacuna* in the law of evidence. Judges and defence lawyers are intimidated and threatened by observers.[31] In this environment in which allegations of blasphemy are considered criminal, court officials, police, and members of the judiciary have been known to condone violence perpetrated on the accused. One high profile statement was made in 2000 by Acting Chief Justice of Lahore High Court, Justice Mian Nazir Akhter, who succinctly stated that 'no one had authority to pardon blasphemy and that anyone accused of blasphemy should be killed on the spot, as a religious obligation.'[32] There is a mounting catalogue of both individual and collective violence occurring outside of legal processes. The Shantinagar tragedy in 1997 in Khanewal district provides an illustration of the victimisation of Christians due to blasphemy laws. In this incident, there was an unsubstantiated claim of a Qur'an being burnt. As a result of this rumour, 13 churches were burnt down and 1,500 houses destroyed in the two Christian areas of Khanewal and especially in Tibba colony.

Another incident of collective violence took place on 11 November 2005 in Sangla Hill, District Sheikhupura (now part of Nankana Sahib District), when a certain Yousaf Massih was accused of burning pages of the Holy Qur'an, leading to the worst anti-Christian violence seen in the district. Three churches, a convent, a girl's hostel, Saint Anthony School, and a priest's home were set ablaze by a mob estimated to be between 1,000 and 2,000. The pattern persisted and in Chungi Amar Sadhu, Lahore Yunus Massih was charged with blasphemy in September 2005.[33] He was attacked by a gang of 30 or 40 with clubs. In 2009, mob violence in Kasur and Gojra against Christians occurred on an unprecedented scale. In Bahmniwala village, nine miles from Kasur city, nearly 110

Christian families (about 700 people) were forced to leave their homes on the night of 30 June 2009, due to the allegation that Christians had showed disrespect towards the Prophet Muhammad. The houses of eight Christians were set ablaze.[34] A similar pattern was witnessed in Gojra the same year when mobs attacked a Christian neighbourhood killing nine Christians and ransacking houses. The case of Asia Bibi (b. *c.*1971), perhaps most poignantly highlights the contentious position that blasphemy occupies in contemporary Pakistan. Asia Bibi was a Christian agricultural labourer from Sheikhapura district in the Punjab, some 30 miles from Lahore, who was accused of blasphemy for allegedly making insulting remarks about the Prophet. She was sentenced to death by hanging in 2010 and her case became highly publicised. It resulted in the assassination of the Governor of the Punjab, Salman Taseer (1944–2011, Governor 2008–11), on 4 January 2011 for having made promises to intervene in the case. Subsequently, the Minister for Minority Affairs, Shahbaz Bhatti (1968–2011, Minister 2008–11) was assassinated almost two months later on 2 March for declaring that he would make serious efforts to reform the blasphemy laws. In all of these cases, it was the threat of accusation of blasphemy rather than actual evidence of blasphemy charges which were at the root of individual and collective violence, showing how the status of minorities is far from being one of protection, but rather of victimisation and threat under the aegis of state policy and discourse.

This chapter has explored how the erosion of the protective space of minority status has occurred since 1947. Over time, minority discourse on Christians has shifted from being one which acknowledges difference, freedom, and rights to one which, through Islamising forces of constitutional reform, has led to the victimisation of Christians and other minorities. The space for religious otherness has been relegated to the stigma of deviance whereby proximate status as a minority has been denied through constitutional reforms. Although Pakistan does not implement *sharia* law, Muslim majoritarianism (and its minorities) provides nationalism's requirements for a cohesive majority identity through which challenge and resistance to state power can be exercised. To some extent, this attempt by the state to appear to acknowledge minorities' existence originated out of Jinnah's defence against India's so-called secularism and its criticism of the Muslim League's Pakistan Movement. However, the evolution of the minority discourse on Christians shows that the minority question and the management of religious *otherness* in the bolstering of majoritarianism are still on course to provide state sovereignty over its populace using a narrowing vision of 'society'.

## Notes

1 Philip Oldenburg, '"A Place Insufficiently Imagined": Language, Belief and the Pakistan Crisis of 1971', *Journal of Asian Studies*, 44, 4 (August 1985): 711–33.
2 Shaun Gregory, 'Under the Shadow of Islam: The Plight of the Christian Minority in Pakistan', *Contemporary South Asia*, 20, 2 (2012): 195–212.

3 Iftikhar Haider Malik, *Religious Minorities in Pakistan* (Islamabad: Minority Rights Group, 2002), p. 20; Rasul Bakhsh Rais, 'Identity, Politics and Minorities in Pakistan', in Sabab Gul Khattak and Ahmed Salim (eds), *The Land of Two Partitions and Beyond* (Islamabad: Sustainable Development Policy Institute, n.d.).
4 'The Problem of Minority Groups', in Ralph Linton (ed.), *The Science of Man in the World Crisis* (New York: Columbia University Press, 1945), p. 347.
5 Ahmed Saleem, Nosheen D'Souza, and Leonard D'Souza, *Violence, Memories and Peace-Building: A Citizen Report on Minorities in India and Pakistan* (New Delhi: South Asian Research and Resource Centre, 2006), p. 25.
6 'Chaudhry Chandu Lal, apart from acting as advocate of the community before the Commission, toured Gurdaspur and Pathankot, secured the permission of Christians of the area to be counted as part of Pakistan and presented it before the members.' Ibid.
7 Ahmed Salim's Interview with Cecil Chaudhry, in Ahmed Salim (ed.), *Reconstructing History: Memories, Migrants and Minorities* (Islamabad: Sustainable Development Policy Institute, n.d.), p. 162.
8 Ibid.
9 Ibid., p. 161.
10 Saleem *et al.*, *Violence, Memories and Peace-Building*, p. 113.
11 Mrs. S.P. Singha, Mrs. Najam ud Din, Miss Subey Khan, along with a host of Young Women Christian Association's workers, were conspicuous among such ladies. Father Francis Nadeem, *Yeh Des Humara hai* (Lahore: Humahang Publishers, 1997), p. 137.
12 Ibid., p. 67.
13 Hamid Khan, *Constitutional and Political History of Pakistan* (Karachi: Oxford University Press, 2005), p. 68.
14 When the BPC report triggered violent protests and was labelled anti-Bengal, the report was referred back to the Constituent Assembly for review. It invited suggestions from the public by January 1951 and a sub-committee was appointed to examine those proposals. G.W. Choudhry, *Constitutional Development in Pakistan* (London: Longmans Green and Co., 1959), p. 73.
15 Hamid Khan, *Constitutional and Political History of Pakistan*, p. 104.
16 Saleem *et al.*, *Violence, Memories and Peace-Building*, p. 172.
17 Ibid.
18

> [T]he joint electorate was not an unmixed blessing for minorities. The number of the minority representatives in newly elected assemblies progressively declined as one moved higher. Out of 40,000 Basic Democrats in East Pakistan, there were 4,965 Hindus, i.e. 12.4 percent, as against their ratio in the population at 19.5 percent. Similarly, there were only 4 minority members out of 155 members of the East Pakistan Assembly. There was no minority member in the National Assembly. As opposed to this, there were 11 minority members in the National Assembly (1955–8), 9 from East Pakistan, 1 from the Punjab, and 1 from Sindh, when elections were held on the basis of separate electorates. The 1970 election was also held on a joint electorate basis and again no minority members were elected in the National Assembly. It was clear that minorities stood to lose their direct representation in assemblies in case they chose to seek integration in mainstream politics through the joint electorate. Still, it did not change the long-standing view of the Hindu minority nor East Pakistani leaders in general in support of the joint electorate.
>
> (Ibid.)

19 Two seats were reserved in Sindh, two in Balochistan, and one in the NWFP, Rasul Bakhsh Rais, 'Identity Politics and Minorities in Pakistan,' *South Asia: Journal of South Asian Studies*, 30, 1 (2007), p. 169.

20 Ibid.
21 Mohammad Waseem, 'Religious Minorities: Case for a Pluralist Democracy', in Mohammad Waseem (ed.), *Electoral Reform in Pakistan* (Islamabad: Friedrich Ebert Stiftung, 2002), p. 152.
22 Theodore Gabriel, *Christian Citizens in an Islamic State: The Pakistan Experience* (Aldershot: Ashgate, 2007), p. 5.
23 Malik, *Religious Minorities in Pakistan*, p. 20.
24 Waseem, 'Religious Minorities: Case for a Pluralist Democracy', p. 150.
25 Nadeem, *Yeh Des Hamara Hay*, pp. 71–2.
26 Ibid., pp. 79–80.
27 Ronki Ram, 'Untouchability in India with a Difference: Ad Dharm, Dalit Assertion, and Caste Conflicts in Punjab', *Asian Survey*, 44, 6 (2004): 895–912.
28 Mark Juergensmeyer, *Religious Rebels in the Punjab: The Ad Dharm Challenge to Caste* (Berkeley: University of California Press, 1982).
29 Asad Ahmed, *Adjudicating Muslims: Religion and the State in Colonial India and Post-Colonial Pakistan*, PhD Dissertation, Department of Anthropology, University of Chicago, August 2006.
30 John C.B. Webster, 'Christian Conversion in the Punjab: What has Changed?', in Rowena Robinson and Sathianathan Clarke (eds), *Religious Conversion in India: Modes, Motivations and Meanings* (Oxford: Oxford University Press, 2003), pp. 351–80.
31

> Regularly, mobs of Muslims, often led by Mullahs, crowd into the courtroom, shouting threats at the judge if he does not rule in their favour. Defence lawyers receive death threats for taking on blasphemous cases, as a matter of course. Mobs gather outside the courtroom, and physically threaten the lawyers as they leave.
> (Ibid., p. 3)

32 Ibid.
33 *Human Rights Monitor 2006: A Report on the Religious Minorities in Pakistan* (Lahore: Sanjh Publishers, 2005), p. 61.
34 For more details on the incident in Kasur, see *Herald* (August 2009), p. 32.

# 10 Violence and state formation in Pakistan

*Gurharpal Singh*

The idea behind this collection of essays was first mooted at the British Association of South Asian Studies conference held at Southampton in 2011. A number of us working on communal violence in India and Pakistan, with a strong interest in the historic province of Punjab, floated the possibility of a panel on Partition violence. Our proposal, for a detailed re-assessment of Partition violence in light of new methodological advances, was accepted by the organisers of the European Association for South Asian Studies at ISCTE-Lisbon University in July 2012, with a recommendation that it be merged with another panel proposal on Pakistan. What at the time for organisational purposes seemed a marriage of convenience turned out to be a timely opportunity for a serious overview of the theme of violence in Pakistan's state formation. This chapter, which was originally designed to focus narrowly on Partition violence, now has a different remit; namely, to assess state formation in Pakistan through the lens of violence, in particular the legacy of mass communal violence between 1947 and 1950. This emphasis, inevitably, shifts the *locus* away, to some extent, from the years preceding and after 1947, but it does enable us to identify some striking continuities in recurring patterns of mass violence in Pakistan's history.

The chapter undertakes this exercise by reading the work of Hannah Arendt (1906–75) on violence. Her insights have, surprisingly, remained neglected in the works on Partition or post-1947 political violence in Pakistan. Mass violence was so central to the creation of Pakistan that its subsequent institutionalisation within the structures of the state, as an instrument of state policy, has been the defining characteristic of post-1947 polity. Neither exogenous explanations of Pakistan's insecurity nor indigenous accounts of its thwarted democratisation fully acknowledge the centrality of violence in the idea of Pakistan. What is required is a need to revisit the cycles of violence between 1946 and 1950, and to rethink the relationship between these forms and their everyday routinisation after independence. Since the Soviet intervention in Afghanistan in 1979, academic interest in political violence in Pakistan has focused on three themes. First, that political violence is mainly the outgrowth of the 'securitisation' of Pakistani politics since the late 1970s which introduced a new dimension by making the country a frontline Cold War state in a real hot war that led to millions of refugees and the birth of the 'Kalashnikov culture'. Clearly, much of the sectarian, social, and political violence dates from this period; and since 9/11, the 'war on terror', internal insurgencies, and the rising tide of sectarian conflicts have refocused attention on the subject.[1] Second, for some analysts, Pakistan's geo-political rivalries – with Iran and India in particular – have played a crucial role in fomenting high levels of political violence, both within and beyond the country. Such conflict is traditionally associated with what are euphemistically called non-government actors. Today, however, this violence is seen to be so corrosive that it now infects the whole of the polity.[2] Third, the most overworked explanation for the high levels of political violence in the last three decades is the persistent failure of democratisation. Successive periods of military intervention, it is suggested, have not only encouraged direct action, but such actions have been encouraged by the military to thwart the onward march of democratisation: political violence is, therefore, the necessary bedfellow of militarisation. It does not exist independently.[3]

Although contemporary accounts provide useful insights into some of the proximate causes of why Pakistan has struggled to develop as a stable polity, they rarely, if at all, probe the issue of why political violence, defined here as mass organised violence directed primarily at political goals, has been so pervasive a feature of its polity since 1947. Pakistan's current predicament, therefore, provides an important point of departure to explore the sensitive topic of the role of political violence in state formation, its long-term imprints, and the repeated cycles of disorder and instability. Arguably, as much as urban communal violence against minorities, especially Muslims, has become the signature tune of contemporary Indian nationhood, political violence within and across borders has become the defining feature of Pakistani statehood which has been variously described as 'failed' or 'failing'. The roots of this phenomenon, it can be argued, lie not in some imaginary existentialist threat which has produced a bloated parallel military state, or thwarted democratisation, but in the 'wrong-sizing' of the state itself, which has resulted in a persistent tension between the state and the nation and, into the bargain, has institutionalised a highly instrumentalist use of violence for political ends. Political violence, in short, is deeply embedded in Pakistan's state formation and state-building, in the construction of the post-1947 nationalist ideal, state policies, persistent irredentism, and powerful networks of non-state actors which the state has nurtured.[4] Understanding it is one of the most serious challenges facing scholars specialising on Pakistan and the region.

## What is political violence?

In *On Violence* Hannah Arendt reminds us that violence 'is distinguished by its instrumental character'.[5] As she observes:

> Violence, being instrumental in nature, is rational to the extent that it is effective in reaching the ends that must justify it. And since when we act we never know with certainty the eventual consequences of what we are doing, violence can remain rational only if it pursues short-term goals.[6]

'Violence', she continues:

> ...does not depend on numbers or opinions, but on implements of violence, and the implements of violence ... like all other tools, increase and multiply human strength. Those who oppose violence with mere power will soon find that they are confronted not by men but by men's artefacts, whose inhumanity and destructive effectiveness increase in proportion to the distance separating the opponents. *Violence can always destroy power. Out of the barrel of a gun grows the most effective command, resulting in the most instant and perfect obedience. What can never grow out of it is power.*[7]

For Arendt, the critical relationship is between power and violence, because everything depends 'on the power behind violence'.[8] Power is at the opposite end of the spectrum from violence because it 'corresponds to the human ability not just to act but to act in concert. Power is never the property of an individual; it belongs to the group and remains in existence only so long as the group keeps together'.[9] Power, as Arendt reminds us, is 'inherent in the very existence of political communities; what it does need is legitimacy'.[10]

For our purpose, reading Arendt, the following propositions seem relevant:

1  That violence is not an end in itself but instrumental, rational, and requires justification.
2  That power is the opposite of violence and resides in political communities.
3  That violence can result from contestations about the nature of political communities, but its extent is likely to vary on the implements used and the 'power behind violence'.
4  And that 'violent action is ruled by the mean-ends category, whose chief characteristic if applied to human affairs, has always been that the end is in danger of being overwhelmed by the means which it justifies and which are needed to reach it'.[11]

These propositions, of course, need to be placed against the backdrop in which most movements for national independence in the former colonies were engaged in some degrees of political violence, ranging from muted civil disobedience to outright wars of independence. India's relatively peaceful transition to independence, notwithstanding the carnage of the Partition, was an exception. Many colonial states, on the other hand, experienced bloody liberation movements that extended well into the 1970s. Yet, paradoxically, the post-colonial states that were most successful in eradicating violence as a feature of their polities were those that had undergone prolonged revolutionary struggle. These states were much more systematic in transforming organised resistance into legitimate power, often behind a clear ideology and a highly organised political party or nationalist movement. Whilst the challenges to post-colonial socialist states were to arise in the 1970s and 1980s, notably as result of poor economic performance and the collapse of the Soviet Union, weak and insecure post-colonial states, in contrast, were only too readily prone to internal and external threats. It is among these states that the levels of political violence have remained consistently high. It is also among these states that the project of nation- and state-building has been most contested.

## Studies of Partition violence

In contrast to Arendt's approach, the literature on the Partition represents a sharply narrow focus on the *causes* of communal violence; that is, *on who did it* rather than *why they did it*. In the last thirty years there have been significant advances in our understanding of the causes and consequences of Partition violence. In South Asia the rising tide of communal conflicts since the early 1980s has rekindled interest in the systemic violence which gripped northern India between 1946 and 1950, leading to the displacement of some 17.9 million people, and the deaths of another 1 million.[12] Paul Brass, in his detailed research on Hindu-Muslim rivalry in Uttar Pradesh – India's largest state – has drawn our attention to the complex ways in which communal riots have been constructed, and how in this construction the memories of Partition remain ever present.[13] For Brass, communal violence needs to be viewed as part of an 'institutionalised riot system' in which the existence of political parties, an ideological context, and partisan state actors and institutions create inbuilt incentives to 'produce communal riots'. Brass concludes that

> In every major town in northern India, there are ... symbols of that presence wherever there are large concentrations of Muslim populations. These 'mini-Pakistans' in turn are seen as centres of riot production designed to intimidate Hindus and generate more and more partitions, more and more violence on the Hindu body.[14]

Ashutosh Varshney, in contrast, has applied the social capital framework to explain the persistence, as well as the absence, of communal violence in India's urban settings. He has done so by examining in detail the degree of mutual dependence among Hindus and Muslims, the extent to which the two communities have been tied together by mutual bonds of dependence or lead parallel lives.[15] More recently, Steven Wilkinson's research on elections has highlighted the importance of electoral cycles which precede communal tensions, especially where the competition for office among political parties (religious or otherwise) is close.[16] The closer the contest, the higher is the incentive to cause riots and communalise the campaign. Saumitra Jha and Wilkinson, in the first serious quantitative assessment of the violence, use the proxy measure of ethnic cleansing to provide an overview of violence. According to them, after 1947 it was the length of combat experience of World War II Indian Army veterans located in the Punjab that was the main variable determining the outward and inward movement of religious minorities in the erstwhile districts of the province. The violence of 1947 and beyond was organised, and Army veterans played a critical role in determining the nature and extent of the ethnic cleansing that took place. Dipankar Gupta, focusing on contemporary developments, has re-examined the anti-Muslim riots in Bombay in 1993 and Gujarat in 2002, and has stressed the importance of forensic analysis – rather than grand social science explanations – in identifying the perpetration of violence.[17] In addition to this literature, there has been increasing concern with the victims of violence and, in particular, with its gendered dimensions. This research has pointed to the fact that because women were seen as the upholders of community 'honour', they were especially vulnerable to attacks from the hostile 'other'.[18]

Despite these methodological innovations, however, a more rounded understanding of Partition violence still continues to elude us. It is certainly the case that researchers today are much more sensitive to the previously excluded dimensions – caste, gender, ethnicity, subalternalism, and the need for self-reflection – but some obvious blind spots remain. The injudicious use of concepts such as 'holocaust', 'genocide', 'ethnic cleansing', 'migration', and 'refugees' to describe the events leading up to and after 1947 continues to remain problematic. If, for example, we accept the proposition that the Partition was *realised* by violence, what then are the implications for the role of official authorities in overseeing the disorder, both *before* and *after* August 1947? If mass violence was used as an instrument to achieve Pakistan, and indeed, as some would argue, a truncated India, to what extent did those who used it as a tool of policy realise their objectives? And what were the long-term legacies of mass violence, and why do they continue to haunt nation- and state-building in both India and Pakistan?

## Mass violence between 1946 and 1950

The mass violence which broke out after the disturbances in Calcutta in August 1946, and finally abated in March 1950, was to leave a lasting imprint. Almost one million people – if not more – were killed and 17.9 million were displaced in the largest forced migration in history. It is now quite clear that this violence was qualitatively different from earlier communal riots which tend to remain within accepted limits as normalcy tended to be quickly re-established. Partition violence was not only more extensive, but it was also clearly linked to political objectives. Heated debates about the creation of Pakistan and its consequences shifted from the drawing rooms and legislatures to the streets of north India at the time of the 1946 provincial elections. Violence thus emerged both as a resource and as a reaction to an increasingly politically vitiated atmosphere. Each outbreak created more fear and distrust: the pool of trained killers was larger than ever. But the Partition massacres were also an outgrowth of the dislocation of the war years, the weakening of the e*spirit de corps* it brought to the Indian Army, and the legacy of a flood of weapons and demobilised soldiers in north India. It is now firmly established that the violence was organised with the singular objective of clearing out minority religious communities. The state's response crucially determined whether violent episodes were constrained or spiralled out of control, creating large numbers of casualties and refugees. The transition from a collapsing colonial state to its national Indian and Pakistani successors both reduced the capacity to maintain law and order and created a psychological environment which hindered the ability to protect minority populations. The potential for serious conflict in August 1947 was further increased by the existence of princely states, some of which harboured political ambitions or ideas of independence, thereby resulting, especially in the Punjab, in the assault on their minority populations as well as refugees who traversed their territory.

I will not rehearse the narratives of violence between 1946 and 1950, which are covered at length in our volume on *The Partition of India*.[19] What I want to do is to highlight three points that are crucial to the argument that I am making. First, contrary to suggestions by some historians that the killings during the period were the result of 'spontaneous actions', or the outcome of midsummer madness in 1947, it is now generally accepted that disorders on this scale were carefully organised. Such writers as Javeed Alam have maintained that the Partition massacres were indulged in 'By people at a moment of loss of judgment, of a sense of proportion, at a moment of frenzy'. Alam has also declared that there was 'no involvement of large organisations or the state as the instrument of mass killings'.[20] This reading of the events transforms the Partition violence into a phenomenon that cannot be rationally explained. It also makes it *sui generis*, a unique occurrence that is beyond comparative analysis. Yet, as we have noted above, Brass' work on violence in Uttar Pradesh in such localities as Aligarh and Meerut, and the writings of Romila Thapur, Imtiaz Ahmed, and Dipankar Gupta on the 2002 Gujarat carnage,[21] have highlighted key features in situations of endemic and intensive communal conflict. Among these is the 'functional utility' of riots for politicians, state complicity in the perpetration of organised acts of violence, and delays in securing justice for the victims. The latter sends out a clear message to would-be rioters that no harm will come to them, allowing in Brass' words, the 'repeat performances' of riot production.

All of these features were evident in the cycle of violence committed between 1946 and 1950. Far from it being a spontaneous and temporary aberration, the violence of this period was frequently marked by its cold-blooded planning and execution. Attacks on foot convoys and refugee trains were frequently made with military-type precision.[22] Their attackers were assisted by complicit railway officials who revealed the timing of the refugee specials.[23] The killing was not the work of a few frenzied hotheads, but was carried out, in many instances, by large organisations, for example the Sikh *jathas* (band of volunteers), and Muslim tribal war parties. Such gatherings did not occur spontaneously, nor did they acquire their fearsome weaponry without planning. The March 1947 Rawalpindi massacres, for example, were carefully planned. As the AICC Report noted at length:

> These were not riots but deliberately organised military campaigns. Long before the disturbances broke out secret meetings were held in mosques under the leadership of Syed Akbar Khan ex-MLA, Captain Lal Khan of Kahuta,

> Tehsildar and Police Sub Inspector Kahuta, Maulvi Abdul Rehman and Kala Khan MLA in which *jihad* was proclaimed against the minorities and emissaries were sent out to collect volunteers from the rural areas.... The armed crowd which attacked Kahuta, Thoa Khalsa, and Nara etc. were led by ex-military men on horseback armed with Tommy Guns, pistols, rifles, hand grenades, hatchets, petrol tins and even some carried field glasses.[24]

The following strategy, the Report continues, was used wherever the mobs attacked:

> First of all minorities were disarmed with the help of local police and by giving assurances by oaths on holy Quran of peaceful intentions. After this had been done, the helpless and unarmed minorities were attacked. On their resistance having collapsed, lock breakers and looters came into action with their transport corps of mules, donkeys and camels. Then came the '*Mujahadins*' with tins of petrol and kerosene oil and set fire to the looted shops and houses. Then there were *maulvies* with barbers to convert people who somehow or other escaped slaughter and rape. The barbers shaved the hair and beards and circumcised the victims. *Maulvis* recited *kalamas* and performed forcible marriage ceremonies. After this came the looters, including women and children.[25]

There are chilling parallels of this account with the 2002 Gujarat attacks on the Muslim minority in which RSS activists came equipped with gas, oxygen cylinders, and petrol, and in which 'respectable' people joined in the looting.[26] The behaviour of Huseyn Suhrawardy (1892–1963), Premier of Bengal between 1946 and 1947, during the earlier Great Calcutta Killing of August 1946 also provides a parallel with the Gujarat *pogrom* in that Suhrawardy appeared to be in sympathy with the rioters. Like many a latter-day Indian politician, he interfered with police operations and with his parliamentary associates 'spent a great deal of time in the police control room directing the operations'.[27]

Hindu 'mobs' and Sikh *jathas* were no less organised. The *jathas* led the attacks on Muslims that ethnically cleansed them from East Punjab. From May onwards, there had been a widespread collection of funds, the manufacture and import of weapons, and the establishment of an organisation of 'dictators', 'company commanders', and village 'cells'. Little is known about their total numbers, the second rank of leaders, or their composition, save that many ex-servicemen from both the British Indian Army and the Indian National Army, founded in 1942 by Mohan Singh (1909–89) and revived by Subhas Chandra Bose (1897–1945) the following year, were in their ranks.[28] During the final days before the publication of the Radcliffe Boundary award,[29] *jathas* commenced heavy raids on Muslim villages in 'border' areas.[30] They were ruthlessly efficient killing machines which carefully targeted their victims.[31] They were well armed with sten guns, rifles, pistols, spears, swords and *kirpans* (steel sword/dagger) and were well organised. The largest was around 3,000 strong.

Similarly, the Hindu rioters in Calcutta in August 1946 were directed by searchlights and microphones fixed to housetops. They put Red Cross symbols on their vehicles to escape police detection. Hindu shops were marked so that they were spared the arson attacks and looting.[32] The Congress General Secretary reported the gathering of attackers in Garhmukhteshwar on horses, bicycles, and even camels in a makeshift army unit.[33] The Viceroy, Archibald Wavell (1883–1950, Viceroy 1943–7), informed the Secretary of State that he was also certain that the violence was organised 'and organised very thoroughly' by 'the lower strata of the Congress' without the knowledge of their leadership, just as the Muslim League had been responsible for violence in Noakhali.[34] In Sonepat, in the East Punjab Rohtak district, rich Hindus contributed a *lakh* (100,000) rupees to finance mob attacks on Muslims. Traders and merchants were also prominent in organising violence in Chapra Town in Bihar. *Zamindars* (landowners) also played a role in the incitement and collection of rioters. In Masaurhi, where there were large Muslim casualties, the owner of the rice and flour mills summoned the crowd to attack by means of the factory hooter.[35]

Second, the violence had clear objectives: it was, in short, politics by other means. Once the Congress rejected the Cabinet formula in 1946, it was apparent that Pakistan would not be wrested from the negotiating table but had to be won on the streets of Calcutta, Lahore, and Rawalpindi. Implicit in the slogan *Le kin rehing Pakistan* (we will secure Pakistan), a slogan shouted by demonstrators during the Calcutta killings, was a threat that anything less would not be countenanced. Whether it was the street violence in Calcutta or the communal violence in the Punjab in the summer of 1947, or still, the use of irregulars in the Valley of Kashmir in 1947–8, mass violence was a handmaiden of politicians.

The Muslim League was not alone in using violence as a political means. After the fall of the Unionist government in the Punjab in early March 1947, and the subsequent massacre of Sikhs in Rawalpindi, the possibility of a division of the province became a distinct possibility, and in this changed context, the Sikh leadership was determined to ensure that areas of Sikh settlement, including the prosperous Canal Colonies, should be awarded to East Punjab. As the Boundary Commission was established, the Sikh leadership made their intentions clear. In an interview with the Governor of the Punjab, Sir Evan Jenkins (1896–1985, Governor 1946–7) on 10 July 1947, Giani Kartar Singh (1902–74), the prominent Akali leader, outlined the basis of the Sikh territorial claim:

> He said that they [the Sikhs] must have at least one canal system; they must have Nankana Sahib; finally the arrangements must be such as to bring three-quarters or at least two-thirds of the Sikh population into Eastern Punjab. An exchange of populations on a large scale was essential.... Property as well as population should be taken into account in the exchange [as] the Sikhs are on the whole better off than Muslims. The Giani asserted that unless it was recognised by H.M.G., the viceroy, and party leaders that the fate of the Sikhs was a vital issue in the proceedings of the transfer of power, there would be trouble.[36]

A day later, the Sikh leaders argued that there was only one possible way out:

> The only solution was a very substantial exchange of population. If this did not occur, the Sikhs would be driven to facilitate it by a massacre of Muslims in Eastern Punjab. The Muslims had already got rid of Sikhs in the Rawalpindi Division and much land and property there could be made available to Muslims from the East Punjab. Conversely, the Sikhs could get rid of the Muslims in the East in the same way and invite Sikhs from the West to take their place.[37]

Thus, Jenkins was left in no doubt what the Sikhs were planning to do. In the run-up to the 15 August 1947 deadline, ethnic cleansing of Muslims in the *doaba* (tract of land between two rivers) of Kapurthala, Jullandhar, and Hoshiarpur had already gone on apace.[38] And when the Boundary Award was announced, excluding most of the Sikh areas claimed in West Punjab, the Sikh leaders, true to their word, decided to 'turn the Muslims out'.[39]

The role of the Congress, and its proxies, was no less important. That leading spokesmen like Vallabhbhai Patel (1875–1950) and Baldev Singh (1902–61) were simultaneously engaged in undermining the civil and military administration in the Punjab, while accusing it of partiality or incompetence, was dramatically demonstrated in the accusations they levelled against Jenkins in August that he was being deliberately negligent in enforcing law and order. Jenkins' considered response systematically demolished these leaders' accusations while drawing attention to the practical difficulties of imposing martial law in conditions where the 'two nations' were fighting 'one and another in the streets, in the markets, and in the fields and villages'.[40] In this 'communal war of succession', orchestrated by the Congress, the Muslim League, and the Akalis, claimed Jenkins, the administration was hopelessly overwhelmed. To accuse it of deliberate neglect was to accept the double-speak of politicians who had first inflamed the passions which had made the division of the province possible. As Jenkins tersely put it, the critics of his administration themselves were 'participants in the events in which they profess[ed] to deplore'.[41]

Third, although mass violence was used instrumentally and for political ends, it was only partially successful, and accompanied by more unsettling developments that were to endure as permanent legacies. For one, mass violence failed to deliver the state of Jammu and Kashmir to Pakistan and, in fact, led to a retaliatory response from the Indian state which ultimately led to the division of the Valley; for another, organised ethnic cleansing in West Punjab brought forth an unanticipated ethnic cleansing on a more systematic scale in East Punjab. Political leaders who encouraged the use of violence were largely oblivious of its potentially disastrous consequences for their own communities, for once ethnic cleansing was unleashed it was difficult, if not impossible, to direct it to specific ends. The infinitely complex nature of Partition-related violence suggests that in large measure it was not *only a means to an end but a means that soon became an end in itself.* Detailed studies now available suggest that the mayhem created in the years between 1946 and 1950 was used to settle personal scores, appropriate property on an unprecedented scale, abduct hundreds and thousands of women, and create new cultures of violence for which the 'new normal' was mass ethnic cleansing and permanent stigmatisation of minorities, religious or otherwise.[42] Of course, in time, this cult of violence would be overlaid by new narratives of nationhood, but mass political violence would continue to stalk the successor states as an ever present partner in the troubled enterprise of independence. This presence would regularly manifest in the challenging project of nation- and state-building. Perhaps more worryingly for a new nation created on the basis of religion, it would continue to come to the surface around the unresolved issue on the most appropriate role of religion in public life.

## Political violence and Pakistan after 1950

Like India, Pakistan was created as the result of a violent rupture with itself: the Partition in a sense marked the 'end of history', and severed, once and for all, the organic connection between community, locality, and the past in preference to a historicised construction of these categories. Islamic modernism was the new template on which the new nation-state was to be inscribed. As in the case of India, Partition as a legacy was no less influential in the nation- and state-building process because Pakistan's creation against heavy odds marked the successful culmination of the 'two-nation theory' but it also became the nation's chosen trauma,[43] the epic struggle that has ever since served as the ideological resource for all regimes. However, the emergence of the military-bureaucratic combine that has dominated state polity since 1947 has laid bare the fundamental contradiction at the heart of the idea of Pakistan, its negative nationalism and, until 1971, unpromising state boundaries that arose from its vision as a loose, sub-continental federation. Ironically, transforming the Pakistan movement into a nation and a state was to result in the neat reversal of the Lahore Resolution of 23 March 1940: the creation of an authoritarian centralised state that shared the characteristics of other South Asian states.[44] At the same time this reversal was accompanied by a determination that there would be no secessions of recalcitrant nationalities, no more Partitions, and an external politics of 'wrongsizing' in which Kashmir, and now Afghanistan, have become the permanent *casus belli*.[45]

Partition historiography, especially in India, has opened up new departures in understanding the legacies of communal violence between 1946 and 1950. The range and scope of this work is beyond the purview of this chapter, suffice it to say that similar work still remains to be undertaken in Pakistan.[46] What I want to do is outline three areas that I think are worthy of further study.

First, we need to examine critically how Partition-based violence is important to the post-1947 nation- and state-making. It is a truism to say that colonial self-determination movements have defined the post-colonial state. The struggle for Pakistan and its dramatic, violent climax was not without profound, long-term consequences. Again as noted above, the violence of the years 1946–50 has become the chosen 'national trauma', an ideological resource of such richness that it defines the dominant national narrative of its establishment. At the heart of this narrative is a deep sense of victimhood, a feeling of injustice, and the saga of a heroic pursuit of self-determination against overwhelming odds fighting a perfidious enemy (the Indian state) which has remained unreconciled to the division.

The other side of this narrative of nationhood is the construction of the Indian 'other' rooted in religious and civilisational essentialism. Though the lineage of this narrative lies mainly in the All-India Muslim League's fears of Hindu majoritarianism, its logical end point was the absurd caricature conjured as a result of 'Islamisation' by Zia-ul-Haq (1924–88, President 1978–88). As a former examiner of Pakistan Studies, I was dismayed to learn how a subject introduced to inculcate a sense of nationhood regaled in a selective understanding of the past. The sections on Partition violence were so ideologically loaded as to render the events as historically meaningless. For instance, in describing the violence in East Punjab, *Introduction to Pakistan Studies* narrated:

> The Sikhs were clearing East Punjab of Muslims, butchering hundreds daily, forcing thousands to flee and burning Muslim villages. The Sikh *jathas* always attacked Muslim migrants on their way to Pakistan.... The Sikhs slaughtered the poor men, women, young and old in cold blood. The minor children were killed in a ruthless manner in the presence of their helpless parents. Women were raped and young girls were abducted.[47]

Now this, as we have seen above, is not to argue that these events did not occur. Quite the contrary. A contextual understanding, however, is completely absent in these essentialised ideological accounts. These accounts, moreover, were also qualitatively different from the post-independence versions produced by the governments of India and Pakistan and the Sikhs to justify their own actions. What distinguishes them is not only the blood-curdling partisanship, but also a deliberate attempt to tie Partition violence to the project of Islamisation of the state. It is true that since 9/11 (2001), as a result of external pressure, some efforts have been made to revise the representation of minorities in school textbooks. It is unlikely, however, that these will lead to any radical revisions. Whether it is the modernists or the Islamicists, the temptation to draw on Partition violence for political objectives is far too strong to lose its resonance in the medium term. It will always remain a rich resource for the nation's 'chosen trauma', the lens through which mass violence is both understood and inflicted (on others).

Second, the instrumental use of mass political violence has become a regular feature of post-independence Pakistan state policy. From Kashmir to Afghanistan, from East Bengal to Karachi, from the North-West Frontier Province to the Punjab, and from non-state actors to religious minorities and sects, the logic has been the same: to use overwhelming violence to control political opponents. Notwithstanding the contextual nature of events in these regions, which no doubt needs to be understood, it is also necessary to highlight the continuities with Partition violence. Whilst researching *The Partition of India*, for example, I was struck by the conscious efforts of the state to suppress the independence movement in East Pakistan, even if it required ethnic cleansing. According to one senior Karachi-based journalist this strategy consisted of ethnically cleansing Hindus and using their property as a 'golden carrot' to win over the underprivileged Bengali Muslim middle classes. In the event, this policy led to 10 million refugees crossing the border to India, and ultimately the short-lived Indo-Pakistan war of 3–16 December 1971. East Pakistan/Bangladesh is but one example. The strategy of overwhelming groups, religious minorities, sects, and recalcitrant nationalities by the use of force, or the force of mass political violence, is so well established that it really needs to be better understood.[48]

Finally, we need to revisit the unintended consequences of the Partition's mass political violence. The failure to secure a negotiated post-colonial Pakistan precipitated mass agitation. But in the words of Mohammad Ali Jinnah (1876–1948, Governor-General 1947–8), the President of the All-India Muslim League (1936–47), and the leader of the Pakistan Movement, this produced a 'moth eaten' state with ambiguous boundaries and a negative nationalism. While violence, as Arendt reminds us, had rational objectives, its outcomes were beyond the control of politicians who had unleashed it in the first instance. Consequently, as I have argued elsewhere, both India and Pakistan were wrong-sized, creating permanent tensions between national ideals and the territories, especially in their peripheral regions, that these states have sought to govern.[49] Indian and Pakistani nation- and state-building in these peripheral regions has been exercised through 'hegemonic'and 'violent control',[50] often reproducing the repertoire of violence in the name of national ideals that command precious little legitimacy. The post-1947 history of Kashmir, Balochistan, the NWFP, Sindh and the Indian Punjab, and northeast India, for instance, all illustrate how contested the post-colonial settlement continues to remain. Tragically, the logical end point of the instrumentalisation of violence to achieve political objectives in South Asia that began with Partition is a nuclear-armed region with the largest concentration of poverty in the world.

In revisiting Partition violence through a reading of Arendt's work On *Violence*, one is left with one inescapable conclusion:

> [that] violent action is ruled by the mean-ends category, whose chief characteristic, if applied to human affairs, has always been that the end is in danger of being overwhelmed by the means which it justifies and which are needed to reach it.[51]

Has the violence which was so necessary to *Le ke rehing Pakistan* now come back to haunt the state itself? To what extent can a state continue to use high levels of force against its own citizens, and those beyond its borders? Why has Pakistan failed to develop a legitimate justification of violence?

The extreme instrumentalisation of violence which today finds its absurd manifestation in the existence of Pakistan as a nuclear state stems largely from the failure of the idea of Pakistan to be grounded in a sense of a community, a community from which the legitimate exercise of power behind violence could be justified. Nearly seven decades after independence, the sense of community on which shared ideals of common statehood can be established continue to elude Pakistan's politicians, with large sections of the country in a state of internal insurgency. Arguably, this has resulted from a wrong-sized state that has, by design or default, become the centre of global terror. Sadly, it seems neither comprehensive democratisation nor Islamisation of the state is likely to provide a panacea to this chronic malady. Violence in the form that it currently exists in Pakistan in its manifold forms can ultimately destroy the future. It can also force its victims to settle for any form of government that gives them protection from attack. Recognising this fact should be sufficient grounds for specialists on Pakistan to explore the phenomenon of political violence beyond contemporary concerns.[52]

## Notes

1 See Husain Haqqani, *Pakistan: Between the Mosque and Military* (Washington, D.C.: Carnegie Endowment for Peace, 2005).
2 See Vali Reza Nasr, 'The Rise of Sunni Militancy in Pakistan: The Changing role of Islamism and Ulema in Society and Politics', *Modern Asian Studies*, 34, 1 (2000): 139–80.
3 See Mohammed Waseem and Mariam Mufti, 'Religion, Politics and Governance in Pakistan' (University of Birmingham, Religion and Development Research Programme, 2009), Working Paper 27. Available at www.religionsanddevelopment.org/files/resourcesmodule/@random454f80f60b3f4/1245229076_working_paper_27.pdf (accessed 21 December 2012).
4 Ideally, reliable quantative time-series data on post-1947 political violence in Pakistan, and beyond Pakistan, by its non-state actors would provide further factual support for the argument. Unfortunately no such data sets are available, and it is only recently that data on political violence has been collected and analysed systematically. For one such study, see Jacob Schapiro and Saad Gulzar, 'Political Violence in Pakistan: Myths vs. Realities', available at www.princeton.edu/~jns/papers/political_violence_policy_brief_120329.pdf (accessed 21 December 2012).
5 Hannah Arendt, *On Violence* (London: Penguin, 1963), p. 46.
6 Ibid., p. 79.
7 Ibid., p. 53 (emphasis added).
8 Ibid., p. 49.
9 Ibid., p. 44.
10 Ibid., p. 52.
11 Ibid., p. 4.
12 See P. Bharadwaj, A. Khwaja, and A. Mian, 'The Big March: Migratory Flows after the Partition of India', *Economic and Political Weekly* (30 August 2008): 39–49.
13 Paul. R. Brass, *The Production of Hindu-Muslim Violence in Contemporary India* (Seattle: University of Washington Press, 2003).
14 Ibid., p. 84.
15 Ashutosh Varshney, *Ethnic Conflict and Civic Life: Hindus and Muslims in India* (New Haven, CT: Yale University Press, 2003).
16 Steven I. Wilkinson, *Votes and Violence: Electoral Competition and Ethnic Riots in India* (Cambridge: Cambridge University Press, 2004).
17 Dipankar Gupta, *Justice before Reconciliation: Negotiating a New Normal in Post-Riots Mumbai and Ahmedabad* (New Delhi: Routledge, 2010).

18 Urvashi Butalia, *The Other Side of Silence: Voices from the Partition of India* (London: C. Hurst, 2000). For reflection on contemporary episodes of violence, see Vena Das, *Mirrors of Violence: Communities, Riots and Survivors in South Asia* (New Delhi: Oxford University Press, 1996).
19 Ian Talbot and Gurharpal Singh, *The Partition of India* (Cambridge: Cambridge University Press, 2009).
20 Cited in Gyanendra Pandey, *Remembering Partition* (Cambridge: Cambridge University Press, 2001), p. 58.
21 Brass, *The Production of Hindu-Muslim Violence*; Dipankar Gupta and Romila Thapur, 'Who are the Guilty? Punishment and Confidence Building in Gujarat', in Asghar Ali Engineer (ed.), *The Gujarat Carnage* (New Delhi: Longman, 2003) pp. 108–11; and Imtiaz Ahmed, 'Has Communalism Changed?', ibid., pp. 137–41.
22 In one such attack on a train outside Khalsa College, Amritsar, 1,200 Muslim refugees were massacred. *Civil and Military Gazette* (14 September 1947).
23 See Swarna Aiyar, '"August Anarchy": The Partition Massacres in Punjab, 1947', *South Asia*, 18 (1995): 13–36.
24 Report on the Disturbances in the Punjab (March/April 1947), AICC File No. G-10/1947, Nehru Memorial Museum and Library, New Delhi.
25 Ibid.
26 K.N. Panikkar, 'The Agony of Gujarat', in Asghar Ali Engineer (ed.), *The Gujarat Carnage* (New Delhi: Sangam Books, 2003), p. 93; and Udhay S. Mehta, 'The Gujarat Genocide: A Sociological Appraisal', ibid., p. 191.
27 Suranjan Das, *Communal Riots in Bengal, 1905–1947* (New Delhi: Oxford University Press, 1991), p. 178.
28 See Ian Copland, 'The Master and the Maharajas: The Sikh Princess and the East Punjab Massacre of 1947', *Modern Asian Studies*, 36, 3 (2002): 657–704.
29 This demarcated the new international border in the Punjab region. Its judgements were controversially delayed until after the British transfer of power.
30 Punjab Fortnightly Report, 30 July 1947, 13 August 1947. L/P&J/5/250, India Office Records, British Library, London.
31 Copland, 'The Master and the Maharajas', p. 687.
32 Das, *Communal Riots in Bengal*, p. 180.
33 Yasmin Khan, 'Out of Control? Partition Violence in Uttar Pradesh', in Ian Talbot (ed.), *The Deadly Embrace: Religion, Politics, and Violence in India and Pakistan* (Karachi: Oxford University Press, 2007), p. 45.
34 Ibid., p. 47.
35 Venita Damodaran, *Broken Promises: Popular Protest, Indian Nationalism and the Congress Party in Bihar 1935–1946* (New Delhi: Oxford University Press, 1992), p. 345.
36 Quoted in Lionel Carter (ed.), *Punjab Politics: 1 June–14 August 1947 Tragedy. Governors' Fortnightly Reports and other Key Documents* (New Delhi: Manohar, 2007), p. 145.
37 Paul R. Brass, 'The Partition of India and Retributive Genocide in the Punjab, 1946–47; Means, Methods, and Purpose', *Journal of Genocide Research*, 5, 1 (2003), p. 88.
38 Carter, *Punjab Politics*, pp. 173–5.
39 The words of Master Tara Singh, quoted in Brass, 'The Partition of India', p. 77.
40 Carter, *Punjab Politics*, p. 201.
41 Ibid., p. 195.
42 The psychological dimensions of this violence have received most attention, especially with reference to the impact on women. See Butalia, *The Other Side of Silence*. For the long-term consequences on nation-building in both India and Pakistan, see Talbot and Singh, *The Partition of India*, chapters 5 and 6.

43 On the importance of chosen traumas in nation-building, see Catarina Kinnvall, 'Nationalism, Religion and the Search for Chosen Traumas: Comparing Sikh and Hindu Identity Construction', *Ethnicities*, 2, 1 (March 2002): 79–106.
44 See Ayasha Jalal, *Democracy and Authoritarianism in South Asia* (Cambridge: Cambridge University Press, 1995).
45 Talbot and Singh, *Partition of India*, chapter 5.
46 For one particularly inept effort which makes rather grand claims to originality see Ishtiaq Ahmed, *The Punjab Bloodied, Partitioned and Cleansed: Unravelling the 1947 Tragedy through Secret British Reports and First-Person Accounts* (Karachi: Oxford University Press, 2012).
47 M.I. Rabbani and M.A. Sayyid, *An Introduction to Pakistan Studies* (Lahore: Caravan Book House, 1992), p. 107.
48 This would require, for example, a more detailed assessment of patterns of violence against minorities dating from the anti-Hindu riots in East Pakistan in the 1950s, the anti-Ahmadiya riots of the mid-1950s, anti-Shia campaigns of the 1980s and 1990s, attacks on minorities after 9/11, especially Christians and Hindus, and the persistent violence in Karachi. It would also address the patterns of violence via non-state actors sponsored by the state to engage in violence in proxy wars in Kashmir and Afghanistan.
49 Gurharpal Singh, 'The Partition of India as State Contraction: Some Unspoken Assumptions', *Journal of Commonwealth and Comparative Politics*, 35, 1 (March 1997): 51–66. For a more detailed discussion of 'right-sizing' and 'wrong-sizing', see Brendan O'Leary, Ian S. Lustick, and Thomas Callaghy (eds), *Right-Sizing the State: The Politics of Moving Borders* (Oxford: Oxford University Press, 2001).
50 Hegemonic control implies the use of coercion and consent, as well as the manipulation of consciousness, to exclude certain possibilities. When hegemonic control breaks down, over-coercion and domination ('violent control') replaces it. Hegemonic control, therefore, is more than overt domination by ordinary means. For the distinction between hegemonic and violent control, see John McGarry and Brendan O'Leary (eds), 'Introduction', *The Politics of Ethnic Conflict Regulation* (London: Routledge, 1993).
51 Arendt, *On Violence*, p. 4.
52 Pakistan, along with North Korea and Israel, is a partitioned, nuclear state. All three states are the *locus* of a high degree of internal and external violence attributed to them. The commonalities of 'wrong-sizing', however, are rarely used to explore the underlying impulses to use violence in domestic and international political environments.

# Index

Abassi V, Nawab Sadiq 81
*Ad Dharmi* 186–7
*Afaq* 27
Afghanistan 1–2, 5, 8, 76, 119, 124–6, 128–9, 133–4, 139, 141, 201–2
Agent to the Governor General (AGG) 86–7, 91
Agricultural Pricing and Taxation in Pakistan 58
Agriculturalists 15, 41, 51–2
Agriculture 47, 49–50, 58, 90; Income Tax Act of 1997 53
Ahl-e Hadith 161
Ahl-i-Sunnat Khidmat Committee 175
Ahl-i-Sunnat wal Jama'at 172
Ahmad, Nurullah 50
Ahmadi 187–8
Ahmed, Justice Fayyaz 121
Ahmed, Khalid 154
Ahmed, Shaikh Rashid 153
Akalis 200
Akhter, Justice Mian Nazir 188
Akhter, Professor Salamat 186
Ali, Chaudhry Asghar 51
Alienation of Land Act 48
All-India Muslim League 1, 3, 14, 32, 77, 182, 203
All-India Sunni Conference 167
All-Party Conference 136
Amin, Mawlawi 173
Amin, Mian 52
Aminuddin 87
Anjuman-i-Sarfaroushan-i-Islam Pakistan 171
Antofagasta 127
Arendt, Hannah 192–3
Army 4, 6–7, 44–5, 60, 118–19, 133–6, 138, 140, 170
Assistant/Additional Political Agents (APA) 87, 89, 91–3

Awami League 6
Awami Muslim League 26–7
Awami National Party (ANP) 41, 61, 66–75; contest elections 72–3
Awan, Akram 160
Awqaf 152, 169, 172, 175
Ayaz, Shaikh 114
Ayub Khan *see* Khan, Ayub
Azad, Abdul Qadir 170
Azad Pakistan Kanfarans 166
Azad Pakistan Massih League 186
Azad Pakistan Party 26
Aziz, Shaukat 157

Bahawalpur 6, 77, 81, 83–6, 89–90, 93–4, 100; Amir of 84–6, 89–90, 94–5; government of 85, 100; ruler of 83–4
Bahrain 126, 129
Baksh, Pir Illahi 109
Baloch 11, 98, 118–19, 121–3, 126, 128–9, 130, 134–5, 139–40, 144; activists 120–1, 131; diaspora 130, 139; militants 124–5, 130–2; Liberation Front 126, 131; Musla Defai Tanzeem 123; National Front 120, 123; National Movement 120, 123; nationalism 12, 130, 140–2; nationalists 7–8, 123, 130, 134–6; Republican Army 124; Republican Party 120; states 87–8, 91
Baloch, Abdul Malik 136
Baloch, Faiz 126, 131
Baloch, Ghulam Mohammad 120
Baloch, Lala Munir 120
Baloch, Mehran 126, 131
Baloch, Sher Mohammad 120
Balochistan 7, 8, 11, 93–4, 96, 118–19, 121–3, 125, 127–8, 131, 134, 139–45; -Brahui confederacy 134; Economic Report 142; government of 124, 127, 141–2; independent 131–2; insurgency

Balochistan *continued*
  in 118–19, 121, 123, 125, 127, 129, 131, 133, 135, 137, 139, 141, 143, 145; Liberation Army 125; National Party (Mengal) 123, 126; Package 135; Republican Party 123, 125; States Union (BSU) 88–9, 91, 93–4, 99; Student Organisation-Azad 123
Barelvi 147–8, 159–62, 166–7, 169, 170–2, 174–7; leaders 161–2; mosques 159, 169, 173, 177; organizations 175–6, 179; Pakistani 166–7, 169, 171, 173, 175, 177, 179; Parties 172, 177; ulama 167–9, 171–2, 177
Barelvi, Ahmad Raza Khan 166
Bari, Mian Abdul 52
Barrick Gold 127
Basic Democrats 46
Basic Principles Committee (BPC) 93, 184
Bhatti, Shahbaz 189
Bhopali, Zahurul Hassan 169
Bhutto, Benazir 7–8, 35, 62, 66, 70, 113, 116, 154, 185
Bhutto, Mumtaz Ali 112
Bhutto, Shah Nawaz 81
Bhutto, Zulfiqar Ali 7, 35, 39, 41, 45–7, 53, 62, 70, 96, 113, 122, 134, 152, 168, 185, 187
Bhutto government 40, 43, 45, 50
Bibi, Asia 189
Bizenjo, Ghaus Bakhsh 91, 122
Blasphemy 162, 186, 188–9
Bloc, forward 61, 63–4, 66–7, 74
Bombay Presidency 101, 103, 105, 115–16
Bose, Subhas Chandra 198
Bugti, Akbar 118–19, 122, 124, 134
Bugti, Brahamdagh 124, 131
Burki, Shahid Javed 46–7

Candidate 42, 60, 63–5, 67–70, 71–5, 124, 174, 186; selection 70, 72–3, 75; selection processes 73–4
Caste 183–4, 188, 191, 196
Central Working Committee 70
Centralisation 77, 82–3
Centre-province relations 14, 24, 108
Chabahar Port 125
Chattha, Hamid Nasir 62
Chaudhry, Iftikhar 154
Chief Commissioner 79, 93, 96
Chitral 81, 83, 88–9, 91, 93, 96; Mehta *see* Mehtar of Chitral

Christians 11, 175, 180, 182–4, 185–6, 188–90, 206
Chuhan, Gulzar 186
Citizen Report on Minorities in India and Pakistan 190
Cold War 3
Combined Opposition Parties 66
Commission 19, 120–1, 185, 190
Communal riots 195–6, 205; violence 107, 192, 195, 199, 201
Conference Muslim League (CoML) 38–9
Congress, Indian National 51, 77–8, 80, 104, 131–2, 182, 199–200
Constituencies 40, 42, 44, 55–6, 64–5, 67–73, 75, 186
Constituent Assembly 3, 80, 99–100, 108, 183–5, 190
Constituents 67, 69, 71, 73
Constitution 3, 7, 64–5, 87, 89, 91–3, 97, 131, 135, 137, 184–5; interim 85, 91–2, 94, 100
Council of Rulers 88
Crown lands 27

*Daily Gazette* 106
*Daily Times* 74–5, 140, 163–4, 178
Dar, Shujat Zamir 119
Daultana, Mian Mumtaz 26–7, 52–3; ministry 39, 45, 50, 52
*Dawn* 97–8, 100, 116–17, 140–5, 156, 164, 177–9
Defence 2, 6, 11, 29, 31, 82, 99, 111–14, 146, 155
Delhi 31, 79, 99, 105, 138, 158
Democracy 11, 35–6, 39, 55–6, 60–1, 82, 91, 93, 97–8, 111, 206
Deobandi 5–6, 10, 147–8, 157, 159, 161, 166–7, 169, 172–3, 175–6; ulama 9, 166–8, 172, 175–6
Dhofar insurgency 129
Diasporas 121, 128–9, 160
District Board 46
Dring, Colonel 84–5
Dubai 129–31
Dundas, Sir Ambrose 96
Durand Line 124

East Pakistan *see* Pakistan, East
East Punjab *see* Punjab, East
East Punjab States *see* Punjab, East Punjab States
East Punjab States Union *see* Punjab, East Punjab States Union
Elahi, Chaudhry Pervaiz 157

Index 209

Election Commission 55, 65–6, 75
Elections 8, 35, 37–41, 55–7, 62–5, 67, 71, 74, 91, 174, 186
Elective Bodies (Disqualification) Act (EBDO) 4
Electoral campaigns 68, 72–3
Ethnic cleansing 132, 195–6, 200–1; regulation of 133, 135, 138, 143–4
Evacuee property 14, 23–5, 29
*Express Tribune* 142, 144, 178–9
Extra-judicial executions 119, 124, 136–7
Extremism, violent 177–9

Factionalism 13–14, 30, 39, 61–2, 64, 67
Fazl-i-Karim, Sahibzada Muhammad 169
Federally Administered Tribal Areas (FATA) 130, 134
Fell, D.Y. 86
Fikr-i-Ahl-i-Sunnat 171
Finance 26, 55, 68–9, 73–4, 129, 132
First Five-Year Plan 27
Frontier Corps 119, 121–2; regions 82, 96, 99; states 88–9, 91–2, 95–6, 98

Gandhi, Mohandas 81
Gandhi, Samaldas 81
Garrison state 11
Geertz, Clifford 146
General Election 55, 65, 93, 98, 136, 168, 174
Ghuri, Muhammad Shahid 172, 177–9
Gibbon, C.E. 18
Gilani, Yousaf Reza 125, 135
Gilgit Agency 95–6
Goharshi, Riaz Ahmad 171
Government 23, 28, 44–5, 51–3, 55, 82–100, 136–8, 144, 173; central 24, 26, 83–4, 86–8, 92, 94–5, 97, 108–10, 114; federal 38, 44, 50, 53, 123, 127, 135, 177; local 44, 47, 54; representative 35–7, 39, 47, 93; responsible 89, 93
Government of Bahawalpur Act 1949 90
Government of India Act 1935 80, 93
Government of Khaipur Act 1949 90
Green Revolution 2
Gross Domestic Product (GDP) 2, 127
Gujarat 105, 196–8, 205
Gulf, Persian 126, 129–31
Gurmani, Mushtaq Ahmed 81
Guzara Scheme 15
Gwadar 8, 120, 126, 128–30, 132, 134, 143
Gwadari, Abdul Majid 130

Hamdam, Aziz 186

Hamid, Agha Abdul 88
Hanafi jurisprudence 166, 168
Haroon, Hameed 156
Hawala network 130
Hayat, H.L. 186
Hayat, Sardar Shaukat 23, 38, 98
Haq, Walter Z. 186
Haq, Zia *see* Zia-ul-Haq
*Herald* 74, 178, 191
Hindus 13, 17, 24, 32, 81, 103–4, 185, 187, 190, 195, 198–9, 204, 206
Human Rights Commission of Pakistan 119–21, 123, 139–40
Human Rights Watch 120
Hunza and Nagar 82–3, 89, 95; states of 93, 96
Hussain, Altaf 69
Hussain, Chaudhry Shujaat 156
Hussain, Mushahid 118, 157
Hyderabad 79, 82, 112, 114, 169, 170

Idarah-i-Minhajjul Qur'an 169
Identity politics and minorities in Pakistan 190
Iftikharuddin, Mian 10, 13, 22, 25–6, 98
Ijaz-ul-Haq 62
India 1–3, 11, 30–1, 80–2, 115, 124–5, 141, 201, 204–6
India States People's Congress 99
India-Pakistan wars 186–7
Indian Army 12, 125, 196
Indian National Congress *see* Congress, Indian National
Industrialists 9, 36, 40–1
Integrated Rural Development Programme (IRD) 47
Intelligence agencies 1, 69, 119–21, 136
Intelligence Bureau 119
Inter-Services Intelligence (ISI) 1, 6, 60, 119
International Covenant on Civil and Political Rights (ICCPR) 137
Iqbal, Javaid 151
Iqbal, Muhammad 112, 147–51, 157, 163
Iran 57, 124–5, 127, 129, 131–2, 139, 193
Iran–Pakistan–India Gas Pipeline 127–8, 142
Irfani, Soroush 154
Islam 6, 56, 146–7, 149–50, 153–5, 160–4, 167; popular 167–8
Islamabad 124, 131–2, 136
Islamic: heritage of Pakistan 154; law and democracy in Pakistan 55; moderation 9; reassertion 162; state 3, 51, 179, 191; system 169; terrorism 136–8, 179; welfare state 175

Islami Jamhoori Ittehad (IJI) 42, 55, 62, 66
Islamisation 5, 33, 181, 168, 186–7, 202, 204
Islamism 148–9, 159
Istakam-i-Pakistan Kounsel 169

Jagirs 27–8
Jaish-i-Muhammad 170
Jam'iyyat-i-ulama-i-Hind (JUH) 167–8
Jam'iyyat-i-ulama-i-Pakistan (JUP) 159, 164, 168–9, 174, 177–8
Jama'at-i-Ahl-i-Sunnat Pakistan 169, 177
Jamaat-i Islami 149
Jamali, Zafarullah Khan 65
Jamhoori Wattan Party 123
Jamiat-ul-Ulama-e-Islam (JUI) 8, 160, 168
Jammu and Kashmir 95, 200
Jamrao Canal Project 103
Javed, Tahir Ali 63
Jenkins, Sir Evan 199–200
Jhangvi, Haq Nawaz 2
Jihadist groups 1–2
Jinnah, Mohammad Ali 1, 3, 80–2, 84, 99, 181–3, 203
Jiye Sindh 111–12
Jiye Sindh Mahaz 111–13
Jiye Sindh Student Federation 111
Junejo, Muhamaad Khan 62

Kalashnikov culture 192
Kalat 77, 80–3, 86–8, 90–1, 93, 95, 99, 129, 131, 134, 136, 144; State National Party 91
Karachi 7, 12, 30–2, 55–7, 99, 107–8, 116, 169–71, 173–4, 177–9; madrasas 177–9
Karim, Prince Abdul 82, 134
Kashmir 1, 2, 5, 76, 79, 81–2, 95, 97, 116–17, 199, 200–3
Khairpur 81, 83–4, 86, 89–90, 93–5, 100
Khan, Ahmed Yar 82, 99, 134
Khan, Aslam 86, 88
Khan, Ayub 5, 35, 38–9, 45–6, 58, 98, 152, 185
Khan, Chaudhry Akbar Ali 19
Khan, Chaudhry Mehtab 17
Khan, George Ali Murad 81
Khan, Hamid 190
Khan, Imran 7
Khan, Ishratul Abad 171
Khan, Liaquat Ali 2, 24, 26, 88, 97–8, 109
Khan, Mahbub Ali 96
Khan, Mohammad Zarif 87
Khan, Nusrat Fateh Ali 158
Khan, Raja Ghazanfar Ali 24

Khan, Rao Abdul Rehman 20–1, 25
Khan, Sardar Bahadur 94
Khan, Sir Shah Jahan 81–2
Khan, Sir Zafarullah 26, 182
Khan, Yahya 38, 96
Khanji III, Nawab Mohammad Mahabat 81
Kharan 82–3, 87–8, 95, 99, 134
Khuhro, Mohammad Ayub 94, 108–10, 116
Khyber Pakhtunkhwa 62
Kisan Party 26
Kizilbash, Khan Bahadur Mumtaz 84, 86, 90

Laghari, Jamal 50
Lahore 31, 33–4, 55, 140, 158, 162–4, 170–1, 173, 176, 177–8
Lahore Resolution 6, 182–3, 201
Land 16–22, 25, 28–30, 32, 44–6, 57, 59; agricultural 20–2, 25, 111; ceilings 20, 32; in West Punjab 16, 32; grants 14, 26–8, 44; reforms 10, 13, 15, 22–3, 27, 29, 48, 54, 58, 113; revenue 19, 24, 49–51, 53–4, 59; Revenue Act 53
Landed, elite 10, 31, 36–8, 40, 42–4, 46–9, 51–4; politicians 36–40, 42–8, 50, 54; power 10, 37, 39, 43–4, 47, 54
Landlords 3, 16, 18–19, 22–4, 27–8, 36, 39–40, 46–7, 51–3; big 19, 20; local 17, 19–21
Landowners 14, 19, 21, 31, 38, 50, 52, 55, 199; big 14–15, 52–3; interest 28–9
Lashkar-e-Jhangvi 5, 171
Law 35, 47–55, 66, 87–90, 93, 137, 170, 184
Liaquat Ali Khan *see* Khan, Liaquat Ali
Ludhianvi, Muhammad Yusuf 171
Lyallpur 18, 20–1, 52

Madaris 173, 175
Magsi, Zulfiqar Ali 123
Mahmud, Hasan 94
Mahmud, Mufti 168
Majlis-i-Shura 168
Makran coast 123, 129–30, 136
Malik, Bishop Alexander John 185
Malik, Ghulam Murtaza 171
Mamdot, Nawab of 24–6, 30, 52–3; government 23, 26
Mansoor, Qamar 152
Maqbool, Khalid 153
Markaz-i-Ahl-i-Sunnat 170–1, 178–9
Marri, Hyrbyair 126, 131

Marri, Khair Bux 122, 134
Marri tribe 118
Massih, Yousaf 188
Mehsud, Baitullah 125
Mehtar of Chitral 81, 88–9, 92
Mekran 82–3, 87–8, 95, 99, 134
Mengal, Akhtar 126
Mengal, Ataullah Khan 122, 134
Mengal, Shafiq 123
Menon, V.P. 78
Mian Iftikharuddin *see* Iftikharuddin, Mian
Minhaj-ul Quran (MUQ) 161
Ministry of Refugees and Rehabilitation 33
Minorities, religious 181–2, 185, 191, 195, 202–3; discourse 11, 180, 186–9
Mirza, Iskander 96
Mohammed, Khalid Sheikh 130
Mohajir Qaumi Mahaz (MQM) 7, 41, 61, 66–73, 75, 170–1, 173
Mosques 5, 169–70, 172–3, 175, 178, 183, 197, 204
Movement for the Restoration of Democracy (MRD) 113
Mudie, Francis 24
Muhammad, Justice Din 182
Multan 6, 19, 21, 127–8, 158, 177
*Musawat* 5
Muscat 130
Musharraf, Pervez 4, 7–9, 35, 47, 62, 71, 119, 124, 126, 131, 135, 152–4, 156–8, 164
Muslim League 3, 6, 8, 23, 38, 41, 46, 54–5, 80, 105–6, 111, 182, 199–200; provincial 25, 26
Muslim League (Convention) 38
Muslim League (Councillor) 38
Muttahida Majlis-e Amal 159
Muttahida Qaumi Movement 170
Muzaffar-ul-Mulk 89

Na'imi, Muhammad Sarfaraz 172
*Nai Zindagi* 110
Naqshbandi, Abdul Karim 174
Naqvi, Ayeda 154
National Action Plan 138
National Awami Party 118, 168
National College of the Arts (NCA) 154
National Sufi Council (NSC) 9, 156–9
Nationalism 12, 31, 56, 99, 101–11, 143–4, 179–81, 206
*Nawa-i-Waqt* 178–9
Nawaz, Salim 119
Nawaz Sharif *see* Sharif, Nawaz
Nazimuddin, Khwaja 26

Nehru, Jawaharlal 77
New Delhi 11–12, 31, 33, 125, 142–4, 179, 190, 204–5
Niazi, Abdul Sattar 18
Nishtar, Sardar Abdur Rab 80
Nishtar Park 170–1, 174
Nizam-i-Mustafah 168
Noon, Feroz Khan 44–5, 50
North-West Frontier Province (NWFP) 81, 83–5, 94, 96, 135, 156, 168, 190, 202–3
North-West Frontier Province and Punjab Provincial Civil Service 87
Nurani, Shah Ahmed 159

Objectives Resolution 184–5
Oman 129
One Unit 91, 94–5, 102, 107, 110–11
Operation Enduring Freedom 124
Operation Searchlight 7
Orissa 78–9

Pakistan: Army 5, 7–8, 124, 130, 157, 165, 172; East 1, 3, 6–8, 12, 102, 111, 185, 190, 203, 206; political parties in 39, 57, 61, 75; political violence in 192, 204; Constituent Assembly (PCA) 80, 98, 106; Democratic Alliance (PDA) 63; Islamic Student Federation 174; militarism 12, 57; Ministry of Refugees 31; Movement 3, 22, 27, 31, 106, 116, 167, 182–3, 189, 201, 203; Muslim League 8, 11, 61–2, 67–73, 75, 118; Ordinance 137–8, 145; Penal Code 5, 171; Punjab Refugee Council 24; military economy 12, 144; political economy 11, 31, 99; state formation 192–3
Pakistan Awami Tehrik 169
Pakistan Inqilabi Tehrik (PIK) 174
Pakistan Islamic Student Federation 174
Pakistan Massih League 186
Pakistan People's Party (PPP) 5, 7–8, 35, 42, 55–6, 61–75, 113, 122–3, 185
Pakistan Sunni Tehrik 166, 171, 173–6, 178–9
Pakistan Tehreek-e-Insaf 7
*Pakistan Times* 15, 25
Paleejo, Rasool Bux 113
Parties, political 7–8, 38–40, 42, 60–75, 157, 169
Partition 1, 11–14, 30–3, 51–2, 110–11, 116, 183, 195, 197, 201–2, 205–6; massacres 196–7, 205; violence 56, 192, 195–7, 202, 205

## Index

Parveen, Abida 158
Patel, Sardar Vallabbhai 78–9, 200
Patiala and East Punjab States Union 79
Patronage, political 31, 36–7, 42–7, 55, 61, 66, 68
People's Works Programme 47
Pir Pagaro 62, 160
Piracha, Sheikh Fazal Ilahi 28
Presidency 7, 103, 105, 115
Princes 77–8, 80, 83, 85, 95, 98
Protection of Pakistan Ordinance 138
Public and Representative Offices (Disqualification) Act (PRODA) 4
Punjab 10, 13–14, 20, 24–5, 31–3, 36, 41, 44, 48, 53–7, 63, 102–3; Agricultural Income Tax Act of 1951 51; camps 109; dominance 56, 106, 111; East 10, 24, 31–3, 64, 198–200, 202; East Punjab States 33; East Punjab States Union 79; government 17, 19, 26–7, 44, 51–2, 59; identity 12, 55; Indian 32, 203; Institute of Language, Art and Culture (PILAC) 157; landlords 27, 43; land ownership and cultivation patterns 16; Legislative Assembly 17, 41, 48, 75, 182; ministers 26; Muslim League 13, 22, 25–6; poetry 156; politics 26, 39, 42–3, 205; Provincial Civil Service 87; service class 133; Revenue and Tenancy Act 48
Punjab Unionist Party 12, 31
Punjabis 6–7, 10–11, 36–8, 42–3, 54, 56, 107, 113–14, 133
Punjabization 4, 56, 133, 144

Qadeer, Mama 136
Qadri, Abdul Wahid 171
Qadri, Engineer Sarwat Ijaz 174–5
Qadri, Ilyas 159
Qadri, Muhammad Abbas 159, 170
Qadri, Muhammad Altaf 171
Qadri, Muhammad Ilyas 169
Qadri, Muhammad Salim 169
Qadri, Muhammad Tahirul 169
Qadri, Mumtaz 162, 171–2
Qadri, Salim 159, 170–1
Qadri, Serwat 159
Qadri, Sheik Hussain 53
Qatar 127
Qaumi Bugti Jirga 122
Qaumi Watan Party 63
Qizilbas, Nawab Sir Muzaffar Khan 23, 51
Quotas for Sindhis in government jobs 111
Qureshi, Shah Mehmud 160

Radcliffe Boundary Award 198, 200
Rafi Peer Theatre Workshop (RPTW) 158
Rahman, Mufti Munibur 170
Raisani, Muhammad Aslam Khan 121, 123
Raisani, Siraj 119, 123
Ramay, Anwar-ul-Haq 64–5
Rashid, Abdul 94
Rashid, Mian Abdul 166
Rawalpindi 12, 21, 178, 199
*Reconstruction of Religious Thought in Islam* 150, 163
Red Mosque 5, 154
Refugee 13–14, 17, 20–6, 31–3, 59, 107–10, 183, 197; landlords 10, 19–20; rehabilitation 10, 13, 18, 24, 28, 31–3, 110
Religion 112, 114, 156–8, 164, 178, 180, 182–5, 204–6
Religious minorities 190–1; parties 8, 185; question 180, 182–3, 187; thought 150–1, 163
Resettlement, refugee 15, 22, 24, 26, 32, 108
Round Table Conference 105
Rural Works Programme (RWP) 46–7

Sahibzadi Naseema Begum 21
Saif-ur-Rehman 89
Saindak Metals Limited (SML) 127
Saints 149, 152–4, 162–3, 167, 173
Salahuddin, Youssaf 156, 158–9
Salam, Abdus 172
Saldanha, Father J. 182
Sangla Hill 188
Saqib, Attaur Rahman 171
Sardari Abolition Ordinance 122
Sardari system 121–3
Sarfaraz, Abbas 156
Sarfaroushan-i-Islam Pakistan 178
Sattar, Pirzada Abdus 94
Savidge Cecil A.V. 96
*Secrets of the Self* 150
Security agencies 119, 121, 137; forces 118–20, 133, 137, 161; studies 120, 140
Separate electorates 181–2, 185–6, 190
Separation: of East Pakistan 12, 185; of Karachi 108, 116
Shafqat, Saeed 40
Shah 84, 91, 96, 99, 121, 140
Shah, A.S.B. 96
Shah, Sabir 65
Shah, Sahibzada Saeedul Hassan 153
Shah, Syed Imran Ahmed 65

Shahabuddin, Khwaja 110
Shafiq Chaudhry Mohammad 28, 53
Shakoor, Chaudhry Abdul 64
Shakoor, Naurez 64–5
Shantinagar tragedy 188
Sharaf, Major General Sharafuddin 129
Sharif, Nawaz 7–8, 35, 62, 66, 70–1, 74, 136, 185
Sherpao, Aftab Ahmed 62–3, 65
Sherpao, Hayat 62
Shohaz, Hussain 130
Sikhs 10, 17, 24, 199–200, 202
Sindh 4, 5, 8, 24, 30, 68, 94, 97, 101–17, 152, 158, 168, 173, 174, 190; Awami Mahaz (SAM) 111; Awami Party 111; Awami Tehreek 113; Azad Conference 104; Muslim League Council 108; Muslim Students Federation 108; separation of 104–5; Sujag Jathas 112; United Front 111
Sindh government 109, 158, 170; and governor 171; failure of 174; Legislative Assembly 110–11; ministry 94
Sindhi identity 101, 102; interests 101, 103, 113; Muslims 104, 106, 107; nationalism 11, 101, 102, 106, 110, 113, 114, 115; nationalist parties 113; nationalist rhetoric 114, 115; nationalist sentiment 102, 106, 114; politicians 107–8, 111
Sindhis 101–8, 110–16
Sindhu Desh 111, 114, 117
Singh, Baldev 182, 200
Singh, Giani Kartar 199
Singh, Manmohan 125, 198
Sipah-i-Sahabah Pakistan 2, 5, 170, 177
Sosheel, Isac 186
South Asian Studies 190, 192
Special Services Group 119
Staatsvolk 133, 135, 138
State formation 11, 13, 76–7, 192–3, 195, 197, 199, 201, 203, 205
Sufi music 156, 158; Order International 158; orders 149, 155, 160, 163, 166, 167; saints 152–3, 163–4; shrines 151, 153–4, 159, 161, 164, 167; Islamism 159; tradition 148–9, 162, 163
Sufis 148, 150–1, 155, 156–9, 161, 163
Sufism 10, 146, 147–52, 154–60, 163–5; ideologization of 152, 155–6; in Pakistan 10, 146–7, 149, 151, 153, 155, 157, 159, 161–3, 165
Suhrawardy, Huseyn 198
Sui gas field 127

Sukkur Barrage 104
Sunni Ittihad Kounsel 172
Sunni Tarjuman 177–9
Sunni Tehreek (ST) 10, 159–61, 166, 168–79
Supreme Court 55, 120–1, 127, 137, 142, 154, 169
Swat 77, 81, 89, 92–3, 95–7, 100, 174; government of 92, 100
Syed, G.M. 101, 106, 111, 113
Synott, Sir Hilary 76

Tablighi Jama'at 172
Talimaat-i-Islamia 184
Taliban 152–3, 155, 160–1, 172
Talpur, George Ali Murad 90
Tanzimul Madaris Pakistan 9
Taseer, Salman 162, 171, 189
Taxation, agricultural 49, 50–1, 58
Teaching, Promotion and Use of Sindhi Language Bill 112
Tehreek-e-Nifaz-e-Aman Balochistan 119, 123
Tehreek-e-Nifaz-e-Fiqh-e-Jafaria 5
Tehreek-i-Nizam-i-Mustafah 169
Tehreek-e-Taliban Pakistan (TTP) 6, 141
*The Integration of the Indian States* 78
Tiwana, Khizr Hayat 15, 25, 28–9, 45, 52
Tozy, Muhammad 155
Tribal leaders 7, 40, 121, 138
Tribes 88, 122–3, 163
Turkmenistan 127–9

United Kingdom 126, 131
United Nations Working Group on Enforced and Involuntary Disappearances (WGEID) 136
United States 2, 76, 88, 124, 126, 132, 141, 181
Ulama 3, 5, 162, 167, 170, 172, 177, 179, 184
United Nations 112, 137
Untouchables 186–8
Urdu 6, 106–7, 112, 156

Village Industrial Development Programme 46
Violence: collective 188, 189; patterns of 206; state 19; and state formation 11, 192–3, 195, 197, 199, 201, 203, 205; in India and Pakistan 192, 205; mass 11, 192, 196, 199–200, 202; political 11, 192–5, 201–4
Voice of Missing Baloch Persons 136

Wafaq ul Madaris ul Arabia 6
Wattoo, Manzoor 62–3, 65
Wavell, Archibald 199
Waziristan 134
West Pakistan, unified 93–4; Land Revenue Act 50
White Paper on Indian States 99
Working Group on Enforced and Involuntary Disappearances (WGEID) 136–7

Wyne, Ghulam Haider 65

Yousef, Ramzi 130
Yussuf, Jam Mohammad 156, 158

Zafar, Emmanuel 186
Zardari, Asif Ali 70, 113, 121, 135
Zardari, Bilawal Bhutto 70
Zia-ul-Haq 5, 7, 35, 39, 47, 50, 62, 113, 168–9, 172–3, 185–7, 202; era 5, 8